THE ASSEMBLIES OF GOD

A Chapter in the Story
of American Pentecostalism
Volume 1–To 1941

Edith L. Blumhofer

Gospel Publishing House
Springfield, Missouri
02-0457

About the Author

Dr. Edith L. Blumhofer is the project director of the Institute for the Study of American Evangelicalism and assistant professor of history at Wheaton College, Wheaton, Illinois. She received her Ph.D. in American Religious History from Harvard University. She is a member of the American Society of Church History, the American Historical Association, and the Society for Pentecostal Studies. As Assemblies of God historian, Dr. Blumhofer wrote this two-volume work and an earlier, briefer work, *The Assemblies of God: A Popular History.* She has written articles for several periodicals as well as for the *Dictionary of Pentecostal and Charismatic Movements.*

Library of Congress Cataloging-in-Publication Data
(Revised for vol. 2)

Blumhofer, Edith Waldvogel.
  The Assemblies of God.

  Includes bibliographies and indexes.
  Contents: v. 1. To 1941—v. 2. Since 1941.
  1. Assemblies of God—United States. 2. Pentecostal churches—United States. 3. United States—Church history—20th century. I. Title.
BX8765.5A4B58   1989   289.9'4   88-39626
  ISBN 0-88243-457-8 (v. 1)
  ISBN 0-88243-458-6 (v. 2)

Printed in the United States of America

In tribute to Helen (1890-1985) and Joseph
(1895—   ) Wannenmacher, Pentecostal pioneers
through whose lives I first encountered the Assemblies of God. They were copastors of Calvary
Assembly, Milwaukee, Wisconsin, from 1921 to
1985.

Table of Contents

Foreword   7

Preface   9

Introduction   13

1. Origins of Pentecostalism: Restorationism, Premillennialism, Healing   17

2. Origins of Pentecostalism: The Holy Spirit as "Pentecostal Fire"   39

3. Charles Parham and the Apostolic Faith   67

4. The "Nazareth" of Los Angeles: Azusa Street and Beyond   97

5. Some Early Pentecostal Centers   113

6. The Pentecostal Life-style: "Days of Heaven on Earth"   141

7. The Pentecostal Life-style: "Let Us Labor for the Master"   161

8. "Is the Present Tongues Movement of God?" Evangelicals Encounter Pentecostalism   179

9. The Formation of the General Council of the Assemblies of God   197

10. Defining Doctrine, 1914–1918   217

11. Communicating the Faith: Proceeding into the Second Generation   247
12. "Into All the World . . . Unto All People": Publishing and Missions   279
13. Education and Home Missions   313
14. Pilgrims and Citizens: Some Dilemmas of Dual Allegiance   343
Appendix   373
Endnotes   379
Bibliography   439
Subject Index   453

Foreword

It has been seventy-five years since some three hundred people answered the call to attend a gathering of Pentecostal saints in Hot Springs, Arkansas. Few at that convention could have dreamed the organization they founded—the General Council of the Assemblies of God—would become in so short a time the largest Pentecostal denomination in the world. From those three hundred delegates, the church has grown to encompass over eighteen million members and adherents worldwide.

The story of the Assemblies of God includes testimonies of exceptional commitment by those early leaders as they struggled to forge a strong church even as it underwent the heat and pressure of doctrinal differences, economic crises, and growing pains. But this volume is much more than a story of human efforts. It is most of all the story of divine intervention and guidance as those early believers committed themselves wholly to the Word of God and the leading of the Holy Spirit.

Today, just as seventy-five years ago, we recognize that God's work is accomplished "not by might, nor by power, but by [His] Spirit" (Zechariah 4:6). I commend to you this first of a two-volume history of the Assemblies of God, with the prayer that you will see beyond the record of human efforts and events to the mighty power of God—still at work in His church today.

G. Raymond Carlson
General Superintendent

Preface

My academic interest in Pentecostalism began during my doctoral studies in American religion at Harvard University, where William R. Hutchison and George H. Williams especially influenced my thinking. In the course of dissertation research and continued study, I have become indebted to many people.

Grant Wacker, Cecil M. Robeck, and Joel Carpenter have read all or part of this manuscript and contributed much helpful criticism. Wayne Warner, director of the Assemblies of God Archives, has provided not only critical insight but also invaluable help in obtaining primary sources. His friendship as well as his advice and assistance have made my task easier and enjoyable. Consultations with Howard Kenyon during the course of his dissertation research at Baylor University helped shape my thinking on chapter fourteen. Conversations with John Sawin, curator of the Christian and Missionary Alliance archives and principal researcher for the early chapters of the Alliance's new history, *All for Jesus,* stimulated my consideration of the contributions of the Alliance to the Assemblies of God. Like all historians of Pentecostalism, I also owe an immense debt to two fellow historians: Charles Edwin Jones (whose bibliographies on the holiness and Pentecostal movements are indispensable resources) and Robert Anderson (author of *Vision of the Disinherited: The Making of American Pentecostalism).* These academic contacts have been enriched by interviews with many of the men and women, retired and active, who *are* the Assemblies of God. For this volume, conversations with Frank Boyd, Alice Reynolds Flower, Noel Perkin, Ernest S. Williams, Hattie Hammond, and Helen and Joseph Wannenmacher became especially meaningful. J. Robert Ashcroft, Robert C. Cunningham, Adele Flower Dalton, Joseph

R. Flower, R. D. E. Smith, Everett R. Stenhouse, Norma Thomas, and the staff of the Assemblies of God Secretariat deserve special thanks. Two general superintendents of the Assemblies of God, Thomas F. Zimmerman and G. Raymond Carlson, have provided both insight and encouragement.

My father, Edwin Waldvogel, is not only a source of varied historical information drawn from childhood memories of the Christian and Missionary Alliance and Zion City: Forty-five years of ministry in New York City have also given him perspective that he shared with me as he read this manuscript chapter by chapter.

Several Evangel College faculty have influenced my perceptions of the Assemblies of God: Zenas Bicket and Gary Liddle merit special thanks. Students in my courses on Pentecostalism at Southwest Missouri State University and Evangel College prodded my thinking perhaps more than they realized. Jody Loutzenhiser, Joyce Lee, Laura Harless, and Glenn Gohr made my task easier by assisting in countless ways. My research assistant at Wheaton College, Teri Kondo, proved adept at varied tasks.

Parts of my research were supported by a summer grant from the National Endowment for the Humanities and by a faculty research grant from Southwest Missouri State University. The rest was funded by the Division of Publication of the Assemblies of God through my appointment as denominational historian. William G. Eastlake, director of the Divison of Publication, and his secretary, Nancy Cox, graciously helped me at every point. I am grateful as well for technical assistance from Jim Williams of Evangel College and Daniel Moul of the Institute for Evangelism at the Billy Graham Center, Wheaton College.

Librarians and archivists at numerous institutions cooperated generously in my efforts: the Assemblies of God Archives, Apostolic Faith Bible College (Baxter Springs, Kansas), Billy Graham Center Archives, Central Bible College, the Christian and Missionary Alliance Headquarters and Nyack College Library, the Holy Spirit Research Center at Oral Roberts University, Moody Bible Institute, the New York Public Library, and Southwestern College (Waxahachie, Texas). In addition, Cecil Robeck's collection on Pentecostalism, housed in his office at Fuller Seminary, proved a rich source of primary materials.

This book is dedicated to two remarkable people, Helen and Joseph Wannenmacher, who encountered the Pentecostal movement in its formative years and devoted their lives to attesting its meaning and power. Helen Innes Wannenmacher's roots were in John Alexander Dowie's Christian Catholic Church in Zion City, Illinois, and her Pentecostal views were shaped largely by the Christ-centered higher-life-oriented teaching of Dowieites who embraced Pentecostalism and operated independent faith homes in Zion. Joseph Wannenmacher, a Catholic Hungarian immigrant, was desperately ill when he heard the Pentecostal message of salvation and healing in a German Pentecostal mission in Milwaukee in 1917. Converted and healed, he, too, imbibed Pentecostal teaching in the Zion Faith Homes, where he met and married Helen Innes. His testimony (circulated widely as a tract) is included as an appendix to this book. It is typical of the testimonies of the many early Pentecostals who claimed to have found physical healing and hope in their encounter with the restored apostolic faith. The Wannenmachers—and other Assemblies of God pioneers—are considered more fully in my *"Pentecost in My Soul": Explorations in the Meaning of Pentecostal Experience in the Early Assemblies of God* (Springfield, MO: Gospel Publishing House, 1989).

Finally, I am grateful for the support and patience—expressed in many ways during the writing of this book—of my husband, Edwin, and my children, Jonathan, Judith, and Christopher. As a family, we have been enriched by the people we have come to know and the places we have visited.

Introduction

In 1916, ten years after events at a nondescript mission on Azusa Street in Los Angeles gave visibility to the emerging Pentecostal movement, Pentecostal evangelist Bennett F. Lawrence attempted to provide Pentecostals with a historical identity. His work appeared first in installments in the Assemblies of God periodical *The Weekly Evangel*. The compiled articles were published in book form as *The Apostolic Faith Restored*.

Pentecostals ardently affirmed that their movement signaled the return of primitive Christianity to the world. Some acknowledged that aspects of primitive Christianity had persisted (on the fringes of respectable Christianity) throughout history; others, however, insisted that the apostolic purity of the Early Church had been utterly lost. All agreed that the full and final restoration had occurred in their day. Whether they thought in terms of the "latter rain" (see Joel 2:23 and Zechariah 10:1) or the "evening light" (see Zechariah 14:7), they shared a view of history that shaped their identity and informed their assumptions about American culture.

The following excerpt from Bennett's *Apostolic Faith Restored* conveys the early Pentecostals' sense of their place in history:

There is, in the religious world of today, a great activity of the Lord's Spirit known as the Pentecostal or Apostolic Faith Movement. This movement of God has resulted in the salvation of hundreds of thousands of sinners, both in so-called Christian lands and in those called heathen; tens of thousands have been healed of various diseases; other hundreds of thousands have received a Pentecostal Baptism in the Holy Spirit; lunatics and demoniacs have been restored to reason and to peace; believers have been brought into a vital touch with God which has meant a tremendous increase of faith in, and knowledge of, Him; hundreds have felt the missionary zeal of the first evangelists and have gone to the uttermost parts of the earth in one of the most spontaneous and widely spread missionary efforts the world has seen since the days of Pentecost.

The honest-hearted thinking men and women of this great movement have made it their endeavor to return to the faith and practice of our brethren who served God prior to the apostasy. They have made the New Testament their rule of life. This effort, which is so general throughout the movement, has had a peculiar effect upon those who were exercised thereby. The older denominations have a past which is their own in a peculiar sense; they can trace the beginnings of their church and the course of its history subsequent to its foundation. The time between the beginning and the present has been sufficient to establish precedent, create habit, formulate custom. In this way they have become possessed of a two-fold inheritance, a two-fold guide of action, a two-fold criterion of doctrine—the New Testament and the church position. The Pentecostal Movement has no such history; it leaps the intervening years crying, "Back to Pentecost." In the minds of these honest-hearted thinking men and women, this work of God is immediately connected with the work of God in New Testament days. Built by the same hand, upon the same foundation of the apostles and prophets, after the same pattern, according to the same covenant, they too are a habitation of God through the Spirit. They do not recognize a doctrine or custom as authoritative unless it can be traced to that primal source of church instruction, the Lord and His apostles.

This reversion to the New Testament was directly responsible for the Movement. . . . It is also responsible for another thing, viz. the absence of any serious effort on the part of the movement to trace an historical connection with the primitive church. There are those among us who believe that the phenomena of the Holy Spirit, for which we so strongly stand, never was entirely absent from the church; perhaps this is true; but to tell the truth, all of us are indifferent about it. If we can so order our lives that they shall fit the New Testament, we care no more for a lack of evidence that the majority of professors of religion did so in the past than we do for the overwhelming evidence that the majority of them are not doing so today.

And now perhaps you are asking, "In what particulars are you so earnestly striving to revert to primitive Christianity?" The answer is of course, "In every way." We recognize the fundamentals of Christianity, we do not slight them, but in addition, we are laboring to obtain that supernatural character of the religion which was so pre-eminently a mark of it in the old days. We do not mean to say that others who believe in the new birth have wholly lost this, but we desire a return to New Testament power and custom along all those lines of activity which made evident beyond controversy that the church was the living body of a living Christ. We believe that healing for the body, expulsion of demons, speaking in other tongues, were in early times the result of an activity of the Holy Spirit in direct harmony with, nay, stronger still, a direct result of the divine attitude toward the church and the world. Further, we hold that this attitude was the only one consistent with the divine nature. If this is true, then with the writer of the Letter to the Hebrews we say, "Jesus Christ is the same yesterday, today and forever," and expect the immutable nature to maintain an unchanged attitude accompanied by the same glorious results.

Recognizing Pentecostalism as a restorationist movement minimizes the tendency to break the movement's history into Wesleyan and non-Wesleyan components. It places Oneness Pentecostalism in the broad context, too: Oneness Pentecostals were, from this perspective, simply more thoroughgoing restorationists than their opponents. And it affirms, on the one hand, the role that blacks and other minorities played in the movement's early history, for a return to the apostolic faith meant an affirmation of Galatians 3:28: "Ye are all one in Christ." On the other hand, it explains the movement's tendency to limit the acceptable roles for women. Since many Pentecostals read the Bible as restorationists, rather than as holiness people, they frequently asserted—even in the earliest phases of their history—a New Testament warrant for regulating women's participation.

Lawrence located the movement's driving force in its restorationism. After years of careful study of primary sources, I am convinced that he was right. Other streams of nineteenth-century piety—the diffuse holiness movement, German pietism, premillennialism, and "higher life" teaching—intermingled in important ways in the Pentecostal subculture, each contributing an emphasis without which the movement cannot be correctly understood. Overarching all of them, however, was restorationism.

1. Origins of Pentecostalism: Restorationism, Premillennialism, Healing

> We are waiting for the promise of the Master—
> For without it all our sowing is in vain—
> That the deserts of the earth shall yet be watered
> With the showers of a mighty latter rain.
> We have had the early droppings of the springtime,
> But a mightier flood from heav'n shall be out-
> poured,
> When the Spirit in His fulness shall be given,
> And shall usher in the harvest of the Lord.
>
> Albert B. Simpson, *The Latter Rain*

In 1897, the Gospel Trumpet Publishing Company in Moundsville, West Virginia, issued a collection of songs for use in general gospel work. Editors Barney E. Warren and Andrew L. Byers titled the songbook *Songs of the Evening Light*. They wrote a revealing preface that urged readers to understand the times they lived in:

> We are in the evening of the last dispensation of time. In fulfillment of the prophecy—"At evening time it shall be light"—the pure gospel is shining now as it never has shone since the days of primitive Christianity. The ransomed of the Lord are returning from their apostatized condition and are coming "to Zion with songs and ever-lasting joy upon their heads."[1]

Similar language described the convictions of many late nineteenth-century Christians; theirs were the last days, the time of the latter rain. This not only meant impending judgment, however; it also heralded the return of apostolic Chris-

17

tianity. God was about to do a new thing: The "end-times" church, having separated from apostate institutions, would once again enjoy the full experience of the primitive faith. "Nothing can stay the onward march of God and His kingdom," they confidently declared.[2] Pentecostalism emerged among people who shared the conviction that theirs were days of prophesied restoration. The movement is best understood as an expression of restorationist yearning, molded in significant ways by the hopes and dreams of late nineteenth-century restorationists.

This restorationist fervor was informed by various other expectations. Early Pentecostals were premillennialists; to some degree, the broadly-based holiness movement influenced all of them. The doctrines of the "foursquare gospel" (salvation, healing, Spirit baptism, and Christ's imminent return) that later described one denomination's Pentecostal message were all vigorously proclaimed in evangelical settings long before the rise of Pentecostalism.[3] In affirming each of the above, Pentecostals confirmed their participation in a religious heritage having a broad base in American culture. In each instance, the nineteenth-century situation had influenced a reconsideration of expectations.

Restorationism

Restorationism, or the attempt to recapture the presumed vitality, message, and form of the Apostolic Church, has manifested itself in various ways in Christian history. Based on a nostalgic sense of the pristine experience of the first Christians, restorationism articulates a yearning for the return of "the good old days."[4] Some restorationists sought to restore the apostolic faith; others anticipated a divine restoration. Since the people whose restorationist hopes most directly shaped American Pentecostalism were premillennialists, they generally expected God's imminent intervention in history; they also sought to find ways to cooperate in the process.

Among the various historical effects of restorationist thought, four had particular significance for Pentecostalism. First, restorationism was closely related to the hope for perfection and the call for religious reform. It ran counter to late nineteenth-century evolutionary optimism because it assumed that the best had already been realized; it proposed instead an agenda that eliminated patterns associated with progress and development. Perfection meant a return to the norms of an earlier era. History was irrelevant. The church was called to be ahistorical, or at least to exist untainted by historical currents. Restorationist thought, then, tended to advocate purifying religious forms and examining practices and beliefs against the New Testament standard.

In the second place, restorationism promoted assumptions of Christian unity and simplicity. It reminded believers of their fundamental oneness in Christ. In focusing on the unity of the Early Church, it ignored the turmoil and heterodoxy that had marked Christian beginnings. An emphasis on shared origins promoted hopes of renewed "family" harmony.

Third, serious grappling with eschatological issues accompanied American interest in restorationism. Some American restorationists understood themselves as promoting America's destined millennial role. Others considered restorationist emphases an integral part of end-times Christianity, having intrinsic eschatological import. Joseph Smith called his restorationist group The Church of Jesus Christ of *Latter-Day Saints;* Alexander Campbell, father of the Disciples of Christ, titled his publication *The Millennial Harbinger.*

Fourth, restorationist expectations both occasioned and supported antidenominationalism. Pentecostal restorationists tended to find submission to church authority intolerable. Impatient with both tradition and creeds, they insisted that God had long since abandoned organized religion. Holiness advocate John P. Brooks, for example, urged "come-outism," not as an option but rather as a necessity.[5] Similar disillusionment with the contemporary church found expression among Plymouth Brethren. From this perspective, restorationist views molded the subculture in which Pentecostalism flourished; its participants had already separated from the mainstream. Their attitudes about the world were shaped by their conviction that cultural values necessarily opposed the true faith; they interpreted persecution as a measure of spiritual strength. They volubly opposed much in their culture, and the sense that they offered a viable, satisfying alternative to this-worldliness attracted adherents. As restorationists, they believed that they had discovered the biblical way to transcend the struggles of daily living.

To some extent, restorationists encouraged spiritual elitism by insisting that they had recaptured most fully the dynamic, the message, or the form of the Early Church. Claims to restorationist intentions gave identity to struggling new religious movements. Establishing that their distinctive views and practices had apostolic precedent helped them discover a sense of purpose and lent a certain audacity to their pretensions. Thus a miniscule congregation in the mountains of western North Carolina could call itself the Christian Union and avow its objective "to restore primitive Christianity and bring about the union of all denominations"[6]; and the followers of an obscure healing evangelist in Kansas could claim that their movement had for the first time fully restored the apostolic faith.

During the nineteenth century, restorationist hopes surfaced in many places. The largest family of restorationist groups in America centered in the activities of those who identified with the Disciples of Christ, the Churches of Christ, and various other movements identifying themselves with the term "Christian." In another form, restorationism had motivated the expectation of an end-times reorganization of the true church—complete with apostles and prophets. The Church of Jesus Christ of Latter-Day Saints, organized in 1830, for example, maintained that the true church had been divinely restored in 1830. Led by a prophet who was surrounded by apostles, Mormons claimed to participate in a religious culture that fully restored both the dynamic and the form of New Testament Christianity.

While the appeal of such groups demonstrates some of the fruit restorationist goals yielded, other smaller settings more directly influenced Pentecostalism: Frank Sandford's Shiloh, the Christian Union, the Evening Light Saints, to cite a few. One who directly influenced the Assemblies of God was John Alexander Dowie.[7] A Scotsman by birth and education, Dowie had spent much of his life in Australia. In 1888, he arrived in the United States and began to teach divine healing. During the 1890s, he established a headquarters in Chicago. His growing conviction that he lived in the last days resulted in his creation of a new denomination, the Christian Catholic Church. Dowie believed that a full restoration of New Testament experience would occur with end-times Christianity. He expected divine restoration of the offices of apostle, prophet, and teacher as well as of the gifts listed in 1 Corinthians 12.[8] It is hardly surprising that some who had been exposed to the radical emphasis on New Testament restorationism as taught among the Disciples of Christ, the Christians, and the Churches of Christ were attracted by Dowie's belief that a restoration of other facets of New Testament experience was already in progress in his ministry. And the expectations Dowie generated among his followers later made many of them receptive to the Pentecostal version of the restorationist vision.

Efforts to restore New Testament practices—or at least the expectation that God would sovereignly restore them—were not confined to any specific denomination or even to Christian orthodoxy. For many, they were closely related to an eschatological perspective. Precisely because they read their Bibles from a restorationist perspective, increasing numbers of late nineteenth-century evangelicals proved receptive to premillennialism. They believed that premillennialism not only harmonized with Scripture, but that it also enabled them to place themselves historically in a way that specifically reinforced their restorationism. They not only attempted to restore New Testament Christianity, they also expected God's sovereign end-times restoration. Some anticipated the coming of the prophesied latter rain. Others heralded the dawning of the evening light. The conviction that their endeavors coincided fully with God's end-times calendar made them confident of their ultimate success. Furthermore, from this perspective, groups as radically different as the Church of Jesus Christ of Latter-Day Saints and the early Church of God (Cleveland) can be understood to have shared a vital expectation. Both affirmed the teaching that the restoration of the true (i.e., the New Testament) church was emphatically an end-times event.

The hope of full restoration of primitive Christianity through the proclamation of the gospel and the reform of religious institutions—together with the sense that such thoroughgoing reform was uniquely possible in America—had motivated numerous Protestants throughout the American experience. Closely related to their understanding of both America's place in history and its special "mission," this hope continued to attract new advocates in the closing decades of the nineteenth century. Restorationism was compatible with several forms of millenarianism. When it combined in particular ways with premillennialist expectations, it became a powerful incentive to some who hoped for end-times Christian power and unity.[9]

Premillennialism

During the closing decades of the nineteenth century, increasing numbers of people with essentially conservative religious inclinations seemed disposed to accept radical millenarian schemes. Russellites, or Jehovah's Witnesses, described a rapidly approaching end. Promising that "millions living now will never die," they published their prophetic tidings. Adventist groups rooted in the Millerite excitement of the 1840s became more visible. More significantly for the story of Pentecostalism, a growing number of individuals in the traditional denominations, prompted in part by both restorationism and the threats to the certainties of their faith that they discerned in the new theology and the new science, insisted that Christ's physical return was near. While refusing to date His return, they generally concurred with Arthur T. Pierson, who, by twelve independent methods of prophetic calculation, concluded that "some great crisis lies between the years 1880 and 1920, or thereabouts." Pierson noted that "we are now on the threshold of that crisis, unparalleled in the history of the Church and of the world, concerning which Christ bade us to 'watch and pray.' "[10]

Animating the conviction of a rapidly approaching end was a view of history articulated by John Nelson Darby. An Irish Anglican priest who had left his denomination to identify with the Plymouth Brethren movement, Darby had participated in prophecy conferences during the late 1820s.

The political events precipitated by the French Revolution and the Napoleonic Wars had renewed European Protestant interest in prophecy. While pre-Civil War American Protestants optimistically proclaimed that the millennium was about to begin, ushered in by gospel preaching and social reform, European Protestants noted that prophecies about the end times seemed to be coming to pass in the political turmoil and social devastation attendant upon war and deprivation.[11] Prophecy conferences provided opportunities for concerned individuals, both lay and clerical, to read and discuss Scripture in an effort to penetrate biblical allusions to the end times.

Darby concluded that history, which he divided into seven time periods called dispensations, was about to conclude in a calendar of events prophesied in detail in Scripture. These would be inaugurated by the "secret rapture" of the Church. Darby taught that Christ would miraculously remove the Church before a seven-year tribulation, which would be followed by the return of Christ to reign on earth for a thousand years. Darby insisted that Christ's return for the Church was both "always imminent" and "any moment." Refusing to set a date for the event, Darby stressed the believer's obligation to be always ready and to be making the world ready. As he reflected on prophecy, Darby also concluded that Israel and the Church were distinct—that promises and prophecies pertaining to Israel had no bearing on the Church as the "new" Israel. As an incentive to personal holiness and militant evangelism, Darby's teaching played a significant role in shaping the context in which Pentecostalism developed.[12]

Darby ultimately found a religious haven among the Plymouth Brethren, a group that sought to restore New Testament patterns in the church. They disassociated themselves from religious denominations, historic creeds, and traditional liturgies. Stressing the importance of a thorough knowledge of the English Bible, they developed Bible study handbooks that greatly extended their influence. Their biblicism provided the basis for both their silencing of women in religious gatherings and their mandating of head coverings for women. Replacing the typical sermon with a "Bible reading," they devised a teaching form that would have enormous influence on segments of American Protestantism.[13]

In the United States, both Darby's dispensational views and the Plymouth Brethren's emphasis on Bible study found a receptive audience, often influencing people who considered themselves conservatives in the growing dispute over inerrancy and science. Darby's total rejection of contemporary organized religion, on the other hand, proved less popular. To his dismay, his American followers usually remained in their denominations.

Not everyone agreed with Darby's views: Some, for example, felt that end-times prophecies were already being fulfilled; others insisted that their fulfillment had not yet begun; others questioned his teaching on a rapture or disliked his separation of Israel from the Church. Even so, many concurred with his teaching that Christ's coming was, in fact, imminent, and they focused on the significance of that conviction for their lives. Though Darby's intricate calendar influenced the future course the movement took in American religion, early interest in premillennialism often expressed itself in simple expectation of Christ's imminent coming. In this basic form, late nineteenth-century premillennialist teaching molded the lives and ministries of a generation that believed it "lived in the shadow of the Second Coming."[14]

Some who became convinced of the validity of this message claimed that their recognition of the truth of Christ's soon return marked a watershed in their religious experience. Reuben Archer Torrey, Yale-educated associate of Evangelist Dwight L. Moody, noted, for example, that "the blessed hope transformed my whole idea of life; it broke the power of the world and its ambition over me."[15] Individuals claimed that premillennialism radically reordered their priorities. Personal holiness (or preparedness) for Christ's coming, they noted, replaced striving for success and recognition in this world.[16]

For some of its adherents, premillennialism seemed to minimize Christian social responsibility by making social concern irrelevant.[17] Rejecting all attempts to modify the social order, to remedy political wrongs, or to come to terms with the urban power structure, such premillennialists tended to concur with R. A. Torrey's sentiments: "In the Return of our Lord is the perfect solution, and the only solution, of the political and social and commercial problems that now vex us."[18]

While such views invited criticism for apparent social irresponsibility, premillennialists found consolation and comfort in their eschatological preoccupation and in the emphasis on Bible study that undergirded it. They seemed truly to long for Christ's return. One handbook of early American premillennialism, William E. Blackstone's *Jesus Is Coming*, devoted a chapter to the practical consequences of the blessed hope. Most of the forty practical uses Blackstone listed referred to how that hope enriched individual Christian experience and reordered priorities. It is noteworthy that none of the forty suggests that the doctrine should promote evangelistic activity. That it did, nonetheless, motivate home and foreign missionary efforts is clear from the statements of many of its proponents. D. L. Moody, for one, claimed that his grasp of Christ's imminent coming had compelled him to act as if he had been given a lifeboat and instructions to approach a sinking vessel to save all he could.[19]

On the other hand, it is important to note that premillennialists were by no means the only missions-minded Protestants.[20] The late nineteenth century was a period of extensive missionary outreach, most of which was understood in nonpremillennialist terms. Although premillennialism can rightly be understood as one source of missionary fervor, postmillennialism and amillennialism—with their stress on transforming the world through the proclamation of the gospel—influenced the missionary goals of most late nineteenth-century Protestants.

Among the most important early American premillennialist missionary agencies was the fledgling Christian and Missionary Alliance. Born out of the vision of a former Presbyterian pastor, Albert B. Simpson, the Christian and Missionary Alliance was an interdenominational association of people who banded together to support projects at home and abroad. Created in 1887 as separate alliances, Simpson's agencies sent out missionaries in an end-times effort to accomplish the evangelization of the world in their generation.[21] A similar goal motivated the Student Volunteer Movement (SVM) (which came together during the same years): "The evangelization of the world in this generation." Certainly some who directed the SVM's early progress were compelled by premillennialist urgency to prepare the world for Christ's return, but many others were not, and the SVM never adopted the premillennialist eschatological framework. Two convinced premillennialists edited the influential *Missionary Review of the World:* Arthur T. Pierson and Adoniram J. Gordon. Their scope was much broader, however. Premillennialism was a personal conviction, not necessarily an essential viewpoint.

Darby's dispensational form of premillennialism ultimately gained ascendancy in influential segments of American conservative Protestantism. It fostered a worldview that was essentially negative and instructed evangelicals to await cataclysmic events. It also discounted the positive accomplishments of the age, which liberals pointed to as signs of progress. But other worldviews also found expression among late nineteenth-century American premillennialists. A. J. Gordon, for example, insisted that the positive accomplishments of the age were commendable, but that evil progressed even as good advanced. Articulating a view that encouraged affirming the good in the culture, he nonetheless maintained that good would triumph only through Christ's return. And, in rejecting Darby's dispensationalism while affirming faith in a premillennial advent, Gordon devised a restorationist eschatology in which an end-times renewal of early Christian vitality could include the exercising of apostolic power and spiritual gifts.[22] He became an important forerunner of Pentecostalism.

Healing

A third emphasis in nineteenth-century Protestantism that specifically influenced Pentecostalism was the understanding of Christ as Healer. (See the appendix for a testimony of healing.) A renewed interest in healing had several sources. First, a focus on healing as "in the Atonement" and as one of the end-times gifts of the Spirit had become increasingly evident in American religion in the mid-nineteenth century. It later found support among those premillennialists who regarded healing as a gift to be restored to the church in the last days. (Prominent among these were A. J. Gordon and A. B. Simpson.) Second, healing harmonized with restorationist expectations. Just as restorationism supported premillennialism, it also encouraged an emphasis on physical healing (which had demonstrably been part of New Testament experience). Third, as will be seen in the next chapter, healing was closely tied to conceptions of the "higher Christian life." Fourth, interest in healing can correctly be seen as part of a broader cultural focus on health. Fifth, it can also be understood as a partial response to unorthodox healing movements like Christian Science and Unity.[23]

The American evangelical stress on healing in the second half of the nineteenth century was informed by cross-cultural contacts. Evangelicals of many denominations who came together in settings like D. L. Moody's Northfield conferences often had a common set of heroes, and several of those were European advocates of healing. Especially prominent were Dorothea Trudel and Johann Christoph Blumhardt, both of whom had also influenced earlier American advocates of healing like Charles Cullis and William Boardman.

Trudel, a Swiss peasant, offered sick people hospitality, biblical instruction, and prayer for their healing in the tiny village of Mannedorf on Lake Zurich. Hers was emphatically a venture of faith in a hostile religious setting. A woman without theological education, she drew criticism from established religious authorities, who several times temporarily closed her healing homes on the charge that she practiced medicine without a license. Published reports as well as visits to Mannedorf stimulated several Americans to explore the subject of healing.[24]

Accounts of the ministry of Johann Christoph Blumhardt, a Lutheran pastor in southern Germany, also energized American expectations. After a much-publicized, prolonged (and, in his German Lutheran Church, highly irregular) encounter with a member of his parish he claimed was demon-possessed, Blumhardt had begun to sense a spiritual renewal in his congregation. Much to his surprise, attendance at regular church services increased dramatically, and people who had come to receive Communion or absolution left testifying to physical healings. As a result, Blumhardt left his parish and, with the assistance of the King of Wurttemberg, procured a resort facility known as Bad Boll where he spent the rest of his life ministering to people from many countries who sought both spiritual and physical renewal.[25]

Among the Americans who advocated divine healing in the late nineteenth century, four can represent the content of the message and the practice of its application that would have special significance for Pentecostalism. A. J. Gordon articulated the message, asserting its essential orthodoxy and continuity with the Early Church; A. B. Simpson focused on the person of Christ, the Healer, and on the relationship between healing and the higher life; John Alexander Dowie regarded healing as an essential part of his restorationist scheme; Maria Woodworth-Etter pioneered the salvation-healing crusades that later Pentecostals imitated.

Adoniram Judson Gordon—The Healing Message

Boston Baptist pastor Adoniram Judson Gordon wrote an influential book on the subject of divine healing that helped publicize European teaching on the subject across America. Editor of the *Watchword* and founder of the Bible school that became Gordon College and Gordon-Conwell Theological Seminary, Gordon was also a prominent associate of D. L. Moody at Northfield and an associate editor of the *Missionary Review of the World*. In 1882, he published *The Ministry of Healing*, a book that remains in print and that many early Pentecostals accepted as a standard statement of their own views.

Gordon unequivocally located healing in the Atonement; he thus maintained that it was universally available. He taught that as in the Atonement for sin Christ had suffered as a substitute rather than as a sympathizer, so in the Atonement for the body He had "endured vicariously our diseases." Just as faith brought salvation, so faith effected healing.[26]

Gordon regarded his age as the end-times dispensation of the Spirit and insisted that the Spirit's role was to increase the knowledge of Christ, who was the Healer.[27] Claiming that the church had lost, at about the same time, both its commitment to divine healing and its stress on the imminence of Christ's return, he maintained that whenever "primitive faith" was revived, the two emphases reappeared. "There is a grim irony," he wrote, "in the fact, that after death and the grave had gradually become the goal of the Christian's hope, instead of the personal coming of Christ, then we should begin to find miracles of healing alleged by means of contact with the bones of dead saints and martyrs, instead of miracles of healing through the prayer of faith offered to the living Christ."[28]

Faith played a pivotal role in Gordon's view of healing. "If we can get a miraculous faith," he maintained, "the marvelous works will be easy enough to credit."[29] Disagreeing with those of his contemporaries who insisted that miracles of healing had been confined to the Apostolic Age (dispensationalist premillennialists were included among these), Gordon avowed: "It is apostolic men that make an apostolic age, not a certain date of Anno Domini."[30]

Gordon was motivated by one part of the restorationist hope. He longed to see a rebirth of the "primitive beauty and piety" of the Christian faith. Although Gordon prayed for the sick privately, he did not integrate healing into his regular church ministry. He influenced the growing interest in the subject primarily through his book, which even his critics acknowledged as "at once the most readable and the most rational presentation of the views of the Faith-Healers."[31]

A. B. Simpson—Christ as the Healer

A. B. Simpson developed a more practical integration of the gospel of healing into his regular activities. One of the four points of the "fourfold gospel" around which he organized the Christian and Missionary Alliance was Christ the Healer.

Simpson's commitment to healing grew out of his own experience of being healed of heart disease (an experience indirectly influenced by Charles Cullis).[32] After serious Bible study about healing, Simpson accepted it as "part of Christ's glorious Gospel for a sinful and suffering world, for all who would believe and receive His word."[33] He then determined to preach divine healing. Making a written "covenant" to express his solemn intention, he affirmed that he (1) would never question the doctrine; (2) would "take the Lord Jesus as my physical life, for all the needs of my body until all my lifework is done"; (3) would "use this blessing for the good of others" and "speak of it or minister in connection with it in any way which God may call me or others may need me in the future."[34]

His affluent, earnest Presbyterian congregation, which had at first responded wholeheartedly to their visionary young pastor, proved unwilling to follow unequivocally his expanding ministry. He too was restive under denominational responsibilities. As a result, Simpson resigned his pastorate to launch an independent ministry. In 1883, he dedicated a Manhattan residence as the Home for Faith and Physical Healing. A year later, he placed the home under the supervision of two women.

Simpson and his associates conducted daily morning and afternoon services there. In the first thirty months, over seven hundred guests resided briefly at the home, while hundreds more attended services for instruction in healing. To guard against the tendency toward sensationalism, fanaticism, and the "wonder-seeking spirit," Simpson used anointing with oil and laying on of hands cautiously, stressing rather *Christ* as Healer, and endeavored to keep "practical godliness and humble work for the salvation of men" the supreme purpose of his ministry.[35]

Some of Simpson's early supporters disliked his placing healing at the heart of the gospel. They observed: "If you expect the healing of the sick, you must also include the gift of tongues—and if the gift of tongues has ceased, so in the same way has power over disease." To this Simpson responded:

> We cheerfully accept the severe logic. We cannot afford to give up one of the promises. . . . We believe the gift of tongues was only withdrawn from the Early Church as it was abused for vain display or as it became unnecessary for practical use. It will be repeated as soon as the Church will humbly claim it for the universal diffusion of the Gospel.[36]

Simpson's teaching on the relationship between the higher life and healing can be understood as part of his conviction that terms like "faith cure" and "faith healing" should be avoided. Faith had no intrinsic curative power. In healing, the individual received divine life. And further:

> The physical redemption which Christ brings is not merely healing, but also life. . . . Therefore it is as fully within the reach of persons in health as those who are diseased. It is simply a higher kind of life, the turning of life's waters into His heavenly wine. Therefore, it must also be kept by constant abiding in Him. . . . Such a life is a very sacred thing. It gives a peculiar sanctity to every look, tone, act and movement of the body. We are living on the life of God, and we must live like Him and for Him.[37]

In fact, Simpson taught that "the power which heals the body usually imparts a much richer baptism of the Holy Ghost to the heart, and the retaining of this Divine health requires such constant fellowship with God . . . that the spiritual results far outweigh the temporal."[38] Simpson had yearned for such an experience at least since 1879; when he believed he had found it, he felt compelled to share it.

Through the institutions and associations he founded, as well as by his writings and the gospel songs he composed, A. B. Simpson powerfully influenced the early Pentecostal movement. His focus on "Jesus Christ the same yesterday, and today, and for ever" (Hebrews 13:8) that supported his teaching on healing found enduring expression in the song *Yesterday, Today, Forever (Jesus Is the Same)*. (More than any other text, those words became basic to American Pentecostalism. They were often displayed on the walls of Pentecostal storefront missions.) He also gave musical form to his conviction that the gospel of healing had had continuous validity throughout human history. Healing was not a nineteenth-century innovation; rather, it was an appropriate end-times restoration:

> There is an old appointed way
> For those who hearken and obey;
> Above the gate these words we see:
> "I am the Lord that healeth thee."
>
> There is a Great Physician still
> Whose hand has all its ancient skill.
> At his command our pains will flee—
> "I am the Lord that healeth thee."

A premillennialist who stressed holiness, Spirit baptism, divine healing, and missions, Simpson articulated a message with which emerging Pentecostals easily identified.

John Alexander Dowie—Healing and Restorationism

A third advocate of divine healing in the closing years of the nineteenth century was John Alexander Dowie. Dowie spent much of his early life in Australia, where he became a Congregational pastor. A man of uncompromising convictions, Dowie became convinced of the present-day reality of healing and established contacts with others who shared his interest.

In 1893, during the Chicago World's Fair, Dowie moved his efforts to Chicago. He had already achieved a reputation as a fighter. His early American campaigns on the West Coast had sparked considerable local furor. And he had also begun his pattern of public criticism of other teachers of healing, most of whom took a less radical stance than he on the use of "means."

The subject of means, or the place of medicine in divine healing, proved particularly sensitive among American advocates of healing. After moving his efforts to Chicago, Dowie came to regard all use of medicine as sinful. "God has but one way of healing," he insisted. "The Devil has a hundred so-called ways. Zion cannot go to medicine for healing. There is no fellowship between the blood of Christ and medicine."[39] Gordon and Simpson, on the other hand, did not unequivocally oppose medicine. "There is no use in giving up remedies without a real personal faith in Christ," maintained Simpson. "Where persons have real faith in Christ's supernatural help they will not want remedies. And where they have not this faith, I have never dared to hinder them from having the best help they can obtain." Whereas medical remedies were "limited" and "uncertain," God's provision was complete and definite. "To combine the omnipotence of Jesus with a dose of mercury is like trying to go up stairs by the elevator and the stairs at the same moment," Simpson observed.[40]

Initially, Dowie's work in Chicago evoked meager response, but early in 1894, the situation improved. Dowie referred to his efforts as "Zion"; by April, Zion included a tabernacle and a large residence known as Divine Healing Home No. 1. Late in the summer of 1894, Dowie began publishing a weekly report of Zion's progress. Known as *Leaves of Healing,* the magazine circulated his sermons and many testimonies of healing. As more people identified with his teaching, Dowie added more healing homes and moved to successively larger tabernacles. The expansion of his work plus his outspoken attacks on the religious establishment drew the attention of the local press. Dowie later called 1895 a "year of persecution."

According to Dowie, by 1895 the dramatic success of his healing ministry had antagonized the medical profession. "The licensed poison vendors and surgical butchers are crying, 'Our craft is in danger to be set at naught,'" Dowie charged.[41] He spent much of the year in court, defending himself against charges that his healing homes were unlicensed hospitals and that, contrary to a newly passed city ordinance, he practiced medicine without a license.

In fact, no medicine was allowed in any of the homes. People came for instruction in healing and for specific prayer. As a condition for admission, they relinquished the use of medicines. At the end of 1895, Chicago's so-called hospital ordinance was declared unconstitutional. Problems with city authorities were but part of larger obstacles Dowie faced, however. He regarded all opposition as an "attack of the Devil." Confrontations generated publicity, however, and in the end, they attracted many adherents to Zion. In 1896, he organized his followers into a new denomination: the Christian Catholic Church.

As has been noted, in describing his vision for the church, Dowie affirmed a restorationist hope: to rediscover the church's "primitive condition, where the church should be catholic ... in embracing all who were in communion with God by repentance and faith in our Lord Jesus Christ."[42] As Dowie's restorationist vision expanded, he inserted the word "apostolic" into the name of his denomination (1904), and he taught about an orderly end-times restoration of spiritual gifts and apostolic offices to the Church.

Zion expanded to include some twenty thousand adherents. The Zion Seventies (see Luke 10:1) went two-by-two to every home in Chicago to invite people to the services. Dowie and several colleagues worked quietly to plan a community in which members of the Christian Catholic Church could live in a Christian environment. In 1899, he purchased some sixty-five hundred acres of farm land along Lake Michigan. As the twentieth century dawned, Dowie unveiled his plans for Zion City, Illinois, to a crowd of three thousand gathered for his watchnight service. The city without "breweries or saloons, gambling halls, houses of ill-fame, drug or tobacco shops, hospitals or doctors' offices, theaters or dance halls and secret lodges or apostate churches" would, he promised, also exclude "hog raising, selling or handling."[43] In mid-July, 1901, Zion was opened for settlement; some six thousand of the faithful moved in.

By the turn of the century, Dowie had influenced thousands of people, some of whom had identified with his restorationist hopes as expressed in his denomination. Many others had experienced healings or been convinced of the validity of his teaching on the contemporary restoration of the apostolic faith. His emphasis on faith in God was complemented by a stress on "entire consecration" and holiness. He offered women and blacks as well as white males opportunities for public roles in his organization. His outspoken criticism of all who disagreed with him alienated some; others were attracted by the apparent success of his message. In the new century, his followers would provide important leadership in Assemblies of God ranks.

Maria Woodworth-Etter—Pioneer of Salvation-Healing Crusades

The healing evangelist whose style best anticipated later Pentecostal preferences was undoubtedly Maria Woodworth-Etter. Born in Ohio on July 22, 1844, Woodworth-Etter's earliest religious impressions were associated with a local Disciples of Christ congregation. After her marriage, she resolved to enter evangelistic ministry. Precluded from public preaching among the Disciples, and discouraged by her husband, she found in a local Quaker meeting the support she needed. Many Quaker meetings preserved a strong emphasis on religious experience (and numerous Quakers would later accept Pentecostalism), and among them, Woodworth-Etter received what she regarded as a baptism in the Holy Spirit. She had prayed for an "anointing for service" and claimed that in response she was "baptized with the Holy Ghost, and fire, and power which has never left me."[44]

After this experience, Woodworth-Etter determined to begin preaching. She achieved considerable local notoriety. She reported hundreds of conversions as well as strong criticism because of her sex. Her campaigns attracted reporters from newspapers across the country. After a brief affiliation with the United Brethren in Christ, Woodworth-Etter joined the Church of God of the General Eldership which had been founded by John Winebrenner. But her denominational affiliations were relatively unimportant to the story of the expansion of her ministry. In 1885, she began to pray for the sick. Like other contemporary healing teachers, she taught that all who had sufficient faith would be healed. If sick persons were not healed, the fault was their own. Her meetings were also known for the trances that became common occurrences: People would fall to the floor, apparently unconscious, only to testify later to profound spiritual experiences while in that state.

As her reputation spread, Woodworth-Etter received invitations from around the country. She eventually acquired a tent seating eight thousand and traveled from coast to coast, preaching an evangelical message into which she integrated a focus on divine healing. Such salvation-healing revivals would later play a pivotal but controversial role in the Pentecostal proclamation of healing. Woodworth-Etter (who had been dismissed from the Church of God in 1904) did not identify with the Pentecostal movement until 1912.[45] Adherents generally accepted and respected her as one who had anticipated their movement. Woodworth-Etter ministered widely under Pentecostal auspices until her death in 1924.[46]

At the end of the nineteenth century, emphases that later characterized Pentecostalism were prominent in broad segments of the religious culture. A stress on the restoration of primitive Christianity, an anticipation of Christ's imminent return, and a focus on divine healing complemented an evangelistic emphasis on Christ as Savior. And although they regarded with concern evidences of religious and cultural change, evangelicals hoped for success in their efforts to wrest individual souls from eternal damnation. They knew they would triumph ultimately through Christ's imminent return. As is so often true, their music captured their sense of destiny. Songwriter C. Austin Miles put it this way:

> There's a shout in the camp for the victory is
> coming
> O'er Satan's power;
> Through the word of the Lord we the battle are
> gaining
> This very hour.

Even as they awaited judgment, they proclaimed progress in spiritual warfare. Their anticipation of a worldwide, end-times revival prompted them to set aside days of prayer and fasting for its realization. They also identified with a concern for holiness that permeated much of the religious culture, and they sensed a need for spiritual power to energize their end-times activities. A renewed focus on the Holy Spirit as the source of both holiness and power characterized the efforts of many whose religious inclinations found expression in contexts shaped by restorationism, premillennialism, and the message of divine healing.

Healing evangelist John Alexander
Dowie, founder of Zion City, Illinois

Shiloh Tabernacle, Zion, Illinois. Erected by Dowie, originally this
was the city's only place of worship. It seated about eight thousand.

He sendeth His word *PATIENCE* and healeth them.

LEAVES OF HEALING

I am the Lord that healeth thee.

And the leaves of the tree were for the healing of the nations.

A WEEKLY PAPER FOR THE EXTENSION OF THE KINGDOM OF GOD.

EDITED BY THE REV. JOHN ALEX. DOWIE.

VOLUME VIII NUMBER 22 CHICAGO, MARCH 23, 1901. PRICE FIVE CENTS

ZION IN AUSTRALASIA.

IT WAS in 1595 that the adventurous Portugese Mariner, Fernandez de Quiros, saw before him a coast stretching as far as the eye could see.

Day after day he sailed by those hilly shores, and saw the same succession of wooded slopes, and then he felt assured forbidding; hence the Island Continent was neglected and not even its size and greatness known.

It is the southern and eastern shores, and especially the latter, that are, even at this day, the principally inhabited portions of Australia.

The masthead of Dowie's weekly publication, *Leaves of Healing*. The paper featured healing testimonies and helped expand Dowie's support base.

Maria Woodworth-Etter, ca. 1900

2. Origins of Pentecostalism: The Holy Spirit as "Pentecostal Fire"

> There are people almost everywhere whose hearts are all aflame
> With the fire that fell at Pentecost, which cleansed and made them clean;
> It is burning now within my heart—All glory to His name!
> And I'm glad that I can say I'm one of them.
>
> I. G. Martin, *I'm Glad I'm One of Them,* 1906

Early in the 1900s, Arthur Tappan Pierson, a dignified elder statesman of the conservative evangelical world, reminisced about the past half century. A graduate of New York's Union Theological Seminary, Pierson was a pastor, editor, author, and conference speaker who was highly regarded among those who coveted a higher Christian life. It had not always been so. Pierson had pursued other goals during his early Presbyterian pastorates. But an encounter with the revival team of Major Daniel W. Whittle and Philip P. Bliss had made Pierson conscious of his lack of spiritual power and had changed the course of his life. The American tour of George Mueller of Bristol, England, had further convinced Pierson of his need to "depend utterly on God."[1] By the end of the century, he was a familiar figure among those American and British evangelicals who longed to experience more fully the faith they professed.

Pierson's assessment of the past decades differed radically from that of prominent contemporaries. He ignored situations that alarmed other conservatives, and he disagreed with liberals who welcomed the advances of modern science and the liberation of Christianity from the obscurantism of the past. His assessment was positive, and he published it under the title *Forward Movements of the Last Half Century.* First on his list of indicators of evangelical progress was "the increase of personal holiness." In spite of the crises around him, Pierson exuded confidence. In the growing interest in holiness and the Holy Spirit he discerned the progress of God's end-times plan.

The subject of holiness illustrates some of the similarities and differences between the loosely-defined liberals and conservatives in late nineteenth-century Protestantism.[2] Like conservatives, liberals expressed concern about the lack of spiritual vitality around them. Social Gospel theologian Walter Rauschenbusch, for example, wrote compellingly of the Church's desperate need for spiritual power. His indictment of contemporary Protestantism was as severe as that of any conservative:

> The morality of the Church is not much more than what prudence, respectability and good breeding also demand. Nor is the morality of church members generally distinguished by the glow of spiritual fervor. There is less family worship and prayerful life than with our fathers. But with this moral outfit, can the Church authoritatively say to the world, "Repent and become like me?"[3]

Rauschenbusch summoned his generation to find renewed power by reclaiming the "old gospel"—by living and acting "according to the truth which the Church has previously instilled into their minds and which they have long accepted as true."[4]

Conservatives did the same. They insisted that the call to holiness was nothing more than the reestablishment of an integral part of the Christian life. But the benefits of holiness, except among more radical holiness groups, were understood by most conservatives to enrich the individual's quest for personal salvation. Even there, liberals spoke similar language; they simply applied it to the church collectively. In terms that could have been borrowed by conservatives, for example, Rauschenbusch maintained that, throughout history, the Church had repeatedly been "rejuvenated by a new baptism in [the] Spirit." Writing in 1904, he shared Pierson's confidence:

> I have full faith in the future of the Christian Church. A new season of power will come when we have put our sin from us. Our bitter need will drive us to repentance. The prophetic spirit will awaken us. The tongue of fire will descend on twentieth century men and give them great faith, joy and boldness, and then we shall hear the new evangel, and it will be the Old Gospel.[5]

Thus the Pentecost event, with which many conservatives seemed increasingly preoccupied, served as a model for liberal expectations as well. The participation of women in the Upper Room event also encouraged growing numbers of women in several denominations to insist on their right to preach the gospel.[6]

Pierson, on the other hand, noted the attention given *personal* holiness in most denominations by the end of the century, and though the emphasis varied from denomination to denomination, he was optimistic:

> Under different names and from divers sources, like mingling streams merged into one flood, the current has been in one direction. Different names . . . have clung to these movements; some of them have been stigmatized as "Perfectionism," or mildly described as "for the deepening of spiritual life." As certain phrases have become obnoxious to criticism, linked with fanatical extremes . . . others have been adopted; but it is plain that, in all these efforts, the same Holy Spirit has been at work, showing disciples their lack of conformity to God and leading willing souls to new steps of self-surrender and appropriation of Christ.[7]

Wesleyan Holiness Teaching on the Holy Spirit

One "stream" of emphasis on holiness was, of course, American Methodism. Motivated by John Wesley's teaching on Christian perfection and by Charles Wesley's powerful hymns describing the experience, holiness advocates in nineteenth-century American Methodist ranks taught the present availability of "entire sanctification."[8] They referred specifically to a "second definite work of grace" in which the inclination to sin would be uprooted and replaced by perfect love. Their focus on cleansing resulted in a concentration on the blood of Jesus and on the work of the Holy Spirit. Phoebe Palmer Knapp gave the experience popular expression in her gospel song *The Cleansing Wave.*

> The cleansing stream I see, I see;
> I plunge, and oh, it cleanseth me!
> Oh, praise the Lord, it cleanseth me!
> It cleanseth me—yes, cleanseth me.

"Hidden depravity," wrote holiness teacher George D. Watson, "can never be truly discovered by us but by the light of the Spirit shining in a converted heart."[9] Watson insisted that this was an experience that followed conversion—that "one must get a good deal of evangelical religion before he can see and feel his need of heart purity."[10]

Consequently, the Holy Spirit was understood as "the executive, personal Agent in making us holy." And the "second blessing," sometimes termed "the baptism of the Holy Ghost," was the only "infallible safeguard against heresy."[11] In most holiness thinking, the work of sanctification had both progressive and instantaneous dimensions. In a sermon preached at the Vineland, New Jersey, Holiness Camp Meeting in 1867, J. W. Horne explained:

> Sanctification is a progressive work, while entire sanctification is the work of but a moment. There is a moment in which the darkness forever ceases; there is a moment in which the dying Adam is dead and the new Adam is alive; . . . there is a moment in which sanctification passes into entire sanctification.[12]

"In the condition of entire sanctification," Horne further noted, "we are enabled to devote our energies successfully to the great work of . . . strengthening the stakes of Zion at home and abroad;

and to strive after the building up of saints in their most holy faith."[13] In contrast, a "state of partial sanctification" was said to "chain down" the believer's attention to his own spiritual struggles in a way that hindered usefulness in the church or society. "When the preacher has a consciousness of inward purity, and realizes the power of God in his heart, with what energy and success is he enabled to work!"[14]

The call to entire sanctification was frequently presented as a challenge to entire consecration—to the "laying of one's *all* on the altar." As one holiness songwriter expressed it:

> Do you want the "fire of God" to fill your soul,
> Burn up all the dross, and sanctify the whole?
> Make the consecration, trust in God, and then
> Let the Holy Ghost come in.[15]

Increasingly through the nineteenth century, people who pursued sanctification described a facet of the experience that underscored the power of the Holy Spirit. "Make, then, this entire consecration," a New York Methodist pastor, B. M. Adams, enjoined, "and the Holy Ghost will come upon you at this meeting, and fill you with a power that you never had before. The nature of its influence I cannot describe; but 'Ye shall receive power after that the Holy Ghost is come upon you.' And ye shall be witnesses to God, even though you may be unconscious of the fact."[16] Thousands were inspired to claim this power as they sang words penned by Methodist Lelia Morris: "He will fill your heart *today* to overflowing with the Holy Ghost and power." The same people joined fervently in Methodist Charles Gabriel's prayer:

> Lord, send the oldtime power, the Pentecostal
>   power!
> Thy floodgates of blessing on us throw open wide!
> Lord, send the oldtime power, the Pentecostal
>   power,
> That sinners be converted, and Thy name glorified.

Since the early part of the nineteenth century, holiness teaching had been part of a deliberate attempt of some Methodists to nurture their full Wesleyan heritage. From the 1830s it had had clear interdenominational appeal. And the challenge to Christian perfection had harmonized as well with a broad cultural concern for the perfection of America. Holiness advocates had poured vitality into movements for social reform.[17] The pre-Civil War movement had also molded some new denominations as some staunch supporters of the second blessing separated from Methodism. Questions related to slavery had formally split Methodism into northern and southern wings in 1844.

After the war, some Methodists decided that complacency in the church demanded that they renew their commitment to the proclamation of the crisis experience of holiness. They used the camp meeting, which by then had virtually become a Methodist institution, to challenge large interdenominational audiences to pursue a definite religious experience that followed conversion. As before, the experience had many designations, but increasingly it connoted a dual reception of cleansing and power. And it was often accompanied by physical manifestations. J. W. Horne noted: "It makes some people boisterous in their manifestations, and other people still. Some may have power that manifests itself in noise like thunder, and some silent power like the lightning."[18] Holiness lyrics that later Pentecostals often sang described its physical effects in popular terms with which many readily identified:

We find many people who can't understand
Why we are so happy and free;
We've crossed over Jordan to Canaan's fair land,
And this is like heaven to me.

So when we are happy we sing and we shout,
Some don't understand us, I see;
We're filled with the Spirit, there isn't a doubt,
And this is like heaven to me.[19]

Songwriter Lelia Morris regularly attended the holiness camp meeting at Mountain Lake Park, Maryland, where she reported being sanctified in 1892. A camp meeting sermon in 1896 inspired her to describe in song another dimension of the holiness experience. In addition to cleansing and empowering, it initiated believers into a rich daily experience of conscious fellowship with Christ: Like the biblical Israelites, they left struggles behind and, in communion with Christ, entered the "promised land." In Morris's words:

'Tis the Canaanland for our weary feet,
With our wanderings o'er, and our rest complete;
Where we dwell with Christ in communion sweet,
Baptized with the Holy Ghost.[20]

One John Brown also considered the experience "entrance into Canaan" and participation in a perpetual feast. He gave it simple but forceful expression in 1899 in the song *Feasting with my Lord:*

Since my soul is saved and sanctified,
Feasting, I'm feasting,
In this land of Canaan I'll abide,
Feasting with my Lord.[21]

For holiness advocates, salvation was not essentially a rational process: It was a dynamic, transforming experience that brought "heaven" into their lives. Daily fellowship with Christ made real to them by the indwelling Holy Spirit transformed their existence. "Life wears a different face to me, since I found my Savior," they sang. "Golden sunbeams 'round me play / Jesus turns my night to day / Heaven seems not far away, since I found my Savior."[22]

Songs and sermons stressed the satisfying nature of the experience: People whose understanding of the Christian life made them aware of a growing disparity between cultural values and their own priorities found in the holiness message inner "rest."

Denied many of this world's pleasures and goods, they none-theless had what they called true and abiding riches. Their experience of Christ made *Him* more appealing than worldly attractions: "Sin, with its follies, I gladly resign. . . . Give me but Jesus, my Lord, crucified."[23] Among the many hymns that testified to satisfaction, F. G. Burroughs' *I Have Found It* is a particularly clear statement of how holiness teaching offered an opportunity to reinterpret life. "Trials" became "conquests," "sighs" were transformed to "praise":

> Since I came at Jesus' bidding, and received the
>   promised rest,
> I have found His ways most pleasant, and His
>   paths serene and blest;
> Trials have been changed to conquests, sighs are
>   lost in songs of praise;
> And all turmoil, care and conflict are transformed
>   by hope's bright rays.

The experience met basic needs of companionship and as-surance. "I am never lonely anymore, since the Comforter has come," believers proclaimed. Nor did they have anything "to dread or fear" with "the power of Pentecost here."[24] It gave confidence too: "Heaven and earth may fade and flee, / Firstborn light in gloom decline; / But while God and I shall be, / I am His and He is mine."[25]

And the satisfaction could increase, for the "glory never failed." The experience was not static; the faithful constantly sought "higher ground." Like the call to salvation, the chal-lenge of sanctification was addressed to "whosoever will." "Bless God, it is for us all today," wrote L. L. Pickett in 1897.[26]

At times this expanding Wesleyan-based holiness message promoted a spiritual arrogance that alienated others. In 1894, the *Journal* of the Methodist Episcopal Church, South, com-plained:

> There has sprung up among us a party with holiness as a

watchword; they have holiness associations, holiness meetings, holiness preachers, holiness evangelists and holiness property. Religious experience is represented as if it consists of only two steps [i.e., salvation and sanctification]. . . The effect is to disparage the new birth, and all stages of spiritual growth from the blade to the full corn in the ear. . . . We deplore their methods in so far as they claim a monopoly on the experience, practice, and advocacy of holiness.[27]

Certainly the heterodox practices that flourished under the broad banner of holiness troubled its thoughtful spokespersons as well as other Christians. By the latter part of the century, vast numbers of Methodists were involved in an interdenominational movement that was not subject to denominational control, and increasingly they felt pressured to reconfirm their Methodist loyalties. Urged to enrich their denomination by bringing the spiritual vigor of their quest for holiness under its guidance, many holiness Methodists complied. The fact that the northern and southern segments of the Methodist Episcopal Church were also reconsidering the doctrine of sanctification contributed as well to impatience with holiness advocates. By the end of the century, those who rejected instantaneous sanctification had deeply influenced the denominations. The situation was further aggravated during the 1890s by the strong come-outer position that had found support among the more radical holiness people.

Holiness advocates had, in fact, proven to be receptive to many varieties of teaching. The prominence they gave religious experience, for example, had encouraged some to advocate a series of religious crises in the pursuit of perfection. Their stress on Bible study had resulted in the expectation by some of physical healing, or teaching about "faith" living.[28] Some, contrary to generally accepted Methodist teaching, expected an imminent premillennial Second Coming. Some pursued unusual manifestations of the Spirit's presence and power. And some went so far as to reject established denominations entirely. In a book that became the virtual handbook of come-outers, J. H. Brooks maintained that the churches were "too selfish, too bigoted, too far backslidden and fallen to give in . . . to a purely spiritual movement in their midst. . . . Holiness cannot be successfully propagated under sectarian conditions. . . . The time of compromise in connection with the holiness work is past."[29] Deploring those who advocated holiness and yet remained "in bondage to the sects," Brooks issued a stirring call to participation in what he called the "One True Church."[30]

Around the country, many holiness people agreed that the denominations were hopelessly backslidden and that further association with them was not only inadvisable but positively sinful.[31] Tiny holiness associations and missions emerged, each intent on promoting a biblical experiential form of Christianity, sometimes with direct reference to the restoration of New Testament faith. Other holiness ministries were longer established, having separated earlier. Some were highly organized: The Salvation Army, for example, represented a tightly disciplined and socially-aware version of holiness teaching. In practical outlook, and even in religious language, it shared the social concern of evolving liberal Social Gospelers. Yet it carefully preserved the individualistic emphasis that made personal holiness the basis for social concern.

Some come-outer holiness groups had strong restorationist sympathies. The Evening Light Saints, for example, shared the restorationist view that the "apostolic morning" of church history had yielded to "papal night." The Reformation had produced a "cloudy afternoon." The late nineteenth century was the focus of all history, however, for it would see the restoration of primitive Christianity in "pure evening light" that would never fade.[32]

During the last two decades of the nineteenth century, participants in the holiness movement made an impressive contribution to gospel music. The songs they wrote testifying to their experience convey better than any other source the popular understanding of the practical meaning of sanctification and "enduement with power." Many of them became Pentecostal favorites because even those Pentecostals who later rejected the holiness understanding of crisis sanctification identified closely with holiness spirituality.

This broad Wesleyan-based holiness movement, using language that conveyed the necessity of two religious experiences, extended its influence into denominations that were traditionally non-Wesleyan. And it had meaning for blacks struggling to chart their course in post-Civil War America. One such was Charles Price Jones, a Baptist pastor who, under the influence of holiness teaching, claimed sanctification in 1894 in Selma, Alabama. The next year, Jones accepted the pastorate of Mt. Helm Baptist Church in Jackson, Mississippi. While there, he determined to proclaim the holiness message: He concluded that the Baptists he knew were not "toting fair with Jesus."[33]

Jones began by convening a holiness convention in 1897. The group he gathered claimed to be interdenominational and non-sectarian, "serving in the denominations if allowed, but serving Christ in the life of His people" if expelled. The attendance of delegates from Arkansas, Tennessee, Missouri, Illinois, North Carolina, Louisiana, Alabama, and Georgia indicated the extent of this movement. Although this and later conventions were predominantly black, Jones noted that "black and white, Jew and Gentile sought God together."[34]

In 1898, Jones reported that "the fight began hard against us."[35] In fact, participants experienced various forms of persecution, and many left their denominations. After prolonged disagreement over a suitable name for the growing movement, Jones and his followers agreed on Churches of God in Christ. One of Jones's associates, Charles H. Mason, founded a church at Conway, Arkansas, and later became pastor of a congregation in Memphis. Mason assisted Jones as an overseer of the church and was known throughout the association as an effective street preacher. First known as Elder Mason, he later became a bishop and led a substantial percentage of Jones's people into the Pentecostal movement.

Jones found music an effective way to teach the experience he advocated. Songs he wrote (like *Jesus Christ is Made to Me All I Need; Deeper, Deeper in the Love of Jesus; I Would Not Be Denied;* and *Come Unto Me*) captured the essence of his message and made an enduring contribution, extending his influence far beyond what denominational membership statistics would suggest. They have been found in evangelical and Pentecostal hymnals since.

Holiness movements also stimulated a reconsideration of the place of women in public ministries. Study of the Holy Spirit, and especially the Pentecost event, put attention on Joel's prophecy: "Your sons *and your daughters* shall prophesy." While this did not necessarily support ordination or offices for women, it did affirm their proper participation in Bible readings, exhortations, public prayers, and occasional sermons in mixed gatherings. Concentration on the Holy Spirit often tended to create a setting in which the equality of the sexes before God was acknowledged. Methodists Phoebe Palmer and Frances Willard and Salvation Army pioneer Catherine Booth published the case for women in ministry, and their views were endorsed by A. J. Gordon, the prominent Bostonian Baptist pastor who articulated the message of healing. (Significantly, non-holiness women who felt called to public ministries also frequently used the Pentecost event as the basis for claiming the right of public participation.)[36]

Non-Wesleyan Teaching on the Holy Spirit

A concentration on the person and work of the Holy Spirit also characterized some evangelicals who denied the basic Wesleyan premise of the necessity of two works of grace and who rejected the language of instantaneous, entire sanctification. These men and women generally had ties to denominations with roots predating Wesleyan history: They were Congregationalists, Baptists, Presbyterians. They were deeply committed to a view of biblical inerrancy. Most of them had been influenced by premillennialist ideas that had persuaded them of their need for both personal holiness and spiritual power. As these matters directed their attention to the Holy Spirit— and as they read the Bible from a perspective that stressed their being in the last days—they anticipated not only personal renewal and an end-times restoration of the apostolic faith, but also a worldwide revival. Although they shared many emphases with Wesleyan holiness advocates, they regarded themselves as distinct; and their combination of emphases on pre-millennialism, faith healing, and revival had extensive influence on the development of Pentecostalism.

This non-Wesleyan concentration on holiness and the Holy Spirit became central to the ministries of several men of prominence in the growing Bible institute and Bible conference movements. All of them enjoyed a close association with Evangelist Dwight L. Moody, whose influence permeated many areas of evangelical endeavor.

Moody claimed to have had a life-changing baptism in the Holy Spirit. Apparently stimulated in part by the concern of several members in his Chicago Avenue Church about his need for spiritual power, Moody embarked on a spiritual quest that culminated in an intense religious experience: "I cannot describe it," he insisted. "It is almost too sacred an experience to name.... I can only say God revealed Himself to me, and I had such an experience of His love that I had to ask Him to stay His hand."[37] Two months before his death in December 1899, he reflected on the importance of the resulting "enduement with power":

> There are two epochs in my life which stand out clear. One is when I was between 18 and 19 years old, when I was born of the Spirit. There never can come a greater blessing to a man on this earth than to be born again, born from above, to have the God-nature planted in him.

> God has been good to me. He has showered blessing after blessing upon me; but the greatest blessing, next to being born again, came 16 years after, when I was filled with the Spirit, and it has never left me.[38]

Because of the meaning this experience had for Moody, he encouraged others to develop teaching on the subject. Among Moody's associates, Reuben A. Torrey became a prominent advocate of the Spirit-endued life.

Torrey perceived (very wrongly) in American Protestantism a general neglect of the personhood of the Holy Spirit. He insisted that a balanced understanding of the person of the Spirit would enrich one's conception of the entire Christian life, which he conceived as a "walk in the Spirit." If one regarded the Spirit as an influence or a power, he warned, one might well try to "get hold of the Spirit and use it." If, on the other hand, one recognized the Spirit's personhood, one would more likely ask: "How can the Holy Spirit . . . use me?"[39] Those who claimed to "possess" the Spirit, Torrey believed, too often insisted that they belonged to a "superior order of Christians."[40]

For Torrey, however, meditation on the personhood of the Holy Spirit had practical meaning in daily life. Knowing that the Holy Spirit was "an infinitely wise, infinitely holy, infinitely tender" Person who desired fellowship with individuals encouraged awareness of one's personal need for holiness in order to sustain that fellowship. A. B. Simpson agreed. "We are not filled with an influence; we are not filled with a sensation; we are not filled with a set of ideas and truths; we are not filled with a blessing, but we are filled with a person."[41] And true communion with the Holy Spirit destroyed interest in this-worldly pursuits. Torrey wrote: "Anyone who has really received the Holy Spirit, and in whom the Holy Spirit dwells and is unhindered in His working will not want to partake of [worldly amusements]. . . . Why is it then that so many professed Christians do go after these worldly amusements? For one of two reasons: either because they have never definitely received the Holy Spirit, or else because the fountain is choked."[42] One's relationship with the Spirit depended on one's carefulness: Fellowship was something to be cherished; its cost was absolute obedience. "How carefully we ought to walk in all things so as not to grieve Him who dwells within us," Torrey admonished.[43]

Torrey regarded sanctification as a progressive experience that began at conversion and proceeded as the believer "walked in the Spirit." Torrey represents those who insisted that "daily, hourly, constant victory over the flesh and over sin" was possible through the absolute obedience that fellowship with the Holy Spirit necessitated:

> The Spirit's power may be in such fulness, that one is not conscious even of the presence of the flesh—it seems dead

and gone—but it is only kept in the place of death by the
Holy Spirit's power. If we try to take one step in our own
strength we fail. We must live in the Spirit and walk in
the Spirit if we would have victory.[44]

Entirely aside from this dimension of spirituality, Torrey and
others taught that Christians could discover the true source of
spiritual power in a crisis experience that they called the baptism with the Holy Spirit. In his teaching on the Holy Spirit,
Torrey claimed to reject two of the central tenets of the Wesleyan-based Holiness message: He denied that sanctification
was instantaneous (or that, in this life, the believer would ever
be entirely sanctified) and he contended that sanctification was
not the baptism of the Holy Spirit. Holiness advocates, Torrey
insisted, expressed in an "inaccurate . . . and unscriptural way
the great and precious truth after which they grasped."[45] Sanctification was not a work of grace, but a gift of faith: Only as
the believer "reckoned himself dead indeed unto sin" and "alive
unto God," only as long as one consciously permitted the Holy
Spirit to subdue one's will, could the believer be assured of
inward "victory" over sin. Torrey tied this notion of progressive
sanctification to his eschatology: One's attitude toward Christ's
second advent indicated one's involvement in the process of
sanctification. The "earnest cry" of those who were being sanctified was "even so, come, Lord Jesus."[46]
Although Torrey believed Christians experienced but one
work of grace, he concluded that they should also be "endued
with power for service." Throughout the 1890s, Moody encouraged Torrey to present systematic teaching on the baptism in
the Holy Spirit.[47] As a result, Torrey published one of the growing number of books on the baptism in the Holy Spirit during
the 1890s.[48] (Another prominent religious author who advocated crisis experiences of "fillings" of the Spirit was Moody's
close associate, A. J. Gordon.[49]) Torrey insisted that Spirit baptism was essential: It was wrong to attempt any Christian work
until one had been baptized in the Holy Spirit. A daily walk
in communion with the Spirit did not constitute the specific
power for service that Spirit baptism bestowed.[50] The service
for which the Spirit endued was essentially evangelistic. While

the experience included a dimension that offered "power to *be*" as well as "to say and to do," it was understood especially to enable effectiveness in attracting others to Christ and to the walk in the Spirit.

These evangelicals noted a close relationship between submission to God's will and the reception of Spirit baptism. Moody maintained:

> If a man isn't willing to do anything or everything for the Lord, I don't believe he will get the Spirit. God can't trust him with the power. But when a man is completely emptied of self, and is ready to do anything or to go anywhere, then it is that God fills him.[51]

Because Torrey believed that the baptism in the Holy Spirit was essential to the evangelization of the world before Christ's soon return, he sought to convince Christians of their obligation to receive the experience. "If I *may* be baptized with the Holy Spirit, I *must* be," he insisted.[52] Moody concurred: "God commands us to be filled with the Spirit; and if we are not filled, it is because we are living beneath our privileges. I think that is the great trouble with Christendom today: we are not living up on the plane where God would have us live."[53] Torrey cautioned his generation to consider seriously the implications of failure to "seek" Spirit baptism:

> If I am not willing to pay the price of this Baptism, and therefore am not so baptized, I am responsible before God for all the souls that might have been saved but were not saved through me because I was not baptized with the Holy Spirit.[54]

Torrey and other leaders proposed no "uniform initial evidence" of this baptism with the Holy Spirit. Moody listed among the definite proofs of the experience a desire to "learn more about Christ," a love for the Bible, a desire for spiritual knowledge and experience, disinterested love.[55] "You shouldn't be looking for any token," he advised. "Just keep asking and waiting for power."[56]

Torrey noted a relationship between the walk in the Spirit and the retention of spiritual power. "I walk with fear and trembling and cry unto Him daily to keep me from the things that would make the withdrawal of His power necessary." He wrote:

> To see a perishing world around you and to know there is no power in your words to save—would not dying be better than that? . . . Oh, the agony of having known God's power, of having been used of Him, and then of having that power withdrawn, to be laid aside as far as any real usefulness is concerned! Men may still praise you, but God can't use you.[57]

The most immediate theological opposition to such teaching surfaced in the reviews of Torrey's and Gordon's books in denominational periodicals like the *Presbyterian and Reformed Review* and the *Presbyterian Quarterly*. While admitting that the teaching incorporated much that was edifying, reviewers claimed that the Pentecost event had been "peculiar" to the Upper Room and would not recur. Noting that Torrey's teaching inclined to some phases "of the doctrine which, in its grosser forms, is called 'the second blessing,' " reviewers suggested that Torrey's distinctions between his views and those of Wesleyan Holiness leaders were inconsequential: His teaching tended to function similarly and to approach the "insidious [Wesleyan] error."[58]

Beginning in 1881, Moody invited those who shared his desire for the realization of the Holy Spirit's ministry in the believer's life to convene at Northfield, Massachusetts, for summer conferences. The first gathering, attracting some three hundred, was advertised as a time of prayer for "revival and an outpouring of the Holy Spirit." Over the next two decades, thousands of people, attending different kinds of conferences (some for college students; others directed toward Christian workers; some advertised as "general"), reported on meetings of "thrilling character" where they received the baptism in the Holy Spirit. Moody urged them on in their spiritual quests: "Let us pray that we may be baptized with power from on high . . . that we may be always ready—ready for anything."[59] To students anticipating a life of Christian service he appealed:

> Let me beg of you: Get full of the Holy Ghost. Just make up your minds you will not leave these gatherings until God fills you. Don't be afraid. Lots of people are afraid of being called fanatics. You are not good for anything until the world considers you a fanatic.[60]

Northfield Conferences in time incorporated other evangelical emphases. Moody invited speakers from various traditions, some of whom differed radically even on matters like the verbal inspiration of Scripture. He permitted no controversial doctrines—like dispensationalism or divine healing—to be taught from the platform at Northfield. But his emphasis on the Holy Spirit, on the walk in the Spirit that was sanctification, and on prayer for a worldwide revival probably made it inevitable that a strong missions orientation would evolve. Arthur T. Pierson became the dynamic spokesman for foreign missions at Northfield.[61]

In 1885, Pierson urged Moody to sponsor an interdenominational council to facilitate effective, rapid evangelization, proposing that the denominations divide the geographic territory to be covered so that they would not duplicate efforts. Moody appointed a committee, chaired by Pierson, to convene the conference. The call Pierson drafted clearly demonstrated the integral relationship between the evangelical concentration on the Holy Spirit and the foreign missions efforts it supported:

> The first Pentecost crowned ten days of united, continued supplication. Every subsequent advance may be directly traced to believing prayer, and upon this must depend a new Pentecost. We earnestly appeal to all fellow disciples to join us and each other in importunate daily supplication for a new and mighty effusion of the Holy Spirit ... that God would impart to all Christ's witnesses the tongues of fire, and melt hard hearts before the burning message. It is not by might nor by power, but by the Spirit of the Lord that all true success must be secured.[62]

This appeal resulted in the London Missionary Conference of 1888. Meanwhile, Moody cooperated with Pierson's concern by adding a student conference, which preceded the General Conference at Northfield in 1886. Some of the Cambridge Seven, a prominent group of university cricket players who had been converted in Moody's British campaigns and had then devoted their lives to foreign missions, attended the student conference.[63] That conference contributed ultimately to the formation of the Student Volunteer Movement.[64]

Moody's Chicago Bible Training Institute also became a center from which specific emphases on the person and work of the Holy Spirit were promulgated. His school, his revival campaigns, and his Northfield Conferences attracted a wide range of middle- and working-class Protestant participants—including women and blacks—popularized teaching on the Holy Spirit, and offered a forum for the exchange of ideas as well as a setting in which important contacts were made. They also popularized the new gospel songs of people like Fanny Crosby (who occasionally visited Northfield), songs that sometimes dealt expressly with the "outpouring" of the Holy Spirit. *The Comforter Has Come,* with its exuberant assertion, "The long, long night is past / the morning breaks at last," was a Northfield favorite long before Pentecostals claimed it as descriptive of their experience.

Mediating Positions: Charles Finney, The Higher Christian Life, Keswick, The Christian and Missionary Alliance

Among those who articulated an interest in holiness and spiritual power, some held a mediating position between Wesleyans and non-Wesleyans. A focus on Christ, the Holy Spirit, and religious experience obscured the differences between liberals and conservatives (or between advocates of instantaneous sanctification and progressive sanctification) and attracted people of various persuasions who were less concerned with theology than with religious experience.[65] The Northfield Conferences came to demonstrate the degree of compatability between conservatives and liberals who stressed Christocentric experience and the Holy Spirit.

One who promoted these themes was Charles G. Finney. Finney accepted a second crisis experience, maintaining that it was not a cleansing work of grace but rather an enduement with power. He used the Wesleyan term "Christian perfection" but tried to qualify it to suit his meaning.[66] Later Pentecostal periodicals acknowledged their movement's debt to Finney, whose *Autobiography* their periodicals highly recommended. Not only could they identify with his emotional conversion experience; they also appreciated his focus on the Holy Spirit. (In an effort to legitimize him fully, some Pentecostals insisted that the "groanings" that marked his intense spiritual experiences must have included tongues speech.) Others, especially Congregationalists and Presbyterians, shared this commitment to an experience-oriented life-style they called the higher Christian life.

The possibility of this higher life had captured the interest of thousands of Protestants. One of them, Presbyterian William Edwin Boardman, became a prominent advocate of the possibility of an intense spirituality he believed most Christians lacked. He lent emphasis to the growing interest through his book, *The Higher Christian Life.* In the 1870s, Boardman joined forces with two other advocates of this higher life, Robert Pearsall and Hannah Whitall Smith. The Smiths had been influenced by both Plymouth Brethren emphases on Bible study and Wesleyan teaching on holiness. Their message too was essentially Christocentric. "My whole horizon used to be filled with this great big *Me* of mine," Hannah Smith wrote in her autobiography, "but when I got a sight of Christ as my perfect Savior, this great big Me wilted down to nothing."[67] For Smith, the simple message of the indwelling Christ as a *present* Savior became "the Christian's secret of a happy life."[68]

The Smiths and Boardman recognized the similarity of their messages: the constant, conscious, sin- and self-subduing reign of Christ within the believer. They described the experience as present salvation: "Jesus saves me *now.*" They decided to embark on a united effort to extend the teaching in Great Britain.

As a result of their efforts, the Keswick movement emerged in 1875. Originally, Keswick Conventions were directed primarily by evangelical Anglicans. All speakers were university men and ordained clergy. Nonetheless, they aroused strong controversy within the church. Throughout the winter of 1875, numerous clergy maintained that higher life teaching "subverted the whole argument and scope of Romans and Hebrews," that it "impugned God's sovereignty," and "dishonored God's discriminating grace." One writer observed that sinning actually brought glory to God, as "God got honour to Himself by drawing us out of it."[69] In spite of strong opposition, the tradition of annual Keswick conventions was established when a second convention gathered in 1876.

In time, Keswick conventions attracted non-Anglicans as well. Numerous participants eventually found a wide following in the United States as well as in England. The writing and preaching ministries of Keswick leaders like Frederick Brotherton Meyer, Andrew Murray, and G. Campbell Morgan evoked response throughout the evangelical world.

The Keswick message came to stress holiness and spiritual power through a life of overcoming. The secret was simple:

> Let in the Overcomer, and He will conquer thee.
> Thy broken spirit taken in sweet captivity
> Shall glory in His triumph, and share His victory.

Such prospects appealed to a diverse group. Keswick participants did not attempt to agree on eschatology or divine healing. They represented a concern in British evangelicalism for the realization of a walk in the Spirit, or of an overcoming life. It is difficult to describe fully the spirituality that Keswick advocated. Like other mediating movements, it attracted people who individualized its teaching. Because its spokespersons came from diverse backgrounds, they articulated differently the emphases on Christ and the Holy Spirit that Keswick helped them understand. Arthur T. Pierson, who participated in several Keswick Conventions, provided the best-organized summary. He identified seven steps in Keswick teaching: (1) Immediate abandonment of known sin; (2) surrender of the will to Jesus as Master and Lord; (3) appropriation by faith of God's promise and power for holy living; (4) voluntary renunciation and mortification of the self-life; (5) gracious renewal, or transformation, of the inmost temper and disposition; (6) separation unto God for sanctification, consecration, and service; and (7) enduement with power and infilling with the Holy Spirit, the believer claiming his share in the Pentecostal gift.[70] These steps assisted participants in obtaining a "full" salvation.

> Love's resistless current sweeping
> All the regions deep within;
> Thought and wish and senses keeping
> Now, and every instant, clean.
> Full Salvation!
> From the guilt and power of sin.
>
> Life immortal, heaven descending,
> Lo! my heart the Spirit's shrine!
> God and man in oneness blending—
> Oh, what fellowship is mine!
> Full Salvation!
> Raised in Christ to life divine.[71]

During the 1890s, various Keswick representatives accepted invitations to Moody's Northfield Conferences. While in America, they engaged in extensive preaching and teaching tours and thus alerted Americans to the message and method that Keswick represented. Keswick's message, like that of American advocates of a walk in the Spirit, or a higher life, was based on the assumption "that the average Christian life is grievously destitute of real spiritual power and often essentially carnal."[72] Moody noted that most Christians of his acquaintance "lived in Romans 7" (with its frustrated expression: "For the good that I would I do not: but the evil which I would not, that I do") instead of "moving over to Romans 8" (with its positive assertion: "The law of the Spirit of life in Christ Jesus hath made me free from the law of sin and death").

A. B. Simpson, the founder of the Christian and Missionary Alliance and a man whose conception of Christian experience extensively influenced later Pentecostalism, also had close ties to Wesleyan and non-Wesleyan teaching on the Holy Spirit.[73] Simpson tried to disassociate himself from Wesleyan teaching on sanctification in a widely circulated article entitled "Himself."[74] In his thought, Christ-centered religious experience, energized by the Holy Spirit, became the central focus.[75] Perhaps his precise differences with one side or the other on matters relating to pneumatology were not consistently clear in his own mind. He unwittingly emphasized a topic that made his ministry attractive to people who shared his hope for experientially-based Christian unity in the end times.

As noted, Simpson was a Presbyterian by birth and theological training who left that denomination to create various non-denominational agencies for evangelistic work. Over the course of his life, he edited several journals and devotional papers; founded a Bible institute (which was known as a missionary training institute) in New York City; established a faith home where divine healing was both taught and practiced; conducted camp meetings; and, in 1887, organized both the Christian Alliance and the Missionary Alliance. (These he merged in 1897, thus creating the Christian and Missionary Alliance.) Both the Christian Alliance and the Missionary Alliance were conceived as associations of evangelical Christians of many denominations who were dedicated to accomplishing certain tasks. In a sense, they fit the pattern of the voluntary associations that were a conspicuous part of nineteenth-century evangelicalism.

Simpson's Christocentrism particularly influenced his views on healing, sanctification, and the Holy Spirit. In each case, he stressed Christ as Healer, as Sanctifier, as Baptizer. His teaching came to be known as the fourfold gospel: Christ the Savior, Healer, Sanctifier, and Coming King. Songs written by Simpson, some of which became popular in Pentecostalism, expressed the implications of the conviction he described in his poem, *Jesus Only:*

Jesus only is our message,

Jesus all our theme shall be;
We will lift up Jesus ever,
Jesus only will we see.

Jesus only is our Savior,
All our guilt He bore away,
All our righteousness He gives us,
All our strength from day to day.

Jesus is our Sanctifier,
Cleansing us from self and sin,
And with all His Spirit's fullness
Filling all our hearts within.

Jesus only is our Healer,
All our sicknesses He bare,
And His risen life and fullness
All His members still may share.

Jesus only is our power,
His the gift of Pentecost;
Jesus, breathe Thy power upon us,
Fill us with the Holy Ghost.

And for Jesus we are waiting,
Listening for the advent call;
But 'twill still be Jesus only,
Jesus ever, all in all.

For Simpson, the all-sufficiency of Christ became a certainty that motivated his entire ministry. This all-sufficiency, he maintained, could be recognized only through revelation of the Holy Spirit: One needed to receive Christ "in His personal life and fullness." Through the Holy Spirit, Christ would then "flow into every part and live out His own life in all the diversified experiences and activities of our manifold life."[76] The Christian life was to be an experience of moment-by-moment appropriation of Christ as all. It was emphatically a growing relationship with Christ as He was revealed to the believer by the Holy Spirit.[77]

This life of fellowship with Christ had physical as well as spiritual benefits. Simpson noted that the Holy Spirit "quickened" the "mortal body." He thus advocated an experience he called "divine health." He encouraged believers to expect the Holy Spirit to strengthen their bodies and to keep them physically well. He described this as a higher reality than divine healing, something that one should comprehend while physically well.

Simpson wrote on the sanctified life, noting that sanctification was not "the extinction of evil," but rather "the putting off, the laying aside of evil."[78] "Wholly sanctified," or "entirely consecrated," believers had received, not a "work of grace" as many in the Wesleyan holiness ranks professed, but a "gift of faith" (language some Wesleyans also used). Sanctification, from Simpson's Christocentric perspective, "set [the believer's] affections on things above," making "the joys of the world to come" more meaningful than "this-worldly" pleasures.[79] Thus, in this life, full consecration became both the Christian's "solemn duty" and one's "blessed privilege."[80] Simpson insisted further that true spiritual power, the result of the "baptism of the Holy Ghost," manifested itself in holy character. "The baptism and indwelling of the Holy Ghost within us will deliver and keep us from the power of self," he taught.[81] In this he concurred heartily with Moody, who regarded Spirit baptism as a "short cut to holiness."[82] The Spirit revealed Christ, Moody believed, and the "quickest way of getting the world out" was "to get Christ in."[83]

So in various settings, some late nineteenth-century evangelicals promoted an individual encounter with the Holy Spirit. Some regarded the encounter as a sanctifying event and a work of grace; others stressed its empowering and regarded it as a gift of faith. Some understood it within the experiential context of American Wesleyan thought; others saw themselves as differing significantly with Wesleyan thought on sanctification and perceived the contemporary repetition of the Pentecost event as eschatologically significant, a sign of the end times. For them, holiness and spiritual power were specifically end-times necessities. Some expressed their spiritual yearnings in

Christocentric language; some dedicated themselves to the realization of restorationist hopes. But together they helped set in motion thought patterns and experiential expectations that motivated prayer for an outpouring of the Holy Spirit in a worldwide revival and influenced the development of Pentecostalism.

Dr. A. B. Simpson, founder of the Christian and Missionary Alliance

3. Charles Parham and the Apostolic Faith

> The Apostolic Faith Movement stands for the restoration of the faith once delivered to the saints, unity of spiritual Christians, the "old time religion."
>
> Charles F. Parham

On a warm summer evening in 1904, a group of young people marched down the main street of a southeastern Kansas town. Attractively dressed and singing gospel songs, they carried a banner that read Apostolic Faith Movement. When they reached a central location, they formed a group and continued singing. As the curious gathered, the young people sang, testified, and preached. They then invited people to a rented hall for an evangelistic service. Most townspeople had an idea what was in store, for the young people, two-by-two, had visited each home and business in the town during the afternoon to introduce people to the apostolic faith.

Those who came encountered the magnetic personality of the founder of the Apostolic Faith Movement, Charles Fox Parham. Acclaimed as an able preacher, Parham reportedly held his audiences spellbound. He played on their emotions, handily moving them from tears to laughter. But entertainment was not his purpose. His purpose was the restoration of the apostolic faith. And the response he evoked in small towns in the contiguous areas of Kansas, Missouri, and Oklahoma indicated that he addressed effectively the felt needs of many people. His message was not profound, but the experience he advocated seemed remarkably effective in enriching his hearers. Few of the towns that he and his followers visited would be the same after his departure. Wherever he went, he left behind those who believed that they had been transformed by a powerful encounter with the living Christ. To them, the experience brought a foretaste of heaven into their mundane lives.

In some ways, Parham seemed an unlikely leader. A frail person, he had neither financial independence nor extensive formal training. He was not an ordained minister. He leaned toward "private interpretations" of Scripture that did not necessarily coincide with orthodoxy. Temperamentally unsuited to cooperate with established authority, Parham had broken his ties to organized religion. Like other "prophets" in his religious subculture, Parham had attracted a motley following. Yet, in the end, he made substantial contributions to the broader religious culture. Fearless and determined, he showed both sensitivity to religious needs and conviction about God's intention to repeat in America the awe-inspiring phenomena of early Christianity.

An Iowan transplanted in southeastern Kansas, Parham's life was marked by restless activity and intense controversy. Haunted by a sense of destiny, Parham achieved notoriety. Persistent rumors raised doubts about his financial and moral integrity and made him a person most later Pentecostals preferred to ignore. In some ways, however, Parham was a quintessential Pentecostal, and certainly American Pentecostals can no longer ignore (as they once attempted to do) his role in the formation of their movement.

One of five sons of William and Ann Parham, Charles Fox was born in Muscatine, a Mississippi River port town in eastern Iowa, on June 4, 1873. In 1885, the family moved by covered wagon to join the earliest settlers of Cheney in south central Kansas. The tiny community had been started in 1883 and was named for the man whose railroad line had opened the area for settlement. Parham's claim that the pioneer community lacked regular church services is inaccurate: First Methodist Church and Trinity Reformed Church had been organized by the time the Parham family arrived. St. Paul's Lutheran Church, Missouri Synod, was organized nearby the next year.[1] If, as Parham later claimed, he had little exposure to formal religious

instruction or preaching during his youth, the situation resulted from choice rather than necessity.

According to Parham's account, his first meaningful exposure
to religion came in 1885 when an itinerant Congregational
preacher conducted meetings in a local schoolhouse.[2] His account, like most of his memories, exaggerated events as well
as his own significance in them.

The visiting preacher, Parham maintained, had been disappointed in the lack of response to his message and had announced that the meetings would conclude before the scheduled
week had ended. Primarily because the meetings provided a
welcome alternative to long evenings at home, Parham decided
to encourage the visitor by standing when the invitation was
next given. Declared a convert, Parham claimed that his decision was later reinforced by a religious experience that
"thrilled every tissue and fibre of our being."[3] (Parham does
not tell his readers if the meetings in fact continued.)

Late in 1885, Parham's mother died. Funeral services were
conducted by C. S. Bolton.[4] The local obituary provides the first
indication of a relationship between the Parham family and
this remarkable missionary of the Church of God of the General
Eldership. Bolton, appointed a Church of God missionary to
Kansas after service in Ohio and Missouri, provides a link
between Parham and another Church of God evangelist, Maria
B. Woodworth-Etter. Woodworth-Etter's charismatic style, emphasis on healing, "trances," and spiritual gifts (including Spirit
baptism) deeply influenced thousands of Americans. Bolton later
assisted her in St. Louis and Topeka, eventually settling into
the pastorate of a Topeka Church of God congregation that had
been formed out of her meetings. The type of spirituality the
Church of God represented (and which Bolton, through his
association with Woodworth-Etter, would seem to have endorsed)—an inclination toward holiness themes and charismatic experience—apparently provided Parham with a frame
of reference for the future. Such elements would later characterize his meetings.[5]

Parham's religious interests were undoubtedly reinforced
when Bolton united his widower father and Harriet Miller in

marriage in 1886. A lifelong Methodist, Parham's stepmother was the daughter of a pioneer northern Indiana Methodist circuit rider and was known as a devout Christian who "loved the power of old time religion."[6] She and William Parham prospered financially and also opened their home for religious activities.[7] William cultivated his land, raised cattle, and later purchased a business in town. The house he built in Cheney in 1901 was described in the local paper as "one of the finest private residences in the county."[8]

At fifteen, Charles Parham held his first public services, which, he reported, "were followed with marked results."[9] The local paper did not report the gatherings, but did note Parham's employment as a schoolteacher in nearby Norwich for the summer term of 1890.

In 1891, he enrolled at Southwestern Kansas College, a Methodist-affiliated school that had been started five years earlier in nearby Winfield. He attended the academy and the normal school. Although a student from the fall of 1891 through the spring of 1893, Parham recalled that his extensive involvement in "religious work" precluded satisfactory academic performance.[10] On the other hand, he also recalled his decision not to enter the ministry, but rather to become a physician.

Parham's Early Ministry

In Parham's personal religious world, events and decisions were charged with spiritual significance. When his frail health deteriorated, he concluded that God was punishing him for heeding the devil's promptings to disregard the call to preach. In a claim typical among those who shared his preoccupation with spiritual meaning, Parham reported that when he had reached the point of death, he "submitted" and vowed to preach. At the same moment, he was convinced he would be healed. A partial recovery followed. Afflicted with continued weakness in his ankles, Parham finally "brought forcible arguments in prayer," soliciting full recovery. Instantly restored, Parham claimed a "revelation" that education would be detrimental to effective ministry, left school, and sought opportunity in the Methodist Episcopal Church, North.[11]

In mid-1893, Parham accepted an assignment as supply pastor in the Methodist Episcopal church in Eudora, Kansas (a small town between Kansas City and Lawrence), where he served until sometime before March 1895.[12] He also preached Sunday afternoons to the Methodist congregation in nearby Linwood, Kansas. His early ministry in Eudora was apparently well-received. In the end, however, his work was singularly unproductive: He reported only one convert after two years.[13] Restive under "the narrowness of sectarian churchism" and "often in conflict with the higher authorities," Parham repudiated denominational affiliation and launched an independent evangelistic ministry.[14]

Parham was never a candidate for ordination in the Methodist church. It seems, rather, that he was a lay preacher throughout his life. Methodist polity clearly states that a qualified lay person can be licensed to preach in a local church on a supply basis. Such licensing (which Parham apparently acquired) does not, however, confer ministerial status. During his tenure in Eudora, Parham was not listed in the Kansas Conference records as either a probationer or a candidate for orders.

Parham's Itinerant Ministry

Having renounced denominational affiliation, Parham embarked on itinerant evangelistic ministry in Kansas. Like other young men and women across the country, he apparently believed that "true Bible Christianity" (which he called "the Apostolic Faith") could not be practiced in traditional settings. Young Parham was a guest in many country homes. A man of the people, he discussed doctrine and spiritual concerns with his host families. Kansas citizens proved receptive to his holiness orientation; the state was hospitable to various contemporary "prophets."[15] State law prohibited the sale of liquor and tobacco. Overall the culture tended to reinforce Protestant values.

In the little town of Tonganoxie, just west of Kansas City, Parham made several firm friends. Among them was David

Baker, an Englishman with a lifelong attachment to the Society of Friends. Baker and Parham spent long hours poring over various Bible translations, and in the course of their study, Baker convinced Parham that the conventional understanding of hell as a place of eternal torment was unbiblical. Since eternal life came by Jesus Christ, he maintained, only those who received Christ could live eternally; the wicked would be annihilated. Parham became an enthusiastic exponent of conditional immortality.

By 1902, Parham had again revised his views on eternal punishment. In a disjointed statement on the end times, he maintained that the majority of humanity would receive "everlasting human life":

> A promised Savior for mankind: the plan was to restore the mass of the human race to what they lost in the fall of Adam, which the unsanctified and many heathens will receive:—everlasting human life. Orthodoxy would cast this entire company into a eternal burning hell; but our God is a God of love and justice, and the flames will reach those only who are utterly reprobate; for without dogs and sorcerers and whoremongers and murderers and idolaters and whosoever loveth and maketh a lie. (Rev. 22:15)[16]

On December 31, 1896, in a Friends' ceremony, Parham married Baker's granddaughter, Sarah Eleanore Thistlewaite.[17]For about two years, they continued to itinerate, building on contacts Parham had made earlier. In September 1897, their first son, Claude, was born. Shortly thereafter, Parham's health failed, the baby became ill, and two close family friends died. Driven to prayer, Parham sought healing for himself. In another dramatic moment that he invested with spiritual meaning, Parham claimed that he "found the power of God to sanctify the body from inbred disease as well as from inbred sin."[18] Later he would declare, "A sanctified body is as much provided for in the atonement of Jesus as is sanctification for the soul."[19] Parham resolved to preach healing and renounce all medical help. He and his son quickly regained strength, and the family moved to Ottawa, Kansas, where Parham began fully to integrate healing into his message. As an independent evangelist with no regular support, Parham often conducted meetings and prayed for the sick in his rented rooms or in local schoolhouses.[20]

Parham soon moved his base of operations to Topeka. After a period of conducting house meetings, he secured a mission and an office, where he prayed for the sick. In 1898, he moved his healing ministry into a large facility that he named Bethel Healing Home. The theme he adopted for his ministry at Bethel was A Living Christianity. Daily morning and evening prayers from 7 to 7:30 were supplemented by a schedule of mission services. Sunday mornings he conducted a holiness meeting. Sunday school followed at 2 P.M., with a healing service scheduled for 3 P.M. Sunday evenings Parham preached an evangelistic service. A women's Bible study on healing on Tuesday afternoons and sessions on prophecy on Friday evenings completed the announced regular schedule. His ministry emphasized "salvation by faith; healing by faith, laying on of hands and prayer; sanctification by faith; coming (premillennial) of Christ; the baptism of the Holy Ghost and Fire, which seals the Bride and bestows the gifts."[21] The mission apparently occasionally reached out to the socially deprived. On January 1, 1900, the local paper reported that Parham's group had provided holiday food for about three hundred needy people.[22]

On the premises Parham also published a biweekly magazine, *The Apostolic Faith*. By this time, he was clearly aware of others who shared his interest in healing. The first issue of *The Apostolic Faith* for 1900 contained a lengthy excerpt from A. B. Simpson's *Gospel of Healing*. It also advertised a pamphlet discrediting John Alexander Dowie.[23]

The title of the publication indicates the restorationist component in his thought. His message had come to include salvation, healing, sanctification, the second coming of Christ, and the baptism of the Holy Spirit.[24] He had concluded that healing had been a central part of the apostolic experience, and that the proclamation of healing "in the atonement" should be "as much part of the Gospel" as the forgiveness of sins. Parham became convinced that an end-times revival—in which "the multitudes would hang upon the Word of God" and "heathen would flow into the hill of the Lord"—would be the result of an uncompromising declaration of divine healing.

Some of Parham's Doctrines

By the turn of the century, Parham exercised considerable inventiveness with various doctrines. His preference for rooting doctrine in his private meditation on Scripture and his conviction that the Holy Spirit communed directly with him undoubtedly influenced the character of his teaching. His impressionable nature and his uncompromising rejection of recognized religious leaders contributed to his impatience with traditional views that diverged from his own.

Although Parham made no mention of participation in the holiness movement, his views on sanctification corresponded with those of the National Holiness Association. Crisis sanctification had many advocates in the region. Iowa was a stronghold of holiness teaching (the Iowa Holiness Association was the largest regional association in the nation); consequently, the surrounding area had been permeated by uncompromising insistence on the normative nature of the second blessing.

It is uncertain when Parham began to focus on the additional experience of the baptism of the Holy Spirit. It is evident, however, that he conceived of that baptism as essentially related to eschatology. Further, it was neither a cleansing event nor an enduement with power for service. Rather, it "sealed the Bride" for "the marriage supper of the Lamb." The record does not indicate how much he knew of the activities of Iowa Holiness Association member Benjamin F. Irwin, leader of the Fire-Baptized Holiness Association, who advocated several crisis experiences (or baptisms) after conversion.[25]

Parham's views on water baptism remained in flux during the early part of his ministry. Writing in 1902, he claimed that a decade earlier he had not taught water baptism at all, because he had believed that Spirit baptism was "the only essential baptism."[26] This suggests that his interest in Spirit baptism dated at least back to his school days in Winfield at age nineteen.

Like his views on eternal punishment, his attitude toward water baptism may have been influenced by his wife's background among the Friends. His views on baptism certainly reflect no influence from his Methodist associations.[27] He never admitted to having taught or practiced infant baptism. Parham's belief (which apparently developed early in the 1890s) that single immersion was the proper baptismal mode he ascribed to a direct communication from the Holy Spirit. He later temporarily accepted triple immersion. However, sometime in 1900 Parham became convinced of his need to "lay his teachings, creeds and doctrines at His feet and by faith in His cleansing blood trust that every error, false teaching or unscriptural thought may be cleansed."[28] As a result, he discovered that "some of the teachings we had believed to be so scriptural and some we had loved so dearly and had been the most persevering in propagating" were "wiped from his mind."[29] Among them was triple immersion. Parham again practiced single immersion using the formula "in the name of Jesus, into the name of the Father, Son and Holy Ghost." Since the Father and the Holy Ghost had neither died nor been resurrected, he reasoned, one could not be "buried by baptism" in their names.[30]

Parham's doctrinal inventiveness led to his advocating a variety of unusual interpretations of Scripture to meet such age-old questions as "Where did Cain get his wife?" For example, he distinguished between "created" and "formed" humanity, claiming that all "created" humanity perished in the flood, whereas, through Noah, Adam's line of "formed" humanity was preserved. Thus, Cain's wife was created, whereas Cain was formed. Parham also subscribed to Anglo-Israelism, a view that maintained that the Anglo-Saxon peoples were the ten lost tribes of Israel. Fascinated by current movements within Judaism, Parham supported the Zionist schemes of Theodor Herzl, a prominent contemporary who called for the creation of a Jewish homeland.[31] The sense of Anglo-Saxon superiority nourished by his eschatology corresponded neatly with racial attitudes that pervaded much of the turn-of-the-century Protestant culture.

Parham's Topeka Bethel mission and print shop were run on a "faith" basis. In fact, the Parham family and the home (as well as the mission) had no apparent means of support, although expenses on the property averaged $130 a month.[32] Rather, Parham and his family determined to pray for their temporal needs and then to expect a miraculous supply. (Although Parham remained officially committed to the "faith" position throughout his life, later issues of his paper printed urgent requests for funds for specific projects.) Guests at the healing home were charged between four and seven dollars a week for board, unless they were "worthy poor." In a pattern typical in their religious subculture, they accepted any who shared their interest in the "full gospel," readily welcoming strangers to their home and pulpit.

Parham's Bible School and the Sandford Influence

During the spring of 1900, Parham invited visiting evangelists to conduct several weeks of services while he traveled to various places to explore "the latest truths restored by latter day movements."[33] After an absence of several months (during which he traveled to Chicago, Cleveland, New York, Maine, and Winnipeg), Parham returned to Topeka and found that he had lost most of his congregation and his facilities to the visiting evangelists. This turn of events reinforced his determination to implement a plan that had been forming in his mind: He decided to open a Bible school to promulgate and further develop his views. In October 1900, he opened Bethel Bible School. Some forty people (including dependents) responded to the invitation he addressed to "all ministers and Christians who were willing to forsake all, sell what they had, give it away, and enter the school for study and prayer."[34]

Parham located his school in a large mansion on the southwestern edge of Topeka. Built by E. R. Stone, a Topekan who had made (and later lost) a fortune in the fluctuating Topeka real estate market, the house was originally set among fruit trees and gardens on ten acres of land. In 1900, however, the American Bible Society owned the building and leased it to Parham.[35] Its spacious rooms and tower provided ample accommodations for the group's activities. They spent most of their time praying, "giving little heed," the local press reported, "to the present, practical need of making a living."[36]

The educational model for Parham's school was the Holy Ghost and Us Bible School begun in 1895 near Lewiston, Maine, by Frank Sandford. Sandford, a former Free Baptist minister, regarded the school as the focal point of a vision he shared with Parham for the "restoration of all things" and the realization of the kingdom of God.

Sandford had an impressive background in evangelical associations. After briefly attending Bates College, he had been called as a young man to the pulpit of one of his denomination's wealthiest and most prestigious churches, the Free Baptist Church in Great Falls, New Hampshire. He had been selected to travel around the world, inspecting Free Baptist missionary work. But the more he achieved, the less satisfied he seemed. In 1893, he abruptly left his denomination and launched an independent evangelistic ministry. A frequent visitor at D. L. Moody's Northfield Conferences, Sandford enjoyed the confidence of R. A. Torrey and preached several times at Moody Bible Institute. He also participated in A. B. Simpson's efforts in New York City and in Old Orchard Beach, Maine. (Sandford's wife, Helen Kinney, was the daughter of a wealthy businessman. She had been the first Alliance missionary to Japan. Simpson had married the couple in 1892.) Increasingly, however, he became convinced that his mentors had not fully understood God's plan: He was called to do greater things than they had imagined.[37] Sandford's admiring biographer claimed that in Sandford's ministry "at last a truly functional Christianity had appeared on the earth, one that had power to silence the tongues of cynics and cast off the rags of hypocrisy that for centuries had brought shame to the Church of Christ."[38] Most others were less certain: Vocal cynics pursued Sandford throughout his life.[39]

As Sandford's independent efforts expanded, he knew both

humiliation and persecution. Slowly he put together a ministry that he called Shiloh: He constructed a seven-story tabernacle, a healing home, a children's home, a school and a five hundred-room dormitory. As his dreams became more radical, however, he alienated his mainstream evangelical friends. Essentially evangelistic at first, he became increasingly preoccupied with the restoration of apostolic experience. Poring over the Book of Acts, he detected a disparity between "denominational religion" and the "apostolic primitive Christianity" of the New Testament. Like John Alexander Dowie in Zion, Illinois, Sandford would conclude in 1901 that he was Elijah (Malachi 4:1); he later claimed apostleship.[40] Sandford taught the reality of the Holy Spirit's baptism and guidance in the minute details of the believer's life.

Sandford's Bible School

The name of Sandford's school, The Holy Ghost and Us, indicated his intentions for its organization and operation. Founded to contend for the "whole truth" of God (presumably compared to other ministries that might have left out one truth or another, like healing or holiness), the school was intentionally unconventional. "Everything gives way to the Holy Ghost's latest," one participant reported. "And it quickly becomes evident to a newcomer that the Holy Ghost does not intend that His students shall become dependent upon the routine of sleeping and eating."[41] He further described the educational format:

> "Curriculum" there is none: it is the Bible.
> "Faculty" there is none: it is the Holy Ghost.
> "Length [of] course" there is none: students go when the
> Director sends them.
> This is the Holy Ghost's work.
> This is real teaching.
> This is supernatural.[42]

Sandford emphasized the believer's need to receive the Holy Spirit in a distinct experience following conversion. In the school, he attempted to lead students, "not *to* the truth, but *into* the truth." Thus, students read the Bible, "praying the lessons drawn from each personality or anecdote into their own hearts."[43] Classes frequently adjourned for prayer because Sandford insisted that the lessons of one passage must be "prayed in" before the next passage was considered. By 1901, Sandford would claim to restore the true church, which he called the Church of the Living God. On October 1 and 2, 1901, he baptized several hundred mature believers. Among them was A. J. Tomlinson, soon to become the leader of the Church of God, Cleveland. Most (if not all) of them had previously been baptized; Sandford described the experience as both "the first baptism under the Restoration" and "a fresh washing to cleanse out the mixture and confusion of the past."[44] He also expressed a strong commitment to divine healing.

As 1900 dawned, Sandford organized from among his students a group of seventy men and women to evangelize the United States.[45] They adhered to the biblical model, going two-by-two and walking without luggage or plans until they found people who would listen. At the end of April, Sandford and six of his most trusted workers left Maine, traveling by rail west to Winnipeg and then to Tacoma. In Tacoma, Nathan Harriman, a Baptist who, like Sandford, had concluded that loyalty to the "whole Bible" mandated separation from denominations, joined Sandford's party. About forty members of his independent Ecclesia Mission decided to move with their leader to Sandford's center in Maine.

Meanwhile, some of the seventy sent out in January had found response to their message in Kansas City. Two, Edward Doughty and Victor Barton, had won a hearing in Topeka. When the train carrying the party from Tacoma arrived in Kansas City, eighteen more, including Charles Parham and several of his followers, joined Sandford's group. This converging of followers of several independent restorationist ministries encouraged Sandford to believe that Shiloh "would be the rallying point for all such clusters of called-out Christians."[46] With more than seventy converts as recruits for Shiloh, Sandford and his workers returned in triumph.

After spending about a month in Maine, Sandford and seven

others (including Charles Parham) returned to Winnipeg, where Sandford had a strong nucleus of followers; a month later, Sandford was back at Shiloh with five more recruits for the Bible school. He had left several workers to oversee his mission in Winnipeg. Parham had traveled back to Topeka to organize his school.

Other Sandford Influences on Parham

Sandford and Parham were similar in temperament and spirituality. Both men practiced healing; both stressed faith living; both taught a specific experience of enduement by the Holy Spirit; both rejected denominations (Parham called membership in a denomination "churchanity"); each professed dedication to the cause of Christian unity; both sought to recapture fully the apostolic faith in the end times; each reveled in intense religious experience; both followed impressions they considered "leadings" of the Holy Spirit.[47]

Descriptions of Sandford's meetings recount the emotional exuberance that distinguished early Pentecostal gatherings. Participants shouted, clapped, sang spontaneously, stayed indefinitely, fought the devil (an exercise in which they literally shouted, waved clenched fists, and went through violent contortions, directing anger at forces unseen but purportedly present), fasted and prayed, spoke ecstatically (sometimes in tongues, an exercise Sandford later repudiated), and preached and testified extemporaneously. The entire Shiloh community of several hundred commemorated Christ's crucifixion by fasting and praying each Thursday from 9 A.M. until 3 P.M. Parham introduced that custom in Topeka.

On October 15, twenty-seven-year-old Parham began conducting classes. Like Sandford, Parham claimed that his school had only one text, the Bible; he stated further that "its only object [was] utter abandonment in obedience to the commandments of Jesus, however unconventional and impractical this might seem."[48] As at Sandford's school, the students lived together, combining what resources they had. At least one had sufficient means to purchase $100 worth of furniture for the house and seemed willing to sacrifice his farm to keep the school open.[49] Despite the turnover among Parham's students during the fall, the schedule proceeded. All was not harmonious at Bethel; some left the school. One later reported that "sometimes friction and disobedience was [*sic*] manifested."[50] But a strong nucleus remained. By the end of the year, they had begun to study the baptism of the Holy Spirit.

For at least eight years, according to his own accounts, Parham had taught a baptism of the "Holy Ghost and Fire," which he had understood to be separate from sanctification by faith. This baptism, he maintained, "sealed the Bride and bestowed the gifts."[51] Parham taught that the bride of Christ was not the Church but a hundred and forty-four thousand people taken from the Church. Those who desired "deliverance from the plagues and wraths of the last days" needed to be "sealed" by receiving a baptism in the Holy Spirit. The "living membership" of the Bride at Christ's return would all be so baptized, and by virtue of their Spirit baptism would "escape the power of the devil before this age closes."[52]

Agnes Ozman and the Baptism at Bethel Bible School

Among the students who determined late in 1900 to receive this baptism of the Holy Ghost and Fire (their specific use of this term indicates clearly that they prayed for the experience Parham had been teaching for some time) were Agnes Ozman and two other women.

Ozman's name would become familiar to early Pentecostals (she later held credentials with the Assemblies of God). Born in Albany, Wisconsin, September 15, 1870, Ozman had moved the next year to Nebraska. She experienced the hard life of frontier settlers as she grew to adulthood. The family had strong religious inclinations, and Agnes and her five brothers and sisters attended the Methodist Episcopal Church. As a young woman, Agnes joined a Bible study group sponsored by the YMCA. The group's discussions convinced her of her need for baptism by immersion, which she received in the local Christian Church. She also accepted premillennial teaching and experienced healing from pneumonia. Like so many people across the country, she showed a strong tendency toward religious individualism, which made nondenominational, experientially-oriented settings more congenial than traditional denominational involvement.

During the winter of 1892 to 1893, Ozman attended a Bible school in St. Paul, Minnesota. When the school's director, T. C. Horton, closed the school to begin full-time evangelistic work in 1894, Ozman moved to New York to continue her training at A. B. Simpson's Bible institute in New York City. There she became intrigued with Stephen Merritt's strong experiential emphasis on the Holy Spirit and found exhilaration working in rescue missions. After leaving the school, she attended a camp meeting at Old Orchard Beach, Maine, then made her way back to Nebraska via Chicago, where she visited Dowie's healing home. Ozman later engaged in mission work in Kansas City, where she heard about Parham's plans to open a school in Topeka. She decided to attend. Thirty years old, she had no settled vocation, purpose in life, or home; she had fallen into a pattern of wandering from place to place, pursuing some elusive spiritual reality. Despite being enamored of a teaching or ministry, she would soon experience an irresistible urge to move on.[53]

In 1912 Ozman said that in Parham's school in the fall of 1900, she and two others had been praying together when she had spoken "three words in another tongue."[54] "This," she recalled, "was a hallowed experiment and was held in my heart as sacred; the Lord had it treasured up for each of us, and nothing was said about it until later."[55]

Ozman reported that, like other students, she spent much time in prayer. During the evening service on January 1, 1901, having a strong desire to be baptized with the Holy Ghost and Fire, she asked Parham to lay his hands on her and pray that she would receive the experience.[56]

According to her own report, Ozman "spoke in tongues as is recorded in Acts 19."[57] Given Parham's later insistence that tongues speech was *always* in known human languages, this reference to Acts 19 rather than to Acts 2 is interesting, since the Acts 19 account of the Ephesian "Pentecost" makes no claim that Spirit baptism was evidenced by speech in known languages: "When Paul had laid his hands upon them, the Holy Ghost came on them; and they spake with tongues, and prophesied."[58] Parham, however, would later virulently oppose any tongues speech that was not an actual human language, labeling it "jabbering."

Parham subsequently claimed that before the service his students had unanimously agreed that the baptism with the Holy Spirit would always be evidenced by speaking in tongues (known languages, as in Acts 2). He implied that Ozman had desired to be baptized with the Holy Spirit specifically so that she could evangelize effectively on the foreign mission field. Ozman's account differs at significant points, however. *Following* her experience, she claimed, the students began "searching the Word for light" on tongues. She recorded that at the time she spoke in tongues she did not consider tongues "the only evidence necessarily given to those who received the baptism."[59] Contrary to Parham's suggestion that consensus on the subject of Spirit baptism had been reached before Ozman's experience, Ozman wrote: "I did not expect the Holy Spirit to manifest Himself to others as He did to me."[60]

Parham asserted that Ozman spoke Chinese for three days, during which she could neither speak nor write English.[61] Ozman later corroborated his claim, noting that her efforts to write resulted in "automatic" characters "in another language."[62] She had some control over her speech, however: In two separate accounts she recorded that she prayed publicly in English at a Topeka mission on January 2.[63]

Parham's View on Speaking in Tongues

As a result of Ozman's experience, others awaited similar enduement. Within several days, more than a dozen had spoken in tongues. The discrepancies in the various accounts of what occurred and what had been anticipated lend credence to the view that Parham had most likely concluded before December that speaking in tongues was "Bible evidence" for the baptism with the Holy Spirit and that he had purposely created a setting in which others would reach the same conclusion under circumstances in which it would seem to be "revealed."[64] According to his own statement, he had been gripped by a need to know what the Bible really meant when it described a baptism of the Holy Spirit. He later maintained that his eastern trip had afforded him opportunities to examine other ministries that focused on the Holy Spirit.[65] He admitted that for many years he had believed that Christians should possess the apostolic power miraculously to proclaim the gospel in foreign languages they had not learned. Early in January 1901 he acknowledged:

> We have for long believed that the power of the Lord would
> be manifested in our midst, and that power would be given
> us to speak other languages, and that the time will come
> when we will be sent to go into all the nations and preach
> the gospel, and that the Lord will give us the power of
> speech to talk to the people of the various nations without
> having to study them in schools.[66]

Given the urgency about world evangelization that his eschatology supported, Parham's fascination with tongues to facilitate foreign missions is logical. It is interesting, however, that until he publicly advocated tongues as "Bible evidence" of Spirit baptism, he showed little interest in missions.[67] Even if he believed that when "God's time" for missionary work came miraculous speech would be given, his Apostolic Faith Movement's continuing lack of foreign missionary fervor is conspicuous. Comparison of the inconsistent (and even contradictory) accounts yields at least one certain conclusion: He regarded this standard for evaluating Spirit baptism as an enhancement to his Apostolic Faith message rather than as an inconsequential aberrance. He had recovered another dimension of New Testament reality. Parham, at least, was certain that Ozman's tongues speech validated his conclusion about uniform biblical evidence for the Baptism with the Holy Ghost and Fire.[68]

Events at the school attracted the press and disillusioned at least one student, S. J. Riggins of Kansas City. Riggins spoke at length with reporters, accusing Parham and his followers of insanity: "I believe the whole of them are crazy. I never saw anything like it. They were racing about the room talking and gesticulating and using this strange and senseless language which they claim is the word from the Most High."[69] A newspaper reporter who visited the school (which the *Topeka Daily Capital* later dubbed the School of Tongues), recounted that each student who had "received the gift" came into the room and "spoke a few sentences in a strange and unnatural way, outlandish words of which they neither knew the meaning nor the language to which they belong. Their reason for uttering them is that the Lord inspires them."[70]

The Spread of the Apostolic Faith

The claimed restoration of the gift of tongues marked the end of Bethel Bible School. Parham attempted to spread the teaching among his previous supporters. Later in January, he conducted two weeks of meetings in the Academy of Music in Kansas City. He then tried to open a mission in Topeka. When that failed, he rented a theater in Lawrence, where he had set up an earlier base. From Lawrence he reported: "Large numbers came to the meetings and many were saved. The sick were healed and a good number of believers received the baptism of the Holy Spirit."[71] About twenty workers accompanied Parham, who consistently denied that he taught either a new church or a new creed. "He insists," *The Lawrence World* reported, "that his mission is to have people return to the Apostolic Faith. His views are referred to as strange and yet he claims that the country ought not to regard the first principles of the Christian religion as strange."[72]

Despite initially favorable response, few people received his message. Within several months, his ministry had disintegrated. Whereas at first Parham had reported that "it was hard to decide who should stay at the school, for all wanted to go and proclaim that God had fulfilled His promise in pouring out His Holy Spirit," the schedule had abruptly been abandoned, and within a few weeks, the students had disbanded, most of them to obscurity.[73] Some had left in disillusionment; apparently none assisted Parham in his future endeavors, nor did they play a role in the later extension of his teaching.

Agnes Ozman was part of a group that left for Sandford's Shiloh. They traveled as far as Kansas City, when their "lack of the presence of God" and their "powerlessness" deterred them.[74] Noting the tendency of Parham and his supporters to follow "impressions," "spirits," and "voices," Ozman later cautioned Apostolic Faith adherents: "There is a very great need ... to prove the spirits and voices, whether they be of God or not."[75] Those who had set out for Shiloh had "followed a voice which was not the Lord's."[76] Reflecting on the disbanding of the school, Ozman admitted: "We all missed very much that [which] God had for us, by getting out of His will."[77]

For several years, Parham struggled to put together a base from which to proclaim his Apostolic Faith. He suffered personal tragedy in the death of his infant son and public rejection in attempts to discredit his message. "Both the pulpit and the press sought to utterly destroy our place and prestige," he wrote, "until my wife, her sister and myself seemed to stand alone."[78] Parham's lectures on Zionism proved vastly more popular than his stance on the gospel.

El Dorado Springs, Missouri

The tide finally turned during the summer of 1903, when the Parhams went to the popular health resort of El Dorado Springs, Missouri, and conducted open air services in a park. To the many who sought the alleviation of physical suffering, Parham preached healing. His message on the physical merits of Christ's atonement brought response that had eluded his proclamation of the restoration of tongues speech.

Among those who claimed healing was Mary Arthur, wife of a prominent citizen of Galena, Kansas. Arthur had suffered for many years from numerous ailments. Her condition was known throughout Galena, and when she returned from El Dorado Springs (which she had visited previously with no benefit) healed, the town took note. As a result, the Parhams accepted an invitation to Galena. Throughout the winter months of 1903 to 1904, Parham preached, first in the Arthur home, then in a tent nearby, and finally, as inclement weather set in, in a warehouse that seated about two thousand.[79]

Parham maintained a rigorous schedule, conducting two services a day for months on end, and hundreds claimed conversion, healing, and Spirit baptism. The Joplin *News Herald* reported in January that over a thousand had been healed, and eight thousand claimed salvation. In the mining towns of southwestern Missouri and southeastern Kansas, Parham had finally found acceptance. For the rest of his life, the region would provide his most loyal following. For most of those years, his home was near Galena in Baxter Springs, Kansas.[80]

In Galena, Parham recruited a group of devoted workers who traveled in "bands" and assisted him in proclaiming the Apostolic Faith. From Galena, he moved his efforts to Baxter Springs. By the fall of 1904, Parham was conducting tent meetings in Joplin. By the end of 1904, the Parhams could report that "many hundreds of people from Carthage, Missouri through southeastern Kansas to Miami, Oklahoma were now believers in the power of the faith once delivered to the saints."[81] That year also saw the opening of the first frame church built specifically as a Pentecostal assembly. It still stands at a crossroads in the unincorporated town of Keelville, Kansas.

As his work extended, Parham apparently did not stress unduly his innovative doctrines. Or perhaps he was already promulgating the view he later used to silence objections: "Truly spiritual people do not quibble over tenets and points of doctrine; it is a sign of waning spirituality to do so."[82] It is also probable that most of his hearers were barely theologically literate. Since his message brought results and transformed their lives, they accepted it. Later, as others from around the country found Parham's restorationism marred by doctrinal innovations, they thought it necessary to repudiate his more unconventional teachings. In 1904, however, his understanding of eternal life or his views on the bride of Christ and Anglo-Israelism mattered little. Amid the intense emotional exuberance and the grueling physical demands of constant meetings and daily miracles, the thirty-year-old evangelist claimed to

preach a full gospel evangelical message, and he produced results that seemed to duplicate New Testament experiences. His
message evoked response: People *experienced* God. His convert
Howard Goss summarized the simple content of his message:
"Jesus, His teachings, salvation, life, and the power to heal
from Christ's time to the present moment . . . [and] a clean holy
life of victory for all believers" as well as crisis sanctification.[83]

Contemporaries later recalled Parham as "a vivid, magnetic
personality with superb, versatile platform ability." Acquaintances noted his humility. The *Lawrence World* had reported
in 1901 that "Parham does not impress one as being a peculiar
man. Indeed he is a right good fellow and is earnest in his life's
work."[84]

Houston, Texas

Having established Apostolic Faith assemblies in the principal towns around Galena, Parham took twenty-four workers
with him to extend the Movement into eastern Texas. When
they returned to Kansas briefly to attend the first Apostolic
Faith camp meeting there (in Columbus, 1905), they reported
marked successes in the Houston area. After the camp meeting,
a second group prepared to reinforce Apostolic Faith visibility
in southeastern Texas. Again, proclaiming healing and praying
for the sick proved to be the single most effective way to win
a hearing. During the winter of 1905 Parham's workers set up
several missions in the Houston area.

Parham's initial contact with his white Texas supporters had
come through his Galena meetings, which several Texans had
attended. The reports he and his workers sent back to Baxter
Springs from Texas exulted in the "great blessings," "glorious
sermons," and "great shouts of victory" that marked his Texas
outreach. Writing in the summer of 1905, the workers recorded
anticipation that August 1905 would be a month of significant
accomplishments. In fact, reporters for the *Houston Chronicle*
who visited the school that month claimed that miracles occurred regularly and that they heard "speaking in all tongues
known to man."[85] Parham warned his Texas audiences that God

would hold them responsible if they did not "join in this great crusade with our Captain Jesus, against sin & Satan."[86] Testimonies of conversions and healings punctuated his services, frequent street meetings gave regular visibility to his workers, and the Houston area became a center for the dissemination of the Apostolic Faith. Innovative as always, Parham often sat on the platform dressed in Palestinian costume. Unlike many preachers of instantaneous sanctification, he encouraged his workers to dress stylishly and thus demonstrate the attractiveness of the Christian life.[87]

Early in the fall of 1905, bands of five to eight workers scattered from Houston to small communities in Texas, Kansas, and Oklahoma.[88] Late in the fall they reassembled in Houston to participate in a short-term Bible school that ran until the spring of 1906. The weekday schedule included morning Bible study, noon shop and prison services, afternoon house-to-house visitation, and 6 P.M. street meetings followed by evangelistic services, highlighted by protracted altar services. A Methodist lay preacher of six years, Warren Fay Carothers, assisted Parham in Bible teaching.[89]

Farrow, Seymour, and Warren

Among those who were influenced by Parham's ministry in Houston were several black Christians with an intense interest in holiness. One was Lucy Farrow, known as "Auntie" among the workers; another was William J. Seymour,[90] whose background among the Evening Light Saints[91] probably helped make him receptive to Parham's message. Another was one J. A. Warren. The convergence of the efforts of these three to spread the Apostolic Faith among black holiness advocates ultimately influenced the entire Movement's future course.

Despite Parham's denials, his worldview nurtured racist assumptions, which frequently surfaced. Nonetheless, in 1905 blacks attended his evangelistic services.[92] Seymour apparently attended some Bible school classes (some reports indicate that he sat behind a curtain). Parham and Seymour both preached to Houston blacks.[93] Local laws enforced segregation, and Parham's personal inclinations most likely conformed to those of his Texas supporters. Parham's British Israelism also supported his sense of racial superiority. According to his scheme, while Japanese and Hindus shared the high German, Scandinavian, and Anglo-Saxon distinction of being "descendants of Abraham," eastern Europeans were "Gentiles," and "the Black race, the Brown race, the Red race, the Yellow race" were heathen.[94]

Both Farrow and Seymour were known in Houston's black holiness missions. At one of them, Seymour met Neeley Terry, a Los Angeles resident who belonged to a holiness mission whose leader had recently been expelled from a Baptist congregation for espousing crisis sanctification. When Terry returned to Los Angeles, she encouraged the group to invite Seymour to serve them as associate pastor. Parham had planned to send Seymour "to those of his own color" in Texas, but the new opportunity was attractive to Seymour.[95] Parham next tried but failed to convince Seymour to remain in Houston until he had received his baptism. Sometime in January 1906 Seymour left Houston for Los Angeles. Apparently he traveled via Denver, where he sought hospitality among members of the Pentecostal Union (Pillar of Fire). The group's indomitable leader, Alma White, later characterized him as "very untidy," and concluded that of all the "religious fakes and tramps" she had ever met, "he excelled them all."[96] Shortly after Seymour's arrival in Los Angeles, his efforts, later complemented by those of Lucy Farrow and J. A. Warren, in a nondescript section of the city catapulted Parham's Apostolic Faith message to prominence among the various independent missions whose leaders coveted an end-times outpouring of the Holy Spirit.[97]

During his early ministry in Los Angeles, Seymour clearly considered himself subject to Parham's leadership. In July 1906, after three months of daily meetings in Los Angeles, he specifically requested (and received) credentials from Parham.[98] When he compiled a discipline for his Los Angeles mission in 1915, Seymour disavowed the racist views Parham represented: "If some of our white brethren have prejudices and discriminations, we can't," he declared.[99] But Seymour later allowed explicit prejudice to surface in his own ranks: He reserved for "people of color" the right to be officers of his mission, limiting whites to membership.[100]

Some Problems Parham Had To Deal With

Although Parham continued to have a strong following among Pentecostals for several years, the focus of Apostolic Faith activities shifted in 1906 from his efforts to those supervised by Seymour in Los Angeles. In his ensuing encounters with emerging Pentecostal leaders, Parham failed to demonstrate the spiritual or emotional maturity that might have extended his influence. Instead, he proved unwilling to relinquish leadership gracefully (although he professed to abhor acclaim). As the Movement attracted some who were concerned to balance spiritual experience with doctrinal orthodoxy, he responded by emphasizing anew his private interpretations of Scripture. He proved unwilling to work graciously with a black man, writing cuttingly of Seymour's Los Angeles mission, where "big buck niggers" prayed with their arms around whites, and where the exuberant worship represented not the Holy Spirit, but "negroisms."[101] In fact, Parham believed that, among other excesses, "noises as practiced by the Negroes of the Southland" had been "pawned off on people all over the world as the working of the Holy Spirit."[102] At least partly as a result, Parham generally discouraged physical manifestations of spiritual experience, insisting that noise indicated resistance to the Holy Spirit. "There should be a holy enthusiasm and intensity without hysteria," he maintained. "Christianity places us in a normal state with all our faculties consecrated to decency, order and service for God, and not to consume ourselves in riotous sensations of the flesh and a sensual working up of feeling."[103]

Accused of both financial irregularity (probably because of misunderstandings about his faith teaching) and of sexual misconduct, Parham became an embarrassment to a movement seeking to affirm its orthodoxy by demonstrating continuity with New Testament Christianity.[104] He also became the victim of his own restorationist views: If God had sovereignly restored the apostolic faith, then God was its leader. "There is no man at the head of this movement," convinced restorationists insisted. "God Himself is speaking in the earth."[105] Although his loyal followers, who numbered in the thousands, maintained that he was personable and humble, his paper, *The Apostolic Faith* (changed briefly to *The Everlasting Gospel,* a title Sandford also used), became an outlet for his frustration. Relentless attacks on emerging Pentecostal leaders distanced him from a movement that owed much to his vision. For while many accounts record speaking in tongues before January 1901, no one had maintained the association between tongues and the baptism of the Holy Spirit that Parham had introduced. And it was that association that gave identity to the scattered fledgling restorationist, millenarian constituency that became American Pentecostalism.

Charles F. Parham, 1873-1929

A flyer describing Parham's message

An Apostolic Faith "band" in Carthage, Missouri, June 1905. The bands typically paraded down the main street, carrying banners to announce their presence and advertise meetings.

Charles F. Parham (front, center), Apostolic Faith Group, Bryan Hall,
Houston, Texas

Stone's Mansion (also called Stone's Folly), Topeka, Kansas (ca. 1900)

Camp meeting. People in the Houston area proved receptive to Parham's message. Camp meetings like the one pictured here drew participants from a large area (ca. 1906).

Parham (standing beside the right post) and workers at the Houston camp meeting, 1906

4. The "Nazareth" of Los Angeles: Azusa Street and Beyond

> It has been said of the work in Los Angeles that it was "born in a manger and resurrected in a barn.". . .
> "Can there any good thing come out of Nazareth?" "Come and see." This is the Nazareth of Los Angeles.
>
> *The Apostolic Faith,* September 1906

William Seymour reported that "it was the divine call" that brought him from Houston to Los Angeles.[1] The human instruments who mediated that call were members of a holiness mission that had been formed by several families whose holiness sympathies had resulted in their excommunication from the city's Negro Second Baptist Church.[2] Determined to proclaim the truth among them as he understood it, Seymour preached his first sermon on Parham's doctrine of tongues as the uniform initial evidence of the baptism with the Holy Spirit. Most of his hearers considered sanctification to be identical with Spirit baptism. Because none had spoken in tongues, Seymour's message challenged both their theology and their experience. He encouraged them to seek a "third blessing," and he insisted that its reception would be indicated by tongues speech. Making the situation more troublesome, Seymour himself had not experienced the Holy Spirit in the way he preached a believer should.

The response was hardly surprising. Mrs. Hutchinson, the pastor, padlocked the mission, refusing Seymour entrance. She invited the president of the local Holiness Association to "settle the doctrine of the Baptism with the Holy Ghost, that it was simply sanctification."[3] Accompanied by several holiness ministers, he complied.

Seymour, meanwhile, accepted an invitation to stay in Los Angeles and teach, first at the home of an Irishman known as "Irish" Lee, and later at the Asbury family home on Bonnie Brae Street. His audiences were a mixed group: Most were working class people, blacks and whites, some of whom owned their own homes and most of whom held steady jobs.[4] News of the meetings spread first around the immediate neighborhood, where noisy gatherings attracted the curious, and then by word of mouth among the city's independent missions. On Monday, April 9, 1906, Seymour and seven others received the Spirit baptism he had diligently described. Reports of tongues speech spread rapidly; crowds thronged the street to hear Seymour speak from the porch. Participants spread the word through those missions scattered about the city that stressed the need for "New Testament Christianity." Blacks and whites mingled as they sought spiritual renewal, and increasing numbers accepted the logic Seymour used to present tongues as the only "Bible evidence" of an authentic New Testament baptism with the Holy Spirit. Controversy mounted too.[5]

Frank Bartleman, one who persistently sought out "movements of the Spirit," reported that at Bonnie Brae Street he had "found God working mightily." Manifesting the antiorganizational bias typical among independent restorationists, he regarded Seymour's small company as having become the focal point of God's contemporary dealings with humanity:

> Evidently the Lord had found the little company at last, outside as always, through whom he could have right of way. There was not a mission in the country where this could be done. All were in the hands of men. The Spirit could not work.[6]

Needing larger facilities, Seymour discovered an abandoned Methodist Episcopal Church at 312 Azusa Street that, in spite of its run-down condition, admirably suited his purpose. Far enough away from residential neighborhoods and lacking the formality of a well-appointed sanctuary, the building accommodated the crowds that followed him from Bonnie Brae Street: Its utter simplicity made the setting conducive to spontaneity, and its location assured freedom from complaints about noise. The *Los Angeles Times* picked up the story on April 18, under the heading "Weird Babel of Tongues; New Sect of Fanatics is Breaking Loose; Wild Scene Last Night on Azusa Street." The next day, such local news was displaced by coverage of the San Francisco earthquake; however, the meetings continued with new appeal. The San Francisco earthquake, it was maintained, was an act of God's judgment. The natural disaster tended to intensify spiritual concern. "Many are saying that God has given the message that He is going to shake Los Angeles with an earthquake," a bulletin in *The Apostolic Faith* reported. "First, there will be a revival to give all an opportunity to be saved. The revival is now in progress."[7] Seymour and his followers, oblivious to the world around them (or interpreting that world according to their sense of their own historical significance), solemnly affirmed that they were the focal point of God's contemporary dealings with humankind.

In 1906 Los Angeles was in a period of rapid expansion that made it the fastest growing city in the nation. Many of its settlers were recent arrivals from the Midwest. Like other highly mobile populations, its citizens often sought community in religious affiliation. At least a third of the residents held church membership, but official statistics failed to account for the many who participated in newer small sectarian groups. Various holiness organizations as well as independent missions had successfully established themselves in the city.[8]

By 1906, numerous Los Angeles Protestants—especially those in independent and holiness missions—had for some time been praying daily for revival. The diaries of itinerant spiritual seekers such as Frank Bartleman and Florence Crawford provide a sense of the number and variety of religious options Protestant missions offered. Los Angeles, with its sprawling population of some two hundred twenty-eight thousand, was hospitable to many forms of spirituality.

In addition to various holiness missions that had followings in the area, Joseph Smale's New Testament Church figures prominently in the rise of Pentecostalism. Led by Smale, former pastor of the city's First Baptist Church, the New Testament Church explicitly embodied restorationist intent. Advertising itself as "a fellowship for evangelical preaching and teaching and pentecostal life and service," the congregation prayed for revival. They anticipated an event similar to what Smale had witnessed in Wales in 1905.

The Significance of the Welsh Revival for Pentecostalism

Reports of the Welsh Revival stimulated many Americans to expect a dramatic answer to their prayers for an end-times "outpouring of the Holy Spirit." Books like S. B. Shaw's *Great Revival in Wales* circulated eyewitness accounts, newspaper reports, and evaluations by noted evangelicals to interested readers across the United States. In several important ways, the revival contributed to the specific context from which Pentecostalism emerged. First, it directly challenged believers to obey the Holy Spirit. It modeled obedience in unusual ways, such as unstructured services with opportunity for all to express their spontaneous worship and conviction. Second, it was presented as an end-times Pentecost (the first showers of the latter rain), and it focused in practical ways on the Holy Spirit. Third, it helped make familiar the terms Pentecostals later found meaningful, and it gave those terms specific experiential connotations just as the Pentecostal movement gained wider attention. British Keswick leader Evan Hopkins phrased the revival's challenge: "Let believers be as one before God—in unity of life and love—in oneness of purpose and desire—and then the Holy Ghost, who is present, will put forth His power; God's children will be filled with the Spirit, and the unconverted will be saved."[9] Those who later embraced Pentecostalism believed that they had accepted this challenge and that in their experience the revival fires, which waned in Wales, continued to burn brightly.

In fact, spokespersons for the Welsh Revival had understood it as the end-times fulfillment of Joel 2:28: "And it shall come to pass ... that I will pour out my spirit upon all flesh." The

Welsh revival defied description. It ignored the methods with which Christians typically approached revival. Spontaneity and seeming disorder replaced promotion, scheduling, regular preaching, financial planning, and even systematic evangelistic outreach. Congregations crowded the churches and chapels of south Wales with the simple desire to "see what God would do."[10] No one knew for certain who—if anyone—would preach. The revival "anticipated the preacher," the *Times* reported. "The people met and poured out their souls in prayer and praise for hours before the preacher came, if he came at all."[11] Nor could anyone predict where the revival would manifest itself. The degree of unity that its various expressions shared was due largely to the itinerant ministry of a young coal miner preparing for the ministry, Evan Roberts.

Roberts understood the revival as the prelude to a worldwide awakening as well as a contemporary fulfillment of Joel 2. It was only a beginning, he insisted: "The world will be swept by His Spirit as by a rushing, mighty wind." The "great lesson" to be learned, he maintained, was "obedience to the voice of the Holy Spirit."[12] When noted British evangelical G. Campbell Morgan visited briefly, he was deeply stirred by the movement's intensity. "It is Pentecost continued, without a single moment's doubt," he reported. "The meetings are absolutely without order characterized from the first to the last by the orderliness of the Spirit of God."[13] With clear reference to the Acts 2 Pentecost account, Morgan continued: "If you put a man into these meetings who knows nothing of the language of the Spirit, and nothing of the life of the Spirit, one of two things will happen to him. He will either pass out saying, 'These men are drunk,' or he himself will be swept up by the fire into the Kingdom of God."[14]

The spontaneity and fervor of the revival often expressed itself in singing. Repeated choruses of worship punctuated corporate, audible prayers. When the excitement was "at its highest," the London *Times* reported, "the outbursts were not successive, but literally simultaneous."[15] Sometimes eight or nine hours passed before worshipers dispersed.

An unusual phenomenon that received considerable press

was the use of classical Welsh by "ordinary farm servants, common plough boys and practically unlettered youths."[16] J. Morris Jones, Welsh Professor at the University College of North Wales, reported that these individuals spoke with "diction . . . more chaste and beautiful than anything I can hope to attain to."[17] Subsequent arguments offering explanations for this phenomena failed to impress most participants, who preferred to believe they had been part of a supernatural event. Prominent British journalist W. T. Stead concurred. Editor of the British *Review of Reviews,* Stead sat in fascination, watching "what they call the influence of the power of the Spirit playing over the crowded congregation as an eddying wind plays over the surface of a pond."[18] "They say it is the Spirit of God," he wrote. "Those who have not witnessed it may call it what they will. I am inclined to agree with those on the spot."[19]

Its abandonment of scheduling and conventional order of services as well as the intensity of its emphasis on the Holy Spirit attracted Americans who longed for revival.[20] Events seemed to validate the preferences of those who shunned organization. G. Campbell Morgan voiced their sentiments: "I am not at all sure that God is not rebuking our over-organization. . . . [God is saying] See what I can do without the things you are depending on; see what I can do in answer to a praying people; see what I can do through the simplest who are ready to fall in line and depend wholly and absolutely on me."[21]

Widely circulated accounts helped attract to Wales numerous visitors—some who hoped to "help the revival along," others who were simply curious, and some who yearned for spiritual renewal. Among the latter was Joseph Smale, who came from Los Angeles. Returning home convinced that what he had seen would become a worldwide awakening, Smale inaugurated daily prayer for revival in his First Baptist Church. After nearly four months, some objected that his preoccupation with revival precluded his fulfilling his regular responsibilities. Smale resigned, taking his most supportive members with him as the nucleus of his new congregation, the New Testament Church.

By 1906, the Los Angeles *Times* reported that over one thousand attended his Sunday morning services.[22]

Frank Bartleman, a contributor to various holiness periodicals and an occasional visitor at several Los Angeles missions, shared Smale's desire to see a repetition of the Welsh event in Los Angeles. A frequent attendant at Smale's meetings, Bartleman was an early visitor at Azusa Street. Convinced of the authenticity of Seymour's message, he helped publicize it through various holiness publications.

Azusa Street eventually attracted people from across the United States, and reports won adherents in scattered parts of the world. The response of those who later embraced Pentecostal teaching often paralleled A. S. Worrell's. Worrell, a respected Southern Baptist editor and New Testament translator, noted in his publication, *Gospel Witness,* that "personal friends" had written to him about tongues speech at Azusa Street. "Many," his informants claimed, "had been converted as results of these wonderful manifestations." "One might as well try to sweep back the waters of the Pacific, as to attempt to check this mighty display of God's power," his report continued. Like others, Worrell chose both to report and to investigate the events.[23]

The *Apostolic Faith,* a four-page monthly paper circulated without charge to publicize the movement, reported in September 1906 that "meetings begin about ten o'clock in the morning and can hardly stop before ten or twelve at night, and sometimes two or three in the morning, because so many are seeking, and some are slain under the power of God." In time, Bartleman claimed, Smale and other mission leaders had to come to Azusa Street to find their members.[24] They found them singing without musical accompaniment songs like *The Comforter Has Come* and *Under the Blood;* they found some "slain in the Spirit" and others speaking in tongues. Others sought sanctification or healing; some simply reveled in the intensity of spiritual release they discovered in the meetings. Some mission leaders stayed to receive their own "Pentecost." Smale did not. Bartleman called him "God's Moses." He had "led the people as far as the Jordan, though he himself never got across. Brother Seymour led them over."[25]

Several visitors were deeply impressed by Seymour's humility: "He is the meekest man I ever met," William Durham of Chicago reported. "He walks and talks with God. His power is in his weakness. He seems to maintain a helpless dependence on God."[26] Bartleman concurred. Of Seymour he wrote, "There was no pride there."[27] Glenn Cook had been preaching in tent meetings when reports of Seymour's meetings attracted him to the mission "to straighten out their doctrine." He found himself one of several with similar intentions. "But the contention was all on our part," he later acknowledged. Of Seymour he wrote: "I never have met a man who had such control over his spirit."[28]

Azusa Street Mission Developments

Participants at Azusa Street who later devoted their lives to Pentecostal ministries treasured their memories of the early years of this setting, which Bartleman called "a veritable Jerusalem," where fervor, intensity, and a pervasive sense of the supernatural reportedly characterized every meeting.[29] Much was said at Azusa Street about unity, the cleansing blood, and the Second Coming. The mission gained a reputation as a place to come for healing, and Seymour reported that healings occurred "almost every day." "Handkerchiefs were sent in to be 'blessed': one day, nine; another day, sixteen."[30] The expectation was simple: "The mission people never take medicine. They do not want it. They have taken Jesus for their healer, and He always heals."[31] The skeptical confused their healing message with unorthodox approaches: Early Pentecostals took every opportunity to avow their opposition to Christian Science, animal magnetism, Theosophy, spiritualism, and hypnotism.

Seymour originally aligned himself with Parham's Apostolic Faith Movement, not only in his use of the name and in direct references, but also in the general themes he stressed (although he denied Parham's nontraditional views on eternal life and his eschatological claims about Spirit baptism). Like Parham's work, the Azusa mission taught repentance, restitution, sanctification, healing, Spirit baptism as "a gift of power upon the sanctified life," and the imminent premillennial return of Christ. A remarkable percentage of the Spirit-baptized either sensed a call or received a call in prophecy to a foreign country. They went out "in faith." In September 1906 Seymour reiterated his commitment to Parham's faith living, noting that "a dozen or more Christian workers" assisted him, "having been called of God from other lines of employment to devote their time in praying with the sick, preaching, working with souls at the altar, etc. We believe in the faith line for Christian workers, and no collections are taken."[32]

The unity that was ascribed to Spirit baptism was emphatically restorationist in nature; it represented a return to New Testament practice, where believers were simply "Christians." Like Parham's Apostolic Faith, the Azusa Street Mission claimed to stand for nothing new; it advocated, rather, "the restoration of the faith once delivered unto the saints." This implicit indictment of accepted religious institutions (which presumably had failed to retain "the faith once delivered to the saints") manifested itself in many ways. "We are not fighting men or churches," Seymour maintained, "but seeking to displace dead forms and creeds and wild fanaticisms with living, practical Christianity. 'Love, Faith, Unity' are our watchwords, and 'Victory through the Atoning Blood' our battle cry."[33] Their practical Christianity characterized the end times as it had the Early Church:

> When the Holy Ghost fell on the one hundred and twenty, it was in the morning of the dispensation of the Holy Ghost. Today we are living down in the evening of the dispensation of the Holy Ghost. And as it was in the morning, so it shall be in the evening. This is the last evangelistic call of the day.[34]

The pervasive sense that God was using them as part of His specific eschatological purpose both excited and awed participants. "Los Angeles seems to be the place, and this the time, in the mind of God, for the restoration of the church to her former place, favor and power," Bartleman reflected. "The full-ness of time seems to have come for the church's complete restoration."[35]

Countless messages in tongues were interpreted to proclaim the imminence of Christ's return. "Awake! Awake!" they pleaded. "There is but time to dress and be ready, for the cry will soon go forth. 'The Bridegroom cometh.' "[36] Anticipation of the second coming of Christ contributed to interest in evange-lism and stimulated concern for personal holiness. At Azusa Street, the Pentecost event was understood to be inextricably related to evangelistic service. "The gift of languages is given with the commission, 'Go ye into all the world and preach the Gospel to every creature,' " *The Apostolic Faith* noted. Even signing could be supernaturally enabled:

> The Lord has given languages to the unlearned—Greek, Latin, Hebrew, French, German, Italian, Chinese, Japa-nese, Zulu and languages of Africa, Hindu and Bengali and dialects of India, Chippewa and other languages of the Indians, Esquimaux, the deaf mute language, and in fact the Holy Ghost speaks all the languages of the world through His children.[37]
>
> The mission paper solemnly noted as well that "the Lord [had] given the gift of writing in unknown languages," "the gift of playing on instruments," as well as gifts of singing with "new voices" and translating "old songs into new tongues."[38]

Each issue of *The Apostolic Faith* told of those who had left for various foreign fields as well as of those who determined to evangelize America. In fact, some people did both. Those who intended to sail from the East Coast frequently broke their cross-country rail journey to evangelize for weeks in towns along the way. All were committed to working "on faith lines." They had been informed that "when Pentecostal lines are struck, Pentecostal giving commences."[39] Expecting miracles, they left for other countries. Some had no clear direction. Informed that they had "spoken the language of Africa" under the inspiration of the Spirit, they would determine to sail for Africa to preach. Others had missionary experience and understood their task.

But all expected a supernatural enablement that would allow them to omit language study or attention to mundane affairs.

Other Missions in Southern California

For several years the revival at Azusa Street alternated between periods of growth and decline. Other missions throughout the Los Angeles area sometimes rivaled Azusa Street in claims to power and miracles. At times fiercely independent "seekers," having a reputation of being unable to work harmoniously with others and seeing the formation of a rudimentary organization, bemoaned the "apostatizing" of Azusa Street, and they separated from Seymour. Bartleman claimed that the mission had "failed God" by hanging a sign outside reading Apostolic Faith Mission.[40] "The Lord," he reported, told him that "there could be no divisions in a true Pentecost."[41] For Bartleman, the sign signaled that "the work had become one more rival party and body, along with the other churches and sects of the city."[42]

Sensing a call "to go deeper than anything [he] had at this time attained to," Bartleman began his own meetings in a mission at Eighth and Maple streets. The withdrawal of several members from the New Testament Church resulted in the creation of the Upper Room Mission under the leadership of Elmer Fisher, to which, Bartleman reported, most of the white believers from Azusa Street eventually made their way.[43]

Such missions maintained full schedules: At the Upper Room Mission, Sunday school was at 9:30 A.M., followed by three worship services—at 11 A.M., 3 P.M. and 7:30 P.M. From Tuesday through Friday, noon Bible studies ran from 11 A.M. until 1 P.M., and evening services were conducted nightly at 7:30. Each evening service was preceded by two or three street meetings.[44] On Mondays, the workers from various missions gathered for prayer and fellowship.

As the movement spawned these and other new missions, it extended its influence. Several of the missions sponsored publications: The Upper Room Mission's monthly was titled *The Upper Room;* the Victoria Hall Assembly published *The Vic-*

torious Gospel. The mission publications carried reports, testimonies, and devotional and instructional articles.

From the fall of 1906, operating out of various centers, the movement claimed thousands of adherents. On one busy day, Seymour and some 500 followers converged on a Los Angeles beach where Seymour baptized 106 in the ocean. Five years after Parham's Topeka experience, it was estimated that some thirteen thousand had spoken in tongues, and, further, that those who rejected "Pentecost" "backslid" and "lost the experience" they had. "Those who are older in this movement are stronger, and greater signs and wonders are following them."[45]

This apparent compliment paid Parham was among the last positive comments *The Apostolic Faith* carried about the absent founder of the movement. Responding to a written invitation from Seymour, Parham arrived in Los Angeles late in October, traveling from Zion City, where he was in the midst of one of his most influential revivals. Parham was appalled by both the worship style and the interracial character of the services. Sitting on the platform, he observed "manifestations of the flesh, spiritualistic controls, . . . people practicing hypnotism at the altar over candidates seeking the baptism."[46] Complaining that all who exercised the gift of tongues did not speak in known languages, Parham insisted that they did not have the baptism in the Holy Spirit. He lamented that his work was being "brought into ridicule" across the country by "fanatics" who accepted "chattering, jabbering, wind-sucking and jerking fits" as the evidence of Spirit baptism.[47]

In a later diatribe against the aspirations to leadership that Parham felt had nearly destroyed the Apostolic Faith Movement, he noted that Seymour had been "made Pope" by his followers and had rejected his mentor, going so far as to assert that "Azuza [sic] was the original 'crib' of this movement, and a Negro the first preacher."[48] The racial issue stayed with Parham. Although Bartleman exulted that "the 'color line' had been washed away in the blood," Parham could not accept the resultant mingling.[49] Years later, his resentment lingered:

> In the Azuza [sic] mission in Los Angeles (where all this

counterfeit Pentecost power was born), in the Upper Room, men and women, whites and blacks, knelt together or fell across one another; frequently a white woman, perhaps of wealth and culture, could be seen thrown back in the arms of a big "buck nigger," and held tightly thus as she shivered and shook in freak imitation of Pentecost. Horrible, awful shame! Many of the missions on the Pacific coast are permeated with this foolishness, and, in fact, it follows the Azuza work everywhere.[50]

Parham had attended no more than three Azusa Street services. His long-harbored bitterness about the mission's success marked the beginning of his ultimate ostracism from mainstream Pentecostalism. Blaming much of the spiritual "confusion" on Seymour's white colleague, Glenn Cook, Parham labeled the Azusa mission "a hotbed of wildfire" in which "religious orgies outrivaling scenes in devil or fetish worship, took place in the Upper Room where deluded victims by the score were thrown into a hypnotic trance, out of which they came chattering and jabbering."[51]

Parham claimed that he had tried unsuccessfully to reason with Seymour. After Parham had preached two or three times at Azusa Street, he was barred from the mission and opened his own services in Los Angeles; through them, he reported, several hundred who had been deluded at Azusa Street "were delivered, and received the real Pentecost teachings."[52] Bartleman admitted that spiritualists and hypnotists did trouble the Azusa Street mission, attempting to influence seekers. It was "a wonder," he noted, "that the work survived at all."[53] But regarding such intrusions as "attacks of the enemy," the faithful nucleus prayed until they "had the victory." Meanwhile, the Azusa Street mission distanced itself from Parham by changing its name to Pacific Coast Apostolic Faith Movement and recruiting its own directors.[54]

Many concurred with Bartleman's view that the early Azusa Street mission was "holy ground." They came to inquire, often stayed to experience the baptism in the Holy Spirit, then left to proclaim its reality across the country and around the world. The view of history outlined at the mission generated excitement and purpose: It appealed to those whose religious preferences or social situations made them uncomfortable in conventional churches. Reinterpreting history, this view insisted that Azusa Street participants were at the center of God's end-time dealings with humanity. It helped them reinterpret their experiences in a way that transformed the meaning of worldly rejection and failure. They reconsidered who they were from the perspective of participation in God's divine plan, and in so doing, they discovered a new sense of purpose, importance, and identity.

The amazing thing was not what was said; most of it had been said before. Rather, the survival and expansion (and modification) of the restorationist vision that characterized Azusa Street in 1906 deserves attention, especially when one considers how many independent missions advocating restorationist schemes have come and gone without much notice on the American religious scene. One reason that the Azusa Street mission became the focus of a larger movement was that across the United States its distinctive teaching was accepted by people whose restorationist inclinations had already prompted their separation from the denominations.

American Pentecostalism began outside the denominations, and it established itself first in scattered ministries across the country that shared its distrust of "man-made organizations." Some of the places it found acceptance later contributed directly to the emergence of the Assemblies of God.

The first edition of William Seymour's paper, *The Apostolic Faith.* It chronicled the Movement's extension for several years.

Front row: William J. Seymour, John Lake. Back row: a Brother Adams, F. F. Bosworth, Thomas Hezmalhalch (ca. 1915)

Caption reads: "These cartoon caricatures appeared in the Los Angeles Times, July 23, 1906, supposedly representing the types of Pentecostals at the First New Testament Church. The photo at the right is of Elmer Fisher, pastor of the Upper Room Mission."

Azusa Street Mission around 1905

A later picture of the Azusa Street Mission

5. Some Early Pentecostal Centers

The Comforter has come,
The Comforter has come,
The Holy Ghost from heav'n,
The Father's promise giv'n;
O spread the tidings round,
Wherever man is found
The Comforter has come!

F. G. Bottome, *The Comforter Has Come*, 1890

Azusa Street functioned as a catalyst. News from Los Angeles stimulated people across the country who already shared a restorationist orientation to consider the validity of the claim that another essential component of early Christian experience had been recovered. Many such people had already progressed significantly in experience and thought patterns that inclined them toward Parham's message; they might well have reached similar conclusions themselves. Among people committed to a full recovery of New Testament Christianity, anything that could establish its continuity with the Early Church tended to elicit serious consideration.

Zion City, Illinois

Among the first places to respond with interest to reports from Azusa Street was Zion City, Illinois. Established by John Alexander Dowie in 1901, Zion was the center of an extensive network of activities sponsored by Dowie's Christian Catholic Church. Tightly organized, the city had strict regulations about religious activities. It contained but one church, a huge facility known as Shiloh Tabernacle, and permitted no other religious teachers within city limits. Dowie held tightly to the reins, until financial disaster and doctrinal controversies resulted in his replacement as general overseer by Wilbur Glenn Voliva. The financial situation deteriorated until the city was placed in receivership. For the first time, a serious religious cleavage surfaced in 1906. A minority remained loyal to Dowie. The majority accepted Voliva and affirmed their continued commitment to Dowie's central tenets of faith: consecration, holiness, and healing. But many desperately sought new associations for expressing their faith.

Various unorthodox religious prophets arrived on the scene but had relatively little success. Some of Dowie's followers had read reports from Azusa Street, however. They invited Charles Parham to bring his message to Zion City. The resulting meetings would have tremendous significance for the future Assemblies of God.

Parham's message had had a hearing in Zion two years earlier when reports of his successes in southeastern Kansas and southwestern Missouri had been brought to the city by two of his women associates. One, Mabel Smith, was especially noted as an evangelist who exercised the gift of tongues and interpretation in every service she attended. A quiet, reserved woman, she was highly regarded in Zion until the authorities of the Christian Catholic Church forced those who received her message to leave the city.[1]

Zion was in considerable disarray when Charles Parham arrived on September 20, 1906, to begin services in the city's hotel. Economic deprivation, social discontent, and religious turmoil had taken their toll. Factions disrupted a long-cherished harmony. The situation facilitated Parham's meetings, which would not have been possible earlier. As usual, the press noted Parham's personal appeal, reporting that he had "a pleasant and convincing manner that makes his discourse almost irresistible."[2] The rapid growth of his audiences seemed to attest this. Overflowing from a hotel room into the halls, the services attracted hundreds during the first week. Voliva responded by prohibiting religious services in the hotel and refusing Parham rental of the city's schools or use of Shiloh Tabernacle. Parham's hometown newspaper reported that while the officers of the church deliberated, Parham continued to preach "and his congregation is numbered by the thousands."[3]

Although that number was probably exaggerated, Parham did find a growing following. (Numbers may well have increased as Voliva's opposition took shape.) He accepted five separate invitations to move his ministry to private homes. He conducted simultaneous services nightly between 7 P.M. and midnight, traveling from one home to another, preaching and exhorting.[4] Hundreds attended, and within a month, some of the most respected citizens had spoken in tongues.

Late in October, Parham left Zion City for Azusa Street. During his absence, the services continued. More disaffected Zionites identified with the Apostolic Faith. Voliva responded by depriving Parham's followers of membership in the Christian Catholic Church, an action that had economic and social consequences.

When Parham returned for the holidays, the city receiver granted permission for his followers to erect a tent seating two thousand in the center of the city. Later, the receiver granted the Pentecostals access to Shiloh Tabernacle on week nights and alternate Sundays.

Early in January, Parham again left, returning in March 1907 when Dowie's recent death gave rise to rumors that Parham intended to assume leadership of the community. In fact, Parham's ministry in Zion City had ended for a variety of reasons, but the teaching he had introduced continued to thrive. As it extended through Dowie's organization, numerous capable and experienced evangelists, teachers, and administrators were won to the Pentecostal movement. Many later affiliated with the Assemblies of God. Among them were F. F. Bosworth, Marie Burgess Brown, F. A. Graves, John Lake, D. C. O. Opperman, E. N. Richey (later Zion City's mayor) and his sons, Charles and Daisy Robinson, Fred Vogler, and Helen Innes Wannenmacher. Motivated by Dowie's precept and example to "take God at His word," they worked in many capacities as Pentecostal pioneers.[5]

Lilian Yeomans, another ordained Assemblies of God minister who had been healed in Zion, undoubtedly expressed a consensus when she stated in the 1930s: "Some people say that Dr. Dowie's work is dead. No! It is more alive today than ever."[6] Those of Dowie's followers who identified with Parham's Pentecostal message concurred that in Pentecostalism the real significance of Dowie's message was preserved and expanded. Shorn of both its communal concerns and its apostolic pretensions, Dowie's focus on the full validity of New Testament Christianity for twentieth-century believers found, they would claim, its logical and fullest development in Pentecostalism.

The Churches of God in Christ

Early in 1907, reports from Azusa Street reached Memphis, where the holiness group known as the Churches of God in Christ, directed by Charles Price Jones and Charles Mason, had a strong congregation. The association's two leaders agreed that the baptism in the Holy Spirit was an experience for all believers. Jones, however, maintained that Spirit baptism would "complete the believer in Christ" by a third work of grace. The specific object of Spirit baptism, he believed, was power for effective service.

Mason later described his association with Jones. He owed much to this simple, humble man. It was Jones who convinced him that he did not have the baptism in the Holy Spirit—that they both lacked power to heal, exorcise demons, and raise the dead (abilities Jones believed would follow Spirit baptism). Jones pointed Mason's attention to the miraculous change the believers experienced at Pentecost and told him that "the blessing was for him."[7] After Mason and Jones had studied the subject together, Mason and two fellow ministers, J. A. Jeter and D. J. Young, left for Azusa Street to examine reports firsthand.[8]

Although he resisted some of what he saw, Mason claimed that when he heard speaking in tongues, he "knew it was right."[9] Shortly thereafter Mason received Spirit baptism, and five weeks later he and his two colleagues returned to Memphis committed to Pentecostalism. They found that during their absence the Pentecostal message had been preached in the Memphis Church of God in Christ by Glenn Cook, a white participant in the Azusa Street meetings who traveled widely, making converts to Pentecostalism. Mason recorded the change that his own Spirit baptism had brought to his ministry: "The Spirit had taken full control of me and everything was new to me and to all the saints. The way that He did things was all new."[10]

But Jones strongly objected to the Azusa Street teaching that speaking in tongues was the uniform initial evidence of Spirit baptism. Although he readily conceded the need for a third "crisis" and had long affirmed most of what Azusa Street taught, he could not accept the idea of uniform evidential tongues. During the annual convention of the Churches of God in Christ in the summer of 1907, Jones's group disfellowshipped those who advocated tongues. Jones changed the name of his non-Pentecostal remnant to The Church of Christ (Holiness) U.S.A.

Mason, meanwhile, became the unchallenged leader of the Churches of God in Christ, a position he held until his death in 1961. Widely respected throughout American Pentecostalism, Mason ministered to blacks and whites.[11] His group's own membership, though predominantly black, was interracial at the beginning.[12] Mason incorporated his denomination, and thus his ministers were eligible for clergy railroad discounts and other civil recognition.[13] Between 1907 and 1914, numerous white ministers sought credentials from Mason's Church of God in Christ.

Southeastern Groups

Several separate associations in the Southeast also shared much that Azusa Street taught. They preached salvation, sanctification, healing, and holiness. Some, more radical than other groups with roots in the National Holiness Association, espoused premillennialism. Publications like the *Way of Faith*, edited by J. M. Pike in Columbia, South Carolina, and *Living Waters*, edited by J. O. McClurkan in Nashville, enjoyed national circulation and were important in maintaining a sense of shared participation among far-flung holiness constituencies.

The first reports of the Azusa Street meetings reached the South through such publications. Pike's *Way of Faith* had earlier carried articles by Frank Bartleman, who began sending enthusiastic reports about events at Seymour's mission. Gaston Barnabas Cashwell, a minister of the Holiness Church of North Carolina, read the accounts in the *Way of Faith*. "I had been preaching holiness for nine years," he would later write, "but my soul began to hunger and thirst for the fullness of God. The Spirit led me more and more to seek my Pentecost."[14]

Cashwell decided to investigate in person. A native of rural Sampson County, North Carolina, Cashwell had been a minister of the Methodist Episcopal Church, South, before casting in his lot with local holiness advocates. Late in 1906 he left for Azusa Street. The rail trip took six days, which he spent fasting and praying.

A middle-aged white southerner, Cashwell was at first disturbed by the interracial character of the Azusa Street mission. He overcame his reluctance sufficiently to request Seymour and others to lay hands on him and pray that he would be Spirit-filled. He agonized in prayer from Sunday until Thursday, when "He filled me with His Spirit and love." "I am now feasting and drinking at the fountain continually and speak as the Spirit gives utterance, both in my own language and in the unknown language."[15] Healing from rheumatism accompanied this experience. A rejuvenated Cashwell returned to Dunn, North Carolina, where on December 31, 1906, he began a series of meetings directed primarily toward the principal holiness groups in the area. Blacks and whites attended the services, people came from South Carolina and Georgia, and most of the local ministers of the Fire-Baptized Holiness Church, the Pentecostal Holiness Church, and the Free-Will Baptist Church accepted the Apostolic Faith message, with its stress on restoration and its focus on evidential tongues.[16] Cashwell sent a jubilant letter to Los Angeles reporting conversions and

Spirit baptisms that deeply stirred the small town of twenty-five hundred.[17]

From Dunn, Cashwell toured the South. He found it necessary to resist the radical holiness teaching that had strong followings in some communities. Writing from Royston, Georgia, he noted: "People have been gulled here by take it by faith, reconsecrate, baptism of fire, 'dynamite,' and 'lyddite' till the faith of the people is almost gone." His response, in contrast, was straightforward: "Get your justified experience all in good shape, then get the sanctified experience of a clean heart. Then when your faith takes hold of the promise of the Father and Son, and the Word of God . . . . you can praise and bless God and the Holy Ghost will come in and praise God himself in unknown tongues . . . ."[18] In another small town, he discovered holiness people strictly keeping the Old Testament Feast of Tabernacles.[19]

During his travels in May 1907, Cashwell preached in Memphis. Some of his hearers had ties to J. O. McClurkan's Nashville-based Pentecostal Mission. As a result two Pentecostal Mission ministers, Henry G. Rodgers and Mack M. Pinson, embraced the teaching of evidential tongues. "We could scarcely wait for the message to end and the altar call to be given," they reported, "as we all sat with ears, eyes and hearts wide open drinking in every word. We must have looked like a hungry bunch."[20]

McClurkan had formed the Pentecostal Mission in 1898. A former Cumberland Presbyterian minister, McClurkan had claimed sanctification under the ministry of a veteran holiness Methodist, Beverly Carradine. In 1898, he had arrived in central Tennessee from California, gathered scattered holiness believers, and formed a fellowship based in Nashville. He endeavored to make Nashville "a center for the dissemination of scriptural Holiness throughout the South."[21] By 1915, the Pentecostal Mission had licensed some sixteen hundred preachers, evangelists, and lay workers, many of whom had received several years of training at McClurkan's Bible school.[22] Given the Mission's uncompromising emphasis on the typical holiness doctrines, enhanced by a strong commitment to premillennialism, it is hardly surprising that some within its ranks accepted evidential tongues. During its 1907 and 1908 conventions, the credentials committee, of which M. M. Pinson had been a member, discussed granting credentials to people who spoke in tongues and indicated some support for doing so.[23] A later decision against distinctive Pentecostal teaching on evidential tongues, however, occasioned the withdrawal of tongues-speaking participants in the Nashville-based mission.[24] Pinson, Rodgers, and Nickels John Holmes left the Pentecostal Mission to assume prominent roles in various tongues-speaking Pentecostal associations.

Rodgers had visions of an association to give identity to those who accepted evidential tongues. He formed a loose regional fellowship for Pentecostals, the Pentecostal Association of the Mississippi Valley.

Later in 1907, Ambrose J. Tomlinson, leader of yet another southern restorationist movement known as the Church of God, was associated with M. M. Pinson in meetings in Birmingham. Amazed to hear Pinson speak in tongues, Tomlinson, at Pinson's urging, invited Cashwell to his small church in Cleveland, Tennessee. Throughout 1907, numerous Church of God ministers received the baptism in the Holy Spirit, but Tomlinson did not. Cashwell finally visited Cleveland in January 1908, and Tomlinson fully embraced his Pentecostal teaching, spoke in tongues, and brought the constituency of the Church of God into the fledgling Pentecostal movement.[25] At about the same time, Pinson and Rodgers visited Tomlinson in Cleveland to discuss appropriate names for newly formed Pentecostal assemblies. The men shared a commitment to restorationist views that made it imperative for them to use "scriptural" names. Pinson and Rodgers had concluded that "Church of God" would be an appropriate designation for independent Pentecostal assemblies and obtained Tomlinson's assurance that their use of the designation would imply no relationship to his own movement.[26]

Cashwell's travels between 1906 and 1909 won many converts to Pentecostalism. Because he addressed a constituency that had already reached many of the conclusions that informed

Parham's Apostolic Faith, it proved relatively easy for him to convince both ministers and lay people that tongues were the biblical evidence of an experience they all affirmed in some way. Those who explicitly longed for restored New Testament norms were often inclined to welcome a movement that endorsed spiritual gifts. And when the experience was forthcoming—when those who agonized in prayer for the baptism of the Holy Spirit spoke in tongues and testified to their assurance of the presence and power of the Holy Spirit in their lives—the case seemed closed.

Although most of Cashwell's converts did not become part of the Assemblies of God, they formed other Pentecostal denominations with which the Assemblies of God would later interact. Those of his converts who did later affiliate with the Assemblies of God had established Pentecostal ministries long before 1914. The General Council would benefit, both by the experience Cashwell's converts had gained and by the people they brought with them into the new fellowship.

The Christian and Missionary Alliance

In May 1907 leaders of Albert B. Simpson's Christian and Missionary Alliance convened on the campus of the Missionary Training Institute at Nyack, New York, for their annual convention. Excitement permeated the gathering in the small town twenty-five miles north of New York to which Simpson had moved his home and his school. During the past year, reports from Azusa Street had encouraged numerous Alliance members to seek and receive the baptism in the Holy Spirit, evidenced by tongues. Alliance teaching was congenial to such an experience, and those who gathered in 1907 to transact business soon saw and felt Pentecostal fervor in their ranks. Numerous students and delegates committed themselves to Pentecostal ministries as a result of the "Pentecostal outpouring" at the Alliance convention.[27]

By any account, that convention had been unusual. One participant wrote: "Meetings ran on day and night for nearly a week without human leadership, no thought of time, trains, meals, sleep, etc. The Holy Ghost did wonderfully quicken and strengthen physically all those who thus fasted and waited upon Him." From the beginning, tongues speech was heard, although the sessions focused, rather, on intercession, "agony for sin and self-life," "visions of the cross, blood, throne" and "deep whole-souled shouts of glory and praise, all testifying 'Jesus is coming soon.' " Most remarkable to some was the fact that tongues speech was interpreted, thus giving the faithful "messages from the throne direct."[28]

Those convinced in the tumult of the convention joined other Alliance men and women who had already made that commitment. David Wesley Myland, for example, first superintendent of the Ohio Alliance, had read accounts from California and received his baptism in the Holy Spirit in November 1906.[29] Myland, a gifted musician, immediately penned a song that became a popular Pentecostal testimony:

> I'm so glad the promised Pentecost has come,
> And the Latter Rain is falling now on some;
> Pour it out in floods, Lord, on the parched ground
> 'Til it reaches all the earth around.

The Alliance proved especially hospitable to Pentecostalism. It shared Pentecostal teaching on Christ, the Holy Spirit, healing, and the Second Coming, as well as a firm commitment to foreign missions. Simpson had written books and songs that had helped popularize the practical dimensions of these emphases. And several faculty at his Missionary Training Institute, most notably William C. Stevens, had espoused a dispensational view that aroused anticipation of a latter rain. Simpson had encouraged expectation of spiritual gifts and had anticipated a miraculous end-times enduement of ability to proclaim the gospel in foreign languages.

The summer of 1907 saw several Alliance gatherings assume a Pentecostal character. At Alliance camp meetings at Beulah Park in Cleveland, Ohio, and at Rocky Springs Park in Pennsylvania numerous Alliance adherents, including Alliance Vice

President John Salmon, received the baptism in the Holy Spirit and spoke with other tongues. People with ties to the strong Alliance branch in Indianapolis, of which G. N. Eldridge was superintendent, accepted Pentecostal teaching from Glenn Cook.[30] Among those who identified with the new movement were Alice Reynolds and her future husband, J. Roswell Flower.[31]

From 1914, men and women with Christian and Missionary Alliance backgrounds made vital contributions to the Assemblies of God. Trained in Alliance branches and camps as well as at the Missionary Training Institute, they brought into the Pentecostal movement a strong commitment to evangelical doctrine and religious experience that served the Assemblies of God well at several critical moments. In striking ways, the Assemblies of God would parallel the Alliance: Doctrinally, the two groups were very close, separated primarily by the Alliance dictum about tongues, "seek not, forbid not"; organizationally, the Assemblies of God would resemble the Alliance. Simpson's books, hymns, and missionary vision articulated what the Assemblies of God affirmed. The Assemblies of God owes an incalculable debt to A. B. Simpson and the Christian and Missionary Alliance.

Elim

In 1906, Rochester, New York was home to the various ministries known as Elim. Consisting of a Faith Home, the Rochester Bible and Missionary Training School, and a local assembly, Elim had been founded in 1895 by the five daughters of a former Methodist pastor, James Duncan. The oldest, Mrs. E. V. Baker (who lived in Chicago), had sensed a "call" to accept divine healing, "faith" living, and a preaching ministry.[32] Shortly thereafter, her four sisters also felt "clearly called" to forsake "secular employment" and "come into His work."[33] Baker returned to Rochester, and the sisters secured the necessary facilities.

The sisters felt uncomfortable about the idea of women assuming the leadership of such a venture. Their father fully supported them as women in the ministry, but they had hoped that their only brother would head the work. His premature death, however, forced the women to accept the responsibility. Though they remained firmly opposed to the ordination of women, the sisters were highly revered.[34] They worked readily with others and commanded general respect among later Pentecostals.

Elim gained a reputation as a place where healing, faith, holiness of life, and the Second Coming were emphasized. A strong interest in missions developed early, and the sisters began to publish their message in tracts and later in a monthly journal called *Trust*. But they learned faith through trials. Encouraged by reading George Mueller's *Life of Trust*, they nonetheless occasionally found themselves short of food, fuel, and rent money. Numerous stories of miraculous provision punctuate their biographical accounts.

The Bible Training School was begun on October 2, 1906, with fourteen regular and six part-time students and a faculty of five. The two-year course covered "Theology, or the great doctrine of the Bible; Synthesis, or an analysis of the Bible by books; Personal Work, or how to use the Bible for seekers; Ancient and Modern History, Church History, Homiletics, Exegesis, Dispensational Truth, Rhetoric, and Greek, if so desired."[35] Organized on "faith lines," the school accepted students without financial resources, believing that teaching them "how to trust the Lord for supplies" was an integral part of their Christian training.[36]

Fearing "fanaticism or the work of the enemy," the sisters responded with hesitation to the first reports from Azusa Street. After vacillating for nearly a year, they concluded, in Susan Duncan's words, "that [God] was responsible for the movement but not for everything that was in it." They decided to "trust [themselves] to God for all that was of the Spirit and to be kept from what was not of His working."[37]

Events at Azusa Street did not necessarily surprise the sisters. Since the Welsh revival had begun late in 1904, they had prayed for a similar awakening in their midst:

> When that remarkable revival broke out in Wales our
> hearts, like those of all Christendom, were greatly stirred.
> The power of God working so mightily, the absence of
> human machinery, the tremendous results in the salvation
> of souls, made us very hungry to know God in His fullness.
> We held special meetings for the purpose of waiting upon
> God in which we were greatly blessed.[38]

During their annual summer convention in June 1907 the
long months of prayer ended in a "manifest outpouring." Two
visitors whose baptism in the Holy Spirit had been evidenced
by tongues explained Pentecostal teaching, and "almost the
entire Convention became seekers at once."[39] All who received
Spirit baptism "were prostrated under the Hand of God." The
Duncan sisters asserted that the "Latter Rain" had begun to
fall: "God was doing a new thing in the earth."[40] The Elim
ministry became thoroughly Pentecostal, and the sisters noted
a transformation in their work. Spirit-filled adherents were
"perfectly free in the Spirit, able to pray or exhort or sing with
readiness and power." Without "straining or working up of
fleshly emotion," they experienced "a glad joyous sense of worship and adoration to Christ flowing out of hearts energized by
the Spirit's presence."[41]

In one significant way the Duncan sisters differed from many
other American Pentecostals. They disagreed with those who
"tried to label and pigeon-hole" the baptism in the Holy Spirit,
"dogmatizing about what other Christians have, or have not."
"Many," they noted sorrowfully, "teach that no one has the
Holy Spirit till they speak in tongues. The experience of God's
most devoted servants throughout the centuries past disproves
this statement."[42] The sisters rejected the distinction between
evidential tongues and the gift of tongues and understood the
Pentecostal movement as a dispensational event. It had, they
noted, "a preparatory bearing on the soon coming of our Lord,
and is indeed the 'Latter Rain.'" After all, "Jesus [was] coming
soon and [could not] translate a people from a lower plane than
Pentecost."[43] Tongues speech for them was "incidental." The
movement was much more than the restoration of a gift: It was
"the restoration of Pentecost ... the lifting up of the Church

to the original plane designed of God, from which they have fallen."[44]

Although the Rochester Bible Training Institute was small, accommodating only some thirty-five students at any given time, it trained several key future Assemblies of God leaders, who consistently paid high tribute to the sisters whose venture of faith made them Pentecostal pioneers.[45]

Chicago Missions

Among the many early Pentecostal outreaches in Chicago, two made especially significant contributions to the early development of the Assemblies of God. Led by strong, young, independent men, both the Stone Church and the North Avenue Mission were widely known as centers where charismatic gifts and Pentecostal teaching predominated. Their respective leaders, William Hamner Piper and William H. Durham, both died before the Assemblies of God was organized, but before their premature deaths, each made a substantial contribution to early Pentecostalism.

William Piper's Stone Church

Piper had been one of John Alexander Dowie's most prominent assistants. After Dowie's downfall, Piper had moved to Chicago and, in December 1906, began conducting services that attracted numerous former Dowieites. Holding to the essential teachings of Zion, Piper eliminated the elaborate trappings that Dowie had incorporated into his ministry and simply ran an evangelical church, which was known as the Stone Church.[46] Formed as the Pentecostal message penetrated Zion, the congregation resisted Parham's teaching. In fact, Piper's people seemed so prejudiced against Apostolic Faith teaching that he deemed it wise "temporarily not to say very much about the Holy Spirit."[47]

The church struggled, however. Attendance reached 600, then plummeted to 125 by April 1907. "Nothing is better calculated to make a minister examine himself than a decrease in his audiences," Piper commented. "After long days and nights of agony of spirit in earnest prayer, I was finally brought to the decision that what was claimed as the baptism in the Holy Spirit and the speaking in tongues was really of God."[48] Convinced that in his reluctance to embrace Pentecostalism he had "failed God," Piper determined to face the consequences of introducing Pentecostal teaching and practice in his church. He conjectured that the decision would most likely cut his membership in half and might well mean that he would have to seek secular employment to finance his continued ministry.

On Sunday, June 30, 1907, Piper startled his congregation with the announcement that that evening three visitors from Zion City would expound Pentecostal teaching at the Stone Church. Piper had carefully chosen three respected and capable individuals: Elder F. A. Graves, Jean Campbell, and Marie Burgess. Best known today for his hymns *Honey in the Rock, He'll Never Forget to Keep Me,* and *He Was Nailed to the Cross for Me,* Graves had been healed of epilepsy under Dowie's ministry. A mature, experienced leader, Graves held the respect of all who knew him. In 1907, though he heartily endorsed Pentecostal teaching, he had not yet spoken in tongues. That experience came to him in June 1908, at Elim.[49] Burgess would soon leave Zion for sixty-four years of ministry in New York City; Campbell married a fellow Zionite, L. C. Hall, and shared his extensive ministry in Texas. Both Burgess and Campbell had spoken in tongues as a result of Parham's visit to Zion in 1906.

From the first meeting, a warm response was evident. The services continued every night for several weeks, and many received Spirit baptism. Attendance increased, and the Stone Church was swept into the Pentecostal movement. Lydia Markley Piper shared public ministry with her husband. The Pipers began a Pentecostal monthly, *The Latter Rain Evangel.* Its editor, Anna Reiff, became one of the most influential lay women in the early Pentecostal movement. Because of its location in Chicago, the church was well situated to host conventions and entertain missionaries. In a day when most people traveling across America changed trains in Chicago, the Stone Church opened its pulpit to innumerable missionaries heading for foreign fields. The thriving congregation was hospitable to visitors, and the assembly became known as a center for spiritual renewal.[50]

William Durham's North Avenue Mission

William Durham's North Avenue Mission (which moved at least once during the brief Pentecostal phase of his association with it) attracted a different constituency. Located in an area populated primarily by immigrants, it attracted various ethnic groups.[51]

Born in Kentucky in 1873, Durham had been called into the ministry shortly after his conversion in 1898. He preached salvation, sanctification, and healing in an independent mission in Chicago. Like so many others, he firmly believed that the denominations were "the greatest hindrance to the advancement of the real cause of Jesus Christ."[52]

Durham's initial positive response in the spring of 1906 to news from Azusa Street gave way to sharp criticism of the teaching that tongues always evidenced Spirit baptism. Never one to doubt his own insights, he noted: "I understood exactly what such a teaching implied and just how widely it reflected on all Christian experience, so far as the baptism in the Spirit was concerned."[53] In the fall of 1906, however, some of Durham's Chicago acquaintances received Spirit baptism and spoke in tongues. Stimulated by their experiences to study the matter, Durham concluded that "all experiences [he] had ever seen, [his] own included, were far below the standard God [had] lifted up in The Acts."[54] The sincerity of his members deeply moved him as they stood "with the tears streaming down their faces," telling "how sweet and precious Jesus had become to their souls, and how real the blessed Holy Spirit had made Him."[55]

Durham decided to travel to Los Angeles to seek the Pentecostal experience. He later recalled that he had been entranced from the moment he entered the door. Hundreds were present, yet none was in charge. In that first service, Durham heard what Pentecostals reverently called the Heavenly Anthem and recognized it as a song he could not sing: "A wave of power and glory seemed to sweep over the place, and a song broke forth in the Spirit, known in this movement as the Heavenly Anthem. It was the Spirit of God Himself. . . . I could not sing in that choir . . . I had not received Him, who was doing the singing. I saw clearly for the first time the difference between having the influence and presence of the Spirit with us, and having Him dwell within us in person."[56]

On March 2, 1907, after much prayer and participation, Durham received the experience he had coveted. He returned to Chicago to assume a Pentecostal ministry, quickly igniting a controversy: Unlike most early Pentecostals, Durham found himself unable to accept teaching on crisis sanctification. He had been uncomfortable with it before his Spirit baptism, he now acknowledged, but after he returned to Chicago in March 1907 he decided to stop preaching the second blessing.[57] Silence on the subject did not suit him either, however. He began to attack the doctrine and articulated in its place what he called "the finished work of Calvary." Maintaining that "when God saves a man, He makes him clean," he insisted that "Christ has finished the work in our behalf."[58] It was, therefore, illogical to believe "that we have been pardoned but that we are left full of sin" and in need of a "second work."[59]

Durham's views aroused sharp controversy. Excoriated by holiness Pentecostals, and especially by the increasingly bitter Charles Parham, Durham nonetheless won a wide hearing and could cite an impressive list of converts to his views, including the most influential segment of Parham's former associates in Texas and Arkansas.[60]

The North Avenue Mission, meanwhile, was widely known as a spiritual congregation. Frederick Link, a thirty-nine-year-old German Methodist pastor from Stevensport, Wisconsin, who later ministered in the mission, recalled his first visit on a fall Sunday morning in 1909: "The glory of God filled the place. Brother Durham rose to preach, but was unable to begin his sermon. He himself was so under the power of God, he could scarcely speak in the English language. Messages in tongues and interpretations [came] by Sister Aimee Semple. I was spellbound and took hold at once."[61]

Among those who received Spirit baptism at the North Avenue Mission were Andrew Harvey Argue of Winnipeg and Eudorus N. Bell of Texas, a Southern Baptist minister who later became the first general superintendent of the Assemblies of God. Durham moved much of his work to Los Angeles in 1911, partly out of a desire to spread his views in the "cradle" of American Pentecostalism and partly because of trouble in his North Avenue Mission. Even so, he continued to have a sizable following in Chicago.

Durham died in 1912 at the age of thirty-nine. His views, however, continued to gain acceptance. This acceptance was so great that when the Assemblies of God was organized in 1914, the sentiments of many of its adherents on the doctrine of sanctification reflected the influence of Durham.

The Apostolic Faith Movement in Texas and Arkansas

Parham's associates throughout eastern Texas continued to proclaim the Apostolic Faith, even as the focus of the movement shifted to Los Angeles and then disseminated across the country. Parham and Carothers conducted a camp meeting in suburban Houston in August of 1906. Lucy Farrow arrived from Los Angeles, on her way to Virginia.[62] Fresh from the excitement of the revival, she attracted large audiences and seemed gifted in assisting seekers to receive the baptism of the Holy Spirit.[63]

Also at the Houston camp, Parham imposed on his ministry the rudiments of an organization. Parham had earlier issued ministerial credentials as Founder and Projector of the Apostolic Faith Movement. Now he appointed Carothers general field director for the U.S.A. Howard Goss became field director for Texas, where some sixty full-time Apostolic Faith representatives worked.[64]

Parham left soon afterward for Zion City, Los Angeles, and other places. His workers continued to evangelize, establishing a mission in San Antonio, where L. C. Hall, a former Zion elder, and D. C. O. Opperman, Zion's former superintendent of schools, joined their ranks. Camp meetings, short-term Bible institutes, and evangelistic campaigns kept the workers constantly busy, itinerating from place to place as the need arose.

During the summer of 1907, when morals charges were brought against Parham in San Antonio, some of his former associates found it advisable to distance themselves from him. Veiled rumors of sexual infraction would haunt Parham for the rest of his life. Shunned by most Pentecostals, he was staunchly defended by his entire family (who insisted he had been framed by Carothers) and the nucleus of his supporters in southeastern Kansas. In Texas, however, the loose organization he had created was temporarily dissolved, and many evangelists "left the field."[65]

A faithful nucleus regrouped, determined to salvage as much of the Apostolic Faith Movement as they could. Shortly after renouncing Parham, they accepted an invitation to evangelize in Arkansas, where they found considerable interest. They began to refer to themselves as Pentecostals, partly to break their ties with Parham and also to clarify what distinguished them from others. The nucleus of workers, among whom Howard Goss, L. C. Hall, D. C. O. Opperman, and A. G. Canada figured prominently, welcomed another capable worker, Eudorus N. Bell.

Bell was the forty-five-year-old bachelor pastor of a Baptist church in Fort Worth when he embraced Pentecostalism. Taking a year's leave from his church, Bell had gone to Chicago to "tarry" at Durham's North Avenue Mission. After eleven months, he had received Spirit baptism. One of the best-trained men to assume leadership in early Pentecostalism, Bell had studied at Stetson University in Florida, the Baptist seminary in Louisville, and the University of Chicago Divinity School.[66]

While Bell was in Chicago, many in his Baptist church accepted Pentecostal teaching. Bell nonetheless resigned to participate in the camp meetings and Bible schools sponsored by Parham's former workers.[67] He married a widow from Fort Worth and quickly distinguished himself in Pentecostal circles. Bell assumed the editorial responsibilities for the movement's paper, *The Apostolic Faith*. He participated in large camp meetings. In 1910, probably in response to Bell's invitation, Durham preached to a camp meeting in Malvern, Arkansas, during which he convinced the workers of his "finished work" views.

Meanwhile, these men and women (Ethel Goss, for example, was recognized as a capable evangelist, far more gifted in preaching than was her husband) had established contact with H. G. Rodgers. The short duration of his Pentecostal Association of the Mississippi Valley had not dampened Rodgers' enthusiasm for organizing a loose network of Pentecostal ministers. In 1908, after discussion with A. J. Tomlinson in Cleveland, Tennessee, Rodgers had set in order several churches using the name Church of God.[68] Rodgers later reported that he had licensed and ordained several ministers using that name and planned to apply for recognition by the Southern Clergy Bureau. Some participants in this Church of God later affiliated with the Assemblies of God.[69]

Sometime in 1910 Rodgers apparently met with H. A. Goss and D. C. O. Opperman in Texas, and they concluded that the name Church of God identified them unacceptably with Tomlinson's work. As a result, Rodgers and the former Apostolic Faith adherents in Texas effected a working arrangement under the name Church of God in Christ. Latent hostility toward organization (Goss reported that some of his colleagues concluded that any structure "when committed to paper . . . was of the devil"[70]) precluded the formation of a meaningful formal structure. Rather, what resulted was "mainly for the purposes of business."[71] Goss termed the arrangement a "gentlemen's agreement," under which it was understood that the "untrustworthy" would be excluded from "fellowship."[72]

The choosing of the name Church of God in Christ was part of the restorationist quest for a biblical name for local churches. Late in 1907, Goss had apparently visited C. H. Mason of the Churches of God in Christ and received credentials from that group. Goss recorded in his diary that he had obtained from Mason permission to issue papers using the name Churches of God in Christ for the "white work" in Texas.[73] Although the name Apostolic Faith Movement continued to be used for several years, Churches of God in Christ gained increasing favor, especially given the restorationist argument introduced in its support. Rodgers and Pinson, both of whom had spent time in Memphis, also knew Mason's work well and had attended his services.

Camp meetings provided the best settings for scattered participants loosely identified under the heading Church of God in Christ to share ministry and highly coveted fellowship. Whereas in May 1911, Bell's *Apostolic Faith* announced "The Sixth Annual Encampment of the Apostolic Faith Movement for Texas and the Southwest," thus clearly identifying the gathering with Parham's earlier efforts, in 1912 his *Word and Witness* announced a meeting of the "Churches of God in Christ of the Apostolic Faith people."

At the gathering in 1911, although it had attracted far fewer participants than that in 1912, a significant decision had been made. Bell and Pinson, each editing a Pentecostal paper representing one of the two major segments of this white Church of God in Christ, had decided to merge their publications.[74] Bell's *Apostolic Faith* was absorbed into Pinson's *Word and Witness,* with Bell assuming editorial responsibilities in addition to his pastorate in Malvern.

In 1912, over three hundred camped on the grounds at Eureka Springs, Arkansas, while others found accommodation in town.[75] Shortly after the camp meeting, *Word and Witness* carried a lengthy article about an appropriate name for the movement. In a strong endorsement of restorationism, the paper editorialized about the appropriateness of the name Churches of God in Christ, explicitly rejecting Apostolic Mission because it was not a "Bible designation." "We believe," the paper noted, "in the Apostolic Movement not as a name for a church, but as a religious reform movement composed of all clean people who will join in our battle cry and reform slogan of Back to Christ and the apostles! Back to the faith once for all delivered to the saints! Back to the New Testament experiences!"[76] As a solution to the challenge of naming a local fellowship or congregation, the paper proposed: "Why not all join with the Bible and with many of the Pentecostal and apostolic saints everywhere and call them Churches of God and Churches of God in Christ as we are doing? Why add to God's names Holiness church, or Pentecostal church? All should be both."[77]

Records from 1913 preserve a list of 361 ministers, at least 84 of whom were women, in association with this Church of God in Christ. They represented twenty states and five foreign countries.[78] The Churches of God in Christ had a school committee, a bureau of information, and a clergy reference committee to make recommendations and offer advice to adherents.[79]

In December 1913, leaders in this predominantly white group (a black missionary couple was listed as workers), sensing a need for more structure to "preserve the work," used the *Word and Witness* to call a convention in Hot Springs, Arkansas, for April 2–12, 1914. Their vision would give birth to the Assemblies of God.

In a sense, focusing on a few individuals and regions is an artificial way of describing what was happening. Across the country people were receiving their "Pentecosts." In Alliance, Ohio, where a Friend, Levi Lupton, ran the World Evangelization Company, a missionary home, a school, and published a paper, *The New Acts,* Pentecostal teaching found acceptance. Lupton used his paper and his school to proclaim Pentecostal teaching.[80] *The Apostolic Faith* and other Pentecostal publications contain hundreds of reports from rural America, small towns, and large cities describing similar responses by individuals and congregations to reports from Azusa Street.[81] Selected because of their later significance for the Assemblies of God, the places highlighted in this chapter can be seen as representative of a much broader movement. Operating primarily outside—or on the fringes of—established denominations, tongues-speaking Pentecostal evangelists, male and female, lay and ordained, infiltrated independent missions, holiness associations, and other nondenominational settings to proclaim the full and final restoration of New Testament Christianity in the onset of the latter rain.

F. A. Graves, noted for his musical abilities, embraced Pentecostal teaching in Zion City; received Spirit baptism at Elim, Rochester, New York; and was the father of three prominent Assemblies of God members: Irene Graves Pearlman, Arthur Graves, and Carl Graves.

1.

Honey in the Rock.

"And with honey out of the rock should I have satisfied thee." Ps. 81: 16.

F. A. G.

F. A. GRAVES.

1. O my brother, do you know the Saviour, Who is wondrous kind and true?
2. Have you "tasted that the Lord is gracious," Do you walk in the way that's new?
3. Do you pray unto God the Father, "What wilt thou have me to do?"
4. Then go out through the streets and byways, Preach the word to the many or few;

He's the "Rock of your salvation!" There's Honey in the Rock for you.
Have you drank from the living fountain? There's Honey in the Rock for you.
Nev-er fear, He will surely answer; There's Honey in the Rock for you.
Say to ev - ry fal-len brother, There's Honey in the Rock for you.

Chorus.

Oh, there's Honey in the Rock my bro-ther, There's Honey in the Rock for you.
my brother, for you;

rit.

Leave your sins for the blood to cover, There's Honey in the Rock for you;
for you.

3

E. N. Bell, leader in the Apostolic Faith Movement in Texas

William Durham (right) and his associate, Harry Van Loon (left)

Ad for Charles Parham's meetings in Zion City

ZION — THE ONLY PLACE WHERE IT IS EASY TO DO RIGHT, AND DIFFICULT TO DO WRONG.

AS ORIGINALLY PLANNED AND ESTABLISHED THE FOLLOWING DECLARATIONS WERE PRINTED AND SCATTERED BROADCAST THROUGHOUT THE WORLD.

IN ZION, WHICH IS TO BE A CITY OF GOD, THERE WILL BE

NO PROFANITY
NO VULGARITY
NO INTOXICATING LIQUORS
NO TOBACCO
NO DRUGS
NO THEATERS
NO DANCE HALLS

NO SORCERERS
NO MEDICAL POISONERS
NO SURGICAL BUTCHERS
NO VACCINATION
OF ALL THE FOUL INVENTIONS
OF THE DEVIL, AND SOME
DIRTY DOCTORS.

NO CUT THROAT COMPETITION
NO SALOONS OR BEER GARDENS
NO CIGARET, CIGAR TOBACCO STORES
NO PLACE " MANUFACTURE " SALE "
TOBACCO IN ANY FORM OR MANNER
NO OPIUM JOINT, NO COCAINE [ENGAGEMENT
NO HOUSE OF ILL FAME ASSICRATION

NO PHARMACY APOTHECARY'S SHOP
OR DRUG STORE.
NO PLACE " MANUFACTURE " SALE "
DRUGS " MEDICINES " ANY KIND
NO PLACE " OFFICE " RESIDENCE
" PRACTICING PHYSICIAN " SURGEON

NO PLACE " RAISING, KEEPING,
SLAUGHTERING " SELLING " SWINE
NO PLACE " KEEPING, " SELLING
FOR HUMAN FOOD " ANYTHING
FORBIDDEN BY GOD
TO BE EATEN ~ 7 ~ 19 ?
VERS." 14 " Or " of DEUTERONMY

NO OYSTERS " SCAVENGER "
UNCLEAN FISH " SHELLFISH " OR
FOOD " SWINE " SEA WEED " EARTH

NO PLACE FOR HOLDING MEETINGS
OR ASSEMBLIES " ANY OATH-BOUND
SECRET SOCIETIES

ALL RIGHTS IN REAL ESTATE CONVEYED UNDER AN ELEVEN HUNDRED - YEAR LEASE, CONTAINING THESE, AND
OTHER RESTRICTIONS. — THESE RESTRICTIONS COVER THE WHOLE CITY SITE, AND RUN WITH THE LAND
FROM THE VERY BEGINNING. THE USE OF TOBACCO HAS BEEN PROHIBITED IN ZION, THEREFORE, NO GENTLEMAN—NO MAN WITH ANY
CONCLUSION SENSE OF FAIRNESS AND JUSTICE WOULD USE TOBACCO IN ZION CITY. LET THE RELIGIOUS CONVICTIONS OF THE PEOPLE WHO
FOUNDED THIS CITY, AND THE PEOPLE FOR WHOM IT WAS FOUNDED, BE RESPECTED.

WILBUR GLENN VOLIVA

One of the many warnings posted in Zion during the years that
Pentecostalism was gaining a place in the city.

Mack M. Pinson's Pentecostal Mission, Nashville. Pinson is in the
back row, the third from the right.

William H. Durham's first (?) Pentecostal tent meeting (ca. 1909). Durham is in the center with his hand raised.

Mother E. A. Sexton, early editor of *The Bridegroom's Messenger.* It published Mack M. Pinson's articles until he began to advocate "the finished work of Calvary."

Camp meeting, Eureka Springs, Arkansas, 1912

Elizabeth Baker, who with her sisters superintended the Rochester Bible Training Institute and related efforts

Rochester Bible Training Institute

6. The Pentecostal Life-style: "Days of Heaven on Earth"

> When you get that rain of the Spirit upon you, don't you begin the days of heaven on earth? You begin to get heavenly tongues, heavenly songs, heavenly choirs, heavenly interpretation, heavenly inspiration, heavenly fellowship; you are in the heavenlies of Jesus Christ.
>
> D. W. Myland, *The Latter Rain Covenant,* 1910

Early Pentecostals eagerly anticipated effecting the renewal of vital Christian experience through both example and precept. The demonstration of the reality of the supernatural in their own lives, they believed, would attract others to similar renewal. If they could not change the denominations, they hoped at least to establish Pentecostal congregations to express charismatic fervor and apostolic polity in preparation for Christ's soon return.

Pentecostals have consistently exhibited a rich diversity in worship, doctrine, and priorities. Some of these patterns have changed significantly over time. But like other comparatively recent movements, Pentecostalism has its share of those who are acquainted with the good old days and long to return to behavioral norms characteristic of early stages in the movement's development. Sociologists of religion maintain that a return is impossible. An examination of the character of the early years suggests that a full return may be undesirable. But as contemporary Pentecostals evaluate the movement, nearing its hundredth birthday, they need to reflect on who they were so they can assess what they are becoming. Some of the things that have changed most radically pertain most directly to the essence of what it once meant to be Pentecostal.[1]

Early Pentecostals at Worship

The service opened with singing of hymns and the Spirit at once began to move upon us, so that several were worshipping in the new tongue, some praying audibly and some breaking forth in song, when Mr. Follette, one of the students, arose and began to speak with great feeling and power in the new tongue.... After this he burst forth in song, which was most beautiful and impressive. When he had ceased, the service went on and a sermon was delivered.... At the close of the service a lady and gentleman... called one of the sisters aside and asked, "Who was that young Jew who spoke and sang tonight?" He was told that there was no Jew present, but that it was one of the students.... With great surprise he informed us, "The young man spoke and sang in the most perfect Hebrew, and we understood every word he was saying."[2]

A brother was testifying at some length when Brother Tom interrupted him. "Hold on, brother; God is seeking to move in our midst." The brother stopped, then continued. Again Brother Tom checked him, kindly but firmly. There was a low murmur of sound from several directions over the congregation. This grew in volume until six persons were on their feet singing in rich harmony a song in the Spirit. Their eyes were closed, but without any confusion these persons moved from their various locations to the front of the hall, where they stood together singing in tongues in beautiful unison, then in harmonizing parts. To me was granted the glorious privilege of being one of this first such manifestation of the Spirit's power. The sensation was like being a pipe from which poured forth the wonderful melody deep within my being. Without effort the heavenly music flowed freely—"out of his innermost being shall flow rivers of living water"—and this was one of the rivers.[3]

Early Pentecostal worship defies simple description, but accounts agree about at least two things: First, worship absorbed one's mind and body and participants claimed it was motivated directly by the Holy Spirit. "[A]ll that wondrous worship and praise which overflowed my whole being came springing up alone from the Holy Spirit within; while my whole heart and soul constantly united with this stream of praise. No effort or work upon my part, my work had forever ceased."[4] And second, the Spirit enjoyed variety: "He does not always want you to be doing the same thing; He does not want things to run in a groove; He wants liberty to have a diversity of operations in the Spirit."[5] "A Pentecostal meeting where you always know what is going to happen next is backslidden," one participant insisted.[6]

Worship burst forth spontaneously wherever the Spirit-filled congregated. "When the power of God got to building up within us, it soon reached the level where vent had to be given to these floodtides of joy," Howard Goss reminisced. "At every opportunity it was instinctive to drop to one's knees and start praying and praising."[7] Train cars, rail stations, street corners, home gatherings—all became hallowed settings for exuberant praise, heartfelt singing, and the exercising of spiritual gifts.[8]

The baptism in the Holy Spirit was understood to facilitate a new dimension of worship. "The Spirit had taken full control of me and everything was new to me," Charles Mason recalled. "The way He did things was new.... He taught me how and what to sing and all of His songs were new."[9]

Intense excitement generally accompanied the initial experience of speaking in tongues (which Pentecostals termed the "Bible baptism" to differentiate themselves from those who considered an experience not marked by tongues to be Spirit baptism). The culmination of a process including repentance, restitution, sanctification, and "tarrying," the baptism in the Holy Spirit represented a release when all latent resistance to the Holy Spirit was removed. Participants claimed to speak many known languages or to sing in tongues as a response to an overwhelming joy that flooded their souls. The experience differed from human joys. As one anonymous testimony from Clearwater, Florida, exulted, "It seemed as if human joys vanished. ... This is something I never had before. It seemed as if the whole world and the people looked a different color. Jesus had come to me."[10]

Like a familiar refrain, those words, "Jesus has come to me," punctuated early written and spoken testimonies. Pentecostalism, in Donald Gee's words, "made the Lord Jesus intensely *real*."[11] Pentecostalism was "His fullness."[12] Exhortations to "seekers" frequently addressed the tendency to anticipate speaking in tongues with reminders to "seek Jesus." "It is not tongues," *Word and Work* maintained. "Tongues is an evidence or a sign that He has come and subdued the man."[13] Writing in 1910, J. R. Flower cautioned: "Too much stress on tongues weakens the argument."[14] "Let us not stress any gift or doctrine out of due proportion," he urged. "Let us preach the Word and leave the rest with God. When the Comforter comes, He will make Himself known, and evidence His presence."[15] Flower voiced a concern that relatively few of his contemporary Pentecostals considered: An overemphasis on tongues, he noted, would "compel us to accept all speaking in tongues as divine," when some was "purely human and other is certainly satanic."[16] (Both Parham and Seymour expressed similar reservations about unqualified emphasis on evidential tongues speech.) Pentecostal leader David W. Myland called tongues "the advance agent, the telltale sign of Pentecost." When, in the experience of Spirit baptism, however, Christ finally "possesses entirely that which He died to make His own," it was "something to shout about."[17]

The "coming of Jesus" made "all things new" in tangible ways. Many even claimed to perceive the natural world differently, as they sang in this song:

> Heaven above is softer blue, Earth around is
>   sweeter green!
> Something lives in every hue Christless eyes have
>   never seen.
> Birds with gladder songs o'erflow; Flowers with
>   deeper beauties shine.
> Since I know as now I know, I am His, and He is
>   mine.[18]

Preachers were urged to be sensitive to the Spirit's new message for the Church: Samuel Jamieson's experience is a case in point. One of the few Pentecostal ministers with traditional academic training, Jamieson had twenty-five years of experience as a Presbyterian pastor when he embraced Pentecostal teaching in 1907. In response to what he considered divine direction, he discarded his sermons to rely on the Spirit: "Burn them up and I will furnish you messages of My own choosing." Next, he found the Bible "practically a new book," "preaching under the anointing" a delight, and an increased "love for souls."[19]

The conviction that "Jesus had come" in a vital way into their circumstances enabled participants to face hardship and encouraged them to attempt the impossible. The Holy Spirit's "revelation" of Christ to their souls made them assert that Christ was more real to them than temporal circumstances. And His presence was what was ultimately important. In their constant quest to be ready for His soon return, they were often reminded of the need to adjust their priorities to correspond with His. Their absolute certainty of His presence within them seemed to give them limitless enjoyment and reckless courage.

Joy typically found expression in enthusiastic, fast-paced, "infectious" singing. Parham's associate Howard Goss appreciated the role of music in attracting converts: "Without it," he claimed, "the Pentecostal Movement could never have made the quick inroads into hearts that it did."[20] Pentecostals sang holiness songs, gospel music, and Charles Wesley's majestic descriptions of Christian experience.[21] Spirit baptism inspired them to sing "new songs" and "old songs in new tongues." The "heavenly choir," joined by various people in spontaneous harmony, attracted considerable interest. Those who heard it or participated in it claimed they could never adequately describe its beauty or sacredness. It occasionally assumed a conversational character: "In the meeting the other night the Spirit began to sing in different ones till it was almost an oratorio," wrote one Margaret Cragin of a service at the Elim Home. "The Spirit fell on those in meeting, on two in another room, and those in the room would answer in songs in the Spirit to those in the meeting."[22]

Some of the earliest Pentecostal creativity took musical form. D. Wesley Myland and Aimee Semple McPherson were among the more prominent of those who claimed to have been "given" songs in tongues and interpretation that achieved a degree of popularity.[23] Countless short-lived choruses, most with little content, were introduced as having been inspired by the Spirit through tongues and interpretation. And some Pentecostals wrote popular gospel songs that captured the movement's fervor and advanced its cause. Most helped popularize specific conceptions of personalized religious experience. Both Thoro Harris and Garfield Thomas Haywood, talented black Pentecostals, won wide acclaim. Harris's *All That Thrills My Soul Is Jesus, He's Coming Soon, More Abundantly,* and *Pentecost in My Soul* became well-known throughout the movement, as did Haywood's *Jesus, the Son of God* and *I See a Crimson Stream of Blood.*[24] Herbert Buffum, a former Nazarene evangelist, authored hundreds of songs both before and after embracing Pentecostalism. Among his most popular were *I'm Going Through, My Sheep Know My Voice, I'm Going Higher Some Day, Lift Me Up Above the Shadows,* and *The Old-fashioned Meeting.*[25] R. E. Winsett and Seeley Kinne became prominent Pentecostal songbook publishers. And of course, many late nineteenth-century gospel songs were sung by Pentecostals with a new sense of meaning. Through the many widely-known evangelical songs Pentecostals sang, they demonstrated their participation in the broader community of faith.

Pentecostal worship services continued indefinitely. The "anointing" to preach, prophesy, testify, or sing could not easily be contained within a schedule. People typically came prepared to stay. Haywood noted that his daily afternoon Bible readings and nightly services attracted many who brought their evening meal and stayed between services.[26] Even conventions to which many traveled hundreds of miles frequently anticipated no specific closing date. Pentecostals dreaded limiting the Spirit. Their general reluctance to follow the pattern of typical Protestant services was part of their effort to assure the continued "liberty" in the Spirit. When Haywood's mission got a pump organ, for example, some thought it was "getting worldly." And "when it went from the pump organ to the piano, it was becoming more worldly. And when the church had its first choir, there was such a revulsion against choirs that it was called the chorus." Even so, the chorus could not sit in a designated place or wear choir robes; rather, its members "sat in the audience and assembled around the piano when the pastor called for their services."[27]

The Faith Life of Early Pentecostals

The excitement the early Pentecostals had about the new spiritual dimension they had discovered in their lives frequently resulted in their neglecting normal responsibilities and pursuing intense spiritual experiences. Taking seriously injunctions to love nothing more than Christ, some virtually abandoned regular family life to "follow the Lord." The movement also attracted its share of men and women who were simply unwilling to work and who regarded the faith life as an opportunity to avoid situations they disliked. It was soon found advisable that responsible voices be raised to encourage men and women to recognize and fulfill family obligations. Denouncing as "false teaching" the idea that God had called wives and mothers "to do mission work, and to leave the little children at home to fare the best they can," *The Apostolic Faith* from Azusa Street was equally critical of men who abandoned their families for the sake of the gospel: "Many precious husbands have left their wives and children at home, and their wives are working hard to support the little children, washing, ironing, scrubbing, and farming, while their husband is claiming to be doing missionary work, and saying the Lord gave him . . . Scripture in regard to forsaking. They take it for granted that the Lord does not want them to be bothered with their families."[28] Urging family responsibility as a biblical principle, the Azusa Street mission attempted to discourage parents from itinerant evangelism. The urge remained irresistible in some, however. Among the more extreme was Frank Bartleman, who left his wife and children at Carrie Judd Montgomery's faith home in Oakland and took a two-year trip around the world. Preaching wherever he had opportunity, Bartleman traveled as far as his funds permitted, stopped to preach and receive an offering, then traveled on.

Early Pentecostal accounts are filled with insistences that believers live a life of radical faith. Whatever their needs, they were instructed to pray. Healing, funds, and direction became the subjects of intense supplication. Failure to obtain the desired object provoked careful self-examination. "If you are not healed," *The Apostolic Faith* editorialized, "the fault is either in you or in Jesus Christ. Which is it? Be honest with yourself and get the fault out of the way."[29] A simple premise motivated their lives: If one did God's will, one could anticipate God's adequate supply.

The movement kindled new expectations in believers, for it offered them spiritual renewal that never ended. There was, as they often sang, "always more to follow." "We are going on to get more of the power of God," *The Apostolic Faith* reported of Azusa Street. This notion that Spirit baptism inaugurated one into a life of growing awareness of God's presence and purpose seemed particularly appealing to people with little vested interest in this world's affairs. Little missions like Haywood's were crowded nightly with "anxious souls" who "taxed them to capacity."[30] Anticipating Christ's imminent return, they considered themselves a privileged people privy to the true meaning of God's dealings with contemporary society.

Few significant events passed without comment about their prophetic import. Earthquakes, economic uncertainty, foreign affairs, political elections, and even world wars were significant primarily for their place in God's prophetic calendar. And Pentecostals contributed prophecies too. With other millenarians, they anticipated that the "signs of the times" would be evident, and some had strong forebodings of dramatic "judgments" close to home. Participants in the Apostolic Faith Mission in Lynn, Massachusetts, forecast the "destruction of the world" to begin in 1908. Of nine people who had prophesied the imminent destruction of Boston ("as a warning to the people"), three were members of the Lynn congregation. They also declared that the destruction of New York and Chicago would follow shortly. One of the mission leaders, Mrs. A. F. Rawson, reported that the congregation was "very solemn in view of the impending destruction."[31] (Such prophecies—like emphases on such unusual "manifestations" as "suspension" or "prostration"—embarrassed segments of the movement. This abuse would contribute to support for organizing the many independent missions to "conserve" the revival.) Pentecostalism offered a frame of reference by which participants could interpret human experience and define ultimate concern. While this perspective shared important assumptions with non-Pentecostal evangelicalism, in significant ways it created a separate world in which Pentecostals affirmed the radical nature of the Spirit's presence in their midst. Speaking in tongues was, of course, vested with a significance that made it the most obvious Pentecostal departure from other evangelical norms.[32] Other "spiritual gifts," however, were just as real to the ardent Pentecostal, who also tended to reinterpret difficulties of any sort as demonic opposition—"attacks of the enemy."[33] The Pentecostal experience initiated believers into a life where spiritual forces were ever present. Everything had religious significance; they perceived themselves as involved regularly in spiritual battles through which they gained a sense of a personal participation in Christ's ultimate victory.

Pentecostals affirmed the present availability of all the New Testament spiritual gifts. Myland maintained: "You need a baptism of interpretation when you get a baptism of tongues, and some need a baptism of discernment, and some will need, especially the leaders, a baptism of wisdom, and you will have to have a baptism of knowledge and a great baptism of faith to lead this kind of life, or you will have a great deal of trouble."[34] Frequent dreams, visions, and transports made the supernatural a vivid part of their daily expectations and mediated interpretations of the divine significance of current events.[35] They occasionally claimed unusual manifestations of spiritual power. The published testimony of a young girl who claimed to have been "taken up two or three feet from the floor by the Holy Spirit and held there until some of the audience became frightened and put their hands on her" was followed by the comment: "Well, the great day is just before us when the laws of gravitation shall be reversed, and we need not be shocked if God shows us a little foretaste of it occasionally in these wonderful days of the 'Latter Rain.' "[36]

In June 1909, *The Upper Room* printed a list of the "marked features" of Pentecostalism that provides a glimpse of early Pentecostal self-understanding. Pentecostals were people who exalted Christ and His blood; who honored the Holy Spirit and "expected His operations"; they "earnestly looked for the coming of the Lord." Missionary fervor compelled them to "pray, and give, and go as only Pentecostal people can"; they lived by "faith," and "the spirit of praise and of worship and of prayer that is manifested in their private lives and in their meetings is phenomenal": their "joy and liberty in the Spirit [were] very marked."[37] "Back to Pentecost" was their watchword.

The Early Pentecostals' View of Latter Rain

It was the Pentecostal view of their place in history that most basically set Pentecostals apart from most other Protestants. Intrinsic to their self-understanding was a carefully articulated view of the contemporary significance of Old Testament prophecies of the "latter rain." The "days of heaven on earth" foretold in Deuteronomy 11 were being fulfilled in their experience, they asserted. Passages like Joel 2 and Zechariah 10:1 defined their worldview. Probably the most important statement of the Pentecostal understanding of the latter rain came from the pen of David Wesley Myland, a former Christian and Missionary Alliance official who became a warm friend of William Hamner Piper, pastor of Chicago's influential Stone Church.

In May 1909, Myland was the featured speaker at a convention sponsored by the Stone Church. His addresses, duly reported in *The Latter Rain Evangel*, consisted of lengthy expositions of Old and New Testament passages that validated the contemporary Pentecostal "outpouring" as the latter rain. They commanded wide respect among Pentecostals as an early defense of the movement. Considered profound in their scholarship, they were compiled in book form and published in 1910.

Myland compared Scripture with Scripture, "under the illumination of the Holy Spirit, to get its deeper sense."[38] "There are many scriptures that are not only double-barreled but triple-barreled," he wrote. "They are literal, typical and prophetical; or putting it in other words, historical, spiritual, and dispensational."[39]

When Myland applied this hermeneutic to his search for a biblical basis for the baptism of the Holy Spirit, he discovered that it enabled him to draw apt parallels between the natural course of events in Palestine and the spiritual momentum of Pentecostalism:

> If it is remembered that the climate of Palestine consisted of two seasons, the wet and the dry, and that the wet season

was made up of the early and latter rain, it will help you
to understand this [latter rain] covenant and the present
workings of God's Spirit. For just as literal early and latter
rain was poured out upon Palestine, so upon the church
of the first century was poured out the spiritual early rain,
and upon us today is being poured out the spiritual latter
rain.[40]

Piper, convinced that his generation lived "in the time when
the Latter Rain truths [were] due," warmly recommended Myland's views. "Our studies in Exegesis have revealed nothing
which in uniqueness and originality equals this exposition of
the blessed Latter Rain truths," he noted. Insisting that "Latter
Rain truths" represented another epoch in church history, similar in significance to Luther's teaching on justification and
Wesley's on sanctification, Piper urged Pentecostals to pray for
a "spiritual understanding" of this all-important subject.

In fact, Myland's insights and even his language were duplicated in other publications, especially those sponsored by
the Christian and Missionary Alliance. W. C. Stevens, principal of the Alliance's Missionary Training Institute, had encouraged anticipation of the latter rain since 1892. In 1907, the
Christian and Missionary Alliance carried an editorial in which
Simpson explicitly encouraged expectation of an imminent
"outpouring" of the Holy Spirit:

> We may . . . conclude that we are to expect a great out-
> pouring of the Holy Spirit in connection with the second
> coming of Christ and one as much greater than the Pen-
> tecostal effusion of the Spirit as the rains of autumn were
> greater than the showers of spring. . . . We are in the time . . .
> when we may expect this latter rain.[41]

More than most of his contemporaries, Simpson recognized
the tendency among those who pursued "deeper" religious experiences to discount earlier convictions as they apprehended
"new" truth. His exposition of the latter rain included a strong
reiteration of his firm commitment to the doctrines and experiences he had learned to treasure. He attempted to assist
Christians to "progress" in truth rather than to discredit long-

cherished teaching whenever a "deeper" truth was presented. "The new does not discredit the old or necessarily cause any confusion in regard to the things in which God has already led and taught us," he maintained. In a warning that might well have saved Pentecostals considerable grief, he pleaded: "Do not ... tear up the foundations of your peace, your holiness, your victory and your settled Christian experience because you are seeking some larger blessing at your Father's hand.... There is no better preparation for the higher enduements of the Holy Ghost than to be settled and established in Christ Jesus and able to rear upon the secure foundation of the indwelling Christ the superstructure of all the fulness of God."[42]

Simpson presented the believer's experience of the Holy Spirit in a way that made many in his constituency (including Myland) receptive to Pentecostal teaching. The Spirit "with us," he taught, described the converted; the Spirit "in us" described believers who were "consecrated and Spirit filled"; the Spirit *on* us described "the yet higher manifestation of God in clothing us with power from on high for special ministry in the kingdom."[43] Simpson's convictions about the extent and significance of the latter rain encouraged him to anticipate the imparting of both the "unknown tongues" of 1 Corinthians 14 and (like Parham) "real missionary tongues like those of Pentecost." According to Simpson, the Apostolic Faith Movement in all of its various expressions represented only "the sprinkling of the first drops of a mighty rain."[44]

Pentecostals heartily concurred, assured that their movement was both part of an extensive end-times revival and the promised latter rain: Never since Pentecost, one wrote, "until the marvelous and solemn visitations of the Spirit of God in the past three years, beginning with the revival in Wales," had the world experienced "anything answering to the promised Latter Rain."[45] Furthermore, failure to "join this forward movement of God's Spirit" would result in "terrible spiritual desolation and uselessness." The "real place of safety" was "under the very center of the cloudburst."[46]

Simpson's *Living Truth* carried several articles on the subject in 1907 that also insisted that the latter rain was "due."[47] But it was Myland who conveyed Simpson's views to Pentecostals and developed them further to embrace the current revival, and Pentecostals eagerly accepted his explanation of their movement in history. The correspondence between early Pentecostalism and the prophesied latter rain became the subject of numerous songs, provided titles for hymnals and books about the movement, and sketched the general outlines of Pentecostals' understanding of history.[48] Pentecostal (and, for that matter, early Christian and Missionary Alliance) dispensationalism was dispensationalism with a difference. While they unquestioningly embraced most of Darby's view of history, early Pentecostals rejected his insistence that the "gifts" had been withdrawn. They introduced into his system their own dispensational setting where the gifts could again operate in the church: The device through which they legitimated those gifts was their teaching on the latter rain.

The Early Pentecostals' View of the World Around Them

Participation in the "Latter Rain outpouring" involved rejection of "the world." The principal of the Missionary Training Institute, W. C. Stevens, declared that the latter rain separated participants "unto a life of ceaseless intercession within the veil ... and of ceaseless witnessing without the veil."[49] Views on worldliness generally paralleled those of contemporary holiness advocates, who had demanded "separation" in various conspicuous ways. H. Richard Niebuhr's phrase "Christ against culture" captures their self-perception: True Christianity could never harmonize with culture. In spite of their rejection of its values, however, early Pentecostals mirrored their culture in important ways. Robert Anderson noted that their list of taboos originated in their economic dislocation: What they could not afford to do, they labeled "sin."[50] Recent tendencies among increasingly affluent Pentecostals to embrace life-styles that blur old distinctions between "the world" and "believers" lend credence to Anderson's view.

Early Pentecostals, however, anticipated no such blurring. While legalism was always a problem, an equally persistent, positive stress on nurturing a love relationship with Christ characterized their subculture. They seemed to strive to be as different from the world as possible as part of their effort to be like Christ. Naturally this found expression in songs intended to reinforce their determination. While they sang their share of songs that urged believers to avoid smoking, tobacco chewing, or fancy dress, they also asserted in music a determination not to allow "this vain world's golden charms" to stand "between their souls and their Saviour." Such songs often recounted the struggle believers could expect as they sought a life-style that modeled clearly their conviction that they were simply pilgrims on earth, seeking "a glorious home on high." Constantly reassuring themselves that this world's pleasures were "fleeting," they admonished one another to forsake worldly pastimes for eternal gain:

Take the world, but give me Jesus;
All its joys are but a name.
But His love abideth ever,
Through eternal years the same.

Although behavioral norms often did correspond with economic realities, Pentecostals claimed that their contemporaries failed to comprehend their separation: "The personal holiness, the purity of principle and motive demanded of each of us was so great, comparatively speaking, that many onlookers believed we were either insane over religion, or drunk on some glorious dream."[51] Clearly a restorationist movement from the start, early Pentecostalism was also millenarian, anticipating God's imminent, miraculous intervention to bring human affairs to a triumphant conclusion. Adherents withdrew—in ways they considered meaningful—from the world, awaiting God's final solution to contemporary problems. Convinced that nothing they did would achieve a righteous society, they either poured their energies into attempts to address humanity's spiritual needs or segregated themselves and "enjoyed the blessings" of the "deeper" life.[52] Certain that the world was about to face judgment, they looked for ways to express their separation from its mores.

They did not seek to avoid struggles or hardship. They discovered a way to transcend it. They affirmed no right to wealth; they did not "name and claim" prosperity. Rather, in their various needs they affirmed Christ's sustaining presence. This too was part of shunning their culture.

Many early Pentecostals expressed their relationship to the world in terms of their understanding of "living in Christ's presence." Since they believed that their movement was a vehicle through which humanity would have its final opportunity to see God's power in action, they shunned whatever they thought would hinder "the flow" of the Spirit. If fellowship with Christ was one's highest priority, if the "joy" of the Spirit's manifestation of Christ truly satisfied, they urged, then mere worldly amusements, producing transitory joy, should be avoided. Effective "soul winning" and spiritual power mattered most. Whatever might hinder the "power of the Spirit" must be shunned. A strong sense of purpose informed their convictions. Since Christ's return was imminent, being ready and making others ready was all that mattered. Dancing, gambling, and theater attendance, then, distracted one from more important concerns, exhibited poor stewardship of time and money, and might well entice one into immorality. Furthermore, pursuit of such pleasures indicated spiritual poverty. The truly spiritual person required no "amusement"; rather, "[w]hen He comes in He brings His own entertainment and you have a continuous banquet. You have no desire for the amusements of the world or of the church."[53]

Pentecostals seemed to harbor special aversions toward "church amusements." Parham's *Apostolic Faith* as well as other papers repeatedly published sarcastic comments about "church sprees." The Christian Workers' Union issued numerous tracts dealing with the subject. Abbie C. Morrow's writing captured the typical argument: "The sons of God should be as fearless as was the Son of God in putting away from His house everything that defiles it. Our Lord does not look with any more favor upon those in the church today who countenance fairs, festivals, dramas, and cantatas than He did upon those defilers of His temple 1900 years ago."[54] Not only was it ridiculous to "think of Peter giving a dramatic reading in the court of the temple" or to imagine "[Jesus] writing to the women of a certain city and asking them to get up a neck-tie social to pay His expenses to come to them"; such customs also "robbed the people of the privilege of giving to the Lord." Morrow did not mince her words: "Ecclesiastical amusement and money-making blight the spiritual life, influence, activity and usefulness of the church and promote almost every species of carnality and worldliness."[55]

Carnality posed the most ominous threat. Spirit baptism "required the crucifixion of the purified natural man and the revelation of Christ in us, in the physical, affectional and mental realms."[56] While holiness people also had to "guard diligently" against exhibiting such "carnal traits" as pride or anger, Pentecostals had a more demanding obligation. "The battle," they were frequently reminded, "is not so much to keep out of sin as it is to be led by and walk in the Spirit—to keep from gliding down out of the supernatural into the natural."[57] Avoiding carnality was not merely a challenge: It was a matter of life and death, vital to preserving the movement's meaning. Commenting in 1910, one writer lamented about waning Pentecostal power in the movement's brief history. Backsliding, as commonly understood, was not the problem. Carnality was to blame for a "cooling of ardor, a lack of positiveness, aggressiveness." While Pentecostal meetings remained "good," "the power" no longer fell and persecution too had waned.[58] Walking in the Spirit, then, demanded "delicate," "tender" response that found its source in self-discipline, which too many shunned.

The determination to "walk in newness of life" expressed itself in many ways. One was in a general concern about modesty, which differed in detail from region to region. While all Pentecostals—like other Christians—urged modesty as biblical, they differed somewhat in their ideas of what modesty mandated. In general, they subscribed to the more conservative customs of their culture. And they blamed "pride in the heart" for interest in contemporary fashions: "What greater proof have we that much of the religious profession of today is a sham than the outward ornamentation and putting on of apparel? It clearly shows we love the praise of men more than the praise of God."[59] At a time when few women had short hair or wore makeup, for example, Pentecostals made social custom almost a matter of faith. Some sought to uproot pride by enforcing plain dress or by objecting to adornments like ties or jewelry. Occasionally women testified that the Holy Spirit "interfered" with their wearing of jewelry: "A sister while under the power took the fancy pins out of her hat and threw them away. Another sister who was baptized, when she came to change her clothing, attempted to put on her jewelry again, but the Spirit would not let her, so she left it off."[60] "The Spirit," then, worked "in harmony with the Word, teaching His people how to dress according to the Bible."[61]

Haywood himself was known for wearing dark suits, white shirts and ties. His reason was simple, and articulated another concern some Pentecostals shared as they sought to convey the conviction that God's Spirit lived within them: He believed that his dress should never "betray his high calling." "Everything about him," his biographer noted, "magnified his office as the man of God."[62] One Bertha Hisey maintained that she lost the desire to dance.[63] "We cannot keep Him in our hearts . . . and indulge in theaters, etc.," Herbert Buffum cautioned.[64]

To some extent, restorationism nourished such ideas: Early Pentecostals took literally biblical injunctions to dress simply and to have a detached attitude toward material things. They remembered the biblical observation that "friendship of the world is enmity with God." Their general attitude, applied sincerely if occasionally somewhat inconsistently, stressed the need to demonstrate their separation from the "fads" that seemed to emphasize unduly the "things of this world." Numerous gospel songs as well helped keep alive the conviction that their religious experience had separated them from the things that others considered important. They had new values and new goals. "I can't feel at home in this world anymore," they asserted.

Even when early Pentecostals attempted to acknowledge the

danger of overemphasizing "outward adorning," they came back to advocating plain dress as an evidence of "normal woman-liness," if not of godliness. An editorial in *The Household of God* in 1909, for example, urged women to covet "a meek and quiet spirit" rather than to stress the virtues of plain dress. This, in turn, would dispel "the desire for outward display." "For women to dress plain is of no value at all," the author insisted. "She must have the heavenly attire of meekness and quietness. . . . Having lost her frivolous, superficial, worldly desires, to please the world and waste [her husband's] hard-earned money on gaieties, she now becomes normal, and assumes womanliness and love which is genuine, and which wins him to Christ."[65]

A related concern about appropriate foods was apparent among some Pentecostals. Former Dowie followers as well as numerous holiness people refused to eat pork or pork products. Some Pentecostals objected to coffee, tea, and other items containing caffeine: "Dearly beloved, I want to tell you that coffee is a stimulant like unto whiskey. . . . Tea . . . will surely cause nervous trouble. . . . Now as we are to live for the glory of God, my better sense tells me I cannot glorify God in this, as it is constantly destroying God's temple."[66]

Tracts with titles like *The Great Ruination Railway* and *A Smoker's Story* detailed the evils of smoking, drinking, and general "worldly pleasures."[67]

The ways early Pentecostals chose to express their separation from the world could—and frequently did—become oversimplified forms through which they evaluated spirituality. Resenting such "legalism," later generations often responded by embracing more of this world. Institutionalization contributed to this process of acculturation. Recalling the objectives of the movement's first generation, however, is vital to understanding how many in the movement understood themselves as being against culture. They perceived themselves as purposely out of step with their times. (To them, waning opposition signaled their own waning power.) They claimed to affirm rather than to proscribe. They firmly believed that they had a simple choice, and that in choosing Christ they necessarily relinquished things that brought pleasure to and expressed the values of those who rejected Him. They had chosen the "better part." Its "cost" was separation from this world, and to God. But its costliness, they believed, made it precious.

7. The Pentecostal Life-style: "Let Us Labor for the Master"

We'll work till Jesus comes,
We'll work till Jesus comes,
We'll work till Jesus comes,
And we'll be gathered home.

Elizabeth Mills, *We'll Work Till Jesus Comes,* ca. 1900

Ceaseless activity characterized most early Pentecostals. It almost seemed that the baptism of the Holy Spirit compelled one to action. Of course, others on the fringes of the denominations exhibited a similar restless urge to "redeem the time." But Pentecostals not only rooted their action in the Bible or the imminence of the end, they responded to repeated audible proddings of the Spirit "to *do* as well as to *be*."[1]

Their activity had several sources. Primarily it came from their sense of the imminence of the end. Time was short; the harvest was *now.* Second, messages in tongues and interpretation as well as prophecies urged them to evangelize quickly. Third, urgency came from their efforts to restore the biblical model. Advocates of the New Testament church model had maintained a relentless pace. A fourth source, at least for some, was their own restlessness. The early Pentecostal movement attracted people with well-developed behavior patterns that discounted contemplation and stressed *doing* things in which they found meaning. Some had long-standing habits of moving from place to place, briefly undertaking one project or another and then moving on.[2]

The activities that they engaged in took different forms. Most bore some relationship to "soul winning"—or at least to convincing those who already pursued the "deeper" life to embrace Pentecostal views. Participants gathered almost nightly for prolonged services. Often their meetings were preceded by street evangelism. Services, climaxing at simple altars where people prayed themselves and others "through," took them away from families and normal social relationships. Living constantly with intense awareness of the supernatural heightened their sense of being "in the world but not of it."

Early reports from across the nation claimed that numerous Pentecostals experienced a measure of ability to use foreign languages to communicate with immigrants.[3] In such instances, it was maintained that the "sign" of tongues attracted hearers to the gospel. Sometimes this gift was apparently used unwittingly, as in a service one and another exercised tongues spontaneously. At other times, a Pentecostal would feel compelled to go to an individual and would then begin to speak in tongues, sometimes claiming the ability to carry on a conversation. Irene Piper, the daughter of the Stone Church's founder, reportedly "could converse with the Chinese and invite them, in Chinese, to her church to accept salvation, all by the power of God alone."[4] Another who claimed such ability was Mabel Smith, a pioneer evangelist who was noted widely for her frequent use of tongues speech. During street meetings in her home city of Galveston, Texas, reportedly while she preached, "her language would soon change from English into tongues. Sometimes she would preach almost her entire sermon in one foreign language; sometimes she would use perhaps as many as three or four. Always there was someone in the audience who understood what she was saying."[5]

Carrie Judd Montgomery, a participant in the founding of the Christian and Missionary Alliance who later became an Assemblies of God pastor, was said to have used tongues to conduct conversations on the street with foreigners.[6] In April 1907, New Acts noted the regular experiences of two workers in Cleveland, Ohio, who, "when they [came] to the home of some foreign family whose language they [did] not understand, [knelt] down and [asked] God to give them this new language, that they may preach Jesus to them. God invariably answer[ed]."[7]

Those who accepted Pentecostal logic about Spirit baptism occasionally embraced the idea, became ardent "seekers," and began to proclaim the message long before they themselves had received biblical evidence. Seymour, for example, had not spoken in tongues before coming to Los Angeles. D. C. O. Opperman proclaimed the Apostolic Faith for two years, with dramatic results, before he "received his Pentecost"; J. Roswell Flower spent several months in active Pentecostal endeavors before his seeking culminated in speaking in tongues. If those who apprehended the idea felt compelled to share it, those who received the experience sensed an even stronger need to proclaim the message. Although in some places the movement attracted primarily those evangelicals who were already pursuing a deeper life, in other places workers reported the conversion of sinners.[8] The movement extended through networks of people who had been acquainted earlier as well as through the activities of countless lay and ordained evangelists who felt "called" to preach.[9] The interrelationships that quickly emerged gave an informal unity to a movement that, in many ways, was remarkably diverse.

Traveling Ministers

Pentecostal workers traveled frequently, stopping for several weeks or months at one place or another to accomplish a task. Southern holiness Pentecostal leaders like Joseph Hillary King shared camp meeting responsibilities with people from the north, like Levi Lupton of Alliance, Ohio. At the popular campground in Durant, Florida, in 1910, A. J. Tomlinson of Cleveland, Tennessee, ordained an independent Pentecostal, Lillian Trasher, for missionary service. Campgrounds were meeting places for Pentecostals from around the nation, and local leaders regularly traveled from one to another.[10]

Without "visible means of support," Pentecostals pioneered full gospel missions in small villages as well as major cities. Many endured much personal hardship.[11] Some seemed unable to settle into pastoral responsibilities. They agreed repeatedly to serve as a local pastor, only to leave after a brief tenure to return to evangelistic work. Some of their most dramatic success—as well as vehement opposition—came in areas that had accepted earlier restorationist teaching through groups like the Churches of Christ.

Their approach to a new field showed a great amount of resourcefulness. Sometimes an evangelist would seek out an organized mission and try to introduce Pentecostal teaching. Glenn Cook, for example, returned briefly to his native Indianapolis from Azusa Street and convinced people with ties to the strong local Christian and Missionary Alliance branch to accept his teaching. G. B. Cashwell brought the Pentecostal message to small Holiness organizations in the South. In other instances, Pentecostals would simply arrive in a town—sometimes by invitation of a local resident, sometimes without—conduct a street meeting, rent a mission, set up a tent or use a schoolhouse or church that had fallen into disuse.[12]

Pentecostal fervor seemed uncontainable: It demanded an outlet. Missionaries crossing the country to embark from the East Coast, for example, evangelized at train stops along the way and frequently prolonged their stay in a community for several weeks because their message had inaugurated a revival.[13] Early Pentecostals demonstrated considerable audacity, too. Sometimes they gained a local hearing by offering to pray for the healing of a sick person.[14] The simple confidence that God would heal in answer to believing prayer resulted in numerous congregations.

Women in Ministry

Women proved especially adept at pioneer work. In some places, the movement had numerous women preachers, some of whom won substantial acclaim. This did not necessarily indicate general approval of the ordination of women as pastors, however.[15] Even the established and respected Duncan sisters in Rochester, New York, firmly opposed the ordination of women. Although Pentecostals believed and taught that their "sons and daughters would prophesy," most balked at a general endorsement of the full ordination of women but approved their credentialing as evangelists and missionaries, especially if they would be working under male supervision.

Attitudes varied by region and religious background. Dowie had permitted women to engage in various public ministries, and Zion women who embraced Pentecostalism provided limited leadership. The Christian and Missionary Alliance allowed women less prominence. While it licensed them as official workers, it conferred no ordination. Nonetheless, numerous Alliance women—as missionaries and, in one instance (Minnie Draper), as a member of the Alliance Board of Managers—made substantial contributions to Pentecostalism. Women workers were somewhat less conspicuous among Parham's bands, although both Millicent (nee McClendon) and Ethel (nee Wright) Goss gained acclaim as evangelists.

Pentecostal periodicals document the activities of numerous women who evangelized in small, struggling missions, helping to "establish" believers. Some had the distinction of introducing Pentecostal teaching into their relationships, churches, and communities. Mary Arthur had invited Parham to Galena, launching his fully Pentecostal ministry. Later known as Mother Arthur, she affiliated with the Assemblies of God. Rachel Sizelove brought her testimony from Azusa Street to her relatives in Springfield, Missouri.[16] Mabel Smith helped evangelize New England, where women either led or figured prominently in several small missions in the greater Boston area.[17] Marie Burgess, at Parham's request, became the foremost pioneer of Pentecostalism in New York City, where she remained as a pastor for sixty-four years.

In the initial fervor of the revival, then, women fulfilled a vital role in proclaiming the message. Some (like Lilian Yeomans) had been credentialed by independent missions before they had become Pentecostal; others (like Elizabeth Sisson) simply stated that they had been "ordained by the Lord"; still others received Pentecostal recognition at one or another of the many camp meetings or missions; and many—probably most—worked undeterred by their lack of official credentials. Some insisted that "the anointing" was more important than any license to preach. Most served as evangelists and missionaries.

Missionary Efforts

Of course, Pentecostal evangelism was not confined to the United States. The movement's early understanding of its significance contributed to a growing awareness of the missions task. Missionary efforts posed specific problems, however. Ardent believers often based a call to foreign service on prophecy or on a language someone told them they had spoken "under the anointing."[18] Some seem to have been totally ignorant about speech communities. They "had the language of Africa," for example, so they decided to sail. Without financial backing, and with minimal biblical or linguistic training, they traveled to distant places, confident that "God would provide." They believed that supernatural enablement to preach in foreign languages would facilitate the rapid evangelization of the world.

A few seemed troubled by the fact that they spoke in tongues but could not go abroad. The *Word and Work* offered an explanation which suggested that these men and women also played a role in foreign evangelism. The magazine published a "revelation" that their tongues speech, in an event labeled "Pentecostal wireless telegraphy," was spiritually "transmitted" through dreams and/or visions to individuals whose language the Pentecostal believer had been "given."

"Faith" missionaries, although they professed utter dependence on God for their material needs, actually depended on American financial support, which was not always forthcoming. The Azusa Street mission, as well as various other missions and publications, offered to forward all donated missionary funds. Various Pentecostal magazines carried letters from different missionaries and solicited support.[19] Some Pentecostals reported miraculous supply. John Lake, a former Dowieite, for example, recruited a group of missionaries for South Africa, "prayed in" the funds necessary for their fares, and embarked. As the ship neared its destination, however, Lake lacked the $125 he was required to have in hand to land. He claimed that he nonetheless stood in line; a fellow passenger came up to him and after a brief conversation handed him $200, and the party landed.[20]

Such testimonies heartened others to expect similar dramatic intervention. They tended to deemphasize responsible reflection on material things. The Azusa Street mission encouraged would-be missionaries: "God is solving the missionary problem, sending out new-tongued missionaries on the apostolic faith line, without purse or scrip, and the Lord is going before them preparing the way."[21] In time, of course, agencies evolved that took much of the missions orientation in hand. Faith missions came to have a different meaning. In spite of the hardships and failures that would-be missionaries experienced, however, their fearless—and almost reckless—obedience to their call to service demonstrated a basic assumption of American Pentecostalism. God could be implicitly trusted for miraculous daily intervention.

Discerning Guidance

Discerning whether one was following God or impressions and voices from another source became the issue, however. And Pentecostals did not always use the Bible in traditional ways. In fact, some claimed, "The Bible becomes a new book to those who are baptized with the Holy Ghost. You absolutely lose your own judgment in regard to the Word of God. You eat it down without trimming or cutting, right from the mouth of God."[22] Former Alliance worker Daniel Kerr developed a distinction between systematic theology and "spontaneous theology." "Spontaneous theology" was "given by inspiration of God" and was to take precedence over systematic theology because it represented God directing spiritual understanding to "proceed spontaneously without labor or study from the hidden fullness of His divine nature."[23]

Given the obvious need, some Pentecostals engaged in efforts to provide biblical training through which experience in the Spirit could be understood. While they concurred heartily with the viewpoint implicit in Donald Gee's later insistence that the baptism in the Holy Spirit was, in the final analysis, an experience rather than a doctrine, they recognized a need to provide guidelines to sort out the various teachings that arose within the movement.

Several of the doctrines that troubled early Pentecostal assemblies were not peculiar to Pentecostalism, but they surfaced anew in a climate that valued "fresh revelations" and that sought to renew and reform doctrine and practice through a nebulous experience in the Holy Spirit. Some represented "recurring errors"; others, "recurring truths." The problem came in distinguishing between the two when both were presented as revelations.[24] Among the earliest problems was the matter of "discerning of spirits." Events forced Pentecostals to admit that spiritualists and hypnotists duplicated some of their manifestations. Several sources concurred that both of these forces were manifested at Azusa Street. Parham excoriated the Azusa Street workers precisely because he thought they failed adequately to discern the difference. His own discerning, however, apparently took the equally unacceptable form of a systematic discouraging of emotional exuberance, until he was accused of "quenching the Spirit."[25]

In some settings, participants either needed frequent teaching on what was "of the flesh" and what was "of the Spirit" or they resented any suggestion that their practices, however unusual or unseemly, were less than authentic demonstrations of spiritual power. In other places, there was more of a consensus that spiritual gifts and worship practices were consistently "in the Spirit." Elim in Rochester, New York, for example, had a positive reputation for intensely spiritual worship. Such distinctions, though virtually meaningless to outsiders (who generally regarded Pentecostal efforts to discriminate between the spiritual and the "counterfeit" as an exercise in futility), carried tremendous weight within the movement.

Events also forced insiders to question the proper use of newfound spiritual gifts. Instances where couples were instructed through tongues and interpretation to marry, for example, created some tragic consequences. Schools where instruction was carried out by tongues and interpretation appalled others within the movement who insisted that the gifts were not for instruction. Careless theological language invited criticism and misunderstanding.

Beliefs about the end times and the eternal destruction of the wicked varied. While the majority of Pentecostals undoubtedly accepted traditional Protestant views, some introduced alternatives. Parham's teaching on conditional immortality has already been noted. Charles Hamilton Pridgeon, founder of Pittsburgh Bible Institute, used his school to promulgate ultimate reconciliation. Hell was not eternal, Pridgeon maintained. Although a real place, it would ultimately yield to God's final victory.[26]

Other teachings that aroused concern pertained to the marriage relationship. With strongly worded appeals to those who pursued the distinction of being spiritual, numerous advocates of "marital purity" extended their teaching throughout the movement. As early as January 1907, *The Apostolic Faith* found it advisable to declare: "It is no sin to marry. . . . There are those today in the marriage life, since they have received sanctification and some the baptism with the Holy Ghost, who have come to think that it is a sin to live as husband and wife."[27] At the other extreme were people who, though already married, found their "soul mates" outside their marriage. "Spiritual marriages" (which sometimes were evidenced by such material tokens as wedding bands) brought numerous Pentecostals into disrepute. Almost from the movement's beginning, various Pentecostal publications found it necessary to denounce these and related views.

Pentecostal Bible Schools

Consequently, efforts to articulate a Pentecostal response to such issues as well as the need to train workers and establish believers often gave rise to short-term Bible institutes. These schools were operated "by faith," thus making it possible for anyone to attend. Gradually a few individuals gained acceptance as people with special teaching gifts. Several created schools that had a significant impact on the Assemblies of God.

T. K. Leonard's Gospel School in Findlay, Ohio, later became the Fellowship's first headquarters. Levi Lupton, a Quaker who became a prominent early Pentecostal leader, ran short-term schools at his home base in Alliance, Ohio. He drew his faculty from the ranks of experienced workers and furloughing missionaries, and he designed the sessions to equip students for evangelism.[28] "Many are really panting in spirit to get a better knowledge of the Word and God's most complete equipment that they may speedily be scattered to the ends of the earth," he observed in 1908.[29] Others agreed with Lupton's assessment of the desire for Bible training. Two men, David Wesley Myland and D. C. O. Opperman, and five women—the Duncan sisters— had a strong direct influence on the Assemblies of God and illustrate some of the ways this earliest interest in Pentecostal education was expressed.

Myland was a successful Christian and Missionary Alliance leader when he embraced Pentecostalism. Already acknowledged as a gifted teacher, in 1912 he decided to launch a new endeavor. His repute as a student of the Bible established by his book *The Latter Rain Covenant,* he issued, through the July 1912 *Latter Rain Evangel,* an invitation to those "who desired sound scriptural teaching, healing and help in the Christian faith and life" to attend a summer Bible school of "at least three months" duration in Plainfield, Indiana.[30] Known as Gibeah, the school accommodated some twenty students. Those who could paid four dollars a week for room and board; those without funds assisted with housekeeping chores.[31]

Convinced that, important as it was, the Pentecostal experience could not stand alone, Myland developed course work in biblical exposition, theology, and practical ministry. The first group of students included several with ministry experience who would devote their lives to ministry through the Assemblies of God: J. Roswell and Alice Reynolds Flower, Fred and Margaret Vogler, and Flem Van Meter. At the close of the term in September 1912, Myland ordained them. They, and others, stayed for the two additional terms offered at the school. In 1914, the benefactor who had donated the home and land that had made the school possible rescinded her offer, and Gibeah closed.

Undaunted, Myland moved to Chicago where he opened Ebenezer Chapel and Bible Training Institute. Beginning with weekday classes open to the public at 3 P.M. and 8 P.M., Myland slowly developed a more typical institute structure.[32] The school continued until 1917, when the Mylands accepted pastoral responsibilities in Philadelphia. In spite of the relatively short duration of these efforts, Myland's influence extended through his students into the Assemblies of God (with which he never affiliated). He both encouraged Flower to begin producing a Pentecostal weekly paper, *The Christian Evangel,* and became its first associate editor. His teaching, developed through years of experience in the Alliance, facilitated the transition of several gifted young men and women from enthusiastic converts to Pentecostal views to expounders of its distinctives within a broader Christian context. Through Myland, the Alliance made one of its most far-reaching contributions to the Assemblies of God.

Opperman had a different background. He spent much of his youth in Goshen, Indiana, near his rural birthplace. Influenced deeply by local Dunkards, he briefly attended their college in Mt. Morris, Illinois.[33] In 1899, while a student at Moody Bible Institute in Chicago, he visited Dowie's services and joined Zion. A school teacher by profession, Opperman became principal of Zion City's elementary school in 1901. The next year, Dowie ordained him to the ministry. In 1905, seriously ill with tuberculosis, Opperman left Zion for San Antonio. There he sensed a call to preach. After experiencing healing, he returned briefly to Zion City, then left for Texas, to preach among Zion adherents there. Early in 1906, he came into contact with Parham's Bible school that had been in session in Houston since the fall of 1905. Opperman became convinced of the truth of Pentecostal teaching and became its diligent advocate among Zion people in Texas.[34]

He found considerable response, especially in San Antonio where L. C. Hall oversaw Zion's outpost.[35] After more than two years of effective Pentecostal evangelism, Opperman finally received his own baptism in the Holy Spirit. In July 1908 he became state director of the Apostolic Faith Movement in Texas.

Early in 1909, Opperman began to conduct short-term Bible schools. The *Latter Rain Evangel* announced his first effort:

> It will be a faith school, no charges for board, room or tuition, but each student will be expected to contribute his all to the common fund. Thence we shall trust God to supply all needs.[36]

Opperman's colleague in the extension of the Apostolic Faith, Howard Goss, described how Opperman used his teaching "gift":

> He would announce a school by faith, fully expecting God to meet every need, whether five came or five hundred. . . . He trained and put hundreds of workers into the Pentecostal harvest field. His schools were a "cutting out" station also, where those not called to active evangelism could painlessly find it out without regrets.[37]

Opperman's second school, conducted in Hattiesburg, Mississippi, at the end of 1909, attracted and enrolled a young local: It was fourteen-year-old Ralph M. Riggs' first contact with Pentecostalism. (Riggs later became the seventh general superintendent of the Assemblies of God.) From his third school in Joplin, Missouri, late in 1910, Opperman sent fifty-five workers "into the field." Later schools in Armiston, Alabama; Des Moines, Iowa; Fort Worth, Texas; and Hot Springs, Arkansas, not only trained new workers (some one hundred workers were commissioned from his Ft. Worth effort in 1912 alone, including thirteen for foreign missions) but also helped establish local converts in their new faith. And the schools contributed to the extension of the movement. Evangelistic activity was an integral part of the students' training. Street meetings and nightly services both made the students part of a practical environment and stimulated local renewal.

Several institutions that predated Pentecostalism embraced the movement and offered a more structured environment for learning. Nickels John Holmes' Altamont Bible and Missionary

Institute (which eventually became Holmes Theological Seminary and permanently located in Greenville, South Carolina) affiliated with the Pentecostal Holiness Church. The Rochester Bible Training Institute (which never affiliated with any organization) had more immediate influence on the Assemblies of God. Opened in 1906, the school offered a two-year program, with the Bible as its chief text. Supervised by the five Duncan sisters, the school was essentially a faith venture, with students "taught to trust the Lord for supplies."[38] Offering courses in "Theology; Synthesis; Personal Work; Homiletics, Exegesis, Dispensational Truth, Tabernacle Studies and Missionary Studies," the school seemed an ambitious program for five lay women to oversee. Their own respected lectures were complemented by those of capable assistants. John Wright Follette especially left his mark on students who prepared for the ministry at Elim.

Some early Pentecostal workers had received Bible training before they affiliated with the movement. Among the best trained were those who had completed a program at either Simpson's Missionary Training Institute or Moody Bible Institute. Few had any academic credentials that carried credibility in mainline denominations; those who did—like E. N. Bell—tended to emerge as leaders in a movement that struggled for credibility.

On the other hand, however, like other restorationists, many Pentecostals did not approve of Bible school training. William Durham maintained unequivocally that the local church was "the only place God ever provided for the training of His people for the work of the ministry."[39] Insisting that the money some gave to Bible schools should rather be used for evangelism, Durham was also of the opinion that schools and "training homes" tended to be run by people who "wanted to build themselves up"; though they began as places exclusively devoted to Bible study, they soon expanded curriculum and became "petty theological seminaries" from which students expected "as much as do the students of the seminaries of the sects." Durham discouraged formal training primarily on restorationist grounds. Bible schools were not "according to Scripture" nor did they have "any place in the plan of God as outlined in the New Testament."[40]

Anti-Organizational Attitudes

The renewal that Pentecostals endeavored to realize through their worship and work helped extend the movement across the United States and around the world. Proliferation exposed serious weaknesses, however. In the Southeast, where Pentecostal teaching on Spirit baptism had simply been imposed upon existing religious structures, organizational channels through which the small denominations addressed difficulties were in place. Even so, southern holiness Pentecostals faced numerous divisive issues that defied easy solution.

The vast majority of Pentecostals were not directly tied to any organization, however. Many of the leaders knew one another. They traveled widely in the United States, attending conventions and camp meetings or participating in short-term schools. They contributed to the same growing list of Pentecostal publications. Previous associations—such as those in the Alliance or in Dowie's Zion—bound some to one another in informal loyalty. But many had a strong distaste for organization. Some were simply temperamentally unsuited to submitting to the decisions of others; others maintained a conviction that organization always "quenched the Spirit." Both kinds of Pentecostals phrased their hesitation in the spiritual terms Pentecostals were most responsive to.[41] William Durham, for example, claimed that organization "will kill the work," because "no religious awakening . . . has ever been able to retain its spiritual life and power after man ha[s] organized it and gotten it under his control." In Durham's opinion, the movement needed "everything else more than it need[ed] organization."[42] But to others, Pentecostalism, like other movements intent on reform and renewal, seemed increasingly to need stability and guidance in order to conserve its dynamic. Thus, while some believed that organization would jeopardize the restored apostolic faith, others thought that only organization could salvage it.

In spite of Parham's strong denunciations of people he thought aspired to leadership, he had provided a rudimentary framework in which his farflung missions came under the supervision of state directors like W. F. Carothers and Howard Goss.[43] The many men and women familiar with Christian and Missionary Alliance practice had discovered through participation in that movement the advantages of loose association and cooperation. Others became convinced that the situation demanded an effort to provide structure. Nevertheless, others continued strongly to oppose all formal efforts to find strength in unity.

Internal disunity raised concerns about doctrine and practice. External rejection raised questions about the essence of the movement. Was it, in fact, God's vehicle for the realization of Christian unity, God's final restoration of New Testament Christianity? Its more thoughtful friends shared the alarm of its critics over the divisiveness it seemed to foster.[44] Moreover, its general failure to penetrate any of the mainline denominations, coupled with their tendency to simply ignore the movement's existence, seemed to bode ill for its pretensions. They reassured one another by observing that Satan could be expected to oppose God's renewed church.

Apostolic Faith Directory.

It is our aim to keep in touch with all Apostolic Faith Missionaries, workers, missions, home and foreign, and papers. Beloved, we can only keep this list revised and up-to-date by your help. We ask your co-operation to this end.

MISSIONARIES.

Thos. Hezmalhalch, J. O. Lehman and John G. Lake, P. O. Box 1159, Johannesburg, S. Africa.

Louie Schneiderman.—48 Sivenright Ave., Woornfontein, Johannesburg, Transvaal, S. Africa.

Geo. E. Berg.—Mukti Lodge, Andheri, Bombay, India.

A. H. Post.—Colombo, Ceylon.

B. Bernstein.—Cheng Ting Fu, Chi-li, N. China.

M. L. Ryan.—Yokohama, Honmoku, Ushigome, Japan.

Miss Lucy Leatherman.—Care American Consulate, Jerusalem, Palestine.

These missionaries are sent out by God, without any salary or dependence upon man. They rely solely upon God for their existence. Let us bear them up in our prayers, that He will supply every need and pour out His spirit upon them in mighty power, using them in the salvation of many heathen souls for His name's sake.

MISSIONS.

New York, N. Y.—325 W. 41st St.; 443E. 118th St.; Glad Tidings Hall, 454 W. 42nd St.; 22 W. 100th St.

Brooklyn, N. Y.—234 Putnam Ave., Mr. C. Trumpler.

Albany, N. Y.—Pentecost Mission, Broadway S. of State St.

Yonkers, N. Y.—Pentecostal Mission, 8 School St.

Watertown, N. Y.—W. H. Standley, 658 Mundy St.

Syracuse. N. Y.—Mr. Harry King, 314 Hamley Ave.

Manchester, N. H.—Bethesda Mission, B. S. Wheeler, Supt. 58 Massabesic St.

Philadelphia, Pa.—Cor. Waharton & 21 Ave.

New Haven, Conn.—Apostolic Tabernacle 65 Park St.

Baltimore, Md.—5 W. West St.

Lynn, Mass.—Apostolic Faith Mission, 260 Maple St.

Atlanta, Ga.—Pentecostal Mission, 136 Marietta St.

Detroit, Mich.—The Bible Mission, L. C. Grant, 701 E. Jefferson Avenue.

Cincinnati, Ohio.—Christian Assembly, 4th and John Sts.

Alliance, Ohio.—Missionary Training Home, Levi R. Lupton.

Dayton, Ohio.—Pentecostal Gospel Union Mission, 767 S. Brown St.

Indianapolis, Ind.—The Christian Assembly, corner Alabama and New York Streets.

Chicago, Ill.—The Stone Church, Wm. Hamner Piper, Pastor, 37th & Indiana Ave; Full Gospel Mission, W. Durham, Pastor 943 W. North Ave. St. Clair Mission, 328 W. 63 St. near Wentworth Ave.

Zion City, Ill.—The Christian Assembly.

Minneapolis, Minn.—1500 E. Franklin Ave.

St. Paul, Minn.—Jackson & 7th Ave.

Joplin, Mo.—Apostolic Faith Mission.

Galena, Kansas.—Apostolic Faith Mission.

Topeka, Kan.—C. E. Foster, 924 N. Kansas Ave.

Colorado Springs, Colo.—The Christian Assembly, Corner Kiowa and Nevada Aves.

Denver, Colo.—The Christian Assembly Corner 19th and Welton Sts.

Doxey, Okla.—Beulah Home,

Oklahoma City, Okla.—Holiness Mission

Stuttgart, Ark.—Apostolic Faith Mission.

Houston, Texas.—Apostolic Faith Mission.

San Antonio. Texas.—Apostolic Faith Mission.

Los Angeles, Cal.—312 Azusa St.

Portland, Ore.—Apostolic Faith Mission, 224 Madison St.

Spokane, Wash.—The Gospel Mission, 921 Mallon Avenue.

FOREIGN MISSIONS.

Toronto, Ontario, Canada.—The Church of God, 651 Queen St. E; Spadina Mission, Cor. Spadina Ave & Cecil St; Pentecostal Mission, Cor. Concord & Hepbourne St.

Manitoba, Canada.—Home & Foreign Mission, 319 Alexander St; Apostolic Faith Mission, 501 Alexander Ave.

Sunderland, England.—All Saints Vicarage, Rev. E. A. Boddy.

PENTECOSTAL PAPERS.

The Pentecost.—437 N. Jefferson Ave. Indianapolis. Ind. 50 cents a year.

The New Acts.—Missionary Home, Alliance, Ohio. 50 cents a year.

Household of God.—Dept. A. 710 Wayne Ave., Dayton, Ohio. 50 cents a year.

Good Tidings.—Dept. C, 710 Wayne Ave., Dayton, Ohio. 50 cents a year.

The Bridegroom's Messenger.—78 N. Broad St., Atlanta, Ga. 50 cents a year.

The Apostolic Witness.—Dallas, Oregon. Free.

Trust. Elim Home, Rochester, N. Y. Free.

The Apostolic Faith.—Houston, Texas. Free.

The Apostolic Faith.—Formerly of Los Angeles, Cal., but now of Portland Ore. Free.

The Pentecostal Record and Outlook.—H. R. Bursell, Publisher, Spokane, Wash. Free.

The Apostolic Standard—Beulah Home, Doxey, Okla. Free.

The Christian Assembly.—4th and John Sts., Cincinnati Ohio. Free.

The Midnight Cry.—Seattle, Wash.

The Latter Rain.—J. E. Sanders, editor, 8 Wait Ave., Watertown, N. Y.,

The Spirit of Truth.—W. L. Lake, editor, Emsworth, Hants, England,

Confidence:—E. A. Body, editor, Sunderland, England.

The Cloud of Witnesses.—Max Wood Moorehead, editor, Bombay, G. P. O. India.

Pentecostal Truths.—A paper published entirely in the Chinese language. Mok Lai Chi, Morrison English School, 7 Ladder Street, Hong Kong, China. Free.

The Apostolic Light.—Published partly in the Japanese language, M. L. Ryan, editor, Yokohama, Japan.

God's Latter Rain.—P. O. Box 1159, Johannesburg, Transvaal, S. Africa.

Spade Regen.—G. R. Polman, editor, 15 Domselaerstraat, Amsterdam, Holland. Printed entirely in the Dutch language.

SONG BOOK PUBLISHERS.

W. Elmer Bailey, Pub. "The World Revival Songs and Hymns," Findlay, Ohio. We can recommend this book as it is used by the Christian Assembly of this city.

Daniel Sloan, Zion City, Ill.

Beulah Home, Doxey, Okla.

✦✦✦✦✦

The Christmas Pentecost.

The "Christmas Pentecost" will be a sixteen-page paper containing some of the best scriptural articles and testimonies that can be secured. We have received a glorious letter from Africa giving a full account of the work with illustrations. You cannot afford to miss it. This edition alone will cost us about $60 and you can help much by sending in your subscription at once. Will you?

Apostolic Faith Directory (1908) published in *The Pentecost*, edited by J. Roswell Flower

Bible school at Hot Springs, Arkansas, led by D. C. O. Opperman,
January through February 1914

T. K. Leonard's Gospel School and publishing house, where he published *The Gospel School Review,* in Findlay, Ohio. It later served as
the first headquarters and publishing house of the General Council
of the Assemblies of God.

Fort Worth Bible School, February 1912, directed by D. C. O. Opperman

8. "Is the Present Tongues Movement of God?" Evangelicals Encounter Pentecostalism

> Here is plain, open blasphemy. . . . It is clearly a lying spirit who is propagating it, and attesting it with "signs and lying wonders."
>
> H. A. Ironside, *Apostolic Faith Missions and the So-Called Second Pentecost*

Pentecostalism developed primarily outside of the major denominations, attracting restorationist millenarians who had already decided that organized religion would never approach "Bible Christianity." Most of America's religious world ignored (if they even suspected) the Pentecostal presence. But some whose attitude mattered greatly to Pentecostals felt compelled to respond. Numerous Pentecostals had had ties to respected interdenominational evangelical frameworks that had espoused teaching with which Pentecostals later closely identified.

The major Pentecostal theological contribution had been the insistence on evidential tongues. Several prominent conservative evangelicals who shared the Pentecostal view that tongues could—and even should—occur in the end times strongly objected to this concept of "uniform initial evidence." Assertions about the latter rain and restorationism also distinguished Pentecostals from those evangelicals who accepted dispensationalism. By assessing the movement's strengths and weaknesses, other evangelicals accelerated the growing disparity between Pentecostal pretensions to unity and the movement's practical sectarianism.

Probably the earliest opposition came from independent holiness teachers. But by 1907, A. B. Simpson and A. T. Pierson publicly cautioned about the movement's excesses. Somewhat later, R. A. Torrey and Harry Ironside published their rejections of what they perceived the Pentecostal movement to be. These evaluations remain significant, for they not only indicate how Pentecostalism was perceived but they also helped mold both the attitudes of future generations of evangelicals toward Pentecostalism and Pentecostals' perceptions of themselves.

The Holiness Response

Early Pentecostals were dismayed by the fact that holiness missions rejected their teaching. Those that did not, as in the South, for example, became the earliest Pentecostal denominations. Because many Pentecostals had participated in holiness activities and continued to affirm the necessity of the "second blessing," they hoped easily to convince the numerous proponents of holiness of the validity of their message. They discovered, however, that holiness adherents were reluctant to admit that they did not already have the baptism in the Holy Spirit. Since the second blessing they prized had frequently been called a Spirit baptism, and since their perception of that Baptism had come to include a dimension of "enduement with power," they concluded that that Pentecostal teaching struck at the core of their own conception of Christian experience. It maintained that the second blessing was not Spirit baptism; it added an additional crisis experience to normal Christian expectations; and it insisted on *uniform* evidence. They consequently vehemently denounced both "third blessing heresy" and the "tongues movement."

William Seymour's experience in Los Angeles is a case in point. Before anyone in his meetings had spoken in tongues, he found himself barred from the mission in which he had proclaimed the apostolic faith. Early Pentecostal accounts are replete with stories of persecution and rejection by holiness advocates. Partly because their missions were torn apart by Pentecostal teaching, holiness preachers not only refused to endorse Pentecostal doctrine but also openly accused Pentecostals of fanaticism, spiritual arrogance, and demon possession.

Among the most outspoken was Alma White, founder of a vociferous holiness group known as the Pillar of Fire. White, who claimed to be the first American woman to be ordained a bishop, held a personal grudge against Pentecostals. They had won her estranged husband, a former Methodist minister whom she had displaced in the pulpit, to their cause. In a stinging indictment that she published in 1919 under the title *Demons and Tongues,* White denounced both Pentecostal theology and Pentecostal practice.

White objected on eschatological grounds to the identification of the Pentecostal movement with the latter rain: "This Tongues heresy," she wrote, "familiarly known ... as the Latter Rain, is a gigantic scheme of Satan to supplant God's ancient people in the promise of the latter rain that is to come to them."[1] Her bitterness about her husband's experience found expression in her association of tongues and demons: "Had it not been for his ... taking up with the Tongues heresy, I perhaps could never have fully understood the power of evil spirits working under a cloak of religion."[2]

White's paper, *The Pillar of Fire,* had carried numerous articles opposing "tongueism" well before her book was published. Claiming that "Mrs. Eddy's teaching and the present day 'Tongueism' [were] leaving spiritual death and devastation everywhere," for example, White declared that the movement that "had started with a black man" and had come "like a simoon from the African desert" was "better adapted to tropical climates where there is plenty of water to immerse the victims of this hellish power."[3]

Such vehemence seemed particularly ironic to former holiness advocates who were well aware of the excesses that characterized Pillar of Fire worship. Evangelist Herbert Buffum, who had been in White's meetings, recalled having seen "people going through every form of gymnastic exercise ... students playing leap-frog while in prayer, [which] we actually witnessed in one of the services in Denver."[4] Pentecostal responses to criticism were correspondingly untempered. Referring to White's opposition Buffum commented: "But thank God! This turkey-buzzard vomit can not hinder the great work of God."[5]

The charge that the Apostolic Faith, or "Pentecostal," Movement was actually a "tongues movement" and that tongues were demon-inspired was fairly widespread among holiness advocates. When prominent Quaker Pentecostal Levi Lupton committed adultery and lost his place of leadership in the fledgling Pentecostal movement, the circumstances provided occasion for broader criticism. Expanding on the situation, for example, Free Methodist Jennie Jolley (who lived near Levi Lupton's home in Alliance, Ohio) maintained that the "tongues demon" blinded "its subjects to the truth of God's word and to the law of the land also."[6]

Others claimed that utterances in tongues and interpretation, when understood by foreigners, were "vile," some of "the worst things that could be said." These, of course, substantiated the view that the speakers were demon possessed.[7] E. E. Shelhammer, a pastor in Atlanta at the time of the early Azusa Street meetings, took several of his holiness congregation's members to attend one of the first Pentecostal services in that city. Insisting that people came "to obtain . . . a spectacular thing," he claimed also that demons conversed with him during the service. Concluding that the tongues movement "was the best counterfeit the devil had ever gotten up," Shelhammer became its uncompromising foe.[8]

Predictably the respected holiness evangelist and teacher Beverly Carradine expressed a broader grasp of the situation. Claiming that contemporaries who pursued the "gift of tongues" exhibited a "spirit, conduct and object" in "perfect contrast" to those manifested in the Upper Room, he noted further that the "gibberish" called "tongues" only mocked the known languages spoken at Pentecost, that tongues seekers "put a gift above the Giver," and that the Pentecostal movement lacked the results in "sweeping revival and salvation of men" that had accompanied the manifestation of tongues in the Early Church.[9]

As tongues-speaking Apostolic Faith people appropriated the name Pentecostal, holiness advocates gradually deemphasized their own Pentecostal character. The deletion of the word "Pentecostal" from the name of the Church of the Nazarene, for example, symbolized that group's rejection of "third blessing heresy" and their desire to disassociate themselves from Pentecostals. While a few holiness associations (e.g., the Pentecostal Mission in Nashville) evidenced some early tolerance for proven workers within their ranks who had spoken in tongues, they ultimately denied the proposition that tongues were a uniform initial evidence of Spirit baptism. For some, evidential tongues posed more of a problem than a restoration of tongues speech.

The Christian and Missionary Alliance Response

In Christian and Missionary Alliance founder A. B. Simpson, many Pentecostals believed they had a kindred spirit. Simpson helped shape the Pentecostal understanding of the latter rain. He shared fully the expectations of those who awaited an end-times "outpouring" of the Holy Spirit. Early in the 1880s, he had admitted that his espousal of healing necessitated an openness to the possibility of tongues and other spiritual gifts. His keen interest in spiritual experiences that energized Christians to evangelize found expression in various formats: publications, camp meetings, conventions, local "branches" (i.e., groups) for the "deepening" of spiritual life, and missionary outreach. Probably more than any other single body of American Christians, participants in Simpson's Christian and Missionary Alliance nurtured a faith that made them responsive to Pentecostal teaching.

Eschewing denominationalism, Simpson had formed branches wherever interested Christians lived. Alliance constituents usually held membership in mainline denominations and attended the regular services of their choosing. Meetings in Alliance branches convened on Sunday afternoons and during the week when local churches had no activities. These branches attracted people from many denominations who shared Simpson's interest in the deeper life and found in it an incentive to support evangelism. A firm believer in divine healing, Simpson also stressed the imminence of Christ's return and the need for consecrated Christian living. His focus on the Holy Spirit as potentially with, in, and on believers generated expectations of knowing the Holy Spirit's power in all dimensions of life and service. In time, some independent congregations affiliated with the Alliance, thus creating Alliance branches that functioned like local churches.

Intrigued by reports from Azusa Street and other places, Alliance people expressed an interest in Pentecostalism. Pentecostals also sought out Alliance affiliates, among whom they found ready response. Records suggest that several Alliance branches became, for a time, essentially Pentecostal gatherings, places where people came both for evangelical teaching and the opportunity to "seek" the baptism in the Holy Spirit. Many Alliance people spoke in tongues. The experience, however, eluded Simpson, who sought a tongues experience for several years.[10]

In September 1906 in reference to Los Angeles, the weekly Alliance publication noted "a remarkable manifestation of spiritual power" in the West and urged its readers to guard against two extremes: at the one end, "credulity and fanaticism" (claiming that God would "not be displeased" by "conservative and careful" investigation) and, at the other, obdurance ("refusing to recognize any added blessing which the Holy Spirit is bringing to His people in these last days").[11] Alliance people had prayed fervently for "the outpouring of the Holy Ghost in all His fulness"; now they were enjoined to "keep . . . hearts opened to recognize the answer in whatever form it comes."[12]

Throughout the fall of 1906 the Alliance branches experienced renewal. In both the Missionary Institute and the Gospel Tabernacle in New York City, people noticed a profound "sense of God." They came, Simpson reported, "not to hear anybody, but because God is there." The paper noted reports of a similar movement at Moody Bible Institute.[13] By January 1907, the paper carried several articles on tongues by a prominent Alliance superintendent in Chicago, William T. MacArthur. Urging caution about a movement that had "brought much real blessing to many" and "possibly only fancied blessing to others," MacArthur summoned his readers to participate in its blessings while avoiding its pitfalls.[14]

Alliance spokespersons had an almost uncanny way of discerning potential difficulties that enthusiastic Apostolic Faith adherents seemed prone to overlook. Within several years, some Pentecostals would echo Alliance appeals for prudence and balance. For the moment, however, the cautions seemed to go largely unheeded. Almost from the outset, Alliance publications warned against "the tendency to seek some special gift rather than the Giver Himself."[15] Reminiscent of Simpson's earlier concern about "the wonder-seeking spirit" with which people often approached divine healing was his sense that the Pentecostal movement encouraged Christians "running after some man or woman with the idea of receiving through the human instrument some wonderful gift."[16]

Late in the spring of 1907, the Alliance held its annual Council at the Missionary Institute in Nyack. Attendance was largely confined to delegates representing branches from Indianapolis to the east. Their numbers were augmented by some twenty missionaries, the Nyack student body (which then numbered approximately two hundred), the faculties of the Institute and the Alliance-sponsored Wilson Academy, and the guests at the Berachah Home. The workers' reports convinced the assembly "that God [was] now visiting His people in many places with a special manifestation of power" and that Alliance branches embraced some who had manifested an "authentic" gift of tongues.[17] Simpson's Annual Report in March had recorded, "In many places there has been apparently a revival of the gift of tongues. . . ."[18] During an all-night prayer meeting on the last night of the Council, "the Holy Spirit came with great power on all present," prostrating many and bestowing a tongues experience on a young missionary candidate for the Congo. The paper reported that she had spoken a Congo dialect that was understood by an attending missionary. Although the Council adjourned, the meetings continued.[19] The Council expressed its consensus that "manifestations" characterized "by the 'spirit of power and of a sane mind' " (such as the one they had seen at Nyack) were appropriate in Alliance ranks; "wild excitement," however, they unequivocally excluded.[20]

Throughout the summer of 1907, as Pentecostal teaching radiated from several centers and diligent evangelists itinerated to spread their message, many Alliance settings assumed a thoroughly Pentecostal character.[21] The Beulah Park Convention in Collinwood, Ohio, for example, saw "God [pour] out His Spirit upon the people in general and upon others in particular, so that they spoke with new tongues and magnified God. The sick were healed and demons were expelled."[22] And this was only "the earnest" of what could be anticipated: "It is the time of the latter rain. Jesus is coming soon. Perhaps the next convention will be in the air."[23] Even the annual camp meeting at Old Orchard Beach, Maine, which had become a celebrated focal point for Alliance supporters, became a setting in which people sought the baptism in the Holy Spirit evidenced by tongues.

Alliance men who toured the districts and attempted to establish guidelines to help them discern between the fanatical and the acceptable in the strong contemporary emphasis on the Holy Spirit brought little criticism of the experiences they found in Alliance branches. Some Alliance men did, however, differentiate among the various Pentecostal groups, noting excesses and extreme teaching. And some questioned whether the tongues movement adequately met the criteria for a spiritual "outpouring." Missionary Robert Jaffray, for example, spoke in tongues in 1908 and declared the next year that the "anointing abideth." Nonetheless, he maintained in 1909 that "subtle dangers" accompanied Pentecostal teaching.

The first danger he noted later became the reason for the separation of some Pentecostals from Alliance ranks: He objected strongly, not to tongues, but to the insistence that tongues were the sole evidence of Spirit baptism. As early as 1907, Simpson had concurred in this view: The espousal of tongues as "an essential evidence of the baptism of the Holy Spirit," he observed, had "led to division, fanaticism, confusion and almost every evil work."[24] Jaffray's second caution addressed another area that concerned many earnest and thoughtful participants in the movement: "There is a subtle danger of attaching too much importance to supernatural utterances and interpretations of tongues, considering that they are the very infallible Word of the Spirit of God."[25] Third, Jaffray noted the failure of Pentecostalism, with its focus on a tongues experience, to promote unity. Charging that "tongues speakers" often separated from earlier church associations because they were "more holy" or constituted "a sacred, select few," Jaffray expressed disappointment in the apparent lack of commitment to Christian unity. Fourth, Jaffray noted something that few Pentecostals admitted: His mission had been "swept" by a Pentecostal revival, and missionaries and Chinese had spoken in tongues. Yet the event had not "empowered for service." It had, rather, spawned "small select meetings" where some tried to "enjoy the blessing selfishly." Missionaries had "backslidden" in their "missionary zeal." From Jaffray's perspective, the Pentecostal experience, while meaningful in his life, had been a disappointment on his mission station.

Jaffray had also encountered the independent missionaries who had sensed a "call" to a field for which they claimed to "have the tongue." Noting that such missionaries had been deceived, their supporters had been misled, they had become a burden on regular missionaries, and money had been diverted from support for established missions, Jaffray urged his readers to be cautious.

Each year, the Minutes of the Annual Conferences reported Pentecostal effusions in Alliance work around the world as well as in the United States. Generally favorable, the comments also consistently urged "watchfulness against counterfeits, extravagances and false teaching."[26] In 1912, the Annual Report said that "marked deepening of the spiritual life of our members and an encouraging increase in their missionary zeal and liberality" had accompanied the movement wherever it had been "wisely directed." Increasingly, however, concern over the central question of uniform initial evidence had surfaced in the Alliance. The insistence on evidential tongues, Alliance leaders concurred, was rooted in an inaccurate view of Scripture; furthermore, such a position maintained that only tongues-speaking believers had received Spirit baptism ("thus leading many sincere Christians to cast away their confidence, and plunging them in perplexity and darkness, or causing them to seek after special manifestations of other than God Himself") and it encouraged "seekers" to pursue "signs and wonders and special manifestations."[27] The conviction that Pentecostals misread the Bible—that the Bible, although affirming the presence of tongues speech in the Early Church, neither advocated any uniform initial evidence of Spirit baptism nor distinguished between evidential tongues, the gift of tongues, and the use of tongues in private worship—was central to the crystallizing of an Alliance position on Pentecostalism.

With such reservations in mind, Alliance leaders decided to treat tongues speaking as they did several other controversial matters: "It would be wise," the report concluded, "to leave the question of 'The Latter Rain' and related doctrines, as matters of personal liberty, just as we do the question of Baptism, Church Government, and other differences of belief among the Evangelical bodies."[28] On April 13, 1914, the Alliance articulated its official position:

> We believe that the gift of tongues or speaking in tongues did in many cases in the apostolic church accompany or follow the Baptism of the Holy Spirit. We believe also that other supernatural and even miraculous operations on the part of the Holy Spirit through His people are competent and possible according to the sovereign will of the Holy Spirit Himself throughout the Christian age. But we hold that none of these manifestations are *essentially* connected with the Baptism of the Holy Spirit, and that the consecrated believer may receive the Spirit in His fulness without speaking in tongues or any miraculous manifestations whatever; and that no Christian teacher has the right to require such manifestations as evidence of the Baptism of the Holy Spirit. The teaching of the Apostle Paul in First Corinthians, chapters 12–14, makes this exceedingly plain.[29]

Over a number of years, several men and women who strongly favored evidential tongues broke their ties to Christian and Missionary Alliance branches and affiliated with Pentecostal missions. Some of them became influential Assemblies of God leaders. Several young students who had recently completed training at the Missionary Institute decided to pour their energies into Pentecostal ministries. Because the Alliance was not yet a structured denomination and because it had not denied the validity of the tongues experience, most people who had spoken in tongues retained their ties to the Alliance. The list of the tongues-speaking leaders who remained with Simpson is certainly as impressive as the list of those who left. And those who eventually decided to sever their ties did not leave en masse. To some, a parting of the ways seemed inevitable; to most, and especially to A. B. Simpson, it was extremely painful. Some twenty-five workers resigned in 1912, but in the same year, a young Pentecostal, W. I. Evans (later dean of Central Bible Institute), graduated from Nyack and began a fruitful ministry as superintendent of the Alliance branch in Richmond, Virginia. George Eldridge, a prominent Alliance leader, continued to serve the Alliance in California through 1916.[30] Pentecostals were not forced out of the Alliance; in fact, Simpson's diary indicates his personal empathy with much that they experienced, and the pages of Alliance publications repeatedly supported contemporary manifestations of the gift of tongues. Several years after Simpson's death in 1919, however, the hostility toward tongues that had come to characterize some local branches won the support of an Alliance leader with wide evangelical influence, Aiden Wilson Tozer. Tozer probably coined the phrase "Seek not, forbid not" that came to summarize the official Alliance position on tongues.[31] By the time he did so, his own opposition coincided with other factors that had virtually eliminated tongues from Alliance experience.

The Responses of Arthur T. Pierson and Reuben A. Torrey

The ranks of those evangelicals who, in the late nineteenth century, had come to advocate a crisis experience of Spirit baptism as "enduement with power for service" naturally included some who felt compelled to respond to the early Pentecostal insistence on evidential tongues. In fact, during the first decade of the movement's history, it shared its claim to "Pentecostal" experience with numerous Protestants who never endorsed tongues speech. Only gradually did the term come to connote acceptance of evidential tongues.

Arthur T. Pierson figured prominently among those evangelicals who used Bible institute and conference settings to promote evangelism and "deeper life" teaching. A Keswick speaker, and popular throughout the United States as well as in England, Pierson edited an important missions journal, *The Missionary Review of the World.* His spiritual pilgrimage had brought him from the pursuit of acclaim as a literary pulpiteer to the espousal of faith living, missions, premillennialism, the Spirit-filled life, and divine healing. Early in the twentieth century, his lifelong Presbyterian connections were severed as a result of his baptism by immersion in Charles Spurgeon's famed Metropolitan Tabernacle.[32] A spiritually sensitive man, Pierson responded in 1907 with concern to the excesses he believed accompanied contemporary tongues speech. Avowing his determination never to "hinder any genuine work of the Spirit of God," Pierson urged sensitivity to the Spirit as the only appropriate response.

Pierson's articles provide a sense of how Pentecostalism was perceived among those who shared some of its basic concerns, and document how widespread the movement's influence had become.[33] His earliest comments about tongues speech were part of a small notice about the Pentecostal revival Thomas B. Barratt led in Norway in 1906. Even as he praised its accomplishments, he cautioned about potential excesses. Later closer encounters with Pentecostals yielded a critical evaluation.

Truly spiritual gifts, he noted, "are promotive of peace and harmony" and lead to "humility and docility of temper."[34] Like other interested observers, he noted the "divisive and centrifugal tendency" that expressed itself in facets of the tongues movement. And, like his friend A. B. Simpson, he cautioned against seeking gifts rather than the Giver and against following messages in tongues instead of the Bible. "The Infallible Scriptures alone," he insisted, "can be our ultimate court of appeal." Nebulous experiences in the Spirit, promoting disharmony and stubborn resistance to authority as well as discounting "the Word," failed to meet biblical requirements and were, rather, "satanic disguise and counterfeits."[35] Noting especially the impact of Apostolic Faith teaching on missions, Pierson admitted that tongues-speaking missionaries were "unusually serious and earnest." However, he continued, "[s]ide by side with revival scenes appear Satan's counterfeits, and hence a solemn awe, begotten by the conviction that this movement is one of his devices. . . ."[36]

Later the same year, Pierson expressed a concern similar to that raised by Alliance Missionary Robert Jaffray. The movement had resulted in "little conversion of sinners, or edification or unification of the saints . . . in a word, few of those marks which prove the genuine working of the Spirit."[37] By that time he had amassed considerable evidence, "confidential but reliable," which attested facts "too shocking to print." And he pointed out that friends who had seen the material said what he had printed erred "on the side of mildness and moderation."[38] Pierson offered two general observations. The first was that the Pentecostal movement tended to overemphasize "subjective teaching," which fostered, he claimed, "morbid introspection [and] constant and searching self-examination."[39] Its second weakness was its absorption in "Holy Spirit manifestations," which tended to substitute a "cult of the Spirit" for "the work of the Lord Jesus Christ."[40] In short, Pierson regarded the movement as unacceptable because he believed that it made "the Holy Spirit . . . the focus of spiritual vision," possibly hindering "His work as the *medium* for clearer, fuller vision of Christ."[41]

Such criticism indicates some of the problems Pentecostals faced. Extremes abounded in the movement, and what Pierson objected to can be easily documented. But, as Pierson admitted, his observations did not apply equally to all Pentecostals. A growing sense of the need to provide ways to discriminate among Pentecostal practices and teaching contributed to support for cooperative association.

A harsher indictment of Pentecostalism came from Reuben A. Torrey, a man who had done as much as anyone to arouse evangelicals to pray for an outpouring of the Holy Spirit. As dean of Moody Bible Institute, pastor of Moody's Chicago Avenue Church, conference speaker, and worldwide evangelist, Torrey could claim with some validity to have assumed Moody's mantle.

Torrey had strongly affirmed the obligation of Christians to pursue a baptism in the Holy Spirit, and he had even considered whether tongues might be the biblical evidence for that experience. But long before Charles Parham rose to prominence, Torrey had emphatically rejected evidential tongues. Certainly the extremes he observed in Pentecostal ranks only confirmed for him the accuracy of his decision.

Torrey's perception of Pentecostalism differed radically from the way some Pentecostals understood their movement. Focusing on the common tendency to seek tongues and other gifts, Torrey rejected the movement as a "tongues movement." To him, the distinctions some Pentecostals tried to preserve between seeking tongues and seeking "the Giver" had little practical significance.

Like his friend A. T. Pierson, Torrey believed that the gift of tongues could appropriately be expected in the last days. But he shared Pierson's conviction that conditions in the contemporary tongues movement clearly proved that it was not "of God." Like Pierson and Simpson, Torrey insisted that Spirit baptism could manifest itself in many ways. He therefore condemned the tongues movement for its position on initial evidence. Torrey shared the Christian and Missionary Alliance view that Pentecostals misread Scripture. His objections went further than either Simpson's or Pierson's, however. Torrey considered the movement to be "accompanied by the most grievous disorders and the grossest immoralities."[42] Citing Parham's arrest for "an unnatural act" in San Antonio in 1907 and Levi Lupton's disgrace in Ohio in 1910, Torrey charged that "the Movement as a whole has apparently developed more immorality than any other modern movement except spiritism, to which it is so closely allied in many ways."[43] Torrey's pamphlet on tongues addressed the simple question "Is the present tongues movement of God?" To it he responded with a resounding no.

Harry Ironside's indictment came in the form of a pamphlet published by the Louizeaux Brothers' Bible Truth Depot in New York City, a press that produced much anti-Pentecostal diatribe. Ironside (whose years in the Salvation Army had predisposed him to dislike anything associated with holiness teaching) applied to Pentecostalism the test of 1 John. He attended mission services in several parts of the country and pored over Pentecostal periodicals, looking for use of the term Lord Jesus Christ or the naming of God as Father. Failing to find such, he insisted that the spirit at work in the movement was unholy. He labeled the movement an "unpentecostal imposture" and urged his readers to "try the spirits by the only safe test—a true confession of Jesus Christ come in the flesh."[44]

Precisely because such criticisms could be amply documented, they proved particularly effective in shaping the response to Pentecostalism of the institutions (e.g., Moody Bible Institute) fundamentalism was emerging from. They also molded Pentecostal perceptions of the evangelical subculture Pentecostalism had emerged out of. When one takes into account the increasing concurrent acceptance of dispensationalism, especially as popularized through the Scofield Reference Bible after 1909, the sources of later fundamentalist hostility toward Pentecostalism become clearer.

Dispensationalism, as articulated by Scofield, understood the gifts of the Spirit to have been withdrawn from the Church. Rejecting the latter rain views by which Pentecostals legitimated their place in God's plan, dispensationalists effectively eliminated the biblical basis for Pentecostal theology; and although Pentecostals embraced most of Scofield's ideas (and enthusiastically promoted the Scofield Reference Bible in their periodicals), they remained irrevocably distanced from fundamentalists by their teaching on the place of spiritual gifts in the contemporary church.[45]

By 1914, then, the evangelicals from whom Pentecostals might have expected support had distanced themselves. In evangelical circles, the term "Pentecostal" was beginning to have negative connotations. Many disassociated themselves increasingly from anything that might identify them with the excesses they associated with contemporary tongues speaking. It is significant that, at about the same time, advocacy of divine healing and support for women in ministry became less conspicuous within the same broader evangelical subculture.

Pentecostal evangelists reported various forms of popular opposition as well. On June 1, 1914, for example, L. V. Roberts, an Indianapolis pastor, participated in a tent crusade with several other workers, one of whom was a former nun who brought numerous allegations against the Catholic church. Instigated by a hostile mob, police interrupted a service while Roberts was preaching and arrested him and eight assistants. The mob then burned the tent. A. B. Cox experienced similar violence in Cumberland, Maryland.[46] Although these reports of arrests were unusual, hostility found petty ways to make life difficult for some outspoken Pentecostal workers. Evangelist Walter Higgins entitled one chapter of his memoirs "Rotten Egg Evangelism." Garfield Haywood reported that his evangelistic efforts in Indianapolis regularly attracted persecution. Not only did "mischievous boys . . . perform many pranks"; crowded, noisy services in his mission on the corner of Michigan and Minerva streets were frequently interrupted by "a brick . . . strik[ing] against the door . . . or a rotten egg or tomato whizzing through the transom."[47] In rural areas, confrontations occasionally took the form of public debates.[48]

Meanwhile, some Pentecostals (among them several who acknowledged these evangelicals as mentors) shared both the concern about excesses and the conviction that speaking in tongues—and the broader "life in the Spirit" they aspired to— was appropriate in contemporary Christian experience. They took steps to provide a framework for excluding "error" and nurturing experience in the Spirit. Although they refused to compromise on the matter of tongues, they concurred about the need to address untoward situations. Uncomfortable with the polity preferred by Southern holiness Pentecostals, they decided to explore the advantages of cooperating in a loosely-structured fellowship that would largely preserve their cherished independence while at the same time provide a forum for the consideration of concerns that affected them all.

By 1914, serious doctrinal differences had further splintered the movement. Disagreements about sanctification and the baptismal formula raised fundamental theological issues. The untimely deaths of two prominent independent leaders, William Piper and William Durham, jeopardized the future of two leading Pentecostal periodicals. Charles Parham's criticisms of all who refused to accept his leadership became increasingly vocal and vehement. Dissension and disunity seemed, from one perspective, to be rampant. Certainly the situation seemed to justify concerns about "conserving" the revival; yet, some resisted. William Durham had called plans to organize "the great crisis,"[49] listing several harmful effects of organization: It destroyed "the independent New Testament Assembly life"; it unduly exalted those men who held office; "scheming men" rather than the "best men" would gain leadership. "Every man, as far I know, who has attempted to organize the Pentecostal movement or to get it under his control, has lost his power with God and his influence with men, and," he continued, "God has made me to know that this will be the fate of every man who attempts to organize or control this work."[50] At a critical moment, however, some who had been moving slowly to encourage cooperation issued a call to a General Council in Hot Springs, Arkansas, for April of 1914.

9. The Formation of the General Council of the Assemblies of God

> God is revealing His real plan to so many that they will never consent to having the present work turned into a sect.
>
> Wm. Durham, *Pentecostal Testimony,* ca. 1911

> The Holy Spirit who . . . has carried on this glorious Pentecostal work in the earth without organization we believe is able to carry it on and control it in the future. . . . We do not believe [God's people] will ever again submit to human organization, and be brought back into bondage.
>
> *The Gospel Witness,* 1913

> This call is to all the churches of God in Christ, to all Pentecostal or Apostolic Faith Assemblies who desire with united purpose to cooperate in love and peace to push the interests of the kingdom of God everywhere. This is, however, only for saints who believe in the baptism with the Holy Ghost with the signs following.
>
> *Word and Witness,* December 20, 1913

In the chilly early spring of 1914, a mixed group of "workers" and "saints" convened in the old Grand Opera House on Central Avenue in Hot Springs, Arkansas, in response to advertisements that had run in Pentecostal papers since December 1913. Primarily from the Midwest, but representing some seventeen states and Egypt and South Africa, they arrived prepared to consider proposals to facilitate cooperation for extending their movement.[1]

From Thursday, April 2, through Sunday, April 5, they worshiped and prayed together. On April 6, they organized themselves for business. Their mere attendance was an acknowledgement that the Pentecostal movement had unleashed forces that made cooperation advisable. Like participants in other revival movements, they nurtured the hope of conserving and directing the revival's spiritual fervor into meaningful channels while providing guidelines for eliminating excesses.

The general sense that Pentecostalism either had attracted more than its share of visionaries or had somehow encouraged unbalanced and even dangerous emphasis on the Holy Spirit had been evident in Pentecostal periodicals for several years. Increasing numbers of Pentecostals felt both a need to repudiate error and a desire to affirm their distinctive emphases in ways that were best facilitated by cooperation.

The Call for a General Council

Hot Springs already had a thriving Pentecostal assembly, which in 1914 was led by thirty-year-old Howard Goss, looked upon as a veteran Pentecostal. A major promoter of the concept of cooperative fellowship and of the call for the General Council, Goss served the gathering as financial secretary. His congregation provided hospitality and supervised on-site arrangements. Local Pentecostals were becoming accustomed to gathering at the Grand Opera House in Hot Springs. In the fall of 1913, Evangelist Maria Woodworth-Etter had conducted several weeks of meetings there, in cooperation with D. C. O. Opperman, who preceded Goss as leader of the Pentecostal outreach in the city. Having come to Hot Springs immediately after their arrest in South Framingham, Massachusetts, on charges related to the practice of divine healing, Woodworth-Etter and her colleague, Cyrus Fockler, seemed primed to engage adversaries. But she noted, "God was with us in power. . . ."[2] Opperman, having secured a six-month lease on the property's auditorium (the first floor housed a saloon), prepared to follow the Woodworth-Etter campaign with a short-term Bible school.[3] In April, the same commodious facility accommodated the Council delegates.

The initial call for a Council had been signed by men identified with the loosely organized, predominantly white Churches of God in Christ. This association had set up several committees through which business could be expedited. A Clergy Reference Committee, for example, composed of Eudorus N. Bell, Archibald P. Collins, Howard Goss, and D. C. O. Opperman, had been elected at a large camp meeting in Meridian, Mississippi, in June 1913; and a Bureau of Information that included Editors Bell (*Word and Witness,* Arkansas), Robert Brown (*The Midnight Cry,* New York City), Lydia Piper (*The Latter Rain Evangel,* Chicago), G. B. Studd (Los Angeles), and A. H. Argue (*The Good Report,* Long Beach) served the associated ministers who numbered over three hundred and sixty by the end of 1913. But the loose ties this association offered were inadequate to address felt needs. Yet the reluctance to organize proved a powerful restraint.

Attitudes Toward Organization

Attitudes toward organization varied widely in American Pentecostalism. Some previously organized associations superimposed Pentecostal teaching on existing (however precariously) institutional frameworks. Most Pentecostals, however, had no organizational loyalties beyond their ties to a local assembly. While their subscriptions to Pentecostal periodicals and their attendance at frequent camp meetings and conventions helped them identify with the movement, these structures did not attempt to provide the discriminating direction that seemed to be required.

Opposition to organization had several sources: restorationism, through which one could affirm the sovereignty of the local church; "spirituality," which militated against cooperation at least partly because it might preclude one's following a "leading of the Spirit"; unwillingness to submit to authority (which frequently assumed a noticeably spiritual tone); and a pervasive sense that organization necessarily "quenched the Spirit." To a lesser extent, some rejected organization because organizations rejected them. This, however, had another side. Pentecostal arrogance frequently alienated others. For the most part, however, Pentecostalism did not immediately affect mainline churches. It flourished among those who were already alienated from the denominations and whose experience made them likely to construe Pentecostal teaching as a negative commentary on denominational structures.

The Purpose of the General Council

The men who decided to extend and build on the loose ties already present were well-known throughout much of the Pentecostal constituency. E. N. Bell, a former Baptist pastor, led an assembly in Malvern, Arkansas, edited a monthly periodical, *Word and Witness*, and preached regularly at camp meetings and conventions; Howard Goss, converted during Charles Parham's meetings in Galena, Kansas, in 1903 had evangelized widely in Texas and Arkansas and had founded several assemblies; D. C. O. Opperman, one of the movement's prominent Bible teachers, conducted schools in various places and also evangelized; A. P. Collins, another former Baptist, frequented camp meetings and was widely esteemed among Texas Pentecostals; M. M. Pinson, a former evangelist in the Pentecostal Mission, had ties to Pentecostals in the Southeast. In 1913 Pinson was serving in Phoenix. These men, like other early Pentecostals, traveled frequently and widely. The contemporary expansion and integration of railroad lines contributed immeasurably to their mobility.

Although the sense that conditions warranted organization had been apparent for some time, these five men issued the call somewhat hastily, "to get the matter before the brethren at once."[4] They anticipated that others would later commend their action by supporting the call. They were not disappointed. Three months later, they added the names of twenty-nine recognized Pentecostal leaders representing fourteen additional states to the call to Hot Springs.[5] They addressed the invitation to "laymen and preachers," especially urging "all elders, pastors, ministers, evangelists and missionaries" to attend. More generally, they welcomed "all the churches of God in Christ" and "all Pentecostal or Apostolic Faith Assemblies" who would "cooperate in love and peace to push the interests of the kingdom of God everywhere."[6]

In spite of the discussion the call aroused—and the accusations it generated—participants arrived in good spirits. Those who first envisioned the meeting did their best to make it possible for all who so desired to attend. They scheduled the meetings to allow participants to use special winter tourist rail fares and encouraged ministers to "lay this before your people and get them to pay your fare to and fro."[7] To those who could not raise sufficient funds, they promised: "We want you to come anyhow, and if you have not faith to get home after you are here, then we will stand with you in trusting God for your return fare or to get out on the field."[8]

Four days of rousing Pentecostal meetings helped allay the reservations of some who feared organization. Although all did not concur fully on doctrine and practice, they discovered unity "in the Spirit." When the Council organized itself for business on Monday, April 6, it had before it several explicit purposes that had been published repeatedly in *Word and Witness*:

> First—We come together that we may get a better understanding of what God would have us teach, that we may do away with so many divisions, both in doctrines and in the various names under which our Pentecostal people are working and incorporating. Let us come together as in Acts 15, to study the Word, and pray with and for each other— unity our chief aim.
>
> Second—Again we come together that we [may] know how to conserve the work, that we may all build up and not tear down, both in home and foreign lands.
>
> Third—We come together for another reason, that we may get a better understanding of the needs of each foreign field and may know how to place our money in such a way that one mission or missionary shall not suffer, while another not any more worthy, lives in luxuries. Also that we

may discourage wasting money on those who are running here and there accomplishing nothing, and may concentrate our support on those who mean business for our King.

Fourth—Many of the saints have felt the need of chartering the churches of God in Christ, putting them on a legal basis, and thus obeying the laws of the land, as God says. See Rom. 13. We confess we have been "slothful in business" on this point, and because of this many assemblies have already chartered under different names as a local work, in both home and foreign lands. Why not charter under one Bible name, 2 Thess. 2:14. Thus eliminating another phase of division in Pentecostal work? For this purpose also let us come together.

Fifth—We may also have a proposition to lay before the body for a general Bible Training School with a literary department for our people.[9]

While the Council was not to be limited by these concerns (its conveners had announced that "the scope of the meeting may be enlarged as the Lord shall lead the brethren"), they remained the underlying purpose for its eventual creation of the Assemblies of God.

The Origin of the Constitution of the Assemblies of God

After appointing E. N. Bell and J. R. Flower as chairman and secretary, the Council began its deliberations. In an early action, it decided to limit voting rights to males. A conference committee, consisting of one delegate from each state represented, framed a Preamble and Resolution of Constitution that Thomas K. Leonard, a pastor, editor, and Bible school teacher from Findlay, Ohio, and J. Roswell Flower presented to the General Council. This instrument served the General Council for more than a decade in place of a formal constitution and bylaws. Specifically designed to dispel hesitations about centralization and creed, the document declared that participants were part of the "GENERAL ASSEMBLY OF GOD (which is God's organism)." It explicitly disavowed sectarian intentions as "a human organization that legislates or forms laws and articles of faith" through which to exercise "unscriptural jurisdiction" over its members.[10] In a clear statement of purpose it declared:

> Be it resolved, That we recognize ourselves as a GENERAL COUNCIL of Pentecostal (Spirit Baptized) saints from local Churches of God in Christ, Assemblies of God, and various Apostolic Faith Missions and Churches, and Full Gospel Pentecostal Missions, and Assemblies of like faith in the United States of America, Canada, and Foreign Lands, whose purpose is neither to legislate laws of government, nor usurp authority over said various Assemblies of God, nor deprive them of their Scriptural and local rights and privileges, but to recognize Scriptural methods and order for worship, unity, fellowship, work and business for God, and to disapprove of all unscriptural methods, doctrines and conduct, and approve of all Scriptural truth and conduct, endeavoring to keep the unity of the Spirit in the bonds of peace, until we all come into the unity of the faith, and of the knowledge of the Son of God, unto a perfect man, unto the measure of the stature of the fullness of Christ, and to walk accordingly, as recorded in Eph. 4:17–32, and to consider the five purposes announced in the Convention Call in . . . *Word and Witness.*[11]

In spite of its cumbersome language, participants welcomed the reading of this Preamble with shouts of praise. Amid the singing of the doxology, the "Minutes" recorded, "The Council broke up into a great praise meeting."[12] Shortly thereafter the Council unanimously adopted the "Preamble and Resolutions on Constitution" as the "Constitution of the General Council of the Assemblies of God." This action renewed the fervor (proprieties being carefully observed nevertheless): "Such joy as is rarely seen in any religious body was manifested upon the unanimous adoption of the . . . PREAMBLE. . . . A great time of shouting, rejoicing, hand-shaking, and even hugging followed; the brethren hugging the brethren and the sisters kissing each other. . . ."[13]

The Appointment of the Executive Presbytery

The assembly further agreed to create an advisory body to be known as the Executive Presbytery. Charged to meet annually, the twelve men who composed the first presbytery were empowered to act on behalf of the General Council "as a Home and Foreign Missionary and Executive Presbytery" for the next year. The Council appointed nine presbyters, and the nine appointed the remaining three. The list included some of the most prominent men in midwestern Pentecostal circles: E. N. Bell, A. P. Collins, R. L. Erickson (pastor of the Stone Church, Chicago), Cyrus B. Fockler (a former Dowie supporter who had pioneered Pentecost in Milwaukee), J. Roswell Flower, Howard Goss, Daniel W. Kerr (esteemed former Christian and Missionary Alliance pastor in Cleveland, Ohio), Thomas K. Leonard (leader of the Gospel School in Findlay, Ohio), D. C. O. Opperman, M. M. Pinson, John Sinclair (Chicago mission pastor), and John W. Welch (a former Christian and Missionary Alliance worker). Secretary J. R. Flower observed that, contrary to the fears of some, twelve "safe, sane and trained brethren" had been selected "to give advice wherever needed" and "to aid whenever asked in helping assemblies to keep in New Testament order."[14] Their capacity remained advisory, and each continued to fulfill a full schedule of non-presbytery-related duties. The executives, Bell insisted, "regarded themselves as only the servants of God and of the saints." Declaring their readiness to "forward mission funds, help the missionaries, give free counsel for Bible order and promote in love the interests of the kingdom of God," they agreed that they had "no quarrel with those who see things differently."[15]

Provision for Ministerial Training

The first General Council dealt with various miscellaneous matters, declaring itself opposed to extreme positions on such divisive questions as appropriate foods. It encouraged "Assemblies of God everywhere" to observe Thursday as a weekly day of prayer; it adopted the *Word and Witness* as its "official organ" and J. R. Flower's *Christian Evangel* as its weekly paper, and made the Executive Presbytery responsible for decisions regarding the vital publications outreach. It recommended the formation of district or state Councils to work in harmony with the General Council.

To address the growing need to provide acceptable training for the ministry, the General Council specifically recommended two schools: the "literary school" run by Rueben Benjamin Chisolm near Union, Mississippi, and the Gospel School conducted by T. K. Leonard in Findlay, Ohio. A specific concern of a committee of three men, including Opperman and Bell, this recommendation probably indicated that no agreement had been reached on a more permanent arrangement. Bell had reported that the committee was considering two "inviting propositions" for locating a combined Bible training institute and literary school "for the whole movement." He had solicited offers, requesting twenty to thirty acres of "good land near a good city" and twenty-five to thirty thousand dollars for buildings.[16] In the absence of concrete plans, the Council recommended existing schools generally, citing two specifically.

The two schools the Council directly endorsed were well-established by 1914. Robert Benjamin Chisolm's Neshoba Holiness School (Pentecostal Faith) had originally had ties to the holiness movement. (It had been known locally since its founding in 1908 as the Holiness Sanctification School.) When its Ruskin College-educated president had embraced Pentecostalism, his faculty had followed suit, and Pentecostal periodicals began to carry recommendations of the institution.[17] The school offered primary, academic, and collegiate courses, with theological and musical training available on request. In the absence of a consolidated school system in Neshoba County, it performed an important local service as well. Recommended by Pentecostals as a place for would-be preachers to obtain basic education, the school focused primarily on the education of children. Chisolm also tutored college and seminary students in Greek and Latin. In an ad that appealed to the antiurban bias of his middle America readers, Flower's *Christian Evangel* encouraged parents who wanted their children "educated in a moral country town away from the vices of the great cities" to contact Chisolm, who offered his services for a hundred dollars a year. (Shortly after the General Council, Chisolm's school was destroyed by arson instigated by local opponents of tongues speaking. The school had been part of a larger complex, including a campground, all of which was rebuilt.)

T. K. Leonard's Gospel School had a different focus. Specifically designed to train ministers, it provided courses in Bible, church history, and English and also offered a one-year home Bible study program. Soliciting those who "earnestly waited on God" for Spirit baptism or "their proper place in the body of Christ" as well as those who felt called to ministry, the school was a faith venture operated out of a two-story brick building in the northwestern Ohio city of Findlay. Leonard advertised seven teachers, and billed the school as one that made "a specialty of the Spiritual."[18] In addition to running the school, Leonard had a local church he called Assembly of God and a small printing plant he had named Gospel Publishing House. He offered his facilities and the printing equipment as the nucleus of a headquarters for the new organization. The executives gratefully accepted this offer, and for the remaining months of 1914, the General Council of the Assemblies of God conducted its business from Leonard's school in Findlay. The expanding needs of the school contributed to the decision at the end of the year to move the headquarters to St. Louis.

Statement on the Rights and Offices of Women

The first General Council dealt with two other issues with long-term significance. It framed a statement on the rights and offices of women, and it declared itself on marriage and divorce. The statement on women bears the unmistakable imprint of E. N. Bell, who had developed his views earlier in *Word and Witness.* The Pentecostal movement had offered opportunities for women to participate in local assemblies. Some rather quickly gained acceptance; others created problems. Bell considered most women "busybodies" who tended not to "settle down" and accomplish anything of enduring worth. Although he could not deny the overall contributions of women to the movement, he believed that those who had established themselves as pastors had no biblical warrant for their office. Noting that "only women of strong character and settled habits" could "open up their own stations with God's blessing," he insisted nonetheless that there was "no scriptural precept or example for such independent leadership by women."[19]

Bell admitted that their participation in the Pentecost event guaranteed women the right to prophesy, and he acknowledged that prophecy was broader than preaching. His objections were rather to women who "[forsook] all other callings and devote[d] their entire time to the gospel ministry" and to those who exerted authority by virtue of "the authority of their office."[20] Exhibiting his strong proclivity for traditional views, he insisted that men were "better adapted . . . to rule and govern assemblies" and that God had wanted "to take these heavy responsibilities off [women's] shoulders."[21]

The General Council reiterated Bell's conviction that women were to be "helpers in the gospel." The sense of its resolution harmonized with Bell's earlier recommendation: "They should be permanently attached to some mission and take up some regular and systematic work for the Lord under the proper oversight of some good brother whom God has placed in charge of the work."[22] The Council also noted that women were "to be in subjection" and should not "usurp authority over the man." Nonetheless, it authorized their ordination as evangelists and missionaries, while explicitly denying them pastoral ministry or any administrative office involving authority over men.[23] Later in 1914, an exception was made allowing women missionaries to perform "baptism, marriage, burial of the dead and the Lord's Supper," only "when a man [was] not available for the purpose." This privilege, to be exercised "in case of emergency only," was carefully restricted. It was extended to ordained women ministering in the United States in 1922.[24] Women were not to have the full range of opportunities the Fellowship would afford men. By male vote (as in many other denominations), it was determined that for some of these responsibilities they were both constitutionally unsuited and scripturally unqualified. Although the General Council reversed itself and permitted the ordination of women pastors, over the years the masculine language of its original constitution and bylaws has been maintained and women have not been elected or appointed to administrative responsibility (above the level of department supervisor) within the denomination.[25]

Statement of Marriage and Divorce

The consideration of marriage and divorce at the first General Council also set a precedent; probably no other issue has been raised so many times through the years. Some Pentecostals had adopted extreme positions on divorce and remarriage, demanding that couples separate, and even, in extreme cases, that they return to their original marriage partner. Some made participation in the local church dependent on a remarried individual's willingness to separate from his or her spouse. Others took a strict stand against divorce and remarriage, but refused to interfere with situations that had developed before the individual's conversion. The Assemblies of God endeavored to find a workable solution to this difficult issue. For those who had "become entangled in their marriage relations in their former lives of sin," the Council recommended that individuals exercise their own conscience and that the church "leave the matter to God"; it discouraged the disruption of well-adjusted families. The Council further disapproved "for the present and the future" of divorce "except for fornication or adultery and (if divorced for any other cause, 1 Cor. 7:15)" recommended "the remaining single of all divorced Christians."[26] (This left open the troublesome question of the right of the innocent spouse to remarry. A considerable variety of opinion on the matter would surface over the years among executive leaders.) It also articulated its consistent position that it would not ordain "those who have remarried and are now living in the state of matrimony, while former companions are living. Ez. 44:22-27."[27] The latter proved to be the only area that the Council failed to reach a unanimous decision, but the dissent was negligible. *Word and Witness* commented, "It is very remarkable that all of the hundreds present agreed, except four—only four!"[28]

"More to Follow"

Having completed its principal matters of business, the General Council adjourned after services on Sunday, April 12. In the minds of its organizers, it had accomplished its goal: It had adopted a name and a framework that would allow it to apply for a charter. It had provided the means to "recognize in a legal way that which [was] already in existence."[29] At the same time, it had strengthened existing ties and proven to the satisfaction of many that cooperation did not necessarily include legislation. In typical restorationist fashion, it had refused to bind by creed, affirming simply that the Bible was its sufficient rule of faith and practice. But the view of Scripture was not necessarily static. In a statement on doctrine, Bell articulated a view of Scripture that allowed "new light": "We must keep our skylights open so as not to reject any new light God may throw upon the old Word. We must not fail to keep pace in life or teaching with light from heaven."[30]

The framers of the Council were never so intent on conserving that they were satisfied with the status quo: They insisted, rather, that "more" could be apprehended. Speaking at a convention at Leonard's Gospel School in the fall of 1914, Daniel W. Kerr expressed a "general belief" that "another outpouring" was necessary "to bring us to the place of real Apostolic usefulness." Kerr anticipated an outpouring that stressed healing much as tongues had been emphasized between 1901 and 1914. He projected a separation, similar to that which Pentecostalism had initially produced in holiness/restorationist ranks, since many Pentecostals would most likely "not take the advance step."[31] The theme of "more to follow" and an accompanying sense of "declension" in their movement are evident in the earliest Assemblies of God literature.

Early participants in the Assemblies of God were not unlike other Pentecostals around the country. They frequently validated their decisions by appeals to evident blessing. With the comment, "the glory came down," for example, they established to their own satisfaction that their actions at Hot Springs had met with divine approval. In Bell's opinion, "nothing was ever more manifestly approved of God."[32] He noted four occurrences in support of his conclusion: the unity of "the body of brethren appointed to consider" proposing the creation of the General

Council; the unanimous approval of the plan by the Council "as a whole"; the "glory of God [coming] down" as manifested by "praises, thanks and shouts as the sound of many waters unto God" and a "message in the Spirit" that had confirmed their action by the interpreted assurance, "I have guided in all this, and my approval rests upon it"; and the "blessing" of the Council "in the power of the Spirit" by the black Pentecostal Charles Mason, a man Bell considered "a real prophet of God."[33]

Throughout the spring and summer, ministers and missionaries identified with the General Council. Credentials were issued to all approved workers by Leonard in the East and Goss in the West. By the fall, the official list included 512 credentialed workers; 142 were women.[34]

One indication of the success on its own terms of the General Council was the way things proceeded as usual throughout the summer of 1914. Short-term Bible schools and the regular list of camp meetings, billed in the same way and featuring the same speakers as in other years, appeared in Pentecostal periodicals.[35] Officially, leaders of the General Council also identified themselves as they had earlier. In response to the question, "Who are we?" Bell stated, "We are simply New Testament Christians who have brushed aside the mental shams and hollowness of the age and in a measure gotten back to the realities of God's grace and power through the atoning blood of Christ."[36] But the two General Council papers, now published in Findlay, Ohio, noted that several of the camp meetings had specifically demonstrated loyalty to the purposes of the General Council. At the Oklahoma Annual Camp Meeting, for example, a district council was formed with W. T. Gaston as its first chairman. At a camp in the city park on the banks of the Grand River in Davis City, Iowa, another district council, which reached into northern Missouri, took shape. The Texas camp meeting also included the organizing of a district council, and in October Howard Goss reported that he had been chosen secretary of the newly formed Arkansas district. At the end of the year, plans to form a district council embracing Indiana, Ohio, and Michigan were announced for January 1915.[37]

Meanwhile, the two General Council editors, Bell and Flower, busily endeavored to convince the reluctant minority among their subscribers of the advisability of cooperation.[38] Flower noted the prevalence before the Hot Springs Council of rumors "that a man-made creed was about to be formed to be forced down the throats of all freedom-loving Pentecostal people; that a strong centralized church government contrary to the Word of God was about to be formed; that some man was to be elected head of the church. . . ."[39] Both men were convinced that events had demonstrated the needlessness of such concern.

The Need for a Second General Council

For several months, Bell and Flower, working out of their cramped quarters at Leonard's Gospel School, were the headquarters staff. They forwarded missionary funds, supervised the publishing work—and occasionally maintained the equipment—in addition to preaching and writing. Both served on the faculty of Leonard's school.[40] By the fall, the expanding list of affiliated workers provided heartening indication that the General Council had won considerable support among independent Pentecostals. However, growth mandated some urgent decisions.

The first General Council had vested the appointed Executive Presbytery with authority to convene the next General Council whenever necessary. Late in the summer the second Council was announced for November 15 to 29. The executives accepted an invitation from the Stone Church in Chicago. Its commodious facilities could easily accommodate the expected thousand participants.

At Bell's request, the second General Council appointed new leadership. Bell's close friend, Arch Collins, accepted a one-year appointment as chairman. D. C. O. Opperman shared the executive leadership as assistant chairman. Secretary J. R. Flower also had an assistant: his old friend and companion in evangelistic efforts, Bennett F. Lawrence. Both Bell and Collins viewed the chairmanship narrowly. Since no specific authority had been allotted them, they assumed none. While they fulfilled schedules crowded with travel and preaching appointments, each was so thoroughly congregational in political preference that he shunned any assumption of authority. The Council recognized "mature"—and presumably ordained or licensed—women in attendance as "advisory members." This honorary designation did not convey the right to participate in formal Council sessions.

In an effort to make its appointed executives more representative of the constituency, the Council increased the number of executive presbyters from twelve to sixteen. It defined the functions of the newly constituted group and promptly charged it with facilitating cooperation among the various centers affiliated with the General Council that supported foreign missions. The Council also authorized the raising of funds for the purchase of printing equipment to be "owned and controlled entirely by the General Council, and to be used solely for the glory of God." This decision demonstrated the strong conviction that "the very life of a movement depends upon the printed page."[41]

The second General Council further clarified decisions made in April. Its explicit purpose was "to lay a firm foundation upon which to build the Assemblies of God." At its conclusion, the executive presbyters decided unanimously to move the headquarters to St. Louis. Bell, Goss, and Collins served as a committee vested with securing suitable premises for the Fellowship. From Washington, D.C., they received a donation of used printing machinery that, together with various purchased equipment, became the nucleus of the Gospel Publishing House. In the spring of 1915, Bell and Flower began publishing from their new location. As a result of the move, the editors were able to expand the staff, and a home was secured where all could live.

At the end of 1914, Bell and Flower had reason to be pleased. Over the year, some ten thousand dollars of missionary giving had flowed through their hands—twice as much as in 1913. Taking nothing to cover their office expenses, they forwarded all funds to designated missionaries, regardless of their formal affiliation with the General Council. Prospects for the General Council seemed bright. The troubled world situation as yet affected them little. They assumed simply that World War I meant that Christ's coming was near. Yet severe problems were on the horizon. At the end of October, *The Christian Evangel* had published "A Letter to the Pentecostal Movement from a Friend" who cautioned the fragile but optimistic Fellowship: "You have nothing to fear from the outside forces that are arrayed against you," the author wrote, "but everything to fear from dissensions arising from within."[42]

In the next few years, internal "dissensions" would wrack the Assemblies of God. Three issues posed particular problems; each predated the formation of the General Council. The first had been largely resolved by 1914, but continued to require clarification. It focused on the nature of sanctification and the practical meaning of holiness. The second proved the most divisive. It questioned the baptismal formula, the doctrine of the Trinity, and the understanding of the process of salvation. This "Oneness" controversy also probed the relationship between "revelation" and doctrine. Through the third issue, though it was less divisive, the Assemblies of God was forced to face the undercurrent of questioning that had long been evident about tongues as "uniform initial evidence" of the baptism in the Holy Spirit. These various crises both contributed to the organizational processes already at work in the General Council and demonstrated how tenuous its unity really was.

Hot Springs Opera House, site of the first General Council, which met on the second floor

SITE OF FOUNDING CONVENTION
ASSEMBLIES OF GOD
APRIL 2-12, 1914

MORE THAN 300 PERSONS MET IN THE GRAND OPERA HOUSE, 200 CENTRAL AVENUE, AND FORMED THE GENERAL COUNCIL OF THE ASSEMBLIES OF GOD. E. N. BELL, FIRST CHAIRMAN.

THIS MARKER PRESENTED BY THE ASSEMBLIES OF GOD, SPRINGFIELD, MISSOURI, ON ITS 60TH ANNIVERSARY. THOMAS F. ZIMMERMAN, GENERAL SUPERINTENDENT.

PLACED IN COOPERATION WITH THE
GARLAND COUNTY AND ARKANSAS STATE HISTORICAL SOCIETIES.

The plaque commemorating the founding of the denomination, laid December 6, 1973, in a special ceremony

First Executive Presbytery of the Assemblies of God,
April 1914. Front: T. K. Leonard, E. N. Bell, Cyrus B.
Fockler. Back: John W. Welch, J. Roswell Flower, D.
C. O. Opperman, Howard A. Goss, M. M. Pinson.

Gospel Publishing House staff at the second headquarters
facility, St. Louis, Missouri (ca. 1916). J. Roswell Flower is
in the back, center. (The black man on the right was a frequent headquarters visitor).

10. Defining Doctrine, 1914–1918

> We come together that we may seek a better understanding of what God would have us teach, that we may do away with so many divisions.
>
> *Word and Witness,* December 20, 1913

Between 1914 and 1918, much of the Western world was preoccupied with the horrors of World War I. Assemblies of God adherents had little difficulty comprehending the general situation; their eschatology provided a frame of reference that gave current events a prominent place on a prophetic calendar. Not so easily resolved, however, were the dilemmas that emerged in their own ranks—dilemmas that played a vital role in shaping the permanent character of the Assemblies of God.

Sanctification

Since the first General Council adopted no statement of faith, it embraced people whose opinions on many issues varied. Although some matters, like abstinence from pork or the washing of the saints' feet, could easily be left to individual preference, other questions seemed to demand clarification. For some problems, cautions issued through the official publications sufficed. During the summer of 1914, for example, *Word and Witness* roundly denounced as unacceptable the prophecies and messages circulated in a series of pamphlets called Yellow Books (one of which, for example, was entitled *In School with the Holy Ghost*). An issue that defied such straightforward handling was sanctification. Early disagreements over that doctrine continued to be raised within the General Council framework for several years.

The call for the original General Council had been given by men who acknowledged the influence of William Durham. Although most of them had earlier maintained the necessity of a "second definite work of grace," each had concluded by 1910 that Durham's rejection of holiness teaching on the subject was biblical. Permeation of the loosely organized, white Churches of God in Christ by Durham's views ultimately proved significant for the General Council.

Equally important in determining the unwritten consensus was the fact that the Assemblies of God attracted to its ranks people from other backgrounds to whom Durham's views proved congenial. Many Pentecostals from Chicago, those from Zion City, and former members of the Christian and Missionary Alliance accepted Christ's "finished work at Calvary" and understood sanctification to be progressive. Bell recognized, however, that Durham represented a potentially troublesome precedent; *Word and Witness* ran an article that carried this observation: "Not a few have tried to imitate William Durham by claiming to have something new for the people; but alas, unless God is behind the message, it is nothing. . . ."[1]

Because the earliest Apostolic Faith adherents had insisted that a discrete work of sanctification precede Spirit baptism, however, the independent Pentecostal congregations that constituted the Assemblies of God in 1914 included many who felt strongly about the need for a "second blessing." The Assemblies of God also embraced some congregations and associations with holiness sympathies.[2] W. Jethro Walthall, for example, brought his holiness Baptist association into relationship with the General Council.[3] The increasing number of ministers who objected on scriptural grounds to holiness views often found it necessary to reaffirm their commitment to the *reality* of the sanctification process as well as to a life of holiness. "It has been told around and published by some that the man that does not teach the Second Work of Grace is a compromiser," M. M. Pinson complained. "Some have gone so far as to say we have quit preaching on holiness. Bless God! The standard God Almighty holds out to you and me is HOLINESS. Glory!"[4] Concluding that holiness was "the lowest standard God has called a person to," Pinson called the new fellowship to ignore differences about the process of being made holy and to unite in their purpose to be holy.

Those who did not recognize any discipline in Durham's teaching on "reckoning one's self dead to sin and alive to God"— which others maintained was inherent—believed that he had granted Christians license to live as they pleased. The strong stand of Pentecostals who continued to maintain the second blessing did not help matters. They warned of the "danger" of spiritual power being "channeled" through "unsanctified vessels." "People who have the Holy Ghost in an unsanctified vessel," warned Charles Parham, "find that their flesh becomes the medium through which fanaticism and wild-fire work."[5] Shortly after Durham's death in the summer of 1912, Parham published a supplement to his monthly *Apostolic Faith* where he recounted his earlier prayers that either he or Durham (whoever was wrong) would die. "How signally God has answered," he declared.

The bitter controversy was duly noted by some outsiders. It figured, for example, in Harry Ironside's published comments rejecting Pentecostal pretensions.[6] For despite repeated affirmations of Christian unity, Pentecostals bickered constantly among themselves.

Both sides within Pentecostal ranks agreed about the "dangers" of an absence of holiness, and Bell and Flower were among many who used their influence as editors to probe the issue and clarify what they believed the Bible taught. It quickly became evident that they objected more to the extremes that had been claimed for the experience by holiness advocates than to the essence of the experience itself. Both parties, they concluded, upheld the necessity of holiness (i.e., separation from sin and separation to God) in heart and life.

In December 1913, Bell's *Word and Witness* carried an article, entitled "The Second Blessing," through which Bell sought to show the differences in holiness thought about the second blessing. Excerpted largely from writings of the respected editor of

The Way of Faith, J. M. Pike, the article documented extremes that Pike claimed would never have been endorsed by John Wesley. Pike further argued that if Wesley "had foreseen what strained meanings would be forced into his words, he would have been more cautious in the use of the term" second blessing.[7] Pike acknowledged that the term was "not used in Scripture," that the subject "as taught by many . . . leading preachers and writers in the holiness movement . . . [served] to arrest spiritual development," that being "filled with the Spirit" was different from cleansing, and that after crisis sanctification itself, " 'the half has never been told.' " Pike concluded by saying to those who professed the second blessing, "Thy present possession is but the earnest. . . . There are rich effusions of the Spirit yet to be received. . . ."[8]

With such sentiments, Bell admitted, he could not find much fault. On the other hand, the doctrine as it was popularly taught seemed to him to demand response. Bell felt that holiness proponents pressured people to realize the experience by insisting that "a man born of the Spirit . . . still has enough of sin in him not only to damn him, but as some put it, [to] 'damn the whole world.' " This, Bell believed, "nullifie[d] the work of regeneration." Bell also cautioned against assuming that "there is nothing *beyond* . . . or *superior to*" what some claimed as their experience of holiness. Citing the New Testament challenge to " 'press on toward the goal unto the prize of the *high calling* of God in Christ Jesus' " (Philippians 3:14), he remarked: "How this puts to shame those who cannot forget their past blessings, who are always harping on their second blessing as the time when they got it all."[9] Noting that Pentecostals tended to regard tongues with a similar finality, he observed: "I honestly believe every child of God ought, from the first moment of faith, to see Christ is made unto him sanctification, to be at once baptized in water, then be filled with the Spirit and be talking in tongues in less than three days from the time he received Christ as a Savior. If the world of professing Christians were *normal* Bible Christians, truly tongues would have come in their babyhood in Christ."[10]

Efforts to find the middle of the road for sanctification were accompanied by a similar concern to refrain from extremes in matters of dress. Although the early leaders of the Assemblies of God (with most American evangelicals) were in favor of a life-style that separated the believer in conspicuous ways from secular amusements and fashions, they deplored the tendency of some to equate "plain dress," and even "poor dress," with holiness. For example, Bell opposed the wearing of jewelry "solely for worldly adornment," but concluded, "The poor-dress gospel has been thoroughly preached before our day, and has never saved anybody yet. You may dress poorly . . . and still go to hell."[11]

When taken together with rejection of holiness language, this failure to espouse uniformly the holiness dress code convinced some that those who formed the Assemblies of God were soft on holiness. However, the early periodicals are full of references to sanctification and holiness, and the oft-repeated assertion that Assemblies of God leaders (in spite of their espousal of Durham) were "believers in holiness" seems well documented in the early literature.[12] When in 1916 the assembled ministers approved a statement on sanctification, the wording was acceptable to those of both persuasions. Rejecting much popular terminology in favor of "Bible language," the statement declared that "entire sanctification" was "the goal for all believers."[13] From its origin, then, the Assemblies of God has embraced those who have expressed their participation in the quest for holiness in different ways. Even so, with the passing of time, the Fellowship's consensus came increasingly to be phrased in language borrowed from William Durham.

The Trinity

A far more divisive issue was already agitating in Pentecostal ranks as the General Council took shape in 1914. From the West Coast, teaching that soon would challenge the existence of the Assemblies of God had been introduced at a large camp meeting. Beginning with a focus on the baptismal formula, the issue had grown by 1915 to include a rethinking of the doctrine of the Trinity and revisions of several common

practices. Many factors helped make early Pentecostalism conducive to the new "Oneness" views; the specific setting in which
the ideas arose helps clarify some of them.

The World-Wide Apostolic Faith Camp Meeting that began
on April 15, 1913, was, by any account, an impressive gathering.
Meeting in Arroyo Seco, near Pasadena, California, the gathering featured the ministry of the well-known evangelist Maria
Woodworth-Etter. The advertisements of the camp claimed divine inspiration even in the planning stages. Wherever the
camp had been announced, "the Holy Ghost [had] witnessed to
it."[14] R. J. Scott, a businessman from Los Angeles, had visited
Etter's recent Dallas meetings where widely-publicized conversions, Spirit baptisms, and healings occurred daily. Impressed, he decided to invite her to Los Angeles—and found
that she "had already heard from heaven that God was going
to gather His saints together in one place and deal with them,
giving a unity and power that we have not yet known."[15]

Crowds thronged the meetings from the start. M. M. Pinson
estimated that about a thousand camped on the grounds, while
others rented nearby rooms. Prolonged, intense meetings ran
constantly; on occasion numerous people preached simultaneously in different parts of the camp. Participants estimated
that weeknight attendance was between fifteen hundred and
two thousand, with larger crowds on Sundays. Some one hundred
ministers banded together to assist Etter, who had the primary
responsibility for the plenary services.[16] Scott and his friend
George Studd (who over the years was associated with various
missions in the Los Angeles area) sought to "keep the meetings
on the Apostolic lines, according to the book of Acts."[17]

The conveners of the camp meeting prepared an inexpensive
paperback hymnal for use in the services. Ironically, the song
they chose for the first page illustrated the importance of Jesus
as "ALL" among Pentecostals. It was immensely popular among
early Pentecostals: Charles Price Jones's *(Jesus Christ Is Made
to Me) All I Need*. Little did the organizers anticipate that the
meeting would birth a movement that focused unacceptably on
Jones's theme—Jesus only.

Woodworth-Etter estimated that she laid hands on at least

two thousand people in prayer and recounted that "mighty signs and miracles" showed "His approval of the word."[18] Pinson concurred: "The Devil is raging, saints are shouting, and God is working," he exulted.[19] Visions and revelations seemed almost commonplace. One, however, apparently went largely unnoticed by the featured speaker and the crowds. One John Schaeppe, inspired by the miracles Woodworth-Etter performed "in the name of Jesus," spent a night in prayer. Toward morning, he received "a revelation of the POWER of the NAME of Jesus."[20]

This "revelation" was subsequently considered one factor in the emergence of a new teaching among some California-based Pentecostals influenced by Frank Ewart, an Australian Baptist preacher who came to Los Angeles via Canada. Ewart had served William Durham's Los Angeles mission as pastor until the spring of 1913. Claiming that he then attended the camp meeting convinced that a "new move of God" was imminent, he wrote an account of the meetings—which differed in significant details from the reports published in Pentecostal papers.[21]

According to Ewart, the camp meeting's promoter, R. J. Scott (who held no pastorate but rather sponsored gatherings like the camp meeting), organized a baptismal service nearby and selected R. E. McAlister to preach on water baptism. McAlister, a Canadian, discussed different baptismal formulas and remarked that the Early Church had baptized in Jesus' name. Ewart reported that McAlister's observation that "the words Father, Son, and Holy Ghost were never used by the early church in Christian baptism" were received with "an inaudible shudder."[22] Although McAlister continued his sermon, maintaining that baptism according to Matthew 28:19 was certainly valid, he had fired at least one imagination—Ewart's—and in so doing, to use Ewart's later extravagant borrowing, "the shot had been fired, and its sound was destined to be heard around the world."[23]

Ewart claimed that it was McAlister who convinced him that the three titles Lord, Jesus, and Christ were "counterparts to Father, Son, and Holy Ghost." He became convinced that Jesus was, in fact, "the Name" (singular) of the Father, Son, and Holy Ghost. The exact chronology of Ewart's comprehension of this "New Thing"(see Isaiah 43:19) is unclear; what is certain, however, is that Ewart's fertile mind devised numerous practical implications for his convictions. His persuasive abilities assured both the survival of the sense that something new had in fact occurred and the systematizing of vague and incoherent allusions.

Ewart later claimed that by 1913 he had "for some time" questioned traditional views of God. Convinced that the "new thing" that had begun at the camp meeting demanded breaking former ties to launch new forms of ministry, he severed his relationship to the Seventh Street Mission and opened a new assembly where R. E. McAlister and Glenn Cook (who had once worked with Seymour) assisted him. Another move brought him into association with Warren Fisher at the well-established mission known as Victoria Hall. When McAlister moved on, Garfield Thomas Haywood replaced him as evangelist. A black preacher having a mission in Indianapolis, Haywood was widely respected among white Pentecostals.

Ewart was restive, however. He felt the more traditional attitudes of his associates, especially Fisher, restricted him from proclaiming his developing views about the Godhead. He finally broke his ties to Victoria Hall and, with the initial assistance of its pastor (who disagreed with his views but wanted to avoid controversy), began tent meetings in the northern California town of Belvedere. In a statement consistent with early Pentecostal claims, he felt that "to receive apostolic results on a full time basis," he would "have to preach the apostolic message on a full time basis."[24] To this he dedicated his new efforts. Glenn Cook, recently returned from an eastern trip, wholeheartedly assisted him. The two purchased a baptismal tank and baptized each other "in Jesus' Name." "Soon," Ewart reported, "the candidates for baptism in the Name of Jesus started to flock to the tent."[25] Apparently the noisy, crowded meetings became something of a local sensation. To Ewart, however, they were a "test" of the validity of his message, and events seemed to attest its truth: "The vast majority" of the rebaptized left "the tank speaking in other tongues."[26] Thus assured of God's approval, Ewart began publishing his views in a paper he called *Meat in Due Season*. Glenn Cook, ever restless, left to proclaim this fuller restoration of the apostolic faith elsewhere. In the course of his travels he came to Indianapolis, where he won G. T. Haywood (who had since resumed his mission work) to the cause.

As the teaching proliferated, it became apparent that several issues were at stake. The most obvious centered in the baptismal formula and the significance of baptism. Using Acts 2:38 as their proof text, Ewart and his followers maintained that believers should be baptized in the name of Jesus. They encouraged those who had been baptized using other formulas to be rebaptized in the "New Testament manner." Gradually they came to posit a three-stage conversion experience. Since Acts 2:38 stated, "Repent, and be baptized . . . for the remission of sins, and ye shall receive the gift of the Holy Ghost," they maintained that repentance, baptism in Jesus' name, and Spirit baptism were three elements of one experience. They further came to reject orthodox language about the Trinity, identifying the Jehovah of the Old Testament as the Christ of the New Testament.

The list of Pentecostals who accepted these views over the next several years is impressive. The movement had been consolidating as the General Council was forming, and by 1915 it had begun to make strong inroads among those identified with the Assemblies of God. Howard Goss, D. C. O. Opperman, L. C. Hall, and H. G. Rodgers embraced the new teaching, along with hundreds of lesser-known figures. Even E. N. Bell, the General Council's first chairman and editor of its official publication, was persuaded to accept rebaptism and to reconsider biblical teaching on the Godhead. Bell had hoped in the summer of 1914 that Frank Ewart and R. E. McAlister would join the General Council. But by the next year, Ewart had become the principle source of a movement that ultimately jeopardized the General Council's existence.

Pentecostals have always been prone to take "new truth" seriously. Even as Oneness teaching surfaced, General Council publications found it advisable to warn regularly against other new teachings. Especially in independent Pentecostal missions and in General Council affiliated assemblies where Durham's new teaching had a firm following, precedent existed for the embracing of truth issuing from revelations. Oneness advocates raised some serious questions that few within the General Council recognized as clearly as did Bell's editorial assistant, J. R. Flower.

First—and most superficially—Oneness people agitated about the baptismal formula. This was part of a much broader issue, however: It was couched in terms that appealed to New Testament precedent. For Pentecostals who as a movement held tenaciously to the restorationist insistence of perpetuating New Testament practices, this proved a vital issue. The matter of rebaptism did not in itself necessarily pose a serious problem. Many recognized Pentecostal leaders rather quickly rejected the idea that their entire constituency needed rebaptism. Pentecostals typically rebaptized those who concluded that their original baptism had not followed a true conversion experience. But the fact that some Pentecostals also had acceded to the desire to be rebaptized by someone who shared their particular religious insights did set a precedent within the movement that encouraged multiple baptisms. Thus some sought rebaptism by one who had spoken in tongues. Various formulas, and even different modes of baptism, had been used among Pentecostals for years. The rigid insistence on a single formula, and giving baptism significance in the regeneration process itself, hinted at more serious departures from orthodoxy, which few Pentecostals were sufficiently astute to immediately discern.

Ewart recalled a sermon at the World-Wide Apostolic Faith Camp Meeting in 1913 calling attention to the idea that God wanted to do a new thing. Probably most Pentecostals shared his anticipation of "new truth" and a more powerful "apostolic" revival. Messages in tongues and interpretation sometimes purported to reveal new insights; periodicals occasionally published "revelations" and prophecies. In this expectant, unsophisticated, fervent religious subculture, where "fresh anointings" mattered greatly to most ministers, many responded to

Ewart out of a sincere desire to conform to the biblical pattern. This occasionally assumed arrogant overtones: Those who failed to embrace a new truth might well be told that their "carnality" or their "pride" prevented their understanding spiritual things— or worse, threatened their "missing God."[27]

The way that this restorationist longing combined with an uncompromising exaltation of Christ strengthened its appeal. Pentecostals thrilled to miracles done "in the name of Jesus." In their ranks, Maria Woodworth-Etter most conspicuously asserted "the power of that name," and besides being only one of many who did so, she had many imitators. Precisely because Ewart's new teaching exalted Christ, it gained a strong foothold among Pentecostals. And in the practical application of the doctrine, little conspicuous difference existed. All Pentecostals believed that the Holy Spirit exalted Christ. Their movement had a strong Christocentric heritage. Their shared attitude toward Christ is evident in the Oneness songs that gained currency in the movement at large: G. T. Haywood's *Jesus, the Son of God,* and *Down From His Glory.* No Pentecostals quarreled with the message of Haywood's chorus:

> Preach in Jesus' Name,
> Teach in Jesus' Name
> Heal the sick in His Name;
> And always proclaim, it was Jesus' Name
> In which the power came;
> Baptize in His Name, enduring the shame,
> For there is victory in Jesus' Name.[28]

David Reed has suggested a relationship between the tendency of Victorian Protestants to sentimentalize Christ and the appeal of Oneness Pentecostalism. Pentecostals were not the only evangelicals whose gospel music focused on intense personal experiences and a lover-like relationship between the believer and Christ. Beverly Carradine, a leading preacher in the holiness movement, bemoaned the evangelical tendency to sing songs appealing to "natural affections" instead of those that stressed the "Being and attributes of God."[29] According to him, "Few of the popular gospel meeting hymn books are marked with any broadness as to the great subjects and doctrines of the Bible."[30] This popular Protestant proclivity to stress a sentimentalized Christ and a related failure to emphasize the Godhead was apparent in Pentecostal ranks and undoubtedly contributed to the acceptance of Oneness teaching.[31]

But probably most important of all was the undeniable fact that the teaching seemed to work. It was marked, supporters claimed, by "God's approval." People were healed, people spoke in tongues, people claimed spiritual renewal, as they embraced this new truth and were rebaptized. Blessing, they asserted, depended on their obedience to the Spirit. Rebaptism was presented as an act of obedience that preceded greater blessing. Pentecostals often measured God's approval by demonstrations of spiritual fervor. Whatever made people shout, dance, or prophesy, especially if it was confirmed by tongues and interpretation, could gain currency somewhere in Pentecostal ranks. And Oneness teaching did. Some years later, when several of American Pentecostalism's early leaders expressed disappointment about the Pentecostal movement's general course, they considered the Oneness segment with favor. In spite of their own rejection of the central Oneness doctrine, they found among Oneness people "more genuine spirituality" than in any other segment of Pentecostalism: "The mere fact of their emphasis of Jesus that the other divisions of the movement regard as extreme has tended to bless them in that it has brought them into close touch with the Lord's life and Spirit."[32]

J. R. Flower recognized both the sincerity of those who embraced Ewart's views and the dangerous precedents the spread of the teaching set. A young man deeply committed to the dual concepts of mutual cooperation and individual liberty that the General Council incorporated, Flower understood both the appeal of revelations and the desire for New Testament experience. He concluded that both needed to be balanced by a consideration of the place of Scripture in the movement's self-perception. As one after another accepted rebaptism and maintained that others should follow suit, Oneness teaching threatened the fragile unity that the General Council had fostered.

Men and women of highly varied backgrounds had united in the General Council; all professed loyalty to Scripture. But many had not thought through the relationship between revelations and the Bible. Bell's comment, for example, encouraging his readers to "keep their sky-lights open" in case God wanted "to shed some new light on the old Word" suggests an openness to precisely the kind of teaching that surfaced. The tone of the comment also suggests that the homage paid Scripture—not being uniformly based on a deep conviction of the finality of its teaching—at times became only lip service. Or, put another way, Pentecostals were facing anew the perennial Protestant dilemma over the diverse interpretations of Scripture attributed to the Holy Spirit. Howard Goss acknowledged the pressure among Pentecostal preachers to present "new light" and "fresh insights." While responsible Pentecostals maintained that "new teaching" had to demonstrate continuity with Scripture, they often seemed torn between two sources of authority: the objective Word and the subjective Spirit. Otherwise, they forced Scripture to accommodate their revelations. Flower believed that the two should harmonize. In the end, however, some Pentecostals opted (though most would not admit it) for the Spirit as the final source of authority. Howard Goss (who became a prominent Oneness leader) reportedly admitted: "You'll never get this by studying it out like some other doctrine. This comes by 'revelation.' "[33]

On precisely these grounds, Flower finally determined to assert what influence he could to assure loyalty to orthodoxy. He recognized the rejection of Trinitarian views as a resurfacing of an ancient Christian aberration, and he deplored the disunity fostered by those who made an issue of the baptismal formula. By January 1915, just as the headquarters staff prepared to move to St. Louis, the issue was brought to a head as the teaching reached St. Louis and points east.

At first Flower hesitated. Not until July 1915 did he begin to address the issue directly, although *Word and Witness* began carrying relevant articles in March. But Pentecostals could readily identify with his explanation for delay: He had "desired to hear from God definitely," he wrote, before taking a public stand.[34] Although this reasoning would seem to identify him closely with the methodology Oneness advocates used, several other factors must be taken into consideration. Flower was much younger than Bell and several others on the Presbytery. Deeply committed to both the concept of unity and the liberty of individual believers to act according to their own consciences, he recognized how critical a premature assessment of the situation might be. Early misgivings about the intentions of the General Council had not been entirely allayed. Direct references to him and Bell as well as to their publications by the Los Angeles-based spokesmen for the "New Issue" had not occasioned response, but the arrival from the West Coast of one of the leaders prodded Flower to action. The man preached about the "water test" in a St. Louis mission and then rebaptized six Pentecostals in the Mississippi River. As other evangelists traveled widely, reports of the disruption of local assemblies arrived at Flower's office. He decided at last that it would be "criminal to remain silent."[35] But he also drew courage from the conviction that "the crest of the wave" had passed. In language uncomfortably close to that of Ewart's party, Flower asserted that God had begun to do a "new thing" to bring about deeper unity.[36]

Such optimism proved premature, however. Throughout the summer of 1915, both *Word and Witness* and the *Weekly Evangel* (Flower's *Christian Evangel* had undergone a name change) carried articles on issues raised by Ewart's group. Both Bell and Flower carefully denied speaking for the Council; they sought merely to advise by presenting scriptural views. The first sign of more general concern became evident in a Presbytery meeting in St. Louis on May 11. Disavowing any intention to legislate, the presbyters issued a statement in both *Word and Witness* and the *Weekly Evangel*. As editor (as well as presbyter), Bell added something of a background report on the meeting, saying that the Presbytery was urging the constituency to "work these problems out on their knees before God and with the Bible in their hands."[37] "[I]t was a profound mis-

take," in their opinion, "to make an issue out of modern revelations and humanly coined phrases which could not be clearly
and explicitly justified by the unmistakable utterances of the
written Word of God."[38] Most of the teaching circulated under
the general designation "New Issue" was not new at all, they
asserted. Pentecostals were simply historically naive and mis-
took "rehatched" teaching for "new revelations."[39]

The official Presbytery statement listed several erroneous
views that generally accompanied teaching on rebaptism. The
presbyters rejected specifically references to Christ's "spiritual
blood" and assertions that "Christ is the Holy Ghost" or that
baptism in Jesus' name was "true Christian circumcision." They
discouraged the use of wine in the Communion service, a practice Oneness followers taught as conforming more closely to
the New Testament. They also denounced the view that Jesus
was the name of the Father, Son, and Spirit and that this was
a truth revealed at Pentecost. And they emphatically denied
that baptism according to Matthew 28:19 was not Christian.[40]
But they carefully disclaimed authority; they sought merely
to advise.

Very early in July, "leaving the conduction of the office in
the hands of Bro. J. R. Flower and other worthy helpers," Bell
left St. Louis "for the summer's campaign." The July 31 issue
of the *Weekly Evangel* carried the "Editor's Field Report." In
it Bell covered the progress of his itinerary. At the time, he
was at a camp in Jackson, Tennessee. Afterwards, word began
to circulate—by mouth as well in print (particularly Oneness
papers)—that he had accepted the Oneness position on baptism.
Indeed, he had been rebaptized by L. V. Roberts during the
large (attendance reached some four thousand) Interstate Camp
Meeting in Jackson. (Another presbyter, H. G. Rodgers, was
also rebaptized at the camp.[41])

Then, late in the summer, the *Weekly Evangel* confirmed
the matter with an announcement over its feature article by
Bell: "Editor E. N. Bell tells why he was baptized in the name
of Jesus Christ. . . ."[42] In Bell's article, which continued to denounce the errors earlier condemned by the Presbyters, he explained having "settled a long doubt" about baptism. Convinced

that God would "refuse the anointing" until he obeyed, he had decided to accept rebaptism according to the New Testament formula singled out by Oneness advocates. Reiterating his conviction that one should not "make a hobby out of a phase of water baptism," Bell nonetheless offered the preeminent Pentecostal reason for his action: Spiritual renewal, he claimed, had followed his obedience. Later he would acknowledge that he had also been haunted by the sense that his "baptism by the Baptists was unsatisfactory," that he should be baptized by someone who had received Spirit baptism.[43]

The same issue of the *Weekly Evangel* also carried a statement issued by the seven presbyters (of the sixteen) who had attended the Arkansas state camp meeting in Little Rock. Bell, Collins, Goss, Pinson, Welch, Rodgers, and Opperman all concurred that rebaptism should generally be discouraged and urged that adherents extend to others the "liberty to be . . . baptized with any words" they preferred.[44] During the same period, Flower had been carrying a series of articles addressing pertinent issues.[45] He had also revised an article that Bell had sent into the office for publication. The article ("Who Is Jesus Christ?") demonstrated that Bell had been intrigued by some of Ewart's views on the Godhead. Flower found most of the article suitable for publication, carrying it in both the *Weekly Evangel* (August 14, 1915) and *Word and Witness* (September 1915). But among other things, in the subtitle "Jesus Christ Being Rediscovered as the Jehovah of the Old Testament and the True God of the New: A New Realization of Christ as the Mighty God," he replaced "rediscovered" with "exalted" before printing it (in what Oneness people would call a "mutilated" form[46]). As office editor, Flower had decided that the situation was sufficiently critical to warrant his interference with Bell's responsibilities as editor in chief. The Fellowship would later applaud his action.

In the midst of the growing confusion, the executives exercised their prerogative to convene a General Council. In session on November 23, 1914, the Presbytery had requested Bell, Flower, and Goss to schedule the next General Council, with the understanding that they should attempt to convene in St.

Louis. In September 1915, both official papers published a call to the third General Council, scheduled for Turner Hall in St. Louis, October 1–10.

In a gesture that expressed the unity the Council professed as a goal, the several Pentecostal missions in St. Louis all closed for the duration of the Council to participate in its meetings. As in 1914, the gathering opened with three days of prayer and worship. On Monday, October 4, the delegates organized for business. The official roster listed 525 names: 54 were missionaries, 13 Canadians. The 76 women (in November 1914, there had been 142) had been specifically invited as advisory members: The call had solicited both their attendance and their advice.[47]

In spite of (or perhaps because of) the unsettled situation, Chairman A. P. Collins was absent when the Council convened for business. John Welch was selected to substitute for him, later accepting election as permanent chairman. Bell (who had considered resigning as editor as early as May 1915 to engage in evangelistic work) terminated his editorial responsibilities, which were also assigned to Welch.[48] When Collins finally arrived, he, Haywood, Jacob Miller, and Bell were requested to lead a general discussion on the biblical mode and formula for water baptism. Limited to thirty minutes each, the men voiced their convictions. The Council allotted the remainder of the day to "free and full discussion" of the proper water baptismal formula. (The next day Assistant Chairman William G. Schell, who had withdrawn as a leader of the general discussion "because of restrictions," would gain permission to speak for two hours on the baptismal practices used by the Apostolic Fathers.)

The thorough airing of the issue resulted in a lengthy statement. With the intention of applying "the spirit and liberality of the Hot Springs Constitution" and expressing "the attitude of this Council," they adopted it, the essence of which follows:

1. Slight variations in the formula of baptism did not affect the validity of baptism.

2. Ministers should not urge "general re-baptizing"; re-

baptism should be administered only if an individual considered prior baptism "not Christian baptism."

3. No "New Testament law" mandated the use of a certain formula.

4. Itinerant preachers should not interfere with "the proper Scriptural authorities" recognized in local congregations.

5. No "line of Christian fellowship or of ministerial fellowship" should be drawn by differences on the matter of a baptismal formula.[49]

The Council also disapproved the teachings that Flower and Bell had been repudiating in both the *Word and Witness* and the *Weekly Evangel* throughout the summer: the use of fermented wine for Communion, "confusing" the new birth with Spirit baptism, equating "the blood" with the Holy Spirit, failing to distinguish among the persons of the Trinity, using the title Christ to mean Holy Ghost. General Council participants hoped that the above guidelines would suffice. Flower reported, however, that they recognized that further action would probably be required: "It was the general conviction that we should wait patiently for another year before arriving at a definite conclusion, allowing time for prayerful study of the Word of God."[50]

Unrelated matters filled the remainder of the agenda. When the Council adjourned on Saturday, October 9, it had modified the membership of the Executive Presbytery; it resolved to make the publishing business self-supporting; and it began to implement a missions outreach by devising guidelines on the qualifications for missionaries and their support and furloughs.

The hopes generated by the amicable General Council quickly faded, however. While Flower reported "great victory" and sought to fulfill the spirit of the Council by omitting the controversy from the *Weekly Evangel,* Oneness proponents became more aggressive. They not only threatened those who rejected their message with "missing God" and with ruin, they also continued to present their revelation as "truth." According to Carl Brumback, this violated an understanding meant to safeguard the General Council: Adherents had agreed that "new revelations" would not be promulgated until a consensus had been reached in counsel with "the brethren." This was predicated on "a mutual confidence in each other's judgment."[51] When that confidence had been shattered, the existence of the General Council was threatened.

That that confidence was shattered irreparably became increasingly apparent. Oneness people tended to regard themselves as more spiritual than those who failed to embrace their teaching. The fledgling Assemblies of God was being forced to face the fundamental issue of the relationship between revelation and Scripture. Officially, all affirmed Scripture. But events continued to demonstrate the proclivity of many Pentecostals to find in "spiritual revelations" a more congenial source of authority. Gradually Trinitarians concurred that the situation demanded final resolution. That resolution proved painful, however, and it permanently influenced the direction of the General Council.

When the (fourth) General Council convened again in St. Louis, in a small church known as Bethel Chapel, none had as yet withdrawn from the General Council because of the New Issue. Though its chief advocates—Ewart, Cook, and Haywood—had close ties to many within the Council (Haywood had even addressed the third Council), they had never assented formally to its objectives.[52] Yet Ewart, his friend Harry VanLoon, and Haywood were but three of several non-affiliated Oneness supporters who participated in the 1916 Council. "There was much expectancy as the Council convened," Flower reported.[53]

In spite of the disagreements of past months, the opening service on Sunday, October 1, was marked by typical Pentecostal exuberance. After a sermon by D. W. Kerr on the abiding merits of Christ's death, delegates took Communion and, the official record noted, "the fire of God fell upon them and their hearts burst out in praise and adoration, singing in the Spirit, weeping and laughing and praising God."[54] During three services on Sunday, unity seemed to prevail.

When business began on Monday with Chairman Welch presiding, the Council appointed a committee on resolutions to prepare matters for general consideration. The committee, consisting of Bell (whose enthusiasm for favorite Oneness texts had proved to be temporary), Kerr, Leonard, S. A. Jamieson, and Stanley Frodsham, prepared numerous resolutions. Most important, however, it drew up a Statement of Fundamental Truths.[55] Some immediately challenged the right of the General Council to devise such a statement. Charging constitutional violation on the grounds that the Preamble adopted in 1914 had stated that "the holy inspired Scriptures are the all-sufficient rule for faith and doctrine," Oneness advocates in particular accused the committee of proposing a creed. Others, though they rejected Oneness views, agreed that the Council should not adopt doctrinal guidelines.

The Statement of Fundamental Truths was primarily the work of Daniel W. Kerr. A talented though reserved man, Kerr was also a mature pastor with a long record of successful ministry in the Christian and Missionary Alliance as well as in Pentecostal contexts. For several months prior to the Council, Kerr had studied intensely and taken voluminous notes on the doctrines in question. This unofficial preparation for the task the Council assigned enabled him to assist the committee in preparing a statement that addressed the controversial issues. The ten subheadings in the category "The Essentials of the Godhead" bear eloquent witness to the Statement's primary purpose. Clearly admitting that it "cover[ed] only . . . present needs as to these fundamental matters," the document did not purport to be either a creed or a "basis of fellowship among Christians": it was rather "a basis of unity for the ministry alone."[56]

The Council considered each of the seventeen statements separately and on Saturday, October 7, approved the document. It also adopted a separate resolution recommending that cooperating ministers use the words of Matthew 28:19 in their baptismal formula. These actions forced the withdrawal of Oneness people from the General Council. More than twenty-five percent of the Council ministers ultimately left. The percentage was much higher in the South, where the teaching had gained rapid acceptance among Parham's earlier colleagues. Several who could not support the Statement of Fundamental Truths had served as executive presbyters; others had helped form the General Council in Hot Springs: Howard Goss, L. C. Hall, D. C. O. Opperman, H. G. Rodgers (who later returned), and Gilbert Sweaza, for example. Separation not only broke cherished personal ties, it also adversely affected missionary giving, which plummeted to $4,879.50.[57] The Fellowship found it advisable to regroup. A standing credentials committee consisting of the chairman and the secretary of the Executive Presbytery were instructed to prepare new credentials that included the "fundamental principles" and to recall all old certificates. In another precedent-setting move, the same resolution requested regular fees for credentials renewals.

As a result of the 1916 General Council, an ongoing transition in leadership was furthered. In general, men with backgrounds in the Christian and Missionary Alliance gained more influence in the leadership of the Assemblies of God. After the Council completed yet another reorganization of the Executive Presbytery (this time creating a separate General Presbytery), three of the five executive presbyters (Chairman Welch, Flower, and Kerr) had found their way into Pentecostal ranks through the Alliance.[58] Former Church of God in Christ leaders, on the other hand, had either left the Fellowship over the New Issue or had vacated leadership positions. The change in leadership can also be viewed from a demographic perspective. A higher percentage of northern and eastern men now served the Fellowship. Some who left had made enduring contributions, but in this separation the Assemblies of God also began to distance itself from those Pentecostals, like Ewart, Cook, or Frank Bartleman, who were essentially restless, unstable, and visionary, always pursuing more revelations.

In general, those who left permanently (many individuals returned in the next few years) were more radically restorationist, imposed more restrictions on women as well as on dress, and were more inclined to pursue and nurture charismatic experiences. It is perhaps significant (holiness Pentecostals at least thought it was) that all had first accepted William Durham's revelation on sanctification.

Oneness Pentecostalism has often been viewed by other Pentecostals as an aberration. Although its doctrinal distinctives distanced it from the mainstream of classical Pentecostalism, from another perspective its adherents must be understood as participants in a valid expression of Pentecostal experience. And the doctrinal departure aside, if one admits the strong restorationist component at the heart of the definition of Pentecostalism, Oneness proponents were more zealously restorationist, more doggedly congregational, and more Christocentrically spiritual—in short, in some important ways more essentially Pentecostal than the mainstream. Their view of the salvation process (which incorporated speaking in tongues) was based explicitly on their reading of the New Testament. Radical restorationists before them who had appealed only to Scripture as the source of truth (like Alexander Campbell or Barton Stone) had also been uncomfortable with Trinitarian language. And their spiritual restlessness, their longing for new insights, was not necessarily a desire for novelty but rather a way of expressing their continuing need to relate the human and the divine. Had the Oneness movement not been perceived as a "forward move," the prominent Pentecostals who embraced it, like G. T. Haywood, L. C. Hall, and Daniel Opperman, would have rejected it. Its appeal to deeply-held Pentecostal norms seemed so authentic that it attracted others like Kerr and Bell—who later repudiated it more because of Ewart's innovations than because of its original apostolic stress. In a sense, those who left the General Council were accusing it of forsaking the apostolic faith.

During the several years after it had denounced the doctrinal innovations espoused by Oneness followers, the General Council rapidly extended its influence. Resolving the New Issue attracted new adherents who were pleased with the Council's trend toward doctrinal stability; in addition, some who had left returned. As measured in both numbers of workers and missionary giving, the growth was substantial. Welch's annual report to the fifth General Council held in St. Louis (for the third consecutive time), September 9–14, 1917, indicated a roster of 620 ministers and 73 missionaries and missionary receipts in the amount of $10,223.98.[59] The same Council authorized the moving of the headquarters and commissioned E. N. Bell to recommend a suitable location for the publishing house. Bell, having spent some time in Springfield, Missouri, had discovered adequate premises there at a reasonable price. When Flower confirmed Bell's report to the Executive Presbytery, Flower was authorized to oversee the move.

The 1918 General Council convened September 4–11 in the new headquarters city. Using the second story of an old theater on Commercial Street, the Council heard reports of rapid progress. Secretary Frodsham noted that $29,630.51 had been given for missions; more district councils had been established and their chairmen recognized as associate general presbyters. Late in 1915, *Word and Witness* had ceased publication, Flower's *Weekly Evangel* becoming the sole official organ of the General Council (Flower had resigned as office editor in September 1917). The sixth General Council decided to give it a name "in keeping with the character of the movement" and designated it *The Pentecostal Evangel*.[60] But these and other changes to help the General Council better serve its constituency occurred in a setting once again agitated by doctrinal disunity. As before, a former executive presbyter rejected a widely held view: F. F. Bosworth had decided that the "uniform initial evidence" teaching that had shaped the Pentecostal distinctive was wrong. But two factors changed the nature of this controversy. One was Bosworth's distaste for strife; the other was the existence of the Statement of Fundamental Truths.

The Initial Evidence

In 1918, Fred Francis Bosworth was among the best-known men in the Assemblies of God. Former director of Zion City's award-winning band, Bosworth had embraced Pentecostal teaching during Parham's visit to Zion in 1906 and had received his Spirit baptism, evidenced by tongues, on October 18, 1906. Shortly after this experience, Bosworth began conducting evangelistic services.[61] He came to know deprivation and persecution. In one eventful campaign, he had been tarred and feathered by a mob opposed to his meetings. He became a popular speaker at camps and conventions and then established a thriving Pentecostal church in Dallas. Ardent Pentecostals across the country followed accounts of Woodworth-Etter's ministry with Bosworth in the summer and fall of 1912. Even before her arrival had drawn the general attention of Pentecostals, Bosworth had reported "a continual revival," nightly meetings being marked by conversions, healings, and Spirit baptisms. For nearly three months, Woodworth-Etter capitalized on Bosworth's thorough preparation for her coming. As many as twenty states were represented in a single service, and people arrived in Dallas regularly to attend the meetings.[62]

Bosworth had attended the Hot Springs General Council; in November of 1914 he had been appointed to a one-year term on the Executive Presbytery. In the course of his participation in constant revival, however, Bosworth became troubled about Pentecostal teaching on the evidence of the baptism with the Holy Spirit. He thought that it promoted seeking a "gift" instead of the "Giver," that it tended to result in "shallow" baptisms, and that it was the source of considerable confusion. Bosworth further came to reject the distinction most Pentecostals made between evidential tongues and the gift of tongues. He wrote a persuasive tract and began to circulate his views.

Others had expressed similar reservations throughout the Pentecostal movement's history. Before the General Council had brought many independent Pentecostals into a cooperative relationship, various prominent, independent Pentecostals had regretted the way the teaching was expressed, for the same reasons now given by Bosworth.[63] And the many who had spoken in tongues but stayed in the Christian and Missionary Alliance tended to share these feelings.

Bosworth remained intensely loyal to the Pentecostal experience. Charging, however, that too many had "NOISE without the power," Bosworth maintained that Pentecostals held to a serious doctrinal error "which, if eliminated, we are certain will solve many of our difficulties, besides opening the way for . . . a much deeper work of God."[64] After more than a decade in Pentecostal ministry and seeing "thousands receive the precious Baptism in the Holy Spirit," Bosworth claimed, "I am absolutely certain that many who receive the most powerful baptism for service do not receive the manifestation of speaking in tongues. And I am just as certain . . . that many who SEEM-INGLY speak in tongues, are not, nor ever have been, baptized in the Spirit."[65]

After giving the subject long consideration, Bosworth decided essentially that the Christian and Missionary Alliance stance on tongues was correct: Tongues were a gift of the Spirit, but not necessarily the only evidence of Spirit baptism. As Bosworth shared his views, several of his friends (among them Arch Collins, W. T. Gaston and M. M. Pinson) seemed to give them serious consideration. In 1917, the General Council noted that questions had been raised about evidential tongues. For the moment, however, the Council applied the "uniform initial evidence" criterion for receiving credentials only to candidates for the mission field.

During the summer of 1918, several prominent Assemblies of God leaders wrote articles for the official periodical (once more *The Christian Evangel*) maintaining what had become the "classical" Pentecostal position on tongues. An older article by William Durham was supplemented by the writings of W. H. Pope, D. W. Kerr, and W. Jethro Walthall, a venerable Holiness Baptist who had become Arkansas District chairman. In August the *Evangel* reported that in the forthcoming General Council all of the major doctrines of the Assemblies of God would be discussed.

Meanwhile, on Wednesday, July 24, F. F. Bosworth had typed a letter of resignation. Expressing his regret, Bosworth nonetheless asserted: "If I had a thousand souls, I would not be afraid to risk them all on the truth of my position that some may receive the fullest baptism in the Spirit without receiving the Gift of tongues."[66] In the course of the letter he lamented that some within the Assemblies of God had shown him less than a charitable spirit: A. G. Garr had effectively split Bosworth's congregation and intentionally misrepresented Bosworth; others had informed Bosworth that he had no right to retain his credentials.[67] Such men hardly represented what others conceived the General Council to be. Their actions seemed to give credence to the fears of those who had objected that the Statement of Fundamental Truths was, in fact, a creed.

The General Council was saved a showdown by the force of Bosworth's magnanimous spirit. Having returned his credentials, he nonetheless traveled to Springfield, Missouri, for the Council; and though a nonmember, he participated in discussions and even voted on the Council's resolution. Many made spirited defenses for the Pentecostal position. The forceful arguments of fighters like Robert Brown, general presbyter and pastor of New York City's Glad Tidings Tabernacle; Joseph Tunmore, soon to become Eastern district superintendent; M. M. Pinson; and D. W. Kerr generated considerable enthusiasm. The discussion ended in the framing of a strong resolution:

> Resolved, That this Council considers it a serious disagreement with the Fundamentals for any minister among us to teach contrary to our distinctive testimony that the baptism of the Holy Spirit is regularly accompanied by the initial physical sign of speaking in other tongues, as the Spirit of God gives the utterance, and that we consider it inconsistent and unscriptural for any minister to hold credentials with us who thus attacks as error our distinctive testimony.[68]

With the unanimous approval of this resolution (which Bosworth assented to), the General Council officially declared itself on the question Bosworth—like other Pentecostals over the years—had raised. Bosworth discouraged his minister friends from leaving the Council with him. He had no desire to force the issue. When the General Council ended on September 11, he boarded a train for New York, where he identified with the Christian and Missionary Alliance.[69]

With the framing of a strong resolution on initial evidence, the Assemblies of God had declared itself on the last of the three major issues that agitated widely in early Pentecostalism. Countless lesser matters continued to foment, but beginning in 1918 the Fellowship entered a period of growth and development that the newly articulated doctrinal unity facilitated. Bosworth's departure in 1918 brought to ten the number of executive presbyters who had withdrawn or been dismissed from the Fellowship in the first four years.[70] A large turnover for any organization, the changes posed a serious threat to the credibility of the General Council. In the end, however, they worked in favor of the Council.

By 1918, a growing list of respected men had emerged as leaders in the Assemblies of God. Having contributed creatively to the definition of a General Council stance on troublesome issues, they now turned to the task of implementing their vision for home and foreign missions. Foremost among them was probably J. R. Flower. But the General Council was a cooperative Fellowship, and Flower's vision could be implemented only as it was shared by people like E. N. Bell, Robert Brown, A. P. Collins, Stanley Frodsham, S. A. Jamieson, David McDowell, M. M. Pinson, J. O. Savell, Joseph Tunmore, Fred Vogler, and John Welch. They and many others, their unity reaffirmed through controversy, prepared to address more specifically the challenges at home and abroad that seemed, to them, their reason for being.

SPECIAL SONG SOUVENIR

APOSTOLIC FAITH
WORLD-WIDE
CAMP-MEETING

Commencing April 15, 1913

Los Angeles, California

Revival Selections by R. J. Scott

Hymnal used in the 1913 World-Wide Camp Meeting

Glenn Cook (left) rebaptizing L. V. Roberts in Indianapolis, Indiana, on March 6, 1915

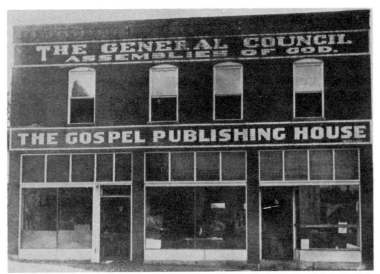

The Assemblies of God moved its national headquarters to this building in Springfield, Missouri, in 1918.

F. F. Bosworth

11. Communicating the Faith: Proceeding into the Second Generation

> Blow ye the trumpet, look about just now and tell someone the message of salvation, the baptism and the soon coming of Jesus.
>
> Aimee Semple McPherson, *The Bridal Call*, March 1918

When the 1918 General Council adjourned on September 11, the Assemblies of God entered a new phase in its endeavor to expand its outreach by cooperative efforts. On the one hand, the General Council had weathered serious doctrinal challenges and had defined more precisely its stance on controversial issues. The requirements for certification, for example, became decidedly more fixed.[1] On the other hand, however, the resolution of troublesome problems simply made possible the realization of goals men and women had worked steadily toward since 1914. Well-established standards for participation enabled appointed and elected leaders to direct their attention toward creating vehicles through which their perceived mission could be accomplished.

Between 1914 and 1921, General Councils convened annually (except for 1914 when pressing needs resulted in the calling of two General Councils). By 1921, the organization had established itself sufficiently so that it could meet biennially. Throughout this period, executive leadership was provided by respected Pentecostal pioneers, each of whom had participated in forming the General Council in 1914. E. N. Bell, chairman from April through November 1914, was reelected to that office in 1920. General secretary since 1919, Bell changed positions with John Welch, who had assumed chairmanship in 1915 and who would resume chairmanship on Bell's unexpected death in June 1923. Archibald Collins, second chairman, presided for only one troubled year (November 1914 to October 1915) when his responsibilities consisted primarily of visiting and encouraging affiliated churches and conventions. Highly regarded as a spiritual leader, Collins did not exhibit executive ability. On the other hand, his negative approach to centralized authority enabled him to fulfill his office to the general satisfaction of a fellowship that continued to disavow its need for strong leadership. From 1925 until 1929, William Gaston presided. The 1929 General Council elected Ernest Williams, who reluctantly left his Philadelphia pastorate for Springfield, where he served until 1949.

From 1918, both the ministerial and the missionary lists increased annually. By 1925, there were 1,155 credentialed ministers in the United States; 235 missionaries represented the constituency abroad. In 1929, the General Council roster included 1,641 ministers and 279 missionaries. By 1941, there were 4,159 ministers, including 394 missionaries.

Early in the 1920s the Executive Presbytery began appointing men known throughout the Fellowship (like Archibald Collins and Evangelist A. H. Argue) to serve as General Council field representatives to advise and encourage the stateside constituency and communicate recommendations to the executives. During the 1920s, the idealism of World War I and the furor of the subsequent Red Scare yielded to American fascination with pleasure and prosperity. With the exception of segments of the farm population, most Americans had both more money and more leisure. In an era dominated by smug Republican Protestants, the promise of American life seemed limitless. An impressive array of disaffected intellectuals ridiculed religiosity and tradition, and prosperity eluded a growing number of farmers, but these discordant notes were scattered and did not seriously disturb the general harmony. As usual, Americans seemed intrigued by display and sensational causes. If the celebrated Sacco and Vanzetti case dominated the headlines, Prohibition generated popular furor; "flappers" conspicuously modeled changing views of womanhood; new art forms like jazz heightened the contrast between the old and the new. In his classic informal study of the decade, Frederick Lewis Allen noted the consternation with which middle-aged Americans regarded changing codes of behavior and dress: "It was incredible. It was abominable. What did it all mean? . . . There was enough fire beneath the smoke of . . . sensational revelations to make the Problem of the Younger Generation a topic of anxious discussion from coast to coast."[2] Religious and secular denunciations of new trends were as much a phenomenon of the 1920s as the fads themselves.

While Pentecostals generally joined the critics of shifting cultural standards, they nonetheless imbibed much of the fast-paced spirit that vivified the 1920s. Camp meetings, where emotional displays rivaled those associated with nineteenth-century camp meetings, were an important gathering place for the faithful. Taking such popular figures as Billy Sunday for their example, Pentecostal preachers vigorously denounced modernity, especially as manifested in bewildering new patterns of social behavior. The most controversial Pentecostal preacher of the period, widely heralded by the secular press as a consumate entertainer, was Aimee Semple McPherson, whose career was made possible by precisely those social realities most Pentecostals thought they rejected.

The Influence of Aimee Semple McPherson

The notoriety attached to Aimee Semple McPherson's name came later. When she affiliated with the Assemblies of God in 1919, the twenty-nine-year-old evangelist had already earned a reputation among Pentecostals for spirituality and energy. Born Aimee Kennedy in Ontario, Canada, October 9, 1890, McPherson had embraced Pentecostalism in 1908 and had married the evangelist, Robert James Semple, who had converted her. Ordained at Durham's North Avenue Mission in Chicago in 1909, Aimee left for China with her husband in 1910. Robert died in Hong Kong three months after their arrival; the next month, September 1910, their daughter, Roberta, was born. Early in 1911, Aimee returned to the United States. On February 28, 1912, she married Harold McPherson. A son, Rolf, was born to them in March 1913.

Restless in the confines of her marriage and home, Mc-Pherson rediscovered her call to preach. In 1915 she left her husband, taking her children to her father's home in Ingersoll, Ontario. (Her mother, Minnie Kennedy, an occasional Salvation Army lassie, shared her daughter's restlessness in traditional roles and left her husband for long periods to preach, later to assist Aimee.) That year she gradually entered the world of itinerant evangelism. When her husband joined her and promised to assist her ministry, her future briefly seemed promising. From 1916 to 1918, McPherson traveled up and down the East Coast, conducting huge tent crusades in which she promulgated a fully Pentecostal message and practiced faith healing, usually by the laying on of hands. Everywhere she went, tumult followed. Dramatic and unpredictable, she proved adept at transfixing her audiences as she presented a simple gospel message. For while her message was unadorned, her delivery was not. Crowds thronged to hear her; they also saw Pentecostal phenomena—"spiritual gifts"—in awesome operation. In 1917, McPherson began to publish *Bridal Call,* a monthly magazine that she wrote, both to communicate her message and to report events in her meetings. From Maine to Florida she gained a public hearing for the Pentecostal message, and wherever she went she strengthened both the visibility and the prospects of struggling Pentecostal missions.

Her ministry in the South brought her into contact with holiness Pentecostals, who quickly recognized the influence Durham had had in shaping her message. It became evident that her teaching resembled that of the newly founded Assemblies of God. In 1918 McPherson, now separated from her husband (they would divorce in 1921), took her two children and her mother on a transcontinental preaching tour that ended in Los Angeles. In 1919 at the urging of a prominent California Assemblies of God leader, Robert Craig, she affiliated with the Assemblies of God. During the next five years, she crossed the United States eight times, conducting some forty revival crusades in tents, theaters, and municipal auditoriums in large cities like Philadelphia; Washington, D. C.; St. Louis; and Denver.[3] Her Denver meetings, in which some twelve thousand people crammed the coliseum nightly for a month, were publicized across the nation. Wherever she went her sensational preaching and dramatic results won her both acclaim and notoriety. In 1920 she preached to the General Council. A 1922 visit to Australia lent an international flavor to her endeavors.[4]

By the time she opened her permanent headquarters, Angelus Temple, in Los Angeles on January 1, 1923, McPherson had established a broad support base. Although she received considerable help from fellow Pentecostals, she claimed that her own converts provided both the principal funds and the incentive for constructing her commodious church. Her Los Angeles audiences, consisting primarily of recent arrivals from the Midwest, filled her 5,300-seat auditorium to capacity long before scheduled services began. She never advertised meetings at Angelus Temple; the facility could not have accommodated the crowds. She filled a grueling schedule with nightly meetings (including regular healing meetings), Thursday night baptismal services, prayer gatherings, youth outreaches, and three preaching services on Sundays.

Meanwhile, however, this popular, flamboyant evangelist had developed hesitancy about her ministry in the Assemblies of God. An unacknowledged but important issue was, of course, her sex. She forced some to confront their latent hostility toward women in the pulpit. Recurrent objections to her construction of Angelus Temple (allegedly diverting funds that could have been better employed among the Fellowship's 234 missionaries) were exacerbated by misunderstandings about the support of a specific missionary family. McPherson's vision and drive—as well as her sex—catapulted her to a prominence that eluded most other Pentecostals. Heralded as one who provided "the best show of all" in a city renowned for its show business, McPherson subtly gave transplanted, entertainment-starved working class people a rich sampling of theatrical skill. Nevertheless, she insisted that entertainment was not her business, and a sincere desire to evangelize permeated her ministry. When she wrote to Assemblies of God executives in 1922, she made a valid point: "Assemblies have been built up and your work established more than I believe you realize. All this adding not only numerically and spiritually but financially for the work at home and in foreign fields."[5]

By 1922, however, the independent character of McPherson's work had begun to generate strong controversy that seemed clearly related to the long-held views of some about appropriate roles for women. Without the full confidence of the executives, McPherson considered further relationship with the Assemblies of God meaningless. In January 1922 she returned her credentials. But her impact on the Assemblies of God was far from over. Throughout the next several years, some who were especially loyal to the Assemblies of God objected to McPherson's tendency to establish rival Pentecostal congregations in communities where Assemblies of God workers preached; she temporarily attracted to her ranks several men with prominent records in the Assemblies of God—John Goben of Iowa and T. K. Leonard of Ohio, for example (while Lilian Yeomans' long association with McPherson's L.I.F.E. Bible College drew repeated criticism from Southern California District officials); and the notoriety attached to her alleged kidnapping in 1926 further alienated her from some who had long criticized her.

Within her own ranks, all was not harmonious either: Some found constant newspaper coverage distasteful, others objected to her domination of her colleagues, and her public rift with her mother delighted her critics. Eventually some of her early supporters separated and formed an association that later merged with another organization to become the Open Bible Standard denomination.[6]

McPherson did not merely serve as a figure of contention, however. Her positive contributions to the Fellowship continued too. In addition to the support her campaigns lent to local congregations, her ministry ultimately gave the Fellowship some of its talented young ministers. McPherson's campaign at San Jose's First Baptist Church in 1922 is a case in point. Invited by the congregation's liberal pastor, D. E. Towner, as part of a ploy to attract crowds and raise needed finances, McPherson managed to convert Towner and then to conduct a campaign that transformed not only that congregation but the lives of hundreds who packed the tent erected to accommodate the masses. Among those who "got the hallelujahs" was the staid Oxford-educated modernist pastor of Lodi's prosperous First Congregational Church: Charles Price. Beginning in 1922, Price's meetings would have a tremendous impact on the Assemblies of God. A popular speaker at district conventions and camp meetings, Price especially cultivated a ministry of healing. Remaining independent of any Pentecostal denomination, Price published a monthly paper, *Golden Grain,* and influenced thousands of Assemblies of God adherents to anticipate increasingly intense and "powerful" evidences of ongoing revival.[7]

Another convert of the San Jose revival was R. D. E. Smith, the son of a deacon at the First Baptist Church. After attending McPherson's L.I.F.E. Bible College, Smith ministered briefly under McPherson's International Church of the Foursquare Gospel before beginning an influential fifty-four years of pastoral ministry and executive leadership within the Assemblies of God in 1933.

Influential Local Congregations

While much of what national visibility Pentecostalism achieved focused on McPherson, numerous ministries emerged within the Assemblies of God that would deeply impress local constituencies. Several congregations gained repute as strong spiritual centers, and several men and women won wide respect. In the East were congregations like Glad Tidings Tabernacle in New York City where Robert and Marie Brown preached; the Full Gospel Tabernacle in Washington, D.C., established in 1907, like Glad Tidings Tabernacle, and led by Harry L. Collier; the Highway Mission Tabernacle, led by Ernest Williams from 1920 until 1930; Bethel Assembly in Hagerstown, Maryland, where Ralph Jeffrey served as pastor for twenty-nine years. The interests of the denomination were advanced in the South by men like James Savell and S. A. Jamieson, whose statement that he did not want "a feathered nest" but rather a place where he could "work hard for the Lord" captured his view of the ministry.[8]

The Midwest had numerous vigorous assemblies, like the one John Waggoner established in Warren, Ohio; it provided the setting where some with tremendous popular appeal within the organization developed their ministries. People like Flem Van Meter, J. Narver Gortner (who later moved to California), Fred Vogler, Joseph Roselli, Gayle Lewis, Willie and Ruth Millsaps, Victor G. Greisen, and Aaron A. Wilson were typical of the many who helped establish Assemblies of God congregations throughout the region. Frank Lindquist, Ben Hardin, and James Menzie laid much of the groundwork that resulted in the organization of the North Central District in November 1922. A remarkable woman from Cumberland, Maryland, named Etta Reckley established assemblies in North Dakota and Montana. In Arkansas and Texas, where the Assemblies of God had its strongest old constituency, the Richeys, William B. McCafferty, W. J. Walthall, Harry Bowley, and Hugh Cadwalder helped extend the Fellowship, and Henry C. Ball coordinated a Latin outreach. Farther west, Wesley Steelberg, Louis Turnbull, George N. Eldridge, Harold Needham, Robert and Mary Craig, Carrie Judd Montgomery, Frank Gray, Mark Draper, and Arthur Osterberg directed thriving outreaches.

At first Canada remained an integral part of the American Assemblies of God and some Canadians became fully identified with the American Assemblies of God. Others later became part of the Pentecostal Assemblies of Canada. In A. G. Ward, A. H. Argue, J. R. Evans, R. E. McAlister, and others, Canada made a vital contribution to the formative years of the American Assemblies of God. Throughout the 1920s, the evangelistic efforts sponsored by Argue and his children, especially Watson, Zelma, and Beulah, nurtured the movement's revival traditions.

Meanwhile, some in the denomination expressed their concern for the youth in whose hands future leadership would rest. In Stockton, California, the growing concern of a twenty-three-year-old pastor, Wesley Steelberg, for his assembly's young people resulted in organized youth rallies using the name Pentecostal Ambassadors for Christ. A. G. Osterberg, an Azusa Street veteran who served as Southern California District superintendent, called participants in his similar youth rallies Christian Crusaders. A Los Angeles youth pastor, Carl Hatch, chose the name Christ's Ambassadors for the youth group in his church. This name (based on 2 Corinthians 5:20) became generally accepted among youth leaders across the country. The 1927 General Council appointed a committee to study the role of youth in the movement. Meanwhile, local Christ's Ambassadors groups gained a wide following. The Southern California District published the first *Christ's Ambassadors Herald,* which by the early 1930s had a national readership.

The Influence of Raymond T. Richey

Of all of these early leaders, Raymond T. Richey undoubtedly had the strongest popular support among the constituency nationwide. Born in Illinois September 4, 1893, he grew up in a home where divine healing was unequivocally accepted. His father, Eli, had claimed healing from cancer and had moved his family from their farm to the faith-charged atmosphere of Zion, Illinois, eventually becoming its mayor. Raymond later moved to Texas, where he sought the prayers of Assemblies of God pioneer Archibald Collins for his own healing of an acute eye disease. Healed and converted in 1911, Richey worked at various jobs before accepting a call to preach.

The call was to the Gospel Tabernacle in Houston, Texas, as an assistant to his father. The congregation had been without a pastor for some time before the Richey family arrived, and attendance had dwindled to less than seventy-five with a committed membership of six.[9] The Richey family worked as a team, with four of Eli's eight children assisting him among the growing tabernacle congregation. During World War I, Raymond established the United Prayer and Workers' League, through which literature was distributed to servicemen and various servicemen's activities were coordinated. During the war years, Raymond worked with the Salvation Army and the Y.M.C.A. as well as in Pentecostal settings. Disqualified from military service because of his poor health, by the end of the war he was ill with tuberculosis. In September 1919 Richey claimed his second healing and committed himself to a healing ministry.

Richey's healing evangelism began inauspiciously. He had traveled to Hattiesburg, Mississippi, to arrange an evangelistic crusade for Warren Collins, a former Assemblies of God evangelist with forty-three years of ministry behind him. Collins had left the Assemblies of God because he rejected evidential tongues, but his meetings were still characterized by charismatic worship, and he retained a following among Pentecostals.[10] Collins and Richey had conducted meetings at Central Baptist Church in Memphis in June, and Collins decided to evangelize in Mississippi in October. Collins, however, failed to arrive, and Richey was forced to fulfill his commitments. The first two services were small; Richey announced that the third night he would pray for the sick, and several claimed healings. The next day's newspaper carried their testimonies, and that evening the hall was full.[11] Thus was launched a ministry of healing evangelism that catapulted Richey to prominence across the nation. In addition to addressing large audiences around the country—in churches, tents, civic auditoriums, and tabernacles—Richey played a prominent role in Evangelistic Temple, a large Houston church that had evolved from his father's Gospel Tabernacle. He also launched Southern Bible School in his church facility.[12]

A Movement in Transition

In spite of the increasing prominence of evangelistic efforts spearheaded by charismatic individuals like Richey, the Argues, McPherson, and Price, American Pentecostals faced numerous problems in the 1920s. The growth in numbers of adherents, workers, and missionaries told only part of the story. In many places, Assemblies of God adherents became accustomed to the hostility of other Christians who misunderstood them.

And all was not "sweetness and light" within the movement.

Some proclaimed the movement's "declension," citing as proof declining numbers of watchnight services or the use in Pentecostal meetings of musicians who had not received Spirit baptism. Some worried about the improprieties of women's dress or "mixed bathing," expressing anxieties more broadly based in the culture. And a group of influential Pentecostal pioneers, some of whom had helped create the Assemblies of God, bemoaned the waning power of the movement at large.

The Assemblies of God, as assessed by John Lake (who had attended the Hot Springs General Council), was commendably efficient, but it was most emphatically not Pentecostal. Surveying the scene, Lake maintained: "Every little man is doing the best he can on a big job." But the movement had "drifted clear away from a true scriptural Pentecostal ideal"; the Assemblies of God was "becoming more and more a little bigoted denomination. The spirit of denominationalism in the Assemblies of God," Lake lamented, "is probably narrower than even in the old churches from which Pentecostal people have been escaping. . . . As a power to bless mankind . . . it does not seem to me they are worth discussing or considering."[13]

The persistent effort to discover the full implications of what Assemblies of God adherents considered an end-times effusion of spiritual power can be traced through the group's history. Lake's concerns were echoed by prominent voices in the denomination, even as others sensed that efficient organization would help assure the movement's integrity. Reports of renewal persisted side-by-side with expressions of deep concern over waning spiritual power. By 1941, a movement that had thrived on the preaching of itinerant evangelists lamented the evident "dying interest" in evangelism. Evangelists settled into pastorates, and few new recruits filled the vacancies.[14]

A transformation was, in fact, in process, but it would be years before its full implications became apparent. The restorationist impulse was becoming less central. The rhetoric that it had generated persisted, but the understanding of how it would be achieved changed in significant ways. Pentecostalism was not so much a way of perceiving and experiencing reality as it had once been: It was becoming more of a point of view.

When Welch and Flower proposed to the 1925 General Council that the Fellowship adopt a constitution and bylaws, the proposal failed, and neither man was reelected.[15] Two years later, however, when the General Council convened in Springfield, Missouri, the same proposal received unanimous approval. This action completed an important phase in the organizational development of the Assemblies of God.

After Bell's death in 1923, veteran preacher John W. Welch had resumed chairmanship. When the General Council convened in Eureka Springs, Arkansas, in 1925, the sixty-six-year-old Welch was replaced by William Theodore Gaston. Associated with the Assemblies of God from April 1914, Gaston was widely acclaimed within the Fellowship as a capable preacher and an able administrator. He continued the tradition of leadership by men who had been at Hot Springs and who had risen to prominence in ministry in Oklahoma, Arkansas, and Texas.

Gaston moved to Springfield from southern California where he had been a pastor and teacher at Berean Bible Institute in San Diego. A friendly, dynamic person, Gaston enjoyed wide popularity among the constituency. Throughout his tenure, he traveled extensively, often crossing the country by train to preach at district councils and otherwise extend the Fellowship. Much of the day-to-day responsibility at the Springfield headquarters was fulfilled by James R. Evans, the general secretary. David McDowell, assistant chairman, spent much time "on the field," encouraging local workers.

Although Gaston enjoyed the esteem of his colleagues, questions about his relationship with a woman pastor who had been his secretary in California resulted in a General Presbytery decision to exclude him from a third term as general superintendent. Confronted with evidence suggesting "conduct unbecoming a minister," Gaston submitted his credentials and resigned from office. Regard for him was evidenced by a General Council vote to give him six months paid vacation; this action was supplemented by a love offering.[16] After the General Council, Gaston returned to California. He never stood trial for any offense, and some confusion about his status resulted. In 1935 he wrote to the executives asking if he would be permitted to accept invitations to minister in Assemblies of God churches. The response was full reinstatement into the Fellowship. Continued confidence in Gaston was expressed in his election as Northern California-Nevada District superintendent in 1945, an office he filled with distinction until his death in 1956.

The incident, however, raised several important issues that surfaced significant differences of opinion. Some advocated forgiveness and restoration: Essentially they hoped to protect the denomination by covering offenses. Others, notably Robert Brown, insisted that indiscretions should disbar one from future ministry. Some thought that even the denomination's executives should not be fully informed of testimony and evidence submitted in morals cases; others argued for full disclosure to avoid misunderstandings. Some objected to the way Gaston's case was handled: They felt that an unfortunate precedent had been made in allowing him to resign without a trial and, if warranted, dismissal.

Executives seemed generally inclined to await the presentation of evidence rather than to follow up allegations against ministers. In 1929 the General Council had no rehabilitation program (which would not come until 1973). Those who disagreed shared a sincere desire to protect the Fellowship's integrity. Above all else, they did not want the media to discover irregularities in their ranks.

Throughout the 1920s, the general secretary's office had notified the Fellowship of the dismissal of ministers through the *Pentecostal Evangel.* As a result of the Gaston case (Gaston strenuously objected to being listed as "dismissed" in the weekly denominational organ, claiming that he was too well-known to recover from the stigma such publication would involve), the executives began to consider the approach they later adopted—that of listing the ministers who have been dropped and added in a ministers' letter.

Also during the 1920s, leaders found it necessary to deal with problems created by those who, as time passed, became restive under the limitations that "cooperative fellowship" imposed on their independent actions. And some expressed concern over the changing priorities of longer-established congregations.

David McDowell, for example, bemoaned a situation in which efforts were poured into producing a Christmas drama, and few found time to attend prayer meetings. From across the country, similar concern about religious complacency and a loss of an eager anticipation of Christ's return surfaced.

Over time, the memories of troublesome situations faded. In later years, adherents would recall the teens and twenties as the good old days, when emotion-charged testimonies and unchecked shouts of praise contributed to ecstatic services and sustained fervor. Separation from "the world" was less conspicuous than participants in that era would later recall, for in eschewing divorce, drinking, smoking, contemporary fashions, mixed bathing, makeup, or bobbed hair, Assemblies of God adherents affirmed a life-style shared by millions of other American Protestants. Yet their frequent references to things spiritual did not preclude the devising of ways to embrace some of the new things their culture offered. Hesitantly, but certainly, they admitted that movies could be used for their own ends; that radio offered a medium for evangelization (Aimee McPherson began broadcasting over the nation's first church-owned radio station, KFSG, in Los Angeles in 1924); in short, that the world's new technology had much for them to appropriate in accomplishing their task.

The Assemblies of God faced new challenges as the influence of a second generation began to become apparent. A movement that had been shaped by its members' immediate experiences had to find a way to embrace growing numbers of children and young people who were on hand simply because their parents were. The first generation needed to communicate its heritage to the second. During the twenties, a steady flow of converts as well as the dominance of the first generation deemphasized such concerns. But institutionalizing processes were well underway as William Gaston left office. As they quietly modified the Fellowship, Christ's imminent return became somewhat less central. The dream of restoring New Testament Christianity was modified by the need to conserve a revival. Although adventist language continued to be widely used, Assemblies of God leaders began to face the likelihood of committing their work to another generation. The challenge of communicating the heritage, then, contributed to the transformation of the movement. One clear indicator of shifting priorities was an increasing focus in the next decade on Christian education.

In 1929, Ernest Williams began twenty years of service as general superintendent. A California native, Williams had received both his Spirit baptism and his ministerial credentials at the hallowed Azusa Street mission in 1907. His wife, Laura, had worked closely with the founder of the Apostolic Faith Mission of Portland, Oregon: Florence Crawford. In 1912, the two accepted a call to the pastorate of a small Pentecostal assembly in Conneaut, Ohio. In April 1915, Williams affiliated with the General Council. In 1920, he accepted a call to Philadelphia's strongest Pentecostal church, the Union Highway Mission (which had affiliated with the General Council in March 1918). He supervised an aggressive evangelistic outreach that resulted in three expansion programs and eventually led to the purchase of a commodious facility, Highway Mission Tabernacle.

Williams' activities brought him into contact with men of increasing prominence in the growing Fellowship. Through the pages of the *Pentecostal Evangel,* adherents across the country learned to appreciate his simple faith and unassuming manner. A leader in the Eastern District and a general presbyter, Williams brought to Springfield a reputation for integrity and spirituality that reassured those who had been troubled by recent events. However, probably no general superintendent has ever embarked on his tenure with the reluctance Williams felt. For ten months after his election by the 1929 Wichita General Council, he wavered, expressing a desire to stay with his thriving work in Philadelphia. But the clear mandate of the General Council, reinforced by the persuasions of his colleagues in national leadership, finally won the day. Unable to fulfill both responsibilities, he resigned his church and moved to Springfield in the fall of 1930.

Some Effects of Economic Hardship

By almost any account, the decade of the 1930s was one of

the most difficult and important in modern American history. The stock market crash of October 1929 ultimately ended an era of Republicanism, hope, and prosperity. In the next several years, disagreements over how to cope with deepening depression resulted in bitter political fights. In 1932, in one of the greatest party reversals in election history, Franklin Roosevelt began his twelve-year tenure as president. The initial excitement of the first hundred days, during which he pushed major legislation through a responsive Congress, gave way to strong opposition to his highly pragmatic philosophy of government. Labor unions became increasingly vocal. While intellectuals flirted with Communism, right-wing folk heroes opposed the New Deal. Events in Europe and the Far East signaled the weakening of the moral suasion by which the United States had endeavored to assure peace. Thousands of disinherited farmers forsook prairie dust bowls to make a new start in the cities, John Steinbeck chronicling their disenchantment in *The Grapes of Wrath.*

By the time Roosevelt took office, about one third of the labor force was unemployed. The poor suffered the most. Assemblies of God adherents were hard-hit by circumstances beyond their control. And the New Deal coalition Roosevelt surrounded himself with seemed to them to be uncomfortably liberal. Although little agreement on a definition of this term existed, Assemblies of God adherents unanimously avowed its negative connotations. It seems evident (though no surveys were made) that most Assemblies of God adherents in the 1930s were Republicans (or, in the South, Democrats who were disenchanted with Roosevelt). Certainly the constituency of the Assemblies of God was predominantly rural, teetotaling white—the kind of people who had supported Republican Herbert Hoover in 1928. And the Roosevelt administration regularly expressed support for minorities and labor unions, two constituencies that made many Pentecostals uncomfortable. Commenting on Roosevelt's landslide victory over Hoover in 1932, Kansas District Superintendent Fred Vogler wrote to J. R. Evans: "The Lord must love the Republicans, for 'whom the Lord loveth he chasteneth.' "[17] Among Roosevelt's first projects was the repeal of the Prohibition amendment, an amendment most Assemblies of God adherents supported.[18] Yet when the indomitable Sara Roosevelt, the president's mother, died, the General Council in session sent a telegram of sympathy. And another General Council forwarded the president its assurance of prayers in behalf of his quest for peace.

In the 1930s, the government collected data from American churches to compile its fourth "Census of Religious Bodies." The resulting analysis of the Assemblies of God demonstrated that the denomination's strongest base was rural (defined as areas with populations of less that twenty-five hundred). Comparisons of data collected in previous census surveys showed extensive growth:

	1916	1926	1936
Churches	118	671	2,611
Members	6,703	47,950	148,043
Church buildings	63	497	1,925
Average members per church	57	71	57
Sunday schools	79	549	2,321

In some ways, in spite of the economic hardship many of its adherents experienced, the 1930s was a peaceful period of steady expansion for the Assemblies of God. General Superintendent Ernest S. Williams was reelected at each General Council by at least ninety-five percent of the vote. Noel Perkin consistently provided strong leadership for the Foreign Missions Department. J. R. Evans served as general secretary until 1935, when his deteriorating eyesight prompted the election of J. R. Flower, who had been voted assistant general superintendent (then a non-resident officer) in 1931. Flower retained the office of general secretary until his retirement in 1959. In spite of sporadic complaints about Stanley Frodsham's British preferences and general pretentiousness, he gave continuity to the *Pentecostal Evangel.* Other offices, however, proved decidely more controversial.

In the early 1930s, the office of assistant general superintendent was primarily honorary; the assistant (J. R. Flower), for example, did not reside in Springfield. When Flower's election on the fourth ballot as general secretary in 1935 made it necessary for the General Council to find another assistant superintendent, it proved impossible for them to agree on a candidate, and the delegates decided to request Flower to fill both offices. Throughout the decade, virtually every election of nonresident executives proved troublesome. Some would maintain that the General Council was, in fact, deeply divided about the kind of leadership it wanted; others would respond with the assurance that its ranks contained so many qualified men that selecting one was difficult; another factor might well have been the strong emphasis on cooperation and a tradition of low-keyed leadership. It is also important to note that a new generation of leaders was emerging through the ranks.

The Influence of Edith Mae Pennington

Among the constituency, people like Charles Price, Raymond Richey, Zelma Argue, and Hattie Hammond continued to enjoy strong support. A popular new face on the Fellowship's evangelistic scene was that of Edith Mae Pennington. Born Edith Patterson in Pine Bluff, Arkansas, Pennington won a national beauty contest in 1921. As a result, she gave up teaching school and accepted an offer to tour the country. She hired a business manager, J. B. Pennington, and accepted engagements in cities around the nation, finally arriving in Hollywood, where she began an acting career. During this time, she "made a start toward God" and found the theater less attractive than she had anticipated. (It is uncertain whether her acting career was promising.) She married Pennington and eventually moved to Oklahoma City.

In 1925, while riding in a streetcar, she noticed a Pentecostal Holiness church with a large sign proclaiming Jesus Saves. The following Sunday she and her husband began attending the small white frame church. After several weeks she had an emotional conversion experience; as a result, she would relate, she was "delivered" from desires to wear jewelry and to attend theaters. The couple moved to Birmingham, Alabama, where Pennington began teaching Sunday school and working with young people.

In 1928, back in her native Pine Bluff, Arkansas, she became the assistant pastor of a newly formed Assemblies of God congregation. Her efforts as an evangelist began in 1930. She quickly discovered that Pentecostals—who preached lengthy sermons about the sinfulness of movies, theater attendance, beauty contests, contemporary fashions, and jewelry—thrilled to her emotion-packed testimony about the emptiness of worldly living. They readily responded to invitations to hear one who had actually tasted a life-style they disavowed. Wherever she went, she was billed as a beauty queen and a former actress rather than simply as a preacher of the gospel. Subtle psychological factors were clearly at work; some would suggest that relinquishing the stage for the pulpit did not involve much re-orientation. And wherever she traveled crowds thronged to hear her, and Assemblies of God adherents claimed renewal.[19]

In 1931, for example, after seven weeks, her campaign in the nation's capital—sponsored by the Full Gospel Tabernacle (Harry Collier, pastor)—continued unabated; meetings had to be moved to larger facilities. Pennington preached every night except Saturdays and also found time to conduct children's services in the afternoon.[20]

Across the country, such local revival campaigns were common, even as the severity of the worldwide depression affected the Fellowship in many ways and the deteriorating political situation also posed new challenges. Ministers tended to share the financial problems of their congregations. Even in the more prosperous 1920s, some pastors were unable to find funds to attend General Councils or to pay credentials renewal fees.[21] Ministerial files contain many letters from those who either renewed credentials late or allowed credentials to lapse because they lacked a one- or two-dollar fee. Bible institute records also hold letters from would-be evangelists who left the schools without making full payment and failed to make more than a subsistence living "on the field."[22] Even district superintendents felt the pinch: Fred Vogler, Kansas District superintendent, expressed some uncertainty about his financial ability to attend the 1933 General Council.[23] Yet other ministers enjoyed a degree of financial security that allowed them to purchase modest summer homes or to travel abroad.[24]

Sunday Schools: A Growing Priority

Among the priorities local congregations established for their ministries to help popularize the movement, under Williams' superintendency Sunday schools became increasingly prominent. Throughout the 1930s, the administration of the Sunday School Department was through Gospel Publishing House. Sunday school efforts expanded, both in scope and in equipment, throughout the decade. By 1941, the publishing house produced nineteen regular periodicals in addition to its regular printing of Sunday school supplies. The *Pentecostal Evangel,* cited in 1937 as the largest religious weekly in the United States, continued to expand its circulation, approaching a hundred thousand copies a week.

As more congregations recognized the evangelistic and educational potential of Sunday schools, the Sunday School Department sponsored regional Sunday school conferences that offered both motivation and training to local assemblies. Gradually old hesitations about both the formalization of church training in Sunday schools and the utilization of such helps as quarterlies and visual aids gave way to an admission of the advisability of such efforts. Increasingly the publishing house expanded its line of material graded for small children; visual aid charts, for example, became available because of extensive demand. Growing interest in vacation Bible schools resulted by 1941 in the creation of a three-year cycle of materials suitable for this newer outreach.

The growing interest in Sunday schools (as well as in other aspects of Christian education) resulted in part from the emergence of a forceful advocate, Ralph Riggs. After coming to Springfield to teach at Central Bible Institute, Riggs became pastor of Central Assembly in Springfield in 1931. Born June 16, 1895, in Coal Creek (now Lake City), Tennessee, Riggs had

spent most of his boyhood in Meridian, Mississippi. He had
attended the Hot Springs General Council in 1914. After receiving training at the Rochester Bible Training School, Riggs
had served as a pastor in Syracuse, New York. In 1920, he had
sailed for South Africa as a missionary. There he married Lillian Merian, a missionary already on the field. Six years later,
they returned to the States. Riggs accepted the pastorate of
Bethel Church in Newark, New Jersey, and taught at the Bethel
Bible Training School. In 1928 he was invited to Springfield.
His book *A Successful Sunday School* together with another by
Myer Pearlman, *Successful Sunday School Teaching*, greatly
facilitated the denomination's Sunday school efforts by establishing goals and training workers. Riggs recognized that congregations needed to appreciate their role in Christian education and vigorously encouraged the articulation of specific
achievable goals. Gospel Publishing House began to offer teacher
training courses as well as adding to its list of Sunday school-
related publications.

In 1935 the General Council approved a resolution to use all
the means at its disposal to encourage the constituency to develop local Sunday schools "in spirituality, efficiency, and numbers."[25] A committee composed of Riggs, Victor G. Greisen,
Kansas District superintendent, and Willie T. Millsaps, a Virginia pastor, recommended the adoption of twelve standards
by which to measure "a good Sunday school":

1. A gain in average attendance of at least 20% each
year.

2. With its enrollment at least equal to its church's
membership.

3. Its pastor present at at least 95% of its regular sessions and monthly business meetings.

4. Its superintendent present at at least 95% of its regular sessions and monthly business meetings.

5. Its regular teachers present at at least 90% of its
regular sessions and monthly business meetings.

6. Conducting a Teacher Training Class and completing
at least one subject a year.

7. At least 90% of whose scholars (over 8 years of age) attend church weekly.

8. With conversions each year at least equaling three percent of its enrollment.

9. With regular offerings increasing at least 25% each year.

10. With missionary offerings increasing at least 25% each year.

11. With its cradle roll at least 5% of its total enrollment.

12. With its home department at least 5% of its total enrollment.[26]

Throughout the decade, Sunday schools contributed to dramatic growth in numbers of adherents. The Fellowship's growth in both members and clergy exceeded that of any other period in its history. Between 1927 and 1941 the ministerial roll grew by 285 percent; the number of churches increased 321 percent, and membership gained 290 percent. At least 2,080 Sunday schools were started between 1937 and 1939.[27] Workers were encouraged not to establish Sunday schools independently of local congregations, but rather to make the schools part of the program of a local church.

As the United States stood poised on the brink of involvement in World War II in 1941, the Fellowship could reflect on its recent past with considerable satisfaction. Only one minor doctrinal issue had been raised to mar the prevailing consensus: The persistence of the teaching that the Church would endure the tribulation (post-tribulation rapture) was noted in 1937 when the General Council officially disapproved that view. Otherwise, general doctrinal harmony prevailed. Executive leadership remained in the hands of men who gave continuity with the Fellowship's earliest history: Ernest Williams, J. Roswell Flower, Fred Vogler, Ralph Riggs. Younger leaders deeply loyal to the Fellowship's purposes had emerged: Wesley Steelberg, Gayle Lewis, Theodore Gannon, Bert Webb. Capable men had found it possible to fulfill their personal visions in ways that complemented the Fellowship's objectives: Peter C. Nelson, Henry Ness, Raymond Richey. A core of evangelists sought regularly to promote spiritual fervor and to facilitate evangelistic endeavors; many among them were young women: Edith Pennington, Zelma Argue, Hattie Hammond, Adele Carmichael. An increasingly structured headquarters operation provided support for rapid growth at the local level. A fellowship whose existence had been so tenuous twenty-five years earlier now not only seemed likely to survive, it had demonstrated its ability to stabilize and expand. It had also completed a chapter in its history. From at least one perspective (and despite each generation's proclivity to have its own nostalgic era), the good old days were over. During the war years, executives made decisions that significantly altered the Fellowship's course; after the war, cultural changes deeply influenced its direction. By 1941, a movement shaped by a restorationist vision had become something its organizers in 1914 had repudiated—a new denomination. Selective restorationist rhetoric persisted, but its implementation proved increasingly troublesome.

Edwin Sikes, Charles S. Price,
J. Roswell Flower, Vernon G.
Gortner, ca. 1935

Young people outside Highway Mission Tabernacle, Philadelphia, Pennsylvania, ca. 1920

Marie and Robert Brown, ca. 1945

Some Assemblies of God evangelists

Edith Mae Pennington

Great Revival, September 25 to October 23

Former Winner National Beauty Prize

Full Gospel Tabernacle

North Capitol and K Streets
Washington, D. C.

HARRY L. COLLIER, Pastor

Sunday, 11:00 and 7:30
Nightly Except Saturday, 7:45
Christian Healing Service, Thursday, 7:45

Choir—Orchestra—Revival Music

COME—BRING YOUR FRIENDS

Charles Price evangelistic party. Price is in the
front row, center.

Aimee Semple McPherson, 1921

The Argue family evangelized widely.

Watson Argue revival, Lighthouse Temple, Eugene, Oregon, 1927

Affiliated churches ranged from large impressive city buildings to small country churches to storefront missions.

Philadelphia, Pennsylvania

Seattle, Washington

Oklahoma City, Oklahoma

Cincinnati, Ohio

Overton, Texas

Brooklyn, New York

De Leon, Texas

Fort Wayne, Indiana

Konawa, Oklahoma

Kentucky mountain mission

Zion, Illinois

Deadwood, South Dakota

Camp meetings have always been popular in the Assemblies of God.

Hurley, Mississippi

Oregon District campgrounds

Wescossville, Pennsylvania

COME TO THE
Union Pentecostal
CAMP MEETING
Of the Sixteenth Inter-State Convention and Central District Council
At West Park, Findlay, O.

In Large Tents on the Gospel School Campus

JULY
7-23
1922
INCLUSIVE

Evangelist Wm. Lambert Brant
OF CHICAGO, ILL.
Special Revivalist
Assisted by many Ministers of the Council and Missionaries with Soul Stirring Messages

SERVICES	Good Vocal and
10:00 A. M. and	Instrumental Music
2:00 and 7:30 P. M.	

OLD TIME
CAMP MEETING
JULY 21 to 31
ASSEMBLY OF GOD
STATE CAMP

HUNDREDS Will Be Camped In Magnolia Park, One - Half Mile East Of Seminole In A Large Tent 60x120 Feet. The Tent Has A Seating Capacity of 2,000. Section Reserved For Colored People.

WE Want All Humanity To Enjoy This Spiritual Awakening. Our Slogan "Get Back To God And The Bible."

COME ALL!
- HUNDREDS SINGING, SHOUTING AND PRAYING TO GOD.
- MANY MUSICAL INSTRUMENTS PLAYING IN THE ORCHESTRA.
- THE MIRACLE CHRIST AND HIS MIRACLE MESSAGE OF POWER GIVING THE MIRACLE OLD-TIME SALVATION TO ALL — IN THE MIRACLE CITY OF SEMINOLE OKLAHOMA.

BERL DODD
Pastor

PENTECOSTAL
Camp Meeting

To be held at Martinsville, Indiana
During the Month of August, 1915
[D. V.]

A Full Gospel Camp Meeting will be held at this place commencing the first of August, continuing throughout the month.

God has wonderfully visited this city in power during the passed few months, and we have the prospects of a wonderful meeting in the future.

We have purchased a large tent which is situated in a beautiful location, and God has been richly blessing us.

Able workers will be with us to give out the Word, and the Gospel of our Lord and Saviour Jesus Christ will be presented in its fullness.

Rooms for light housekeeping, and furnished rooms and board can be obtained at reasonable prices.

Martinsville is located 30 miles South of Indianapolis on the I. & V. railroad, also hourly service on interurban cars. For further information, address:

Pastor Fred Vogler

590 W. Morgan Street   Martinsville, Indiana

12. "Into All the World . . . Unto All People": Publishing and Missions

> There's a call comes ringing o'er the restless wave,
> "Send the light! Send the light!"
> There are souls to rescue, there are souls to save,
> Send the light! Send the light!
> Send the light, the blessed gospel light,
> Let it shine from shore to shore!
> Send the light, and let its radiant beams
> Light the world forevermore.
>
> Charles H. Gabriel, *Send the Light,* 1890

Assemblies of God leaders believed that evangelism was the Fellowship's reason for being. This conviction determined their priorities in mobilizing adherents to address the task. Gospel Publishing House developed as an agency to facilitate evangelism.

Commitment to publishing was an integral part of the earliest phases of the Pentecostal movement. As it formalized its goals, Gospel Publishing House had a tradition to build on. Early Pentecostal promoters of publishing had quickly discerned the varied possibilities of the printed page. They produced tracts by the thousands and inaugurated periodicals by the score. In fact, the earliest Pentecostal leadership was provided by people who published. In some cases, publishing followed recognition of charismatic leadership; in others, however, publishing was perceived as a primary way to extend the movement and to guide its opinions.[1]

Regular publications served several vital needs: They provided news of the extent of the revival, which contributed to a

279

growing sense of identity among disparate participants; they offered devotional and doctrinal articles that helped people understand their charismatic experiences; they popularized the terminology Pentecostals used to describe their religious experiences (words like "tarrying" or phrases with particular group meaning, like "praying through" or "let go and let God"); they publicized needs (some regularly published prayer requests from readers; some solicited evangelists and pastors for specific places) and testimonies; they occasionally exposed both unacceptable doctrines and errant workers; and they greatly enhanced the visibility and influence of those Pentecostal workers whose activities and sermons they reported.[2]

Pentecostal papers were frequently intended for wide distribution. They were both evangelistic and news-oriented. To make them more accessible, many were offered free of charge, published "as the Lord provides."[3] This seeming disregard of money harmonized with a widely-held concept of faith: God would provide for whatever He wanted done.[4] But some believed this approach did not go far enough. William Manley, editor of *The Household of God,* insisted that publishing "as the Lord provided" did not demonstrate faith: "Faith would publish the paper regularly, trusting God fully to supply the money without advertising for it."[5]

Other papers were available for a nominal charge. *Word and Work,* a widely circulated monthly published by the Christian Workers' Union in Massachusetts, cost fifty cents a year. In spite of this small subscription price, its editor, S. G. Otis, sometimes had difficulty collecting. "We have been financially embarrassed and have not had the money needed to print our publication and get it out promptly," he wrote in 1907.[6] *Word and Witness* also cost fifty cents a year; *The Christian Evangel* cost a dollar.

Pentecostal papers varied considerably in extent of coverage. Some presented local ministries only; others published devotional articles; some provided news of many ministries as well as articles by workers from many places on various doctrines and practices.[7] Doctrinal divisions and new "revelations" invariably spawned new papers and tracts. Usually monthlies, the papers provided a forum for presenting a wide variety of distinctive positions.[8]

Gospel Publishing House

Complementing the *Word and Witness, The Christian Evangel* was more specifically designed for Pentecostal readers. It included both a children's page and a Sunday school section, which presented the International Sunday School Lessons with a Pentecostal perspective. Although Bell had academic credentials, pastoral experience, and considerable seniority over his assistant, J. R. Flower, it was Flower who, from April 1914, made these two publications genuine voices of the General Council. Writing in a simple, forthright style, Flower contributed articles that demonstrated both less proclivity for potentially divisive "revelations" and more understanding for those who represented different viewpoints.

The newly combined efforts of Bell and Flower issued from Findlay, Ohio, until early in 1915 when the publishing interests—which all headquarters activity originally revolved around—moved to St. Louis. Although Bell had resigned the chairmanship in November 1914, he continued to serve as editor until October 1915, when the new chairman, John William Welch, assumed editorial oversight.[9] The 1915 General Council also acted to place the publishing house on a self-supporting basis by appointing Welch, Flower, and William G. Schell as a "managing Committee of the papers ... with the threefold object of securing donations, subscriptions and loans for the papers and publishing plant."[10] The St. Louis offices, with newly acquired equipment—some donated, some purchased—became a busy hub of activities for a growing staff.

Gospel Publishing House was far more than an agency for the publication of magazines. It also published tracts and carried numerous evangelical books to assist Christian workers. And, to a great extent, its personnel affected both the general perception and the effectiveness of the movement's endeavors.

By 1917, the publishing house was totally debt-free. *The Christian Evangel* and *Word and Witness* had been combined into a weekly periodical called *Weekly Evangel.*[11] Throughout these years, in keeping with the Council's early purpose to assist all segments of the Pentecostal movement, the *Evangel* continued to carry reports of non-Council ministries that shared the Council's doctrinal and experiential commitments. Increasingly, however, its denominational orientation predominated. In an effort to clarify the paper's espousal of distinctive Pentecostal views about evidential tongues, the 1919 General Council authorized a change of name to *Pentecostal Evangel.*[12] On October 18, 1919, the paper was issued with its new title, the title it has carried since.

The Appointment of Stanley Frodsham

At the 1916 General Council, Stanley Frodsham was appointed to assist Welch in editing General Council publications. While Welch kept responsibility for the *Evangel,* Frodsham assumed an increasing share of the load in addition to his responsibilities as general secretary and missionary treasurer. In 1919, John Thomas Boddy, an older minister who had been ordained as a Free Methodist and had later served in the Christian and Missionary Alliance, accepted the position of editor. (In 1919, all officers—the editor and assistant editor were considered Council officers—were elected from the General Presbytery, which consisted of twenty-seven ministers.[13]) Boddy's frail health necessitated Frodsham's continued involvement, until in 1921 Frodsham became editor in his own right.[14] Except for a brief interval (1928 to 1929), Frodsham served as editor of the *Pentecostal Evangel* until 1949. For most of those years, he was also general editor for all Gospel Publishing House publications. Frodsham's contacts with the Pentecostal movement in Europe and across Canada gave the early *Evangel* a broader perspective than most Pentecostal publications enjoyed. His keen interest in the movement's worldwide progress assured that the paper, essentially a General Council organ, would remain a Pentecostal weekly that non-Assemblies of God readers would also find profitable.[15] To a remarkable degree, Frodsham shared Flower's early perception of the importance of the paper to both the Council and the movement at large.

The *Pentecostal Evangel* continued to function much as many other Pentecostal periodicals had in the period prior to increased organization. Its supporters considered it "at the base of all the work of God in the General Council."[16] Through its pages, the executive officers communicated with the constituency. Because of it, leaders believed, "missionary enthusiasm" was "kept at boiling point."[17] The publication of missionary needs generated response. In 1919, the average *Evangel* reader contributed five dollars to foreign missions. Bell considered soliciting new *Evangel* subscriptions an essential part of the missionary task: Five thousand new subscribers, he noted, meant at least twenty-five thousand dollars more for missions. Withholding nothing for administrative expense, the headquarters in 1919 forwarded $96,973.59 to missions.[18] By 1925 (when missions was fully separated from Gospel Publishing House), the total funds disbursed had increased to $177,103.[19]

The General Council encouraged wide distribution of the *Evangel,* urging that it be placed in "depots, jails and public places" as well as in public libraries.[20] To expand its production of literature with a "distinctive Pentecostal testimony" the Council appointed a Committee on Publications, which in 1925 included John Welch, William Faux, Daniel Kerr, Joseph Tunmore, and J. Narver Gortner. The presbyters also began to consider compiling a hymnal; they issued several before World War II.

Early Growth

Statistics indicate slow but steady growth of Gospel Publishing House. By 1918 Bell, serving as its manager, reported that business between 1917 and 1918 had increased from seventeen thousand dollars to twenty three thousand dollars. By 1919, volume had exceeded thirty thousand dollars, and publishing house assets had increased by fifty percent. Such progress was made possible, in part, by a staff that worked "for a much less figure than they would receive if they worked outside for the world," Bell noted.[21] Their cooperation enabled the publishing house to operate debt-free and prompted Bell to predict a bright future.

At the new headquarters in Springfield, Flower oversaw the installation of the cylinder press, paper cutter, and linotype machine that had been moved from St. Louis. Constituting most of the equipment, they were installed on the ground level of the newly purchased two-story headquarters building on the corner of Lyon and Pacific streets. The second floor housed editorial, missionary, and executive offices.

By 1920, Gospel Publishing House had begun publishing Sunday school literature. The preparation of such materials had been extremely controversial during the Fellowship's brief history, and remained so for at least another decade. Many adherents believed they should read only the Bible, which the Holy Spirit would then enable them to comprehend. They strenuously resisted the use of quarterlies because they allowed a hearing for "man's wisdom." Bell concurred with the general view that existing Sunday school supplies were inadequate. As early as 1916, he had urged readers to make substantial contributions to enable Gospel Publishing House to produce acceptable helps for Sunday school members. His comments reveal the more general Pentecostal conviction, often expressed with considerable superiority, that Bible studies by non-Spirit-baptized Christians were necessarily inadequate. "It is very important," he claimed, "to get Helps printed by Pentecostal people who are filled with the Holy Ghost."[22] Bell also encouraged the use of quarterlies for children who seemed (to the childless Bell) alarmingly prone to lose Bibles. Observing that "if most small children had a Bible, they would tear it up or lose it in three weeks." He further commented that "parents should teach them better, but many do not correct this evil, and we have to face it as best we can."[23] With this rationale supporting its efforts to launch Sunday school publications (Bell found it necessary to assure his readers that it was no sin to read Bible verses printed outside the Bible), Gospel Publishing House slowly began to meet an increasing demand for "spiritual" supplies.

Reports to the 1925 General Council demonstrated that a market for Pentecostal-produced helps existed. The publishing house supplied 111,000 pieces of Sunday school literature per quarter, published two children's papers with a circulation of 37,000 (a gain of 32,000 over four years), and printed more than 5 million copies of Assemblies of God publications annually (an increase of nearly 2 million over two years).[24] An influential associate editor, Charles Elmo Robinson, joined the editorial staff in 1925. He and Frodsham generated a new effort: The production of children's books infused with moral instruction.[25]

By 1927, the growth of Gospel Publishing House resulted in its being placed under the direct supervision of a full-time plant manager. J. Z. Kamerer, an alumnus of the Rochester Bible Training Institute who had been in the printing department since 1919, supervised the expanding operation as plant manager until 1952. Kamerer gained wide respect among the constituency and was largely responsible for the rapid development of publishing capacity. After five expansion programs, the operation was moved to its present location at 1445 Boonville Avenue in 1961.

Foreign Missions to 1941

Implementing a missionary vision had been part of the purpose of those who had assembled at Hot Springs in 1914. They understood evangelism to be the supreme purpose of a renewed Pentecostal experience. Early teaching on tongues as missionary speech had supported the conviction that Spirit baptism was "power for service." Segments of the Pentecostal movement seemed to expect that the ability to proclaim the gospel in languages one had never learned would become widespread, and repeatedly claimed a limited facility to do so. At the same time, others never experienced speech in recognizable languages. They too considered themselves endued for service, and, for some at least, explanations like "wireless Pentecostal telegraphy" did not suffice (see chapter 7). Such men and women accepted the challenge of language study, believing nonetheless that the Holy Spirit had specifically granted them ability to proclaim the gospel with supernatural conviction among non-Christians.

The Missionary Vision

This emphasis on missions had several sources: premillennialism, with its focus on preparing the world for Christ's imminent return; a desire to hasten the Second Coming, based on a literal understanding of Matthew 24:14 ("This gospel of the kingdom shall be preached in all the world for a witness unto all nations; and then shall the end come"); the conviction that Pentecostalism was the "latter rain," which would fall on "all flesh"; and restorationism, which stressed the example of the Early Church. Those Pentecostals who rejected all organization beyond the local church also refused to organize support for missionaries beyond soliciting funds through publications or local congregations.

Most Pentecostal papers carried reports of missionary work; some specifically sought to keep readers aware of the needs of particular people.[26] But frequently papers were discontinued; local assemblies chose new leaders; prominent advocates of missionary activity died, or, occasionally, were repudiated for moral failure.[27] Though some missionaries on the field managed to establish strong outreaches, others found themselves virtually abandoned. Those whose call was rooted in the enthusiasm of an intense religious experience frequently failed abroad; moreover, they burdened other missionaries.

Pentecostalism spread to the mission field both by the arrival of Pentecostal missionaries from the United States and Europe and by the embracing of its message among missionaries already on the field.[28] Just as Christian and Missionary Alliance branches at home proved particularly receptive to the experience of spiritual gifts, so some Alliance missionaries responded positively to the message.[29] (And just as in the States, many tongues-speaking Alliance people never severed their ties to the group—and never accepted evidential tongues—so, many tongues-speaking Alliance missionaries continued to serve under the Alliance.) Because of the concentrations of missionaries in China and India, these countries were among the first to be targeted by ardent Pentecostal evangelists. Thomas Ball Barratt, Norway's Pentecostal pioneer whose influence extended rapidly across Europe after 1906, made an influential trip to India during which missionaries under appointment with many mission agencies received the Pentecostal experience.[30]

Precisely how such missionaries continued to relate to their agencies is unclear, although a general pattern is evident: Some identified with Pentecostalism; others remained under appointment with non-Pentecostal mission boards; and still others opted for independent endeavors. At first, of course, there were no specifically Pentecostal agencies that they could identify with. Some were willing to live by "faith" and accomplished impressive tasks without any official endorsement. Others, however, responded gladly when, with the 1914 General Council, opportunity came to identify with the Assemblies of God. Although many repudiated organization, they nevertheless shared the sentiment veteran China missionary William W. Simpson expressed when he accepted Assemblies of God appointment late in 1916: "I don't care for a mission board to back me up with pledged financial support; but I must have people of like precious faith to uphold me with their prayers and fellowship. . . . I want to be sent forth with the hearty cooperation, sympathy, and prayers of the people of God following me."[31]

Unlike many other Pentecostal associations (an article in the *Weekly Evangel* estimated the existence of some forty distinct Pentecostal groups by 1916) in which missionary goals tended to be diffused and unformulated, the General Council had been formed with several specific missionary objectives in mind. It hoped to generate missionary fervor at home, set guidelines enabling candidates to gain Council endorsement, and ascertain that missionaries obtained adequate support. It sought to advance missions by encouraging coordination and cooperation among those on the field.[32] These goals had been occasioned by the problems missionary work had generated in the first decade of Pentecostal activity. They expressed the desire to assure that candidates were worthy and that they would have the resources to accomplish their task. They understood that task as evangelism—the proclamation of Christ, not the addressing of social problems.

Implementing the Vision

Implementing the vision took time. Numerous Pentecostal centers, generally focusing in either a publication (like the *Latter Rain Evangel)* or a Bible school (like Beulah Heights or Bethel, both in New Jersey), sent out their own missionaries. Some of these centers gradually merged into the General Council, but their missionaries did not necessarily solicit General Council endorsement. Some experienced missionaries who decided to affiliate found cooperation difficult after years of independent ministry.

When the first roster of General Council workers was published in the fall of 1914, it contained the names of sixteen missionaries representing seven fields. By 1915, the affiliated missionary family would number fifty-four, representing nine fields. The first General Council devoted little time to devising ways to address its missions task. When the second General Council (November 1914) convened in the missionary-minded Stone Church in Chicago, Council leaders hoped to climax the sessions with a missions emphasis. However, the pastor, R. L. Erickson (who was also an executive presbyter), was unwilling to cooperate, demanding instead an offering for the church; the missions emphasis was postponed until 1915.

At the 1914 General Council in Chicago, Lemuel C. Hall framed a resolution by which the delegates committed themselves to "the greatest evangelism that the world has ever known."[33] The ambitiousness of the task, in spite of the remarkable advancement of Protestant missions during the preceding "great century" of the expansion of Christianity, did not daunt them.[34] In the audacity of such commitment was part of the secret of decisive action. In spite of general turmoil over Oneness teaching, Council delegates found time to urge presbyters (in 1915 there was no distinction between an Executive and a General Presbytery) to strive for cooperation among the various centers supporting missionary endeavor. The Council did not call upon such centers to identify with Council efforts; rather, it hoped to promote "greater efficiency" within each of them, a curious objective, since its realization mandated interfering in the affairs of others. It is evident that the concept of cooperation had not yet assumed the overtones of loyalty and denominationalism that it would later display.

Meanwhile, Council publications continued to report the efforts of various "worthy" missionaries in many fields, many of whom had not as yet sought the endorsement of the Council. Council publications were sent to missionaries without charge, and the editors handled missionary funds. In return, Bell requested only that missionaries provide him with news that would maintain a high level of interest in missions among his subscribers.

The realities of prolonged warfare between 1914 and 1918 helped the headquarters staff realize their hope that Assemblies of God congregations would channel their missionary giving through the headquarters office. As it became increasingly difficult to ascertain that funds would reach their destination, Bell sought to find ways to assure that missionaries received their support. The situation also encouraged giving in larger amounts since it became advisable to transfer funds less frequently.

The resolution of the Oneness issue in 1916 helped, in the end, to stabilize confidence in the intent of the General Council. Though the general commitment to a cooperative fellowship remained the same, a subtle change began to manifest itself as Council-approved interpretations of specific doctrines became requisites for General Council credentials endorsement. This did not spawn immediate conformity. (Numerous "private opinions" have been held by General Council members; however, usually they have not been propagated or made a source of contention.) The application for credentials required potential Council ministers to affirm both their intention of cooperating with the decisions of the General Council and their commitment to the Statement of Fundamental Truths. Missionary giving in 1917 increased dramatically over the previous year, and seventy-three missionaries (excluding dependents) composed the Council's missionary family.

As in other denominations, a consistently strong percentage of the early Assemblies of God missionaries were women. The

General Council offered women ordination as missionaries and from the fall of 1914 approved of women missionaries administering the ordinances of the church and presiding at weddings and funerals if no man was available. Similar rights were not offered to women in the States until 1919 (the same restrictions were appended). By 1917, however, the General Council had stopped ordaining workers as missionaries. It simply ordained qualified workers to the ministry. Until 1935, when women's full ordination was explicitly granted, their official ministerial status was ambiguous.[35]

In 1917, the General Council formed its first Foreign Missions Committee. Composed of John Welch, Eudorus Bell, Stanley Frodsham, George Eldridge, William Simpson (missionary to China), and Susan Easton (a missionary with thirty-three years of experience when she accepted Assemblies of God appointment to North India in 1918), the committee interviewed prospective candidates in an effort to implement Council policy relative to missionary qualifications and the conducting of missionary work.[36] The committee was short-lived, however, as both Simpson and Easton left for their fields.

The 1918 Council further defined missionary procedure, requiring each missionary to submit quarterly financial reports and deciding to grant missionary appointment certificates. Frodsham, who served as missionary treasurer from 1916 to 1919, was able annually to report substantial increases in missionary giving. When he noted in 1919 that giving had more than doubled in the past year, the Council reacted in typical Pentecostal fashion: "The whole Council arose to their feet and praised the Lord."[37]

In keeping with its purpose to facilitate the efforts of all who shared its vision, the General Council continued both to publicize and forward offerings to missionaries who had not received endorsement from the missionary committee. In 1918 it also set up a fund to support publicity and missionary expenses. Contributions totaling nearly five hundred dollars enabled the denomination to publish and circulate some eighty thousand missionary tracts, used to cultivate missionary interest among the constituency. The mailing of some ten thousand tracts to subscribers of *The Christian Evangel,* for example, had resulted immediately in a "marked increase" in missionary giving.[38]

The Development of a Missions Department

Early attempts to define missionary policy culminated in 1919 with actions that established beyond question the intention of the General Council to function as an "aggressive agency for foreign missionary work."[39] Meeting for the second time in five years at the Stone Church in Chicago, the Council sat for only five days. In those five days, it made its first attempt to create a department of foreign missions.

The decision to separate missions from publishing was inevitable. The rapid increase in the number of missionaries (their number had increased from 16 in 1914 to 195 in 1919) and the extent of their outreach not only overburdened the editorial staff, it also required more concentrated supervision and bookkeeping. The Council heard reports of worldwide progress: Through Missionaries James Harvey and Will Norton the Assemblies of God had contributed over forty-four hundred dollars to famine relief in India; donations of nearly fifteen hundred dollars had paid for a saw mill to facilitate the construction of adequate housing for missionaries in Liberia; over a thousand dollars had been provided to enable sick missionaries to return home; in Japan, where in 1918 none of the native workers had received Spirit baptism, fifty Japanese had spoken in tongues.[40]

Council participants recognized an integral relationship between extension of the work at home and missionary progress. And some had already begun to share the vision of M. M. Pinson, focusing their attention on the ethnic groups that constituted, from their point of view, a foreign mission field in the United States. In 1916 Henry Ball, in Kingsville, Texas, inaugurated *La Luz Apostolica* ("The Apostolic Light"), a Spanish periodical that would eventually become the official paper of the Latin American District Council of the Assemblies of God. Shortly thereafter, Alice Eveline Luce began work among Mexican Americans in Southern California; she would be instrumental in the founding of the Berean Bible Institute of San Diego.

In a decision with far-reaching implications, then, the 1919 General Council created a missionary department, supervised by the Executive Presbytery, to coordinate the Fellowship's varied missionary interests. A nominating committee presented three names as candidates for the office of Missionary Secretary: Archibald Collins, James Evans, and J. Roswell Flower. Flower, who had left the headquarters to engage in convention work in southern Missouri and northern Arkansas, was selected on the first ballot, an election made unanimous on motion.[41] Few within the nucleus of stateside Assemblies of God leaders had done as much to facilitate the growing missionary outreach as had the thirty-one-year-old Flower. Farsighted and noted for integrity, common sense, and spirituality, Flower had already gained considerable experience in coordinating missionary activities; he also enjoyed the confidence of both missionaries and the American constituency.

When he took office, Flower gratefully noted a recent dramatic increase in foreign missions giving. (This was undoubtedly related both to the increase in membership and to postwar affluence.) Even during the war years, however, lack of finances had not hindered missionary appointment. Although all personnel had not been generously underwritten, all of those "whom the brethren deemed . . . profitable for the ministry" had been accepted. Flower regarded as the task of the missions committee the "recognition of the Pauls and Barnabases" and the "elimination of the John Marks who would likely lose heart and come back before they should."[42] Deciding how to assign undesignated funds proved difficult. Flower noted that fully two-thirds of the missionaries qualified for any funds submitted for "the neediest missionary."[43]

Flower's philosophy of missions captured the pervasive, though unacknowledged, persuasion that somehow Pentecostals were called to do something different from other missions agencies. Restorationist dreams (though modified somewhat by the time of the 1920s, a modification accelerated by the culture of that decade itself) sustained the sense that the movement had been charged with a solemn and distinctively Pentecostal mandate; such a mandate both legitimated its missionary efforts as well as set them apart in significant ways from those of non-Pentecostals. "Pentecostal missionaries," Flower insisted, "have a holy calling. They cannot follow the methods of non-Pentecostals who have gone before, neither can they bend their efforts in building up charitable institutions, hospitals and schools. Pentecostal missionaries have a Pentecostal commission—to be witnesses in Jerusalem, in Judea, and to the uttermost parts of the earth. Witnesses!"[44] Executive Presbyter Daniel Kerr concurred: "It is not wise to construct much machinery. We have enough! What we need is a lubricant—oil from heaven."[45]

Missionaries rather quickly discovered the advantages of "machinery," however. Lillian Trasher, for one, channeled her missionary efforts through a charitable institution: She founded an orphanage that over the years provided for thousands of children and widows. Missionaries in North China began a Bible school in 1922 to help implement their commitment to train native workers; such institutions soon became characteristic of Assemblies of God efforts abroad. During the 1920s, Harold Waggoner, who had been in North India since 1913, brought his leper colony under the General Council. Gradually some Assemblies of God missionaries overcame early fears that efforts to meet human needs through traditional channels were necessarily inferior to direct evangelistic outreach.

As missions efforts became established with concentrations of missionaries in specific fields, missionaries formed district councils. The earliest were in North China (where W. W. Simpson and George and Harriet Slager were among those whose reports inspired the Fellowship), North India (where Christian and Violet Schoonmaker, Harold Waggoner, and James and Esther Harvey were prominent Council representatives), Japan (where Carl Juergensen, ably assisted in his outreach by his daughter Marie's fluency in Japanese, established the Assemblies of God presence), Egypt (where W. I. Doney and Lillian Trasher were among those who labored), and Liberia (to which Methodist missionaries John and Jessie Perkins returned from furlough convinced Pentecostals and where they pioneered for the Assemblies of God). These early foreign districts were conceived as districts of the American Assemblies of God, and their full membership was limited to missionaries.

Motivated by restorationist hopes, millenarian urgency, and Christian compassion, such missionaries nonetheless often shared assumptions of cultural superiority with other Westerners. Stories of their adventures, sorrows, and triumphs regularly appeared in the *Evangel* and helped prompt missions giving.

In 1921, Missionary Secretary Flower made the first attempt to grapple with the realities of missions finance by computing a basic budget. Such scrutinization of financial needs seemed, to some, to betray the Pentecostal commitment to faith living; Flower realized, however, that financial responsibility would be requisite to the development of an extensive missionary outreach. His early efforts bore no relationship to either available funds or requirements for appointment; they were simply the first projection of the real financial needs of a growing missionary force. In a year in which missionary giving reached $107,953.55, Flower estimated that some $233,800 was needed as a base budget. His projections were minimal: $40 per month for each missionary, $20 for each child, $25 per month for maintenance of mission property, $500 travel expenses for each missionary going to or returning from the field. Many missionaries lived on far less than the projected budget would have allowed. While some received support that was not channeled through the Council, and others obtained indigenous assistance, most experienced some degree of financial need; some knew real economic hardship for prolonged periods.

When they left the United States, many early Pentecostal missionaries were uncertain when—or if—they would return: Some considered Christ's return so imminent that they believed they would be raptured before their furloughs; some simply decided that the magnitude of the task mandated their remaining on the field indefinitely. This is characterized by an Alice Wood—in Argentina for fifty years without a furlough; an Anna Ziese—in China despite Communist advance; a Jessie

Wengler—in Japan during World War II. They considered themselves called and committed for life. (Professionalization would later contribute to a significant modification of that perception.)

The annals of early Assemblies of God missions include numerous accounts of those whose missionary commitment cost them their lives. Exposed to unsanitary conditions and unprepared for extremes of climate or diet, some succumbed early to such sicknesses as dysentery and cholera. Among the best-known of those who died on the field was Eric Booth-Clibborn, grandson of General William Booth, founder of the Salvation Army. Entrusted with the sensitive task of reorganizing a troubled field, Booth-Clibborn and his wife arrived in French West Africa (now Burkina Faso) on June 19, 1924; nineteen days later, Booth-Clibborn died of dysentery.[46]

By 1925, when both the General Council and its foreign missions program experienced a change in executive leadership, the groundwork had been laid for the building of an extensive foreign missions outreach. With one missionary for every five stateside preachers, the Assemblies of God had a growing missionary presence in several fields. In addition to the larger efforts in China, India, and Africa, outreaches were scattered across Central and South America and the Middle East. Working under a philosophy of "establishing self-supporting native churches in each field," the foreign missions department also endeavored to promote missionary fervor at home.[47]

The mid-1920s were no exception to the persistent Pentecostal tendency to seem gripped by a conviction that "the whole structure of civilization" was threatened by unprecedented cultural change. Optimistically and naively they proclaimed "native religions" inadequate to meet the crisis.[48] To their way of thinking, Christianity was "the only adequate force." Their reports would leave the impression that the task of rapid evangelization could—and should—be relatively easy. Though reports continued to note the "victories" Pentecostals expected, some of them learned through hardship the inevitability of conflict and the loneliness of rejection. Often criticized by their more secular contemporaries for disdaining and undermining ancient cultures or for seeking to impose Western values on their Third-World converts, missionaries actually (if inadvertently) made vital contributions to indigenous movements striving to disown colonial allegiances.[49] For its part, the Assemblies of God noted that emerging nationalist movements tended to encourage native Christians to support the Council's efforts to create self-supporting national churches.[50]

Reports of progress were tempered by the reality that in some years as many as fifty percent of affiliated American congregations contributed nothing to foreign missions. For those who understood the movement in terms of a compulsion to engage in end-times evangelism, this fact should have raised questions about the adequacy of the generally-accepted Assemblies of God opinion that foreign missions was at the core of the Fellowship's reason for being. Though unacknowledged, the issue focused on an essential aspect of the commonly held understanding of the meaning and function of Pentecostalism.

From 1922 through 1925, adherents in the same seven states gave in record amounts to missions: California, Ohio, Pennsylvania, New York, Illinois, Missouri, Texas.[51] By 1925, New York City's Glad Tidings Tabernacle led Assemblies of God churches in missionary giving. Other congregations consistently among the top contributors were The Christian Church, Cleveland, Ohio, (D. P. Holloway); Bethel Temple, Los Angeles (Louis Turnbull); Highway Mission Tabernacle, Philadelphia (Ernest Williams); The Gospel Tabernacle, Minneapolis (Frank Lindquist).

Although offerings reaching Springfield were larger than ever, the practice of deducting nothing for office expenses resulted in a continuing need for operational funds. These were met through an account that accepted donations for office expenses, through the sale of missionary literature and offering barrels, by interest on bank accounts, and through small grants from the general fund. Missions personnel recognized the need for future development of a sound financial program for the department.

The Appointment of Noel Perkin

At the 1925 Council, Flower turned over the leadership of the foreign missions department to William Faux and moved to a pastorate in Scranton, Pennsylvania. Faux, ordained a Baptist minister in 1900, had affiliated with the Assemblies of God while a pastor in Butler, New Jersey, having received his Spirit baptism in 1914. After spending several years at Beulah Heights Bible School in North Bergen, New Jersey, he had fulfilled various headquarters responsibilities before accepting appointment as missionary secretary-treasurer in 1925. His tenure was brief, however. Disqualified by financial misconduct, he was dropped in 1926 and replaced in 1927 by Noel Perkin, a man whose integrity and dedication during his thirty-two years of service would earn him the title Mr. Missions.

A native of London, England, Perkin had been reared in the Wesleyan Methodist Church. As a young man, he accepted a position in the Bank of Montreal, where he was employed for seven years. Throughout his formative years, people involved in missions influenced him profoundly. In Canada, he "feasted on the truths" presented in Christian and Missionary Alliance gatherings; this contact, he later claimed, provided the "foundation teaching" that made him receptive to Pentecostalism. In cottage meetings and small mission halls, he began to seek his own Spirit baptism. In such settings he met people like Christian Schoonmaker, a former Alliance adherent (later an Assemblies of God missionary, and the father of Assemblies of God Missionaries Paul, Joe, Grace, Mary, Martha, and Ruth Schoonmaker) whose spirituality, Perkin recalled, made him "hungry." But it was in his room in a boardinghouse that he first "found [himself] pouring out expressions in a strange language . . . praying unto God."[52]

Uncertain of his ability to preach, Perkin nonetheless shared the evangelistic fervor that seemed to compel his Pentecostal friends to activity. He and several businessmen rented a large hall, accommodating some twelve hundred people, and sponsored evangelistic services. Evangelists A. H. Argue and Andrew Urshan were the first to provide several weeks of nightly meetings. Other evangelists followed, and the sponsors discovered the need to find assistance in following up the converts. They secured the services of James R. Evans (later general secretary of the Assemblies of God), W. Pocock, and Christian Schoonmaker successively.

Perkin was the growing congregation's treasurer; as the need arose he also preached, learning as he went. With a regular attendance of some six hundred, the congregation's leaders decided to sponsor a foreign missions convention. (All who had roots in the Christian and Missionary Alliance were convinced of the advantages of missionary conventions: prolonged times of emphasis on missions through reports from mission fields, motivational sermons, and an emphasis on sacrificial giving that A. B. Simpson used with remarkable success to raise funds for overseas evangelism.) There Perkin sensed his own call to the mission field. He relinquished his job and in 1918 was ordained by three elders of his mission (known by then as Trinity Pentecostal Assembly), J. R. Evans, C. A. McKinney, and George C. Slager, a missionary to China since 1910. In November 1918 he received credentials with the General Council; shortly thereafter, supported by faith, he left for Argentina. "I had no promise of support," he later recalled, "other than the assurance that my friends at Trinity Pentecostal Assembly would most likely stand back of me as far as they were able."[53] Experience during several years on the field expanded Perkin's grasp of faith living and helped prepare him for a life of sensitive identification with missionary situations around the world.

Returning to the States in 1921, Perkin decided to "seek God's mind" at the Elim Bible Training School in Rochester, New York. An assistant at Elim Tabernacle and a participant in some of the classes, Perkin not only found spiritual succor, he also met and married Ora Blanchard. After serving two pastorates in upstate New York, the couple accepted an invitation to assist in the business management of Gospel Publishing House. They moved to Springfield in 1926, and the next year Perkin assumed the duties of missionary secretary. For the next thirty-two years, he "lived, ate, drank, talked, dreamed and sacrificed for missions." He served with five general superintendents: William T. Gaston, Ernest S. Williams, Wesley Steelberg, Gayle Lewis, and Ralph Riggs.[54]

The newly focused Missionary Department that Perkin agreed to supervise had been given its mandate by the 1925 General Council:

> 1. To extend the knowledge of Christ throughout the world, by utilizing the services of the church, with a view to establishing of self-supporting native churches in each field.
> 2. To promote an interest in foreign missions by approved methods in the home churches.[55]

In retrospect, Perkin commented on the significance of the new approach: "This meant moving away from somewhat unrelated efforts of individual missionaries in favor of a concentrated effort on the part of a united Assemblies of God fellowship working through its established channel, the Missionary Department, with the missionaries cooperating, to effect world evangelization."[56]

Support of the Constituency

As in other denominations, lay women in the Assemblies of God soon saw missionary efforts as an opportunity for direct participation. No movement comparable to earlier Protestant "women's work for women" evolved, however. Assemblies of God women followed the lead of Etta Calhoun, who, like many other early Pentecostals, had served in local Women's Christian Temperance Union chapters. With the blessing of her district presbyter, Calhoun organized a Women's Missionary Council (WMC) at Morwood Mission in Houston in February 1925. Other local congregations emulated her efforts, and in August 1925, the Texas-New Mexico District Council officially acknowledged the auxiliary function of WMC groups. Despite reluctance among those whose restorationist sympathies made them insist that no New Testament prerogative for women's associations existed, other districts authorized similar organizations. After several appeals to the General Council for national recognition in the form of the appointment of a coordinator for local activities, the national office was created in 1951 with Edith Whipple as its first secretary.

The North Central District also introduced a plan to raise funds. Proposing to eliminate separate offerings for home and foreign missions, the district suggested the Busy Bee Plan, under which wooden beehive banks were given to local church members so they could "make honey" for God. After some modification, the Missionary Department introduced the program as the World Missions Plan. All offerings received under the plan were divided so that home missions received twenty-five percent and foreign missions received seventy-five percent.[57]

By 1929, the missionary list had grown to 279. From around the world, workers sent in reports of hardship as well as of success. Civil unrest made China, where sixty-four appointed missionaries served, a particularly difficult field. Bandits constantly threatened; roving bands of soldiers provided little security. Robbers terrorized whole communities, and missionaries saw cannibalism, torture, rape, and murder. Usually, they were horrified witnesses. Occasionally, however, they became victims. In June 1916, Missionary Elmer Hammond was returning by train to Hong Kong from a baptismal service in Nyan Pui Leung in southern China. About a hundred thieves attacked the train, disabling it and robbing the passengers. Hammond was among those who died.[58] In 1932, Missionary William E. Simpson (son of the China veteran, W. W. Simpson), a dedicated worker who had been in China fourteen years without a furlough, was murdered by bandits as he traveled to meet new missionaries who had responded to his appeal for help.

Despite such hindrances, missionaries reported conversions and hope. Eastern Europeans seemed especially receptive to Pentecostal teaching, and the General Council arranged to work in cooperation with the Russian and Eastern European Mission. By 1929, John E. Voronaeff and his wife, Katherine, assisted by local workers, had brought between four and five hundred churches together to create a Russian Assemblies of God.[59] The movement progressed in western Europe (where it was entirely indigenous) and other parts of the world as well.

In the United States, the outreach among Spanish-speaking peoples had expanded sufficiently to warrant its organization in 1929 as the Latin American District Council of the Assemblies of God. The tireless efforts of Henry and Sunshine Ball, complemented by the dedication of Alice Eveline Luce and the vision of non-Spanish-speaking supporters like M. M. Pinson, assured the continued growth of efforts among Spanish-speaking Americans. Luce, who had begun working with the Assemblies of God in 1915 in Texas and Mexico, later moved to California where she became involved in the Spanish section of Berean Bible Institute in San Diego. Bible schools in San Antonio and Mexico City also served this constituency. Ball's publishing efforts in San Antonio facilitated Spanish outreach by providing Spanish periodicals, tracts, and hymnals.

As the missions program had moved toward centralized organization during the 1920s, missions executives had developed ties with established missionary agencies. Representatives of the General Council, for example, attended conferences of the Student Volunteer Movement. Such associations were vivid reminders of the continuing struggle for self-identity. On the one hand, although many local preachers with only the most rudimentary education stirred their congregations with essentially separatist fundamentalist diatribe, at another level, the organization contained some whose loyalty did not blind them to advantages offered by association, however informal, with other Christians. The conviction that Pentecostalism should energize and unify the church managed to resurface occasionally, although it consistently proved troubling. The Fellowship's leaders generally seemed convinced that they needed to work on their own, writing their own textbooks, publishing their own devotional materials, and providing their own tracts. Missionary personnel occasionally conveyed the impression that they were the only missionaries on a given field. But missionary work often tends, in the end, to promote a degree of ecumenism that eludes home churches. Before long, Perkin recognized that the Assemblies of God could best use its resources by concentrating in areas where evangelical missionaries were not already at work.

An Expanding Missionary Force

As the missionary force expanded, the problem of endorsing those whom leaders accepted as having a "genuine call" while maintaining financial accountablity caused growing concern. General Superintendent Ernest Williams insisted that if the foreign missions committee selected candidates carefully, funds would be available. In other words, he posited a "covenantal" arrangement: If the committee chose those who had demonstrated both "consecration" and "ministry gifts," God could be depended on to supply financial needs.[60] Perkin proposed to give more consideration to applicants' "quality" than to available funds. Such reasoning had in it the seeds of various problems, the fruit of which the Fellowship would face later. For the moment, the proposal's simple force prevailed.

The Missions Department, committed to the notion that prayer was the key to advance, enlisted over ten thousand "partners" who pledged to pray daily for both the success of missionary outreach and guidance for missionaries. In a decade of both severe financial need and worldwide political uncertainties, these partners were frequently asked to address specific needs; reports of "victories" circulated in General Council publications. In June 1930, for example, missions giving fell far below the necessary minimum. The prayer bands were mobilized, and July giving was the highest the Missions Department had ever received in a single month. Evidencing a simple faith that marked early Pentecostal "prayer warriors," Perkin attributed financial generosity to the prayers of his partners.[61]

Financial realities at home forced the adoption during the 1930s of what Perkin termed a conservative missionary policy. Although the Fellowship did not recall workers because of financial need, it did delay the departure of new recruits. In 1932, the General Presbytery charged a specially constituted missionary committee to investigate missionary personnel so that the central office could have more accurate information about both the "character and efficiency" of the Fellowship's missionaries. The committee solicited information from foreign district leaders. As a result, some missionaries were removed from the rolls, and channels were set up through which information could be readily obtained.

Concentrated reflection on Assemblies of God missions yielded the fact that far more women served on the foreign field than did men. This had been true of American foreign missions for years, but in the Assemblies of God, the recognition prompted concern. In 1931, Perkin cited the findings of "competent authorities" who had surveyed several Assemblies of God fields and advised him that "the work of the General Council of the Assemblies of God depends too much on women workers." Noting gratitude to the women who "filled the gap" (implying both that men were not fulfilling their calls and that women were only temporarily supplying the need), he encouraged men and married couples to seek missionary appointment.[62]

Several times during the 1930s, Perkin, accompanied by other Fellowship executives, toured Assemblies of God mission fields. The firsthand experience from such trips enabled leaders to better encourage missionary support at home and formulate realistic and practical policies.

The same concern voiced during the prosperous 1920s continued to be heard during the depressed 1930s: Missionary finances would be more than adequate if every member would contribute. In 1933, Perkin estimated that five cents per member per week would "restore our missionary giving to its highest level of the past."[63] Six cents would enable "advanced missionary effort." Yet, almost entirely, missionary funds came from a mere thirty percent of adherents; seventy percent gave "almost nothing."

Such statistics changed little throughout the period. Nor did the basic question, evaded by many: Was the movement, in fact, essentially an evangelistic thrust, rooted in a distinctive understanding of an "enduement with power for service"? Far fewer than half of the affiliated congregations seemed to agree. The statistics laid bare a fundamental disagreement within the rank and file about the practical meaning of Spirit baptism. Another problem, of course, was the growing presence of a second and third generation of Assemblies of God adherents who had not necessarily experienced Spirit baptism. Could one rightly claim to be Pentecostal if one only casually related to the movement's distinctive doctrine? Throughout the decade, although such questions became increasingly relevant, they did not surface. Perkin, rather, reiterated constantly the need for each congregation to adopt a clearly defined missionary policy and the advantages to home congregations of support for foreign evangelism.

The Effects of the Pre-War Years on the Missions Endeavor

When the 1935 Council convened in Dallas, the Assemblies of God had 287 missionaries in 37 countries, assisted by 641 national workers. This represented a fairly large turnover, since by 1935, missionaries under appointment with the Pentecostal Assemblies of Canada had been removed from the General Council list. Of the 235 missionaries on the field in 1925, only 113 remained under General Council appointment in 1933. Wrestling with the perennial problem of meager resources, Perkin advocated the placement of concentrations of workers where they were most likely to succeed in establishing self-governing, self-supporting, and—most importantly—self-propagating churches.[64]

The changing world situation had begun to create serious problems for missionaries in some places. The General Council's direct involvement in Russia ended, for example, when John and Katherine Voronaeff and were arrested and sent into exile during the Stalinist purges; they ultimately spent at least twenty years in Russian prisons.[65]

Reflecting a surge of anti-Communism in the broader culture, Assemblies of God adherents expressed dismay over newly elected President Franklin Roosevelt's determination to extend official recognition to Stalin's government. After the Communist party had seized control of Russia in the revolution of 1917, the United States had refused to recognize the regime, and mutual hostility had marked the relationship of the two powers. The General Council in session in 1933 in Philadelphia took the unusual (and unsuccessful) step of approving a resolution addressed to Roosevelt, urging him not to recognize Russia unless the Russian government committed itself to religious liberty; freedom of speech, assembly and the press; opportunity for Russians to emigrate freely; freedom for the Russian poor to receive clothing packages without paying excessive duties.[66]

Throughout other parts of Eastern Europe, Assemblies of God efforts continued to be coordinated through the Russian and Eastern European Mission. Both the mission's president, Paul Peterson, and its vice president, Gustav Schmidt, were General Council ministers. Efforts to train local workers centered in a Bible school in Danzig, of which Nicholas Nikoloff was president.[67]

Mexico illustrated another accelerating trend in missions administration. The political situation—which had long been plagued by tensions exacerbated by American foreign policy—made it necessary to place the control of Assemblies of God interests in local hands. "When once they begin to look to America for support the whole project takes on a foreign aspect," Perkin noted, "and is branded as supported by foreign funds and therefore does not draw the interest a self-supporting native assembly attracts."[68] In this case, political realities coincided with longheld convictions to facilitate the realization of the goal.

In 1931, as Japan exercised political and military muscle (ignoring, for example, restrictions that arms agreements of the 1920s had imposed on its naval development), Perkin noted with concern that a troubled future seemed assured. "Japan," he explained, "must have room for expansion, or war is bound to ensue. Hundreds and thousands of men are out of employment and the agents of Communism are busy secretly sowing their literature on this fruitful soil."[69] Still, fourteen Assemblies of God missionaries, assisted by twelve national workers, struggled to penetrate this ancient culture with their message.

Each year, however, reports of progress were tempered by the presentation of statistics reminding evangelistically-minded stateside congregations that Assemblies of God missionaries were "only touching the fringe of the unevangelized millions, and that there is yet much land to be possessed."[70] Throughout the period, such militaristic language (which would later have unacceptable imperialistic overtones in some parts of the world) continued to describe Assemblies of God objectives.

In 1941 the General Council convened in Minneapolis amid growing concern about American involvement in war. The Council adopted as its theme Our Place in the Present World Crisis; this meant, essentially, prolonged consideration about how the Fellowship could minister effectively to servicemen. Meanwhile, the Missions Department had been grappling for several years with the worsening world situation. Perkin's somber report noted that "tens of thousands of ministers and devoted Christians... [were] languishing in concentration camps" while thousands more had already been killed in war.[71] Missionaries could no longer enter Europe, and in Syria, Iraq, and French West Africa they faced significant war-related dangers. But few had returned home. Rather, they solicited prayer for "strength... to carry on in spite of conditions."[72]

In spite of the closing of several countries to American missionaries, 394 missionaries were at work in 43 foreign lands. Since 1939, more than a hundred missionaries (more than half of them newly appointed) had crossed the oceans through war zones. All but four who had been passengers on the torpedoed SS Zamzam had safely reached their destinations. They had been rescued and awaited new travel arrangements. War conditions, however, had produced sharp increases in the costs of living abroad; steamer fares had doubled. As in World War I, restrictions on the way money could be transmitted necessitated accommodations in the handling of finances.

By the late 1930s, civil unrest forced missionaries in China to be constantly prepared to leave the field. Typically, however, a worsening situation seemed to spark renewal everywhere. (In fact, early Pentecostals had maintained that an absence of persecution signaled waning group fervor.)

As American entry into the war approached, the Assemblies of God also entered several new fields where, over time, the denomination would grow dramatically. Brazil is a case in point. Pentecostal teaching had been introduced in this country, which would ultimately be home to the largest number of Assemblies of God adherents in any nation, primarily by Scandinavian missionaries. In 1936, in response to appeals from Assemblies of God workers already in Brazil, the missions department approved six missionaries for appointment to Brazil. In 1986, 51.9 percent of the total worldwide Assemblies of God constituency was in Brazil.

In 1939, Everett and Dorothy Phillips accepted missionary appointment to Nigeria, where the circulation of literature like copies of the *Pentecostal Evangel* had produced a strong nucleus of believers before missionaries arrived. Over the years, through the dedicated efforts of missionaries like the Phillipses, Nigeria became the foremost Assemblies of God field in Africa. Shortly after his arrival, Everett Phillips launched Central Bible Institute of Nigeria, a timely project that developed into the largest Assemblies of God ministerial school overseas.

Farther north, in Egypt, Lillian Trasher was already becoming a legend as her orphanage expanded, winning recognition from various sources. Much of the recognition was verbal, but occasionally large gifts—like the twenty-five thousand dollars donated by an anonymous titled Briton—heartened this hardworking, unselfish woman.

As America entered the war, then, Assemblies of God overseas efforts continued to expand wherever possible. More missionaries went to the field every year; few returned home to evade crises. An era of intense suffering was about to begin for some, as they would come to share in the experiences of the citizens of other countries whose governments were already at war. Unknown to them, they had come to the end of an era. For Assemblies of God efforts at home and abroad, the war years would be transitional. The growing debate over education revealed some of the underlying tensions that stimulated change.

Some early Pentecostal periodicals

Employees of Gospel Publishing House at their new office in Springfield, Missouri, 1918

Pentecostal Evangel staff, 1928. Left to right: Marjorie Head, Stanley Frodsham, Charles Robinson.

The Assemblies of God work in Suva, Fiji, was begun by Albert and Lou Page, here with their children in 1917.

Prayer cards like these have always been used by Assemblies of God missionaries.

**J. Elmor Morrisons
Missionaries to China**

MISSIONARIES TO
CHINA

Glenn and Pauline Dunn

*Stir me, O stir me Lord, I care not how;
But Stir my heart in passion for the world;
Stir me to give, to go, but most to pray;
Stir, 'till the Blood-red banner be unfurled
O'er lands that still in heathen darkness lie,
O'er deserts where no Cross is lifted high.*

And this Gospel of the Kingdom shall be preached in all the world for a witness unto all nations; and then shall the end come.
Matt. 24:14.

Home Address	In Fellowship With:
2914 Jones Street	General Council
Greenville, Texas	of the
	Assemblies of God.

"The harvest truly is great, but the labourers are few. Pray ye, therefore . . ." Luke 10:2.

Anne R. Eberhardt

Missionary to India

*Rev. and Mrs. Nicholas Nikoloff
and son Paul*

Missionaries to Bulgaria

Foreign address:	Home address:
"Antyme I" 37	580-23rd Street,
Bourgas, Bulgaria.	West New York, N. J.

MR. and MRS. H. B. GARLOCK

John and Ruth

FOREIGN ADDRESS

Tamale, Northern Territories
Gold Coast, West Africa

HOME ADDRESS

1139 So. Market St.,   Wichita, Kansas

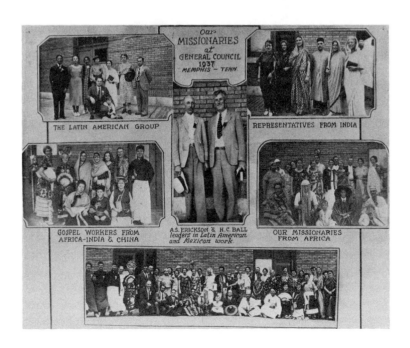

Our MISSIONARIES at GENERAL COUNCIL 1937 MEMPHIS - TENN

THE LATIN AMERICAN GROUP

REPRESENTATIVES FROM INDIA

GOSPEL WORKERS FROM AFRICA-INDIA & CHINA

A.S. ERICKSON & H.C. BALL leaders in Latin American and Mexican work.

OUR MISSIONARIES FROM AFRICA

Missionaries sometimes formed national district councils of the American Assemblies of God in their adopted countries. This is the Egyptian District Council in 1937.

13. Education and Home Missions

> The motto of the school is: "How to pray. How to study the Word. How to know the Lord and walk with Him." The standard of consecration is found in Luke 14:26–27. Read it. You will be expected to live in Mark 12:30, John 13:34–35, and I Cor. 13:1–13. Memorize these scriptures before you come.
>
> D. C. O. Opperman, *Ozark School Herald,* April 1916

A concern for providing biblical training for potential workers had motivated various Pentecostals long before the creation of the Assemblies of God. D. C. O. Opperman, W. F. Carothers, Andrew Fraser, T. K. Leonard, and other early Bible school promoters had carried their enthusiasm for Bible teaching into the Assemblies of God. But in the disharmony of the first few years it proved impossible to find meaningful expression for a cooperative educational effort. Various men and women who identified with the General Council continued to sponsor or to cooperate with non-Council schools. Unable to immediately create a school—or even to reach a consensus on operating one—the General Council in 1914 had set an early precedent by recommending that the constituency pursue training in any available "full gospel" school.

However, virtually no one considered such training essential. Numerous men and women achieved their goals without it; some of the constituency explicitly rejected the notion of training for ministry outside a local assembly. But many early Assemblies of God leaders recalled with appreciation their own training, however informal or nontraditional, either in well-established or in short-term (and probably long-gone) Bible institutes. Such men and women believed that cooperation could facilitate the provision of practical training that would help assure the movement's future.

The Council did not define education; the nature of the training they wanted to provide was essentially indoctrination in fixed truth as perceived by the Fellowship. Their sense of imminence of the end convinced them that they had no time for anything more; a fear of the unknown also influenced their rejection of the liberal arts. From one perspective, the Bible school training endorsed by early Assemblies of God leaders fit into the model contemporary fundamentalists were establishing: It set out to proclaim fixed truth and to locate where those who differed were in error. Its concerns were more practical than theoretical.

Encouraging Attendance at Existing Schools

During the Council's first several years, its leaders continued the custom of recommending either existing schools or schools that resulted from the vision of such widely-accepted teachers as D. C. O. Opperman.[1] In 1915, Opperman acquired the Grand Hotel in Eureka Springs, Arkansas, and convinced Ben Chisolm, founder of the Neshoba Holiness School near Union, Mississippi, to join him in launching a school that would offer elementary education as well as Bible training.[2]

The *Weekly Evangel* began to advertise the venture, known as the Ozark Bible and Literary School, during the summer of 1915.[3] Declaring that the school would "honor the Holy Ghost as General Superintendent, Teacher and Leader," Opperman apparently hoped to found a permanent General Council school. He chose as its motto: How to Pray. How to Study the Word. How to Know the Lord and Walk with him.[4]

Hugh Barbour's observation about the early Quakers— "Friends conceded that the Bible was authoritative and then talked about the Spirit"—applies as well to the way people like Opperman envisioned Bible training.[5] He insisted that the Bible was authoritative, but his schools were occasionally criticized for the practical stress on the Spirit as the present Revealer—the Spirit behind the Word—as he stressed direction through "gifts" of tongues and interpretation. Convinced that Christ would return "within this generation," Opperman's approach was emphatically practical. During the doctrinal disagreements of 1916, both Opperman and Chisolm endorsed Oneness views, closed the school, and opted for other activities. Chisholm returned to his farm in Mississippi; Opperman continued to preach among Oneness Pentecostals until his death in 1925.[6]

Even as Opperman's attempt to create a General Council school became a casualty of the doctrinal dispute (as well as his restlessness), the executives continued to envision such a school, centrally located and amenable to the General Council of the Assemblies of God. Before the General Council reached any decisions, however, several other schools that contributed extensively to the training of Assemblies of God workers were founded independently. On the East Coast, two Bible institutes in New Jersey attracted the support of prominent local Assemblies of God congregations: Beulah Heights Bible Institute and Bethel Bible Training School. Bethel, in particular, influenced the Assemblies of God. This school resulted from the combined visions of three esteemed Assemblies of God pioneers: Christian Lucas, pastor of an assembly in Ossining, New York, and son-in-law of John Thomas Boddy, an early editor of the *Pentecostal Evangel* (1918–1920); Allan Swift, who had identified with Pentecostalism as a student at the Christian and Missionary Alliance school in Nyack; and Minnie Draper, an influential woman with years of experience in many kinds of Christian leadership.

A strong Assemblies of God nucleus on the West Coast shared this concern for preparation for ministry. Robert and Mary Craig, ordained ministers who served as pastors of Glad Tidings mission in San Francisco, saw their new converts class expand dramatically until they resolved to meet a growing demand for Bible training by creating Glad Tidings Bible Institute. Like other such institutes, Glad Tidings sought to combine classroom training with practical experience. Its program integrated local evangelism with classroom studies. Its academic component essentially expanded on the subject matter one encountered in Pentecostal sermons and Sunday schools. That was considered sufficient, not only because few Pentecostal educators had more to offer, but also because the prevalent Pentecostal mindset disdained formal training as potentially "quenching" the Spirit. For a time, D. W. Kerr and his son-in-law, Willard Peirce, assisted the Craigs at Glad Tidings. The school attracted as faculty and students men and women who made lasting contributions to the Assemblies of God—people like J. Narver Gortner, Leland Keys, Emil Balliet, and Myer Pearlman.

Kerr and Peirce also participated with Harold Needham, George N. Eldridge, and others in the creation of Southern California Bible College in Pasadena in 1920. From their inception, these schools trained missionaries as well as stateside workers. At first, no departmentalized curricula complicated the programs. All students studied the same basic subjects.

Farther south, Alice Luce helped organize a Spanish-language Bible institute in conjunction with efforts spearheaded by William McPhair to provide English training in San Diego. In addition to her involvement in the school, which was called Berean Bible Institute, Luce saw a need to extend training to those who could not participate in a local campus setting. She became a pioneer in the field of Assemblies of God correspondence education, which was readied in Spanish while plans for English correspondence courses were still being discussed.[7]

Creating General Council Schools

Meanwhile, in Springfield, Missouri, executive leaders considered ways of realizing their goal of creating a Bible school under the jurisdiction of the General Council. In 1920, they hoped they had found a way to do so. They decided to participate in the formation of a Bible school in Auburn, Nebraska.

With only three of eleven votes on the board of directors, the presbyters had little direct influence on school policies. The school had been envisioned by leaders in the Nebraska, Kansas, Missouri, and Iowa district councils. While still in the planning stages, it had been endorsed by the Executive Presbytery, with the understanding that the district councils involved would assume financial responsibility for the institution. Two general superintendents, Bell and Welch, served as directors.[8] In September 1920, the General Presbytery confirmed district appointments of directors and trustees, added Samuel Jamieson (probably the best academically qualified man available, Jamieson was nearly seventy years old) to the district lists, and appointed him chairman of the school's board.[9]

From the beginning, problems plagued the institution. Some were beyond the leaders' control. A coal strike delayed the school's opening once; an epidemic that resulted in a quarantine of the city postponed it again. More seriously, even among "faith"-oriented Pentecostals who were accustomed to economic uncertainty—and in a day when the Fellowship imposed no academic requirements for teaching—it proved difficult to attract faculty. Not only was no salary promised, neither were day-to-day supplies. Nonetheless, a small group of dedicated men and women worked hard to birth the institution. Most of the Fellowship's executives concluded after a year that Midwest Bible School as constituted could never fulfill their objectives for a General Council school. They determined to look for suitable property elsewhere.

Late in the summer of 1922, the Executive Presbytery declined an offer of premises formerly occupied by a Baptist college in Webb City, Missouri (a town in the southwestern part of the state, near Joplin), in favor of a site proposed by the Springfield Commercial Club.[10] With the assistance of the club, the General Council acquired fifteen acres of land in north Springfield, which it developed to create Central Bible Institute (CBI). An immediate outlay of funds for both building and expenses launched the venture; the Executive Presbytery also approved a catalog of courses. The presbyters decided to invite D. W. Kerr to move to Springfield with his son-in-law, Willard Peirce, to lead the new institution.[11] The two had already contributed significantly to the structuring of the California Bible institutes. The perception of the school as a General Council institution was reinforced by the naming of a committee of the

Executive Presbytery, chaired by either the chairman or, in his absence, the secretary, to "cooperate with the active management of the Bible School."[12]

While work progressed at the school's permanent site, CBI was housed in Central Assembly (the city's only Assemblies of God church). Kerr and Peirce supervised renovations to ready the church basement to serve as a kitchen, dining room, and classroom. As CBI approached its second year in 1923, the prospect that at least a hundred students would enroll necessitated the construction of dormitories and mandated the cultivation of all available financial resources. The Executive Presbytery designated six of the Fellowship's most prominent men to publicize the school's needs among the constituency: William T. Gaston, S. A. Jamieson, Bert Williams, Andrew H. Argue, R. E. McAlister, and Hugh M. Cadwalder. It further requested that district council chairmen receive funds for the school. In contrast to the schools on both coasts, CBI was advertised in the *Pentecostal Evangel* and enjoyed from the start a broad—though not always sufficient—base of support.

Early in January 1923, both Kerr and Peirce indicated that they would resign at the end of the school year. The Executive Presbytery commissioned John W. Welch to secure new leadership.[13] Welch invited a young graduate of Simpson's Missionary Training Institute to direct CBI. The next month, Frank Boyd accepted this invitation to Springfield, where his wife, Helen, also joined the school's workers. The remuneration was meager: twenty-five dollars a week (plus housing and board) for Boyd; ten dollars a week for his wife, two other women instructors, and William Faux, who taught part-time in addition to his regular duties at headquarters.[14] But the potential seemed limitless, and the teachers banded together to make the school a success.

Among the first students to enroll at the institute was one who would soon begin a lifelong association with its faculty. Myer Pearlman, a Scottish-born Jew, had migrated to America and had converted to Christianity at the Craigs' Glad Tidings Mission in San Francisco. Standing outside the mission, he had heard the congregation singing F. A. Graves' *Honey in the*

Rock. (Pearlman later married Graves' daughter.) Entering the meeting, he later recalled, he "felt some strange influence ..., indescribable but delightful."[15] Shortly after his conversion, Pearlman wholeheartedly embraced Pentecostal teaching and enrolled briefly at Glad Tidings Bible Institute. A few months later, he followed D. W. Kerr to Springfield. Educated in Jewish schools, Pearlman was fluent in Hebrew, Greek, Spanish, French, and Italian. Instructors at CBI readily noted his abilities, and he was invited to join the faculty immediately after his graduation. Over the years until his premature death in 1944, Pearlman's teaching and writing endeared him to many in the Fellowship.[16] For many years, his books (especially *Knowing the Doctrines of the Bible*) were standard texts in Assemblies of God schools.

In September of 1923, the General Council met in St. Louis and constituted the Executive Presbytery a Bible school commission and charged it with the supervision of all Bible schools operated within the framework of the Assemblies of God. Framers of the resolution hoped to encourage the standardization of training among the several existing schools, and they agreed to make CBI the model for all other General Council institutes. In 1925, the General Council made its position clearer by voting that if other schools conformed to the standards in effect at CBI, their work should be considered among the constituency as equal to that of CBI. Also at the 1925 General Council meeting in Eureka Springs, Arkansas, the Council was given official representation on all recognized regional Bible institute boards of directors.

Despite the lack of strong academic requirements at the Bible institutes, some who desired training could not do the work. In 1925 CBI began to offer a one-year preparatory course to enable such people to enroll in its regular program. A conviction that training should be made available to those who felt called to the ministry shaped an admissions policy (shared with some other fundamentalist and holiness schools) that differed sharply from that of academic institutions.

By 1925, then, the General Council had realized its early goal of setting up a General Council-sponsored Bible school. CBI had become an expanding reality; already several individuals whose efforts would mold perceptions of its achievements had begun their long associations with the school. And strong local institutes were extending their programs too. Growing interest in standardizing curricula attempted to assure a degree of continuity among the various schools, and administrative decisions had established frameworks in which the future course of Assemblies of God education could be deliberated.

For the moment, however, most students obtained only the most rudimentary training. Others, either unconvinced about the need for training (in various ways, the Fellowship's leaders found it necessary to urge persistently that training was advisable) or unable to afford even its modest cost, failed to return for the available second and third years of work.[17]

In 1924, Canyonville Bible Academy in Canyonville, Oregon, was created to provide Bible training in the Northwest.

Southwestern Bible School in Enid, Oklahoma, formed in 1927, was the fulfillment of the dream of one of the Fellowship's most esteemed and energetic men, Peter C. Nelson. Nelson, who was a native of Denmark and a graduate of Rochester Theological Seminary, drew on years of experience as a Missionary Baptist pastor and evangelist in his work for the General Council, which began in 1925. When he had decided to change his affiliation, he was fifty-seven and had been ordained for more than thirty years. His extensive evangelistic campaigns had brought him to the attention of Assemblies of God leaders, who coveted his various talents for their movement. Settling (shortly after their affiliation) in Enid, Oklahoma, the Nelsons assumed primary responsibility for Southwestern Bible School. Associated with Nelson in this venture was a dignified, gracious Englishwoman, Annie Bamford. Known affectionately as Mother Bamford, this dedicated coworker deeply influenced a generation of Assemblies of God young people who were attracted to the school by Nelson's tireless efforts on its behalf. The school moved to Waxahachie, Texas, in 1943. (Just prior to this move, Guy Shields' Shield of Faith Bible School and Raymond Richey's Southern Bible College consolidated with it.) It is now known as Southwestern Assemblies of God College.

The Council's Response to Secular Education

Assemblies of God institutions developed in a period when American views of education were in transition. Their assumptions about secular learning were partially shaped by their sense of rapid change in their culture. By any standard, the philosophy of education in American institutions was in flux during the 1920s. Vocal intellectuals, protesting the "aesthetic starvation" around them, dominated American literature. The writings of Sinclair Lewis—especially *Main Street, Babbit,* and *Elmer Gantry*—and the commentary of H. L. Mencken exposed longheld assumptions to analysis and ridicule. While writers and intellectuals flirted with radical social and political schemes, many conservative Americans worried about radical influence on college campuses. After the Scopes Trial in Dayton, Tennessee, in 1925 exposed fundamentalism's apparent intellectual poverty, fundamentalism became, for many educated Americans, synonymous with anti-intellectualism. Conservative Protestants noted with alarm the welcome on American campuses received by liberal religious leaders. They sensed a basic, frightening loss of their own cultural authority. Among conservative Christians, pervasive fear of radicals renewed the recurrent tendency to label as "radical" any ideas that seemed to challenge long-held assumptions. The Red Scare in the early 1920s encouraged social conformity, but during the "return to normalcy" later in the decade, non-conformity flourished.[18]

In a setting that seemed to Pentecostals increasingly secular and materialistic, then, leaders of the General Council expressed strong support for sheltering Assemblies of God young people in "academic schools" where Christianity and patriotism would inform the curriculum. General Councils did no more than express sympathy with the concept of Christian day schools, however. Not until the resurgence of fundamentalism in the 1970s would a significant number of Assemblies of God congregations have the resources to identify with a broader conservative Christian effort to provide an alternative to the alleged secular humanism of the public school system by forming Christian day schools. (Currently, well over 1,200 schools sponsored by Assemblies of God churches enroll nearly 110,000 children.)

A committee report presented to the 1929 General Council noted that the concerns about secularism in the public schools extended to college education as well:

> On account of the worldliness of many of our High Schools and Colleges and their antagonistic attitude for the most part to the Pentecostal message, there is a growing need of academic schools of our faith in different parts of our country to provide education without contamination of worldly and anti-Christian influences. We believe that our fellowship should look with favor upon the establishment of such schools, and should look foward to the time, if the Lord tarry, when we may have somewhere an institution of college grade, where the most complete and thorough education can be obtained under Pentecostal auspices.[19]

This recommendation, appended to six suggestions for the improvement of Bible school training, was presented by four men prominently associated with infant Assemblies of God education programs: P. C. Nelson, Robert J. Craig, William I. Evans, and A. B. Cox (who conducted a Bible school known as Peniel in his Dayton, Ohio, Bethel Assembly of God). The concerns they expressed were similar to those that had helped shape other parochial school systems, Catholic and Protestant, across the country. But the Fellowship merely agreed with their sentiments; it failed to act. Not until another generation had assumed leadership would the issue of denominationally-sponsored collegiate education be given serious consideration. And even then it would be controversial.

In 1929, the Executive Presbytery invited William Irvin Evans to join the staff of CBI as dean. Born in Philadelphia on August 12, 1887, Evans had received his Spirit baptism during the Pentecostal effusion at the Christian and Missionary Alliance Bible institute in Nyack, New York, where he was president of the Student Missionary Band. He married a Nyack classmate, Hilda Lindberg, and served as superintendent of the Alliance branch in Richmond, Virginia, for four years. When he left the Alliance for independent Pentecostalism, Evans filled pastorates in Ossining, New York, and Butler, New Jersey. By 1917, he had joined the faculty of Bethel Bible Training School in Newark. He became principal of the school in 1923, a position he filled until the school merged with CBI in 1929.

Throughout its thirteen-year history, Bethel had on its staff men and women who would later serve CBI with distinction: Frank Boyd, Ralph Riggs, Hazel Fairchild Forrester, Ernest Williams. Associated with a flourishing assembly in Newark, the institute also utilized the services of Allan Swift, out of whose vision it had been founded, and Missionaries Gottfried Bender and William W. Simpson. Many of its graduates accepted Assemblies of God appointment to mission stations or pastorates. Association with Bethel admirably prepared Evans for his career at CBI.

Already during his tenure at Bethel, Evans had gained a reputation for spirituality that had come to the attention of executives responsible for CBI. Until his death in 1954, he was by all accounts an awesome presence in the growing institute. Although the record decidedly attests his humanity, many students apparently agreed with Historian Carl Brumback, an Evans protégé, who names Evans as chiefly responsible for the school's spiritual reputation. While this assessment is probably unfair to men like Myer Pearlman and Frank Boyd, Evans nonetheless did feel a responsibility for the school's spiritual well-being (probably more than he did for its academic excellence). He—and the school's faculty—influenced the denomination not only through the students, but by spending summers preaching and teaching in camp meetings around the country.

Shortly after his untimely death in 1954, Gospel Publishing House published *This River Must Flow,* a compilation of Evans's musings on the meanings of Pentecostalism. It reveals a man deeply concerned about the critical challenge of communicating a revival's dynamic to second and third generations. "The baptism of the Holy Ghost creates flowing rivers," he wrote. But then "human instrumentality [becomes] a dam across the river. Then God has to work on that dam. . . . Are we building a Pentecostal dam?"[20] Evans concurred wholeheartedly with the later sentiments of a more famous Assemblies of God preacher, David du Plessis: "God has no grandsons." He cautioned students to consider carefully the meaning of being Pentecostal: "Receiving the baptism of the Holy Spirit doesn't make you Pentecostal," he frequently cautioned. "It's what you do after you receive the Baptism that makes you Pentecostal."[21] Evans and the faculty he led shared with Assemblies of God Bible institute personnel everywhere a sense of urgency about creating an environment in which students would learn to live the experience they professed.

Coordination of Council Schools

During the 1930s, a growing number of schools sought General Council endorsement, and one of the primary concerns of the denomination was the development of a systematic approach to education. Between 1930 and 1941, the following schools were founded: North Central Bible Institute, Minneapolis, 1930; Shield of Faith Bible School, Amarillo, Texas, 1931; Northwest Bible Institute, Seattle, 1934; Great Lakes Bible Institute, Zion, Illinois, 1934; Peniel Bible Institute, Stanton, Kentucky, 1935; Eastern Bible Institute, Green Lane, Pennsylvania, 1938.

Throughout the period, denominational executives evaluated these schools using standards established for CBI. In 1931, CBI altered its structure by departmentalizing its curriculum. The school offered five areas of specialization in its regular three-year program: general Bible, pastoral, missions, Christian education, and music. It also made one- and two-year programs of study available.

At the 1931 General Council in San Francisco, the Committee on Bible Schools (consisting of P. C. Nelson, Harold Needham, Ralph Riggs, Gayle Lewis, and James Savell) urged that prospective ministers be encouraged to obtain Bible school training, that a uniform policy for endorsement of schools be adopted, and that an educational commission be formed. In the course of its work, the committee recognized a lack of consensus on Bible school training being advisable for ministers; they determined to raise the issue. Hardly a disinterested group of men, while they appreciated the way many active ministers had "overcome the handicap" of their lack of formal training, as a committee they nonetheless insisted that the absence of "whole-hearted interest and cooperation on the part of pastors and other leaders" was deplorable. In a period when new Bible schools had been formed or were in the planning stages in several places, the men urged the General Council to move slowly in endorsing additional institutions. It recommended, instead, that existing schools be made financially sound by channeling sufficient students into them.[22] Authorized by the General Council and appointed by the Executive Presbytery, the proposed commission was charged with assessing the needs of the Fellowship and devising a philosophy of education.

The next year, John W. Welch accepted the presidency of CBI, and CBI continued to emphasize strongly the practical application of classroom learning. Early in the 1930s, students served as pastors of nine rural congregations. And the Kansas District, under the leadership of its farsighted superintendent, Fred Vogler, began to utilize them during the summers. Vogler purchased tents and assured students that their basic needs would be met if they would spend their vacations in evangelistic work. Among the young CBI students who developed their preaching skills in Kansas was the long-time speaker on the Assemblies of God radio broadcast, *Revivaltime,* C. M. Ward.

During the 1930s, CBI organized a Correspondence School Department to assist local congregations in training lay workers to teach Sunday school and engage in other Christian service. The first two courses were a Personal Workers' Course and Studies in the Life and Teachings of Christ. By 1933, some 550 students from 36 states and 7 foreign countries had enrolled, and additional courses were in preparation.

At the 1933 General Council, the urgent need of coordinating the various educational efforts sponsored through districts, local churches, and the General Council continued to dominate educational concerns. By this time, the early willingness to recommend training in any reputable Bible school had given way to exclusive support of district- or Council-sponsored schools. Others received no publicity in the *Pentecostal Evangel*. Notices about district schools were carried in the *Evangel* only if they had some relevance to the constituency as a whole.

The financial reverses many adherents experienced during the 1930s made paying for Bible school education increasingly difficult. School policies frequently permitted students to proceed through their training and even to graduate without meeting financial obligations. Would-be evangelists and pastors leaving Bible institutes often found it easier to draw crowds than to collect offerings. For the 1934–35 school year, the CBI board of directors decided to take "a bold step of faith": They reduced tuition for those who paid in advance. As a result, the school was crowded with an enrollment of 181, and the year-end financial statement showed that all expenses had been met. During the summer, a new building was completed; tuition was further reduced, and 323 young people applied for admission, promptly making the new facilities inadequate. A large garden helped keep food expenses manageable.

During the mid-1930s, the suggestion that the General Council should sponsor a "literary school" resurfaced. The 1935 General Council, meeting in Dallas, referred this project to a committee, charging it to formulate plans to finance, maintain, and control such an institution. Deep divisions within the General Council on the issue of "literary education" surfaced, however, and the committee reported back to the General Council the day after its appointment that it recommended that all consideration of "literary education" be deferred.

The same Council authorized the work of a new committee to plan for the standardization of all endorsed Bible schools. Participants further agreed that all schools which then conformed to the accepted standards would be entitled to "liberal publicity" in Assemblies of God publications.[23] A committee of three was designated a standing committee on institutions, charged with visiting all endorsed educational institutions, as well as all schools desiring such endorsement. Cooperating institutions were asked to finance the visits. In the end, however, much of the funding came from the earnings of Gospel Publishing House. One member of the committee would have a long-term influence on Assemblies of God education: Fred Vogler, Kansas district superintendent.

Fred Vogler, a remarkable pioneer of Pentecostalism, was a native of Australia.[24] Arriving in the United States at seventeen in 1905, Vogler and his parents settled in Zion, Illinois. In July 1907, Vogler identified with the thriving Pentecostal work that Charles Parham had helped establish in Zion. Vogler immediately became an enthusiastic witness to this newfound experience. A leader among the local young people, Vogler helped extend Pentecostalism into nearby communities. He evangelized with Bennett Lawrence and J. R. Flower in Indiana; traveled with Flower to assist Albert Copley in Kansas City tent meetings; then, with his wife, Margaret Boyer, joined the Flowers, Flem Van Meter, and others at D. W. Myland's Bible school (known as Gibeah) in Plainfield, Indiana. From there, he moved to a seven-year pastorate in Martinsville, Indiana. While visiting a sister in Topeka, he noticed that the Kansas capital lacked a strong "full gospel" witness. He moved his family to Topeka, supported them by working as a carpenter, and started a church. The fledgling Kansas District had, at the time, only seventeen congregations. Three years later, Vogler was elected district superintendent. His passion for evangelism resulted in extensive growth within the district during his fourteen years of leadership. A close friend of the Flowers and others with roots in Zion and Gibeah, Vogler was deeply committed to the concept of cooperative fellowship that was at the heart of the General Council's purpose. A vigorous supporter of several progressive causes like Bible school education and Sunday schools, Vogler was motivated by a broad vision of the dynamic potential of the Assemblies of God.

The Development of the Home Missions and Education Department

In 1937, the committee on institutions recommended to the

General Council in Memphis that the Council create an education department headed by a general educational secretary who would devote his full time to Assemblies of God education and would serve on the board of directors of each General Council school. The General Presbytery had already thoroughly considered the proposal, and veteran leader J. Narver Gortner had voiced support for appointing Vogler to the office of education secretary. This was the first time a General Council had considered creating a totally new headquarters department. Since 1914, the missions department and Gospel Publishing House had been the only two divisions within the General Council's organizational structure.[25]

The proposal also involved adding an executive to the headquarters team, thus demanding financial commitment. In 1937, even the assistant general superintendent was unpaid; his residence in Springfield was not required.

In spite of the reluctance of many adherents (who seemed both unenthusiastic about supporting education and doubtful about its purpose), the new department became a reality in 1937. The issue remained volatile, however. It proved virtually impossible to proceed with consideration of "literary" education at either the high school or college levels. More fundamentally, the Assemblies of God failed to articulate a philosophy of education. While Bible institutes offered specific kinds of training, the level of instruction—as well as the abilities of the instructors—varied widely.

Whereas most American educators assumed that education necessarily included a dimension of critical thinking and an exposure to the vast varieties of human thought, most Assemblies of God educators had had little formal training themselves. They accepted uncritically generalizations that often misrepresented other religious and cultural traditions. Few of them had any concept of either the advantages or the requirements of what most Americans considered education. They wanted, instead, practical, task-oriented training, and they deemed irrelevant the educational models offered by long-established institutions. "The Spirit," they claimed was "the Source of truth." Only the "spiritually minded" could grasp the "sense" of Scripture. Much of what others thought constituted education then, they deemed irrelevant.

The stress on the Spirit had a popular, spiritual ring. That it was sometimes little more than an excuse for laziness disturbed relatively few. Most of the movement's leaders who had any training had received it in one of the several turn-of-the-century Bible schools that proto-fundamentalists had founded. Emphasizing service over academic performance, these schools welcomed virtually all students. Though they filled a vital role, they also testified to the reservations their founders had harbored about the adequacy or the relevance of traditional education.

Education in the Assemblies of God, then, had a specific, localized meaning; even then, some who wanted workers to be "Spirit-taught, led and filled" distrusted it, and its progress was controversial. On the other hand, the denomination generally lacked a reservoir of educated people to draw its educators from, and its sense of alienation from the prevailing culture fostered the view that secular education jeopardized spirituality. Those who enrolled at Bible schools (both Pentecostal and non-Pentecostal) often had not completed a high school education, and some had never even begun one. In a sense, Bible institutes offered would-be religious workers practical training similar to what many new training institutes offered in typing, nursing, or teaching. Those who might not have qualified at traditional institutions because of sex, money, or background didn't need to be excluded from ministry; Bible institutes made accelerated training inexpensive and practical.

The education report to the Memphis Council in 1937 stressed the necessity for "training our youth as to doctrine and the development of Christian character."[26] Noting that over thirteen hundred students were currently enrolled in the various schools, the men observed that the quality of the schools ranged from excellent to mediocre. While they acknowledged that schools that institutionalized the "individual vision" of prominent leaders had performed an important function, they believed it was time for a "united vision for the future perpetuation of the great Pentecostal message. We must pass this heritage on to our youth that they may go forth in the power of the Spirit. . . ."[27] They dreamed of a day when the Assemblies of God would produce its own texts and encouraged support for continuing education through correspondence courses. They recommended standards for faculty and qualifications for students that reflected their personal priorities, requiring all applicants to "give evidence of a definite born-again spiritual experience" and citing a preference that "they have also a definite conviction of heart that God has called them into His service."[28]

This strong sense of a need to equip the next generation to carry on the movement's momentum heralded a subtle shift in its self-perception. Leaders faced the likelihood that history would not climax in Christ's return before another generation came of age. Educating the next generation seemed vital to the Fellowship's instincts for self-preservation. For the moment, leaders hoped to balance two concepts that were fundamentally in tension: On the one hand, commitment to the imminent return of Christ; on the other, the felt need to provide institutions to preserve the movement's message. In short, by the 1930s, among Assemblies of God leaders a consensus that education was at the core of the church's task was finding broader support. It conflicted directly with the restorationist expectations that had shaped early Pentecostalism.

The growing conviction about the importance of education manifested itself in various ways: On the popular level, one of the most important was the growing support for Sunday schools. Congregations that had been formed with the expectation of an imminent end had frequently disdained training and focused, instead, on the charismatic manifestations Pentecostals enjoyed. Some failed to realize that the question was not whether the church educated; certainly churches educated, whether or not the members thought so. Others focused on the perception of the church's educational role and the determination to organize its educating potential. Gradually, among the more acculturated segments in the movement, the conviction that education was an integral part of church life won wider recognition.

It is not accidental that a growing debate about education

coincided with growing concern about Sunday schools. To put it differently, the Fellowship was entering a new stage, one which sociologist David Moberg has called maximum efficiency. "Statesmen" were emerging within the ranks to voice "group convictions" that led ultimately to "an increasingly rational organization that replace[d] charismatic leadership."[29] But recognition of this transformation was in the distant future. For the moment, a partial rethinking of the church's inevitable role in education sufficed.

When the Committee on Home Missions reported to the 1937 General Council, urging the creation of a home missions department, some Council participants suggested a close relationship between home missions and education. (Presumably, Bible institutes provided practical training that equipped the pastors and evangelists on whose activities home missionary work depended.) They agreed that the substantial minority that had voted against the creation of an education department would be at least partially reconciled by the combination of home missions and education. The Council adopted a resolution calling for the expansion of the scope of the newly created education department to embrace home missions. The new department, called the Home Missions and Education Department of the General Council, was charged with cooperating with the Foreign Missions Department in realizing the broad objective of world evangelization. The Council voted to invite its newly elected assistant general superintendent to move to Springfield and assume the direction of the new department.[30] This action created an important precedent: Thereafter, for over thirty years, the duties of an assistant general superintendent consisted primarily of directly supervising a headquarters department. (The major exception, of course, was foreign missions, which had its own full-time leader who was not considered an assistant superintendent.)

Vogler accepted the challenge and moved to Springfield to supervise the dual programs. He had chaired the committee on institutions whose recommendations had birthed the education department; despite his lack of formal training, he was probably the best qualified man in the denomination to accomplish the purposes the Council had agreed constituted its will for education. The strong practical record of his own ministry reassured those who were hesitant about the value of education. Nevertheless, his name is even more closely associated with the systematic expansion of a General Council home missions program, an outreach he supervised (excepting a brief hiatus) until his retirement in 1954.

The initial educational task Vogler supervised included the formulation and application of detailed standards for General Council endorsement. (These standards became article XII of the constitution and bylaws.) In 1939, the General Council (meeting in Springfield, Missouri) disapproved the ownership by closed corporations of any schools seeking General Council recognition. It urged that such institutions take steps to "tie the ownership of the school" to district councils or the General Council.

Also in 1939, the General Council accepted an offer from the board of directors of Glad Tidings Bible Institute in San Francisco of the facility the school operated in, with the proviso that the General Council should continue to operate the school. The school's ambitious founders, Robert and Mary Craig, were present and cited for their generous contribution to the progress of the institution.[31]

The recurrent concern for "holiness" (understood as conspicuous separation from "the world") also found support at the 1939 Springfield General Council. Men like J. Narver Gortner and Robert Brown represented the continuing effort to keep alive among the diverse constituency the stern dictates they had imbibed as holiness Methodists. Such men hoped to help assure the persistence of particular customs of dress and behavior by imposing them on the next generation of leaders—students in Bible institutes. The resolution the Council adopted captured a majority conviction:

> Be it resolved by this General Council that we condemn such unscriptural conduct as the donning of male attire, or the wearing of shorts or slacks, on the part of the lady students in any of our Bible Schools, while attending picnics, going on hikes, or on any occasion on which they may

appear in public; that we brand such conduct as being, in our opinion, essentially worldly; and that we place ourselves on record as opposing all trends and tendencies that appear to break down, or blot out, or make less outstanding, the line of demarcation between the holy and the unholy, the sacred and the profane; and that we recommend that the standard in dress established by Central Bible Institute be the recognized standard for all our Bible Schools, and that a failure to conform thereto shall subject the school thus failing to censure or disapproval.[32]

This concern over appearance had surfaced before. In 1935, a resolution disapproving "bobbing and undue waving of the hair, use of such cosmetics as tend to change the color of the complexion, plucking of the eyebrows, and the painting of the fingernails" had been introduced. Dress standards imposed at the Bible schools were recommended as a standard for the general constituency.

By 1941, considerable progress had been made in standardizing the education at the various endorsed schools. That year, North Central Bible Institute in Minneapolis surpassed CBI as the school with the highest enrollment (373 verses 333).[33] The education committee's report was presented by Henry Ness. (It was out of his vision that Northwest Bible Institute in Seattle had been founded, which in 1941 was the third largest endorsed institute.) It noted that to date over twelve hundred institute graduates had entered stateside ministries and some two hundred fifty had accepted foreign missions appointments.

At the same Council, concerns Vogler expressed in his capacity as home missions secretary resulted in the framing of several key resolutions. Those who desired to pioneer new congregations were instructed to do so in cooperation with the existing district councils; districts were encouraged to solicit the assistance of Bible institute graduates who would enter communities as personal workers before efforts were made to set up regular congregations; the Council further indicated its support of the view that home missions funds should be invested "with the thought of permanence," rather than in an effort to "see what can be done."[34]

By 1941, Vogler had succeeded in giving coherence to diffuse interests under the broad auspices of home missions. In one sense, the need to have a home missions department represented an evolving recognition of changing conditions. At first, home missions had received little attention. Everyone was assumed to have an obligation to participate in the task of evangelizing the United States. In 1919, for example, the General Council formally urged districts to "press this work . . . of carrying the Pentecostal Message into the neglected districts of this country." It encouraged "brethren who [feel] led" to evangelize in areas with no Pentecostal outreach; the Fellowship's executives consulted with evangelists about "pushing out into new fields."

The 1921 General Council had established a home missions fund. By 1927 some adherents held the conviction that home missions efforts needed coordination, a conviction they expressed by introducing a motion to authorize the Executive Presbytery to appoint a home missionary secretary. Although no formal action was taken, sentiment in some districts strongly favored the idea. Funding a new department, however, proved a major obstacle. Meanwhile, the *Pentecostal Evangel* solicited support for home missions, and executives of the denomination recognized early the relationship between strengthening the home base and advancing the cause of foreign missions. By 1941, home missions was supervising the Fellowship's extension in Alaska and Hawaii among native Americans, Jews, and transplanted Europeans; as the nation mobilized for war, home missions also directed its efforts toward servicemen. Vogler's department would ultimately coordinate the principal Assemblies of God outreaches to military personnel.

Between 1939 and 1941, home missions efforts proliferated. In an effort to provide new funding, executives reassigned the earnings of Gospel Publishing House. Until 1939, those earnings had been used to upgrade equipment, construct buildings for CBI, and supply such headquarters needs as were not met by other sources. In 1939, with Gospel Publishing House adequately supplied (temporarily) with new equipment, the executives decided to distribute among the districts a share of the publishing concern's earnings; the volume of business each district did through the publishing house determined the size of the district's share. In addition, outright appropriations of funds helped supply moneys to the smaller struggling districts that generated insufficient business to qualify for significant percentage returns. As a result, over two years, Gospel Publishing House had been able to return to the districts more than fifty thousand dollars, designated for launching new assemblies. In 1941, the home missions department also reported "definite results" among Apache Indians. The Fellowship's executives noted with satisfaction that the achievements were the realization of a "hope" that dated from 1914, when Flower had been among those who had anticipated a time when "substantial help could be given to the districts to assist them in the spread of this glorious Pentecostal message."[35]

One of the thriving home missions efforts of the 1930s was a Bible school begun in Eastern Kentucky by Oscar E. Nash while a pastor in neighboring Cincinnati, Ohio. Specifically created to provide Bible training for "mountain young folks of the hills of Kentucky," the school began with seven students. Nash charged no tuition, but asked a fifty dollar fee for room and board for each six-month term; even so, many among the growing student body had to pay in kind, and some could offer only a fraction of the fee. In 1938, Nash donated this school, with a house, twenty-eight acres of land, and a church building, to the Kentucky District. By that time, ambitious young people had left the school to do home missionary work in their native region. The school, which could accommodate thirty students, had reached its capacity by 1939. The Kentucky District—led by Nash (still a pastor in Cincinnati) and Theodore Gannon, a hard-working, young Assemblies of God veteran (he had begun preaching at age twelve)—dreamed of a school that would be available to all the Fellowship's young people who could not afford the more traditional programs offered elsewhere. Coming from the school, workers cooperated with one another to expand the Assemblies of God presence throughout the mountain hamlets of Kentucky. Gannon's early involvement in this home missions enterprise became a vital part of his training for later leadership of the denomination's division of home missions.

Although not formally under a national program of home missions, much of the evangelistic work and church-planting of the 1930s was, in effect, home missionary activity. The pioneering efforts of energetic men and women like Bert Webb, Bartlett Peterson, Charles Scott, Ben Hardin, and Etta Reckley resulted in the formation of many assemblies. Throughout the 1920s and 1930s, local revivals, sometimes in out-of-the-way places, won staunch recruits for the Pentecostal ministry. In northwestern North Dakota, for example, Evangelist Blanche Britton helped spark a revival in 1925 out of which over a hundred men and women ultimately entered the ministry. One of them was G. Raymond Carlson. He received his credentials in 1937 and served many years in ministry, becoming general superintendent in 1985. From the time Bert Webb embraced Pentecostalism in 1925, he worked as an evangelist. He began numerous churches and succeeded in stabilizing several struggling congregations; among them was First Assembly of God in Memphis, for many years one of the Fellowship's most dynamic southern congregations. Scandinavians in the north central states proved especially receptive to the Pentecostal message; ethnic outreaches also flourished during the 1930s among Italians and Germans. Joseph Wannenmacher, a Pentecostal pioneer who had migrated from Hungary and settled in Milwaukee, Wisconsin, founded a Hungarian branch. (See the appendix for the testimony of Wannenmacher.) By 1941, then, both education and home missions had strong leadership that sought to implement the General Council's will. However, joint administration of them would not survive, for each area would grow rapidly and demand increasing oversight.

R. B. Chisolm about 1912. Chisolm's school in Neshoba County, Mississippi, was recommended by the first General Council.

OZARK SCHOOL HERALD

Vol. 1   Eureka Springs, Ark., April, 1916   No. 1

Take this child away and nurse it for me and I will give thee thy wages.—Ex. 2:9

Study to show thyself approved unto God, a workman that needeth not to be ashamed. II Tim. 2:15.

Home of Ozark Bible and Literary School

Bible Training School Gathering of Young Evangelists and Christian Workers.

To be held in Eureka Springs, Ark., Beginning April 5, 1916

During 1916, D. C. O. Opperman and R. B. Chisolm operated the Ozark Bible and Literary School with the approval of the General Council.

Central Bible Institute's first year, housed in the basement of Central Assembly. D. W. Kerr is in the first row, fourth from the left.

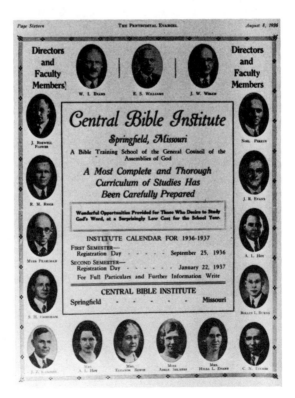

Bethel Bible Training School, Newark, New Jersey, 1925. Bethel merged with CBI in 1929. W. I. Evans is in the second row, eighth from the right.

Peniel Bible Institute, Dayton, Ohio. Operated by A. B. Cox, pastor of Bethel Temple in Dayton, its first class was held in 1929.

Northwest Bible Institue, ca. 1934

Gospel School, Findlay, Ohio. Run by T. K. Leonard, it was recommended by the first General Council. (T. K. Leonard at the far right.)

Glad Tidings Temple and Bible Institute, San Francisco. Founded and operated by Robert and Mary Craig, both church and school were thriving Assemblies of God centers by 1920.

Fred Vogler, first head of the Department of Education and Home Missions

Student body of Glad Tidings Bible Institute, San Francisco, 1933

14. Pilgrims and Citizens: Some Dilemmas of Dual Allegiance

Only a pilgrim here and a stranger,
Seeking a city builded on high,
Sing me the songs of Christ and His glory,
These, only these, my heart satisfy.

Lelia Morris, *Songs of the Kingdom*

We are out today on the firing line,
For the truth and right we will boldly fight;
We are out today on the firing line,
A victorious, loyal band;
See our banners wave, hear the bugles blow,
Sounding out o'er sea and land;
In unbroken line on to victory go,
And shoulder to shoulder stand.

Lelia Morris, *On the Firing Line*

Early Pentecostals tended to profess little interest in society. They often regarded major political, social, and intellectual transitions as significant primarily because of how they seemed to fit the prophetic agenda most Pentecostals subscribed to. Some events and trends prompted their negative commentary; occasionally, however, Pentecostals welcomed even that which they, at another level, deplored. Contemporary human experience, they reminded one another, pointed to the imminent "coming of the Lord," the event they professed to live for. Taking their inspiration from Hebrews 11, they regarded themselves as "pilgrims and strangers" on earth; yet as men and women standing "on the firing line" for God, they sometimes inclined to take sides on cultural issues.[1]

As people living in this world, they were deeply affected by cultural change. And although the written record contains little or no commentary on how they addressed some issues, it provides fascinating insights on how they dealt with others. Confrontations with major cultural issues revealed significant elements in the Pentecostal search for identity.

First, circumstances forced Assemblies of God adherents to address the subject of Christian participation in war. The denomination was formed in 1914, just a few months before the outbreak of World War I. At a time when much of America enthusiastically supported President Woodrow Wilson's efforts to transform the war into a grand crusade, members of the fledgling Assemblies of God were challenged to address complex issues of civil obedience and military participation. The eschatological bases of Wilson's vision for America veered sharply from Pentecostal millennialism. Early Assemblies of God attitudes toward war must be explored if one hopes to gain an accurate understanding of the significance of the denomination's later support for World War II. They illumine both a divergence of opinion and a perception of identity that have been significantly modified over time.

Second, the Assemblies of God was organized as the women's movement entered the final phases of its long quest for women's suffrage. The changing roles of women and new perceptions of womanhood in American culture encouraged Pentecostals to evaluate appropriate roles for women in their own movement. Convictions concerning the proper place of women in the growing denomination's structure were based on certain explicit assumptions apparent in the early phases of the movement's history.

The following pages will examine how the Assemblies of God dealt with these two issues, each of which had roots in a much broader cultural context.

Early Views of War

The way the Assemblies of God addressed issues raised by World War I demonstrates the practical implication of the concept of cooperative fellowship. During the four-year course of the war, the group's periodicals recorded different views of the war experience and offered articles suggesting alternative perceptions of appropriate Christian involvement. The denomination seemed little threatened by disagreements about pacifism; its periodicals published articles airing a variety of opinions on the assumption that the editors should inform the readership of scripturally viable alternatives.

Like other American Protestants, Pentecostals were comfortable with a religious language rich in militaristic symbolism. They considered themselves engaged daily in spiritual warfare: They sang about conquests and victories. In the familiar words of Isaac Watts, they were "soldiers of the cross" with an obligation to fight: "Sure I must fight, if I would reign."[2] And the triumphant cadence of Lelia Morris's *Victory All the Time* captured their confidence:

> In the midst of battle be not thou dismayed
> Though the powers of darkness 'gainst thee are
>   arrayed;
> God thy strength is with thee, causing thee to
>   stand
> Heaven's allied armies wait at thy command.[3]

Pentecostals considered themselves engaged in a conflict infinitely more momentous than any earthly struggle. Their gospel songs popularized its progress. Christians stood daily "on the firing line," participating "in the gospel war."[4] It is hardly surprising, then, that their first response to war was expressed in cosmic terms: They easily incorporated current events into the prophetic calendar they already followed. World War I could be understood as an extension, an outward manifestation, of the spiritual conflict they had been engaged in all along.

Early response to the progress of the war in Europe fueled the Fellowship's intense awareness that theirs were the end times. Articles analyzed how war events fulfilled prophecy and declared the judgment of God in current events. "Wars and

346 / DILEMMAS OF DUAL ALLEGIANCE

rumors of wars" were "signs of the times." Amid rampant excitement about approaching cataclysm, spiritual enthusiasts uttered predictions reinforcing biblical prophecy. Immediate revelations, then, tended to confirm their prophetic views. Although its editors carefully avoided endorsing date setting, the *Evangel* published several testimonies affirming—using both ecstatic utterances and crude mathematical evidence—that Christ would return during the celebration of the Jewish holidays in the late summer of 1917. They introduced an unusual piece of evidence to support their conviction that the world was engaged in a climactic struggle: a vision George Washington had purportedly experienced at Valley Forge. Citing a third-hand account from the *National Tribune* in December 1880, Pentecostals used considerable ingenuity in applying the story to buttress their claims.[5]

Washington, the story maintained, had had a supernatural encounter in which he had seen three great crises challenging America. The third and most severe, he had been informed, would be worldwide in scope. All attempts to stay the trouble would fail. Divine assistance, in the form of the Second Coming, would rescue the world from self-destruction. From this perspective, World War I was Armageddon.[6] The war, then, reinforced Pentecostal identity as "latter rain" people. With renewed conviction they asserted their place in history and counseled one another always to be ready for Christ's return. On April 22, 1916, the *Weekly Evangel* reminded its readers:

> DON'T FORGET these are days of special importance.
> DON'T FORGET that the coming of Jesus for His Bride
> is to be expected daily. DON'T FORGET that many signs
> and many events of the present point to the next great
> coming event. DON'T FORGET the war. DON'T FORGET
> that this is the time of the Latter Rain. DON'T FORGET
> that the purpose of the Latter Rain is to bring in the
> Harvest. DON'T FORGET that Jesus said, "The harvest
> is the end of the world." DON'T FORGET that you must
> be ready.[7]

In addressing issues raised by the war, Pentecostals also expressed explicitly their perception of their relationship to their culture. Tracing the theme of citizenship served as a meaningful way to address questions related to Pentecostals' interest in both the progress of events around them and their changing sense of who they, in fact, were. As citizens of another kingdom, Pentecostals were uninterested in their culture; yet, they soon learned to move handily from operating under the pilgrim model to expressing their concerns as Christian soldiers. These two themes mingle to make the story of Assemblies of God attitudes toward war and country complex. Pacifists declared their identity as pilgrims; others, while concurring, claimed an obligation in that pilgrimage to counter evil; this readily adapted to identifying morality with the Allied cause— or other causes they could conceive of in moral terms.

Generally, the early movement preserved a strong sense that participants were "strangers and pilgrims" in this world. This reinforced strictures against worldliness: Songs and sermons reminded them that radical religious experience made them uncomfortable in this world and gave them a higher calling. The reality that many of them were already economically and socially dislocated made such views more plausible. By the 1930s, however, subtle changes made Pentecostals less strangers than people asserting the responsibilities of dual citizenship: They were pilgrims but also citizens of a nation infused with moralist rhetoric. The world wars laid bare the significance of notions of citizenship, demonstrating how both models of "pilgrim" and "citizen" appealed to Pentecostal sensibilities.

World War I not only supported Pentecostals' predominating sense of identity as "end-times people" and encouraged their tendency (which they shared with others) to attempt to locate God in current events, it also raised difficult practical issues. Adherents of the fledgling Assemblies of God, men and women with a variety of religious and ethnic backgrounds who had purposely avoided articulating firm positions as tests of Fellowship, ultimately had to face the question of appropriate Christian attitudes toward war.

The issue was, at first, decidedly more poignant in Europe. The *Evangel* reported on the war's effects on Pentecostals in war-torn nations. In 1914, Assemblies of God adherents had been following the progress of English Pentecostalism for some time. Alexander Boddy, an Anglican vicar in Sunderland, had visited the United States and toured much of the country, visiting camp meetings along the way. His publication, *Confidence,* circulated in this country, providing news of the progress of Pentecostalism throughout Europe. Since tongues speech had occurred in his parish in 1907, Boddy had become an acknowledged leader in British Pentecostalism. Older and more experienced than most emerging non-Anglican Pentecostal mission leaders, he had ties to the Keswick movement as well as to the Welsh revival. He conducted influential conferences in Sunderland, where Pentecostals gained a sense of participation in a broader movement as he integrated into British Pentecostalism the Christocentric and experience-oriented message he had imbibed in those settings.

The war experience deeply—and permanently—divided British Pentecostals. As a local representative of the state church, Boddy was expected to support the British cause. His own inclinations coincided with this requirement, and he unabashedly wrote and preached about the justice of British participation. Younger men—like Donald Gee and Howard Carter—who in other respects had been deeply influenced by Boddy refused to follow his patriotic support of war. They insisted that Spirit baptism, with its focus on loving concern for the world's spiritual needs, precluded participation in war. Insisting that their citizenship was in heaven rather than in this world, they defended defiance of civil laws that violated gospel principles. After the war (during which some had been imprisoned for their refusal to fight), they displaced Boddy in the leadership of British Pentecostalism.

The Christian Evangel introduced its readers to the practical quandaries accompanying war by reprinting a series of editorials from *Confidence* in which Boddy advocated the Allied cause. Characterizing Germany as a "bully," Boddy argued the need to "bring that bully to his senses in the quickest way possible."[8]

Boddy's editorials provoked responses which revealed that the Assemblies of God, like British Pentecostalism, embraced a pacifistic element. William Burton McCafferty, pastor and prolific writer, responded to Boddy's editorials in an article insisting that the Christian's heavenly citizenship mandated pacifism. Arguing that it was always wrong to fight, either in self-defense or in defense of a weaker nation "in the right," McCafferty insisted that God's word to the church was, "Ye followers of the Prince of Peace, disarm yourselves."[9]

Although *Evangel* editors consistently disclaimed taking sides on the numerous controversial issues that surfaced during 1915, they seemed increasingly inclined to endorse pacifism. In June, July, and August they published three articles by Frank Bartleman presenting an unyielding pacifism.[10] Bartleman—who never affiliated with the Assemblies of God—criticized numerous aspects of American life and fueled internal Pentecostal debate too.

Bartleman considered the war God's judgment on sinful humanity. Whereas few Pentecostals endorsed calls for social righteousness, Bartleman insisted that the absence of such righteousness invited judgment. His language carries some of the concerns that contemporary social gospelers expressed more profoundly. Bartleman called for an ethic of love and decried the absurdity of war. Maintaining that the war was essentially the product of economic rivalry, he examined the propaganda issued copiously by both sides and declared the official American stance of neutrality to be "hypocrisy."[11]

As Bartleman sought to apply a consistent ethic, some considered him unacceptably pro-German. Reflecting on the situation after the war, he complained that to be a Christian in the war years "meant to be denominated 'pro-German.'"[12] Believing that the war made a travesty of Christ's injunction "Love your enemies" (among others), he observed, "It is not right to curse our enemies simply because it is popular." He recalled that "during the war there was little else left for a preacher to do.... The Gospel was scarcely allowed to be preached. One could not preach 'love your enemies.'"[13]

Bartleman believed that participation in war meant rejection of Christ: "War is contrary to the whole Spirit and teaching of Christ," he wrote. "Anyone going into war is bound to lose out.

Christ's kingdom is 'not of this world.' "[14] This issue of the place of the Christian's citizenship played an important role in the evolution of an Assemblies of God position on war. Bartleman and other pacifists emphasized the Christian's participation in an eternal kingdom. Stanley Frodsham carried Bartleman's views of heavenly citizenship further. Such citizenship mandated something more than neutrality: It meant that Christians should live their lives as pilgrims and strangers in any country. Pride in nation and race was an abomination.[15] This impatience with conflict had an emphatic restorationist component: Its advocates ardently sought to imbue their generation with both the ethic of Christ and the cultural disinterest they perceived in the Early Church.

The *Evangel* also both advertised and published pacifistic literature written by members of the Booth-Clibborn family. Several members of this family of descendants of William and Catherine Booth (founders of the Salvation Army) articulated strong pacifistic sentiments. Some became Pentecostals, and three of the grandsons affiliated with the Assemblies of God.[16] Samuel H. Booth-Clibborn argued against Christian participation in war in *Should a Christian Fight?—An Appeal to Christian Young Men of All Nations.* His father, Arthur Booth-Clibborn, expressed similar sentiments in *Blood Against Blood,* a book distributed by Gospel Publishing House.

Samuel Booth-Clibborn addressed his remarks specifically to Christians. In both his book and an article published in the *Evangel* just after the United States entered the war in April 1917, he argued for nonresistance. Urging those who had "nothing higher to live and die for" to fight for their countries, he reminded Christians: "We do have a better cause to live and die for."[17] His pacifism was rooted directly in his Christianity. For the Christian, the outcome of a war made no real difference: "What does it matter under what flag you are? . . . Jesus lived all His life in a conquered country and never objected to paying the tribute of subjection to victorious Rome. If He put up with it, why can't we?"[18] Strongly denouncing "the wretched idolatry of nation-worship where parents sacrifice their young men on the bloody altars of the modern 'Moloch' of PATRIOTISM," he insisted that Christian participation in war involved dire moral and spiritual consequences. Christians had no alternative but pacifism.[19]

Samuel's father, Arthur, a Quaker by birth, concurred. Christians who fought were "assisting the Prince of Hell, who was a murderer from the beginning."[20] On the same note, the *Evangel* also published an unnamed English conscientious objector's conviction that Christians who "measured [their] walk by the Word of God" would not fight.[21]

As time progressed and British fortunes deteriorated, the Wilson administration's poorly disguised commitment to the Allies became overt. The *Evangel* editors used Washington's vision to demonstrate the likelihood of eventual American involvement.[22] Bartleman concurred in 1916 that events pointed toward America's entry into the war. He regarded it as satanically inspired. "Satan seems . . . to be preparing the way for killing here," he wrote in 1916. "For two years our daily papers have been full of killing. Conscience is getting seared. A selfish spirit, refusing the voice of God, is predominating. God must give a rebellious people the sword."[23]

Honest efforts to address the ethical issues raised by war were—as they have always been—controversial. Pacifism became both unpopular and dangerous as war enthusiasm swept the country and the Sedition Act enumerated penalties for a wide range of dissent.

It had become evident too that some Assemblies of God adherents objected to thoroughgoing pacifism. Though pilgrims, they were also patriots. Responses to Bartleman accused him of sympathy for Germany and resulted in an editorial disclaimer that counseled neutrality. Meanwhile, the editors encouraged young men preparing for war: "We are all very proud of our soldiers and our sailors, and of all those who have so nobly responded to their country's call to arms." The challenge was not so much to militarism as to the mortality of those involved, that they might face an imminent "call into eternity." Evangelism among soldiers was encouraged. Some local pastors, like Raymond Richey, became deeply involved in outreaches on military bases.

Meanwhile, the *Evangel* increasingly reflected the diversity of its readers. Although Bell argued that it was spiritually "unsafe" for Pentecostals to join the army, he admitted that there were some "bright Pentecostal lights" among European soldiers. More traditional than some of his colleagues on the subjects of war and women in ministry, Bell believed that either of two factors made military service acceptable: a draft law or the necessity to defend "mothers, wives and children." He was also convinced that the defeat of Germany would benefit righteousness.

Meanwhile, as American war participation became a reality, the Executive Presbytery adopted a resolution on military service. In keeping with the denomination's objective of cooperative fellowship, the resolution was not primarily an effort to deal theologically with the problem of Christian participation in war. Rather, it was framed to secure "the privilege of exemption from military service." (In spite of the formulation of a Statement of Fundamental Truths in the midst of uncertainties about war, the Statement of Fundamental Truths expressed no sentiments about war. Apparently the issue was not even raised.) At the same time, however, editors insisted that those adherents who "felt free to do so" could certainly take up arms.

The resolution, dated April 28, 1917, was accompanied by a letter signed by Stanley Frodsham, who had already made his own pacifistic views evident. The resolution made some startling claims: Scriptures like "Follow peace with all men"; "Resist not evil"; "Thou shalt not kill"; or "Love your enemies" had "always been accepted and interpreted by our churches as prohibiting Christians from shedding blood or taking human life."[24] "[A]s a body," Assemblies of God adherents, then, could not "conscientiously participate in war and armed resistance which involves the actual destruction of human life...."[25] Frodsham, serving as general secretary for the denomination, noted further that the principles of the General Council "were in opposition to war from its very beginning." The introduction of the matter in the *Evangel* tied Pentecostals to the historic peace churches:

> From the very beginning, the movement has been characterized by Quaker principles. The laws of the Kingdom, laid down by our elder brother, Jesus Christ, in His Sermon on the Mount, have been unqualifiedly adopted, consequently the movement has found itself opposed to the spilling of blood of any man, or of offering resistance to any aggression. Every branch of the movement, whether in the United States, Canada, Great Britain or Germany, has held to this principle.[26]

This resolution, framed by several of the executive presbyters (during the brief period when E. N. Bell was excluded from their ranks) and approved by the Executive and General Presbytery, ignored the militaristic strain expressed in Boddy's early defense of the war, implied a Pentecostal consensus by speaking for "all sections of the Pentecostal Movement,"[27] and maintained that Pentecostalism was "one monolithic whole in its . . . nonresistance."[28]

The executives had framed the resolution to meet specific guidelines issued by the War Department, including a date (May 18, 1917) by which such principles had to be articulated. The resolution, though clearly a pacifistic statement, was conceived to coincide with the diversity the Fellowship sought to preserve: It intended only to secure for participants the right to follow conscience.

Later issues of the *Evangel* urged young men to fulfill their obligation to register with local draft boards. Pressure during the war years encouraged some who had avoided affiliation with the Assemblies of God to seek credentials. One such was W. I. Evans, then a young pastor in New Jersey. Like many other early Pentecostals, Evans had had strong reservations about organization. He led an independent mission until the draft law made it advisable for him to affiliate with a registered religious group. He needed an organization through which he could maintain his conscientious objection; the alternative was imprisonment. When the war ended, however, Evans concluded that he had compromised. He returned his credentials and engaged in independent ministry until, his reservations satisfied, he left New Jersey for Central Bible Institute in 1929.[29]

At the 1917 General Council, A. P. Collins informed participants that the Texas District Council had decided to cancel the credentials of any minister who spoke against the government. The General Council "agreed that such radicals do not represent this General Council."[30] Two models of Pentecostal attitudes toward culture were in tension: the Christian as pacifist, having an unyielding commitment to the Christian's heavenly citizenship, and the Christian as soldier, which tended to identify fighting for America with being on God's side. Texas Pentecostals clearly did not wholeheartedly share fellow Texan William McCafferty's commitment to heavenly citizenship.[31]

Neither did E. N. Bell. The August 24, 1918, issue of the *Evangel* carried Bell's advice that Assemblies of God adherents should destroy the tract form of one of Bartleman's earlier *Evangel* articles, "Present Day Condition." Later that year, with the war drawing to a close, Bell found the courage to express more fully his own nonpacifistic views. From his perspective, participation in war was not sinful. Hatred, however, was. If one kept personal hatred out of his heart, Bell believed "a soldier is [not] a murderer when he obeys his country in executing just punishment on the criminal Hun."[32]

Early Assemblies of God adherents, then, expressed diverse attitudes toward war. A strongly pacifistic element, attempting a consistent view, articulated a radical stance on Christian citizenship, locating it entirely in heaven and making strong national loyalties not only irrelevant but sinful. In adopting a resolution to address the conscription law, the Fellowship's executives avowed the pacifistic nature of Pentecostalism everywhere. Sentiments expressed within the ranks—especially by Texans (who had the strongest representation of any state in the early General Council membership)—exposed the falseness of this claim. The espousal of voluntary conscientious objection satisfied many on both sides of the bigger issue. Only a few continued to sense that the movement had "lost something" when it had veered from pacifism.[33] Leaders avoided the fundamental question of appropriate Christian response to war. Commitment to cooperative fellowship took precedence over wrestling with the larger issue. Consequently, a systematic just war theory or theology by the Assemblies of God received an indefinite postponement.

Changing views in the Assemblies of God were part of a profound move in American Pentecostalism at large. Robert Anderson has traced the shift in Pentecostal rhetoric after World War I from challenging the social system to buttressing it.[34] Historian R. Laurence Moore has noted that, in the same years, Pentecostalism's early "egalitarian innovations" were suppressed. "[P]remillennial condemnations of patriotism in Pentecostal journals," he wrote, "gave way to reproductions of the American flag."[35]

The war experience exposed inconsistent views of Christian identity. If that of pilgrims and strangers suited some, others found the battling soldier, at times, more congenial. Two decades later, when the nation again stood at the brink of war, few would admit any sinfulness in strong national loyalties. Most would opt—with considerable pride—to serve their country.

Attitudes Toward Women in the Assemblies of God

It is sometimes assumed by scholars of women in American religion that Pentecostalism has historically been among the religious traditions most hospitable to women in ministry.[36] (Ministry in this sense refers to leadership in public acts of worship.) Some students of Pentecostalism have claimed that the movement at first embraced women in ministry and then moved from that stance as it acculturated.[37] Certainly women played a prominent public role in early Pentecostalism; clearly, however, their public role has diminished over time. Questions related to institutional authority elicited an essentially negative response from the movement's beginning. Questions pertaining to cultural authority were not so clearly formulated. In the cultural sphere, women found ways to exercise considerable authority. An examination of early Pentecostal assumptions yields insights that help explain the situation in the Assemblies of God.

Early Pentecostalism offered lay people, men and women, a

wide range of opportunities for participation. Impatience with hierarchy and denominationalism combined with the urgency of the message to enable women to serve as evangelists, pastors, teachers, editors, authors, and missionaries. The *call* (sometimes discovered through exercising spiritual gifts) and the *anointing* seemed vastly more important than credentials and authorization. Women's activity also had apparent theological warrant in the focal Pentecostal text of Joel 2:28—"Your sons and your daughters shall prophesy." For decades, advocates of women in ministry had used those words to support women's right to preach.

Early Pentecostals claimed that the experience of Spirit baptism made them want to proclaim the gospel. Many eagerly anticipated domestic or foreign service, assured that the Spirit's special enduement would make them effective. In the movement's earliest phases, its periodicals reminded husbands and wives of their responsibilities to one another and to their children. Contemporary conditions seemed to render such advice necessary: Situations in which one spouse neglected family obligations to follow a "leading," leaving a family in economic hardship, were all too common.

Numerous women became well-known in early Pentecostal ranks; their preaching too gained respect. To name but a few, Abbie Morrow wrote tracts and articles that circulated widely; Marie Burgess Brown established a thriving Pentecostal mission in New York City; after her ordination by A. J. Tomlinson at a campmeeting in Durant, Florida, Lillian Trasher chose to apply the training she had received at God's Bible School in Cincinnati and N. J. Holmes's school in Altamont, South Carolina, as a missionary to Egypt; Ethel Goss evangelized; Anna Reiff edited the influential *Latter Rain Evangel;* Florence Crawford dominated the association of missions known as The Apostolic Faith (Portland, Oregon).

Efforts to understand women's prominence must take several factors into account. First, the movement in most places took the form of a lay movement, impatient with hierarchy and denominational structure. Some women held credentials from local missions; some had been set apart for the ministry through prayer and the laying on of hands of a group of sympathetic people in a home or other nontraditional setting; some claimed to have been "ordained by the Lord," an event that to the mind of Elizabeth Sisson, veteran missionary and Bible teacher, needed no human ratification.[38] If early Pentecostal women were ordained, then, their ordinations had often been highly irregular, involving few issues such as their relationship to male pastors or participation in an organized denomination. Ordination was not so much an acknowledging of authority within a specific group as fervent prayer for effectiveness in witness.

To be sure, most considered ordination (or credentialing of any sort) relatively unimportant. The sense that God had called one to a specific task was infinitely more important than gaining human authorization to perform the task. Some participants later recalled meetings that resembled early Quaker gatherings: Whether a man or a woman preached made no difference; the speaker, male or female, was the Spirit's choice, and essentially the Spirit's channel. The anointing, then, validated the message.

Lay men and women accomplished much in disseminating Pentecostal teaching. And it seems evident that, in this country at least, the assertion of women's right to preach and to assist in extending the movement did not generally involve the right to administer the ordinances of the church. Women (and men) regarded their opportunities essentially as Christian service rather than as sources of income. As a more professional concept of the ministry evolved within the movement, the participation of women preachers declined. The professionalization of the ministry is one important aspect of the story of women in American Pentecostalism.

Economic factors form another related consideration: Women frequently accomplished tasks for which financial resources were meager. They proved adept at pioneer work; they performed tasks that some men disdained as women's work. They had already become familiar figures in home missions; their service as city missionaries was recognized in many denominations, some of which provided training as deaconesses for women. The kinds of work Assemblies of God women accomplished did not differ markedly from tasks other religiously motivated Protestant women engaged in. Many in the culture sensed an urgency, not necessarily rooted in premillennialism, to evangelize. For congregations that could support a man to perform the same duties, however, it became increasingly common, over time, to secure the services of men.[39]

A second factor is related to the first. As a revival movement that emphasized the Holy Spirit, Pentecostalism seemed likely to encourage women's activity. Its focal text of Joel 2:28 supported their public speech. Revivals have historically been vehicles through which women have discovered new avenues of Christian service.[40] And Pentecostalism presented itself as a revival with a difference. The latter rain outpouring represented equipment for an urgent task. The expectation of Christ's second coming made the task of recruiting workers essential. Time was short: Women workers were needed. When Christ did not return and concerns related to passing leadership on to the next generation surfaced, new questions became relevant.

Despite the openness toward women in ministry that a superficial survey indicates, deeply rooted prejudices both against women exercising authority over men and against married women assuming responsibilities outside the home thrived within Pentecostal ranks. Men assumed a dichotomy between home and public spheres. Even in its initial stages, Pentecostalism was not entirely supportive of ministering women, except in specific, well-defined roles.

Part of the reason for an apparent discrepancy between theory and practice derives from the mingling of various streams of late nineteenth-century Protestantism in Pentecostalism. Many of the Pentecostal women who preached followed the example of holiness women: They too used Joel 2:28 (a text of the holiness movement itself). Because the Pentecostal movement was predominantly restorationist, however, most of its participants read the Bible from a restorationist perspective. Although Paul had called women "fellow laborers," he had also enjoined subjection. Although he had asserted that in Christ there was "neither male nor female," he had also commanded women to be silent.

An examination of sentiments expressed in three of the settings that produced people who affiliated with the Assemblies of God helps provide perspective essential for understanding how a restorationist reading of Scripture influenced the operative assumptions about institutional authority for women.

W. F. Carothers superintended the Apostolic Faith Movement in Texas: working closely with Charles Parham from 1905 and after the movement disowned Parham in 1907, helping its missions to regroup. A man with an unusual range of interests, Carothers was especially committed to the restorationist character of Pentecostalism. One who cherished the unstructured course of Pentecostal worship and outreach, he also issued a strong call for balance in the movement's perception of the function and use of spiritual gifts.[41] From time to time, Carothers wrote for publications of the Assemblies of God. And in the 1920s he briefly held credentials with them; he left because he concluded that they had lost the restorationist concept of unity.

Restorationist views could be introduced either to support or to restrict the ministry of women. Carothers chose to apply them in a restrictive sense. Writing in 1909, he set out to describe the relationship between men and women "as it should exist, with reference to the government and work of the church."[42] He set the tone of his discussion by introducing it with nine verses (and offering the references of others) that enjoined women to submit to men, to be silent in church, and to respect male headship.

Carothers' views contained most of the traditional arguments that have been used over the years to limit women's roles. For one thing, man's prerogative was rooted in creation: "Man is especially made in the image and likeness of God, and is therefore by right the sovereign of all creation. It is man's prerogative to rule in all things."[43] God, then, had made a distinction between the proper spheres for males and females that, to Carothers' mind, was best preserved "in the old chivalrous Southland."[44] "Nothing," Carothers insisted, "is more heavenly than the sincere observance of this distinction . . . and nothing more of a monstrosity than modern efforts to obliterate and disregard the differences between the sexes."[45]

Second, women were weaker than men, less able to cope with "the shock of the strife of war that is inseparable from sovereignty." God had given woman a "tenderer office and character."[46] Carothers responded to the use of Galatians 3:28 ("There is neither Jew nor Greek, neither bond nor free, there is neither male nor female: for ye are all one in Christ Jesus") to validate women's ministries with the assertion that the passage referred only to the fact that "the woman is as truly a Christian in her place as the man is in his place."[47]

Convinced that the Bible precluded women from either exercising authority over men or teaching men, Carothers admitted only their right to "prophesy." This he understood to be "preaching under direct inspiration from the Holy Spirit." Such preaching, he noted, was always equally appropriate for men, women, boys, or girls. Again, the prerogative was the Spirit's. The individual—male or female, adult or child—functioned simply as a channel the Spirit spoke through. Since woman's intellect was not involved, she exercised no authority while she prophesied. The primary form of public speaking ministry open to women, then, was equally appropriate for children.[48]

The early Pentecostal subculture was penetrated by fear of offending the Holy Spirit. Apparent tensions between the authority of the Word, to which most Pentecostals paid at least lip-service, and the authority of the Spirit, to which they sought to yield themselves, frequently troubled them. Questions about appropriate use of spiritual gifts like tongues and interpretation demanded resolution. Did the radical nature of experience in the Spirit supersede the letter of Scripture? Suppose a woman declared that she had been called of the Spirit to be the pastor of a congregation? What if she offered "the brethren" (note the assumption that the deacons would be males) an opportunity to "test her doctrine by the Word"? Carothers addressed the subject late in 1910 in an article billed as "remarkable and timely" by William Piper, editor of an important Pentecostal monthly, *The Latter Rain Evangel*.

Carothers' response was predictable: Testing such a purported call was simply a waste of time. "The place to apply the test," he insisted, "was at the threshold of error." A biblical basis for women serving as elders (a favorite early Pentecostal term for a local pastor) simply did not exist. "The woman has no business teaching as elder at all, whether she 'teaches' Bible or does not."[49] Claims of calling could not supersede Scripture.

Another center of early Pentecostal activity was Rochester, New York, where the Duncan sisters supervised a growing network of ministries known as Elim. Curiously, the five sisters—who gained a widespread reputation for spirituality and faith—strongly opposed the ordination of women and could not condone women in authority in a local congregation. They illustrate, on the other hand, the extent of the cultural authority women sometimes acquired.

The oldest sister, Elizabeth Duncan Baker, had been deeply influenced by Elizabeth Sisson, a missionary to India and a woman committed to following the call of the Holy Spirit despite obstacles. (In an unusual move, the Assemblies of God later gave Sisson credentials based on her ordination "by the Lord.") When Baker and her sisters independently of each other sensed an urging to open a mission in Rochester, they looked to their brother to lead their public ministry. His untimely death, however, forced them to assume leadership roles in order to implement what they considered the Spirit's leading. For several years, their aging father provided a male presence. As time passed, the sisters expanded their efforts, conducting a faith home, a Bible training institute, and a publishing ministry as well as mission services. In 1907 they embraced Pentecostal teaching and identified their various efforts with the Pentecostal movement.

As their outreach expanded, however, and they decided to construct a church building, their uneasiness resurfaced. They dealt with their antagonism toward women in ministry in an acceptable Pentecostal fashion.

First, they prayed for a male pastor. When no satisfactory male presented himself, they claimed divine instruction to proceed without a pastor. They conducted the church much as they had their mission and claimed that the Holy Spirit was the pastor. They had already established their reputation as "vessels" through whom the Holy Spirit spoke. This conception of their task was comparable to that approved by Carothers. They organized a male board of deacons to officiate at Communion until "regular ordained [male] elders" joined them later and regularized the situation. Confining themselves to "anointed utterance" in the services, then, they were convinced that the ordinances were "properly administered" only after male leadership had emerged. The implication was clear: Local congregations needed male leadership for all but prophetic functions.[50]

The situation in downstate New York was similar. Marie Burgess opened an Apostolic Faith mission in midtown Manhattan in 1907. When she married in 1909, however, she clearly—and gladly—resigned leadership to her husband, Robert Brown. The two shared a view of woman's appropriate sphere of ministry that permitted—and even featured—her "anointed utterance" but left governing to him.

Among the pre-Pentecostal groups that provided both leadership and participants for the Assemblies of God, none figured more prominently than did the Christian and Missionary Alliance. Alliance founder A. B. Simpson shared the conviction that his contemporaries A. J. Gordon and A. T. Pierson had expressed: Women should not be denied a range of public opportunities.[51] In the Alliance, women led rescue missions; one directed Simpson's healing faith home; several did editorial work; many served as missionaries; a few sat on the Alliance's governing board, the Board of Managers.[52]

Women in Alliance outreaches, however, worked under definite restrictions—restrictions that helped shape the expectations of Alliance people who affiliated with the Assemblies of God.[53] Although Simpson admitted that women were "called without restriction to teach, to witness, to work in every department of the Church of Christ," he insisted that man was woman's head. Women were not to "rule in the ecclesiastical government of the Church of Christ, or to exercise the official ministry which the Holy Ghost has committed to the elders or bishops of His Church."[54] He required women to function within their God-ordained (and male-defined) "sphere." When they stepped out of that sphere, Simpson insisted, women "lost power."[55] A woman's proper place was dictated by both "her nature" and "her distinct place in the social economy."[56] Convinced that women were not "adapted to leadership" and affirming a conviction that few—if any—were so called, he nonetheless applauded their service as foreign and city missionaries (which he understood as paralleling the New Testament role of deaconess) and encouraged their cultivation of all opportunities they found within their "true spheres."

Simpson and Gordon enjoyed the friendship of F. L. Chapell, a prominent Bible teacher. Chapell too encouraged women to "respond to the divine call" to preach. He considered their quiet, unassuming participation in church life a "marked phenomenon of the times."[57] Claiming that women's increasing involvement was a response on their part to "the strong impulsion of the Spirit, as He voices the divine purpose in the closing of the age," Chapell nonetheless manifested convictions similar to those held by others who did not share his excitement about women "laborers in the gospel." For one thing, women's involvement demonstrated the essentially simple nature of the gospel. Unqualified for "elaborate argumentative discourses intended to convince the intellect," women showed that "simple, heartfelt" discourse was sufficient. Clearly, Chapell concluded, "the excellency of the power is of God and not in the agent." For another thing, women's activities showed that "genuine Gospel service" could be "free from ecclesiastical ambition." Whereas men were both tempted and taught to covet position or title, such designs were assumed to be absent in women. "Ecclesiastical promotion does not come in her thought at all, and is out of the question in most quarters," Chapell maintained.[58] Ministering women, then, were a "sign of the times," "eleventh-hour laborers" whose assistance, though welcomed, was limited both by her nature and her calling.

When the Assemblies of God was organized in 1914, former adherents of the Christian and Missionary Alliance, Pentecostals with roots in the Apostolic Faith movement, and participants at Elim gained prominence in the new organization. It is not surprising, then, that, from its inception, the Assemblies of God promulgated a view of woman's "proper sphere" that paralleled those considered above. All of its leaders were men. In fact, only male ministers and delegates were originally eligible to vote in denominational deliberations.[59]

The founding Council of the Assemblies of God declared (by male vote) its acceptance of the view that Galatians 3:28—(In Christ "there is neither male nor female"), a passage often introduced in support of women's ministry—meant rather that "in the matter of salvation, the lines of sex are blotted out."[60] Citing 1 Timothy 2:11–15, it affirmed that women were to be in subjection to men. On a more positive note, it acknowledged their call to "prophesy" as well as to be "helpers in the Gospel." The Assemblies of God offered women credentials as evangelists or as missionaries (roles regarded either as prophetic, temporary, or expedient), but not as pastors.[61]

The next year, the General Council created a category of "advisory members" of the Council and invited women who were "mature believers" to register as such. This ambiguous status, which did not allow women to vote, was definitely inferior to that of males. Males, it was assumed, would be mature—a female candidate's maturity was open to question.[62]

The practice of Assemblies of God congregations having women pastors was clearly discouraged, not only in official periodicals but also in the consistent restrictions on their participation at General Councils. In 1919, for example, the Council's male leadership reiterated limiting the vote to "all male ministers." Although by 1919 those women whose qualifications were "accepted by the Roster Committee" were granted the right to engage in discussion from the floor, they could not vote, even if they had been ordained prior to the formation of the Assemblies of God and their ordination had been recognized.[63] And the credentialing as evangelists and missionaries that was officially sanctioned for women neither qualified them to administer church ordinances nor to receive much coveted clergy discount passes on the railroads.[64] In 1920, the General Council extended to women the right to vote at Councils and also added to the list of acceptable offices for women that of assistant pastor (a post that did not require ordination as an elder).[65]

For several of his nine years as a denominational leader, former Southern Baptist Eudorus Bell authored a question and answer column in the denomination's weekly publication. He frequently found opportunity to articulate his opposition to women functioning in ways that gave them authority over men. Given the variety of circumstances—ranging from claims of spiritual authority to a shortage of workers—that encouraged public roles for women in some areas, however, Bell found it necessary occasionally to justify the existence of female leadership.

Such justifications make interesting reading. Layered with qualifying phrases, they grudgingly accorded women no more than the right to be pastors on a temporary basis. The tension between Bell's personal inclinations (which he shared with his friend Carothers) and the movement's commitment to the Holy Spirit's authority within believers surfaces repeatedly. If God should "call her in His sovereignty," if He "[set] His seal" on her leadership "by giving her souls," if she had the ability to "build up the assembly in the Lord and in peace," then "many brethren hold ... this privilege is granted her as temporary. . . ."[66] Even given her charismatic enduement, however, Bell simply could not conceive of female pastors on more than a supply basis. Neither "female rights" nor "New Testament command or example" supported her place as a pastor.[67]

Circumstances forced Bell to agree reluctantly that a woman might temporarily "do a work ... that no man at that place is prepared to do." But "if the woman is wise," he continued, "she will push the man. . . ."[68] The right person for congregational and administrative leadership, every time, was a man. After all, God had "especially designed" the ministry "for stronger shoulders."[69]

In September 1916, Bell suggested a second way of perceiving ministering women: as substitutes for "men [who] fail God." In such cases, women were apparently God's second best option for the task. Among people constantly enjoined to know and experience "God's best," the "second best" had little appeal. If in the absence of male deacons women temporarily served in their place in a congregation (Bell appealed to ancient church history for a distinction between the roles of deacon and deaconess), Bell insisted that such service did not make a woman a deacon. He asserted that she remained "*only* a deaconess" (emphasis added).[70]

A married woman's proper place, then, as portrayed in the official journal of the Assemblies of God during its formative years, was in the home, "in subjection to her husband." When asked directly what Paul had intended when he had instructed women to be silent in the church, Bell responded: "He meant what he said . . . the squabbles in the church, the disputing and disorder, . . . leave this setting things in order to the men in charge."[71]

Early Pentecostal women were admonished to "adorn themselves with a meek and quiet spirit." They were told that the women's movement threatened the social order and represented rebellion against God. Although all were not so outspoken as Frank Bartleman[72] (whose articles on various subjects appeared in the denomination's periodicals throughout its first several years), his strong injunctions to women to accept their role in the home as God's call were echoed in many places. Threatened by cultural changes that they perceived as "signs of the times," many Pentecostals honestly wanted to disassociate themselves in conspicuous ways from the "flapper generation" of "new" women. In this regard, it is probably significant that many Assemblies of God adherents urged certain fashions on women: Among Pentecostals, long skirts, long sleeves, and long hair, Anthropologist Elaine Lawless has argued, had theological significance as tokens of woman's submission to male authority.[73] The familiar refrain of heavenly citizenship, applied somewhat inconsistently, reinforced such visible "rejection" of the world.

As with other Protestant groups, the foreign field of Pentecostal missions provided a setting where American women more successfully asserted their need for official endorsement. But even there, restrictions were a reality. In keeping with the general profile of American missionaries, a large majority of early Assemblies of God missionaries were women. Several months after the denomination was organized, two women missionaries to India requested Assemblies of God executives to grant them the "privilege to fulfill the functions of the Christian ministry."[74] Their request was granted, but with a proviso: They could fulfill those functions only when a man was unavailable to do so. Their authorization was "a special privilege," for use "in case of emergency only."[75]

As time passed, Assemblies of God officials expressed concern about the predominance of women on the mission field. At the denomination's General Council in 1931, Missionary Secretary Noel Perkin cited the findings of "competent authorities" who, he claimed, had advised him that "the work of the General Council of the Assemblies of God depends too much on woman workers."[76] Expressing gratitude to the women "so splendidly filling the gap," he reminded the Council of the need for single men and married couples.[77]

Early in its history, the Assemblies of God ordained people to various types of ministries, or offices: elder (or pastor), evangelist, missionary. In 1917 the General Council voted to drop such categories, and simply to ordain "to the full gospel ministry." It is uncertain precisely how this affected women. Given earlier proscriptions about ordaining women as pastors, it seems likely that it meant, in effect, that the leadership frowned on women's ordination. Women continued to be endorsed as foreign missionaries or evangelists. However, it is evident that some people—and districts—disregarded the ruling. David McDowell, an executive officer and a pastor in Pennsylvania, for example, in a highly irregular proceeding, ordained his wife himself so that she could serve the congregation more effectively during his frequent travels.[78] Other women, like Helen Wannenmacher in Milwaukee, preached regularly and conducted services in their pastor-husbands' absences. It seems evident, however, that their ministry conformed to the denomination's earlier expectation of submission to male leadership.

Several women evangelists also found receptive audiences in the worldwide Assemblies of God constituency. But it is evident that they took seriously urgings to modesty and "womanly demeanor." And usually they spoke in settings controlled by men. Men invited them and when it was time for preaching, turned the service over to them.

It is likely that Aimee Semple McPherson became, at least partially, a victim of the prevalent uneasiness about women ministers operating in settings they controlled. Although several factors influenced her departure from the Assemblies of God, she increasingly defied the norms for denominational evangelists. After a brief, unsuccessful attempt to work with her husband, Harold McPherson, she launched out on her own to minister in an environment she dominated. It is interesting that her early independent ministry attracted a higher percentage of males than did the Assemblies of God.[79] As time passed, she too associated with men in the performance of such acts as baptism. And when Angelus Temple needed someone to substitute for "Sister," Temple leaders turned to men like Paul Rader or Watson Argue.

This brief survey of the limitations on the institutional authority of women from the inception of the Assemblies of God provides context for the decision of the General Council in 1935 to grant full ordination to women. Given a brief statement on women at the 1931 Council, the action of the 1935 Council (which was recorded without comment) is surprising. In 1931, apparently some ordination certificates were issued to women in spite of earlier ambiguity on the subject. The Council ruled that such certificates should "clearly state that women are ordained only as evangelists." It further required that the words "bury the dead, administer the ordinances of the church, and perform the rite of marriage, when such acts are necessary" (language that had been on some earlier women's missionary credentials) be omitted from women's credentials.

The pertinent resolution of the 1935 Council began by noting that "[t]he Scriptures plainly teach" the view that men and women have different ministries within the church. Nonetheless, it continued, "women may also serve the church in the ministry of the Word." Women seeking ordination as either evangelists or pastors were required to be at least twenty-five and "matured." They needed, further, "to give evidence of both development in the ministry of the Word" and "actual service." Their "right to administer the ordinances of the church, *when such acts are necessary*" (emphasis added), was included in their ordination. The resolution was made retroactive, presumably to authorize the actions of some district councils during the preceeding decade when the status of women had been ambiguous.[80]

By 1935, assumptions about proper institutional and cultural roles for women were so ingrained that the resolution made little difference. It was formulated during the administration of Ernest Williams, a beloved leader whose personal views on women in ministry closely paralleled Bell's.[81] The predominance of males in both the denomination's administration and its congregational leadership was not affected by permitting the ordination of women "to the full ministry." The language of the denomination's constitution and bylaws continued to reinforce assumptions that authority should be exercised exclusively by males. And, more often than not, women who obtained credentials and used them ministered in cooperation with their husbands. At any rate, they functioned under male leadership, since all leadership above the congregational level (and often that within the congregation) was male. Probably most importantly, women often agreed with traditional views about their proper spheres.

From one perspective, at least little, if anything, changed in 1935. Altering the denomination's technical rule did not, in itself, negate longheld assumptions. Nor did it change what women wanted for themselves. The small—and declining— number of active ordained women pastors, for example, is only partially due to denominational expectations: It can also be attributed in part to women's occasional reluctance to assume new responsibilities. The failure to address the underlying reservations about women in leadership made the decision to ordain women little more than a technical improvement. One student of ministering women noted in another context: "Emphasis was always on woman's responsibility, not her rights; on her service to the cause of Christ, not her leadership of it."[82] That observation applies to the Assemblies of God as well.

Failure to shift the emphasis assured the existence of a wide gap between technical rights and actual service. In fact, in most major American denominations, the successful implementation of the conviction that women could (and should) minister had come only after a thorough consideration of lay rights and responsibilities. Issues pertaining to women's place in the authority structure of local congregations and districts had been addressed before women had been accepted as pastors.[83]

The credence sometimes given Bell's assertion that the Assemblies of God offered women more opportunities than did most other religious organizations is historically uninformed. Historical perspective must also inform sociological analyses of the situation. In several major denominations, women could be ordained; they exercised leadership through missionary agencies. Belle Bennett championed the rights of the laity in southern Methodism, establishing a basis for women to serve the church at all levels; in 1921, Helen Barrett Montgomery became the first woman to lead the national governing agency of a mainstream denomination when she was elected president of the Northern Baptist Convention. In evangelical circles after about 1920, however, women gradually lost the measure of prominence they had quietly gained during the late nineteenth century. The rapid acceptance of the Scofield Bible is part of that story; the gradual ascendancy of Dallas Theological Seminary alumni in the Bible school movement is another. John Roach Straton's impassioned defense of young Uldine Utley (a teenage evangelist) in 1926 was the last public advocacy of women preachers from the conservative camp for decades.[84]

The early Assemblies of God, then, offered women "restricted freedom." Women exercised a degree of cultural authority that sometimes obscured the restrictions. But the limitations expressed deeply-rooted sentiments; they were symbolized in significant ways. Later generations would rediscover them and learn that the celebration in their history of women evangelists and missionaries did not mean unreserved acceptance of ministering women.

The above information should not obscure the vital contributions women made to early Assemblies of God efforts. They evangelized, served on mission stations, taught at Bible institutes, and served local congregations in countless ways. They often ministered effectively, even if they did so amid restricting assumptions. And most of them apparently found such ministry fulfilling and the environment unobjectionable. The foregoing does, however, suggest that the declining percentage of actively ministering women is not merely a function of sociological change. Professionalization of the ministry went hand in hand with the endorsement of widespread assumptions about woman's proper role. Basic points were never discussed: They were assumed. It is hardly surprising, then, that Pentecostals failed to produce a body of literature comparable to holiness tracts and books supporting the ministry of women. They tended, rather, to find congenial attitudes about women's public ministry that suited as well their assumptions about family life. And Assemblies of God women tended, on their part, to acquiesce. Examples of married women holding a pastorate apart from their spouse and succeeding (in the denomination's terms) in family roles are scarce. The most outstanding (perhaps the only one) in the early years was Carrie Judd Montgomery. In a setting increasingly wary of the cultural implications of feminism, Assemblies of God adherents opted for a moderately authoritarian resolution to the tension between authority and Spirit raised by the subject of women in ministry.

During the late 1930s, Americans watched the world situation deteriorate. The Assemblies of God applauded Franklin Roosevelt's neutrality laws and hoped for peace. The apocalyptic frame of reference that had seemed irrepressible during World War I was less conspicuous in the 1930s; so was the tendency to disclaim cultural responsibility by appealing to heavenly citizenship. Loyalty transferred readily into patriotism. The horrors of fascism prodded American sensibilities and prompted Assemblies of God adherents to rally around the "four freedoms" that Roosevelt and Churchill defined. The Christian's dual citizenship, in a setting less overwhelmed by the imminence of the Second Coming, promoted both patriotic loyalty and evangelistic witness.

World War II contributed directly to further consideration

of the cultural issues the Fellowship had addressed earlier. It also coincided with events in the broader setting of American evangelicalism that ultimately helped mold new directions for American Pentecostalism.

Appendix

This testimony of Joseph P. Wannenmacher has been translated into many languages and circulated by the millions. It is typical in many ways of how early Pentecostals came to their persuasions.

Jesus Christ, My Physician

How thankful I am to God, for Jesus Christ, the Great Physician, who is still the same today. Through His inexpressible Mercy, He forgave my sins, granted me peace of soul and healed me of an incurable disease—"That it might be fulfilled which was spoken by Esaias the prophet, saying, Himself took our infirmities and bare our sicknesses and with His stripes we are healed." Matthew 8:17; Isaiah 53:5.

I was born in Hungary. My parents were devout Catholics. When I was three years old my mother died of tuberculosis of the lungs. Four of the children in our family inherited this sickness from my mother. I was one of them.

My second sister died when she was 17 years old. At the time of her death her body had turned to a festering mass. Her left arm was so swollen and full of matter that it was about three times its normal size.

God gave us a wonderful stepmother who spared nothing that we might be helped. At the age of 5, I suffered an eruption of my right hand and after much physical torture an operation was performed. My condition improved somewhat, but at the age of 9 my foot became swollen and the pain was unbearable. My home town in Hungary was a famous health resort, there were many of the finest physicians there, and I was treated by some of these; but in spite of all their medical science, surgical helps, baths, etc., my condition grew steadily worse and we knew that I too was suffering from the dreaded bone consumption.

In my childish fear, knowing the fate of my sister, I asked my mother if I too would have to die. My hopeless question made her run out to the court yard, throw her hands up toward heaven and implore God to "spare the life of her little boy." God who is "touched with the feelings of our infirmities" heard her earnest plea, and I improved.

MY CHOICE OF PROFESSION

My father was an orchestra leader. From the age of 3, I loved to pick up musical instruments and was encouraged to play them. The study of music was not difficult for me since I grew up in a musical atmosphere. I played in my father's orchestra when I was 10. But because of the easy-going, loose life of most musicians in our country, my father was opposed to my choosing music as a vocation. Therefore, I chose to become a mechanic and was apprenticed under a great master of mechanics. Under his tutorship, I became a journeyman at the age of 14. How proud I was of this! I begged my parents to take me to America so that they would not have to work anymore, for I would support them.

IN AMERICA

In 1909 when I was 14, we immigrated to the United States. I found good work as a mechanic and tool maker and before too long I became foreman in this same shop. But during this time my foot became swollen again, and again I was forced to have two more operations, the physicians finally recommending my foot to be amputated.

You cannot imagine the hopelessness of my condition; nevertheless, I determined with the little faith I had, to die trusting God, rather than be cripple the rest of my life. About this time my brother of 19 died of tuberculosis of the lungs. Before his death he often asked why we children, who were so innocent, had to suffer. Oh, that he too could have heard that Jesus is the Great Physician, before it was too late! Even then, God saw the consecration of my heart, and from that moment on I took no more pills or medication of any kind. I was determined to trust God.

Because of my terribly weakened foot it became impossible for me to continue working as a mechanic. I therefore turned to music and played in various restaurants, theatres, and concert halls in order to make a livelihood.

While still working in the shop a man had told me about Christian Science, saying that if a practitioner would treat me I would be healed. Innocently I turned to Science for help. I paid many hundreds of dollars for treatments and lessons supposedly to teach me how to pray. I even joined the Third Church of Christ Scientist. But instead of becoming better, my condition became worse.

THE REMEDY: THE HOLY BIBLE

In my desperation, as I clung to God, someone brought a Bible to our home; and for the first time I held the Book of Life in my hands. No one will ever know what the Bible meant to me during this trying time in my life. Every night when I would get home from playing in the theatres, I would read and be inspired by the truth of the Word.

In my youth I attended church religiously, going to mass every morning, serving as altar boy, making many pilgrimages and doing penance. I thought I could make myself pleasing to God and earn His favor, but I still had not heard the joyful message of the Bible. My father played the organ, my god-father was the priest of our town, and yet not until the age of 18 did I hear that God is love. I had always thought He was the punisher of man and had singled me out as His favorite victim.

My entire life was just the opposite of love, being very impatient and high strung. This evil nature controlled me and I did not know what to do about it. As I continued to read the Bible it spoke to me of love, hope, and comfort, that which I lacked the most. Finally, I realized that it was God's will that I should not be condemned for He wanted to help humanity. However, in spite of this I remained in the same sad condition. Things went from bad to worse—my father died, and my stepmother and I were left alone.

A terrible fear gripped me whenever I would pass a funeral parlor. I was afraid to die. But our Saviour never comes too late with His help, for at this time, as I lay praying one night, the Lord Jesus appeared to me. His hand was outstretched and He said, "Fear not." This meant so much to me that my fear of death left. Later I had another vision at which time I saw Jesus carrying the cross up the hill of Golgotha. Blazing words appeared over my Lord which read as follows: "Whosoever believeth in me shall not perish but have everlasting life." And I was like a perishing apple. I immediately received strength and courage to believe God and to seek Him more earnestly than before. I decided to live according to the teachings of the Bible and prayed much that God would help me to be pleasing to Him. Physically I was so weak that even my violin bow seemed heavy in my hand. As I continued to pray I would cry to God, "Oh God, help me, God help me. God can't you help me?" The teachings of the Bible gave me courage during my horrible condition and showed me which way to turn in the path of life.

THE HOUR OF MY DELIVERANCE

"He sent his word, and healed them, and delivered them from their destructions." Psalms 107:20.

One morning in the spring of 1917, a good friend of ours, Mrs. M., told my stepmother of a church which preached that Jesus Christ was the living Saviour and the healer of men today—in this present day and age. This church based this claim on the following quotations from the Bible: "Jesus Christ the same yesterday, today, and forever" (Hebrews 13:8); "How God anointed Jesus of Nazareth with the Holy Ghost and with Power: who went about doing good, healing all that were oppressed of the devil: for God was with him" (Acts 10:38); and, "The effectual fervent prayer of a righteous man availeth much" (James 5:16). That same day, I went to that church where a two hour service was being held in the afternoon. The service was about God healing the body. In his sermon, the minister said, "Jesus Christ suffered on the cross for you. He took all of your sins and sicknesses upon Himself. By His sufferings on the cross, and the shedding of His precious blood, He paid the full price for your salvation, so that you could go free and be saved and healed." God never intended for His children to be sick. Then he also quoted, "Christ hath redeemed us from the curse of the law, being made a curse for us" (Galatians 3:13). We are redeemed through Jesus Christ. This I never knew or understood before. The curse of the law included all bodily sicknesses and diseases (Deut. 28:15–62).

This sermon was God-inspired and just for me, for I had been taught up to that time that man—including myself—could please God by suffering much. This message, then, was something entirely new to me. After I had heard it, my faith in God became so alive that I was able to believe that God, at that moment, would really help me. A happiness glowed within me and warmed my innermost being. For years I had not known what it was like to have a good, warm body. My blood was unclean. I was miserable and sick.

After this message, the minister asked, "Is there anyone here today who would like to dedicate his life to Jesus Christ?" I lifted my hand. The minister then continued, "If there is anyone here who is sick and wishes to be prayed for, come to the front."

I immediately accepted his invitation, went to the front with others, and wanted to introduce myself and explain my condition to him. However, he just simply said, "Kneel down here."

No sooner had I bowed my knees before the Almighty God and His Son Jesus Christ—even before the preacher or anyone else could pray with me—than the power of God fell upon me in mighty dynamic healing streams surging through my entire body. "And the whole multitude sought to touch Jesus: for there went virtue out of him, and healed them all" (Luke 6:19). This same power flooded my being and manifested itself in supernatural and ineffable might. At the same time, I felt impressibly [sic] happy. I became a new creature instantly. My body was warm now, my heart pure, and my spirit born again.

Praise God, I now had received the redemption which is in Christ Jesus for my spirit, soul, and body. Christ came to "destroy the works of the devil" (1 John 3:8). All sickness, with all traces of its symptoms, vanished completely as I prayed there on my knees before God. Oh, what an hour of bliss I experienced that day! How can I ever describe it?

Imagine what it was like for my stepmother, who had been so greatly concerned over my health, to see me as I returned home that day. I told her that I had been to the church about which Mrs. M. had told us. She saw in my eyes that a miracle had happened. She cried for joy and became extremely happy. Later, I told her step by step how God had delivered me. Hallelujah!

THE GIFT OF THE HOLY SPIRIT

Two weeks later, after experiencing the grace of God in the saving of my soul and the healing of my body, I heard in a sermon that there was another gift for all believers—the receiving of the Holy Spirit. As I earnestly sought God, praying that He would grant me the gift of the Holy Spirit, which 120 men and women had received on the day of Pentecost, the Holy Ghost fell on me (Acts 10:44–46). I began to speak in other tongues as the Spirit gave utterance (Acts 2:4). I praised God with a loud voice. "For the promise is unto you, and to your children, and to all that are afar off, even as many as the Lord our God shall call" (Acts 2:39). This infilling of the Holy Spirit manifested itself as the Scriptures describe, "Out of his innermost being shall flow rivers of living water" (John 7:38).

Wherever I go, whenever I have opportunity, I tell people of the goodness of God to me through His grace. How faithful God is to have mercy on us poor, sinful creatures and to recreate our lives through His power. That which is impossible with man is possible with God.

Endnotes

Chapter 1: Origins of Pentecostalism: Restorationism, Premillennialism, Healing

[1]Barney E. Warren and Andrew L. Byers, eds., *Songs of the Evening Light* (Moundsville, WV: Gospel Trumpet Publishing Company, 1897), 1.

[2]John W. Welch, introduction to *The Apostolic Faith Restored*, Bennett F. Lawrence (St. Louis: Gospel Publishing House, 1916), 7.

[3]Donald Dayton, *The Theological Roots of Pentecostalism* (Grand Rapids: Zondervan, 1987).

[4]See, for example, E. H. Broadbent, *The Pilgrim Church* (London: Pickering & Inglis, 1931), which documents the restorationist attitude toward the course of history by tracing the fate of apostolic Christianity in church history.

[5]John P. Brooks, *The Divine Church a Treatise on the Origin, Constitution, Order, and Ordinances of the Church; Being a Vindication of the New Testament Ecclesia and an Exposure of the Anti-Scriptural Character of the Modern Church of Sect* (Columbia, MO: Herald Publishing House, 1891; reprint, El Dorado Springs, MO: Witt Printing Co., 1960).

[6]Charles Conn, *Like a Mighty Army* (Cleveland, TN: Church of God Publishing House, 1955), 7.

[7]See Grant Wacker, "Marching to Zion," *Church History* 54 (December 1985): 496–511.

[8]1 Corinthians 12:8–10; 28.

[9]By the late nineteenth century, hopes for Christian unity had, of course, begun to shape formal ecumenical efforts. The American tradition of voluntary associations—purposive agencies supported by concerned Christians of many denominations—was nearly as old as the republic. The Evangelical Alliance and later the Federal Council of Churches represent efforts toward Christian cooperation. But the visionaries attracted to restorationist hopes who later espoused Pentecostalism regarded growing ecumenical concerns warily. Restorationism ultimately enabled some to affirm ecumenical intentions

without joining conciliar Protestantism. Unable to work within established structures, they rejected them and identified with the urge, long present in the American religious culture, toward thorough reform and biblical recreation.

[10]Arthur T. Pierson, *Forward Movements of the Last Half Century* (New York: Funk & Wagnalls, 1900), 411, 409. In 1875, Moody had expressed his conviction that the world was "on the eve of some very great event—some very great change." He predicted that the event would be either "a great war" or "the coming of the Lord." See *Signs of Our Times*, 9 June 1875, 355.

[11]The confidence that the millennium would come through preaching and the hope that it might well begin in America had been expressed most effectively by Jonathan Edwards in 1739 in his *History of the Work of Redemption*.

[12]Darby's dispensationalism was popularized in America in various ways. One of the most effective was the Scofield Bible, which Pentecostals used widely. For an analysis of dispensationalism in America, see Timothy Weber, *Living in the Shadow of the Second Coming* (New York: Oxford University Press, 1979).

[13]It is interesting to note, however, that some Plymouth Brethren participated in early phases of the Keswick movement. Henry Varley, who deeply influenced D. L. Moody, for example, spoke at the Brighton Convention out of which Keswick was organized. *Signs of Our Times*, 9 June 1875, 356. See chapter two for a brief survey of Keswick teaching.

[14]This phrase, chosen by Timothy Weber as the title for his study of American dispensationalism, conveys a sense of the practical influence this "blessed hope" had. People convinced of the likelihood of Christ's "any moment" return often lived in total anticipation of that event. In a real—and, they would have claimed, positive—sense, it cast its glow over their lives.

An example of a prominent premillennialist who differed at significant points with the popular version of Darby's teaching was A. J. Gordon, a man whose writings deeply influenced many first-generation Assemblies of God adherents. For a sense of the various understandings of history and prophecy that coexisted under the aegis of premillennialism, see A. J. Gordon, *Ecce Venit* (New York: Fleming H. Revell, 1889).

[15]R. A. Torrey, *The Return of the Lord Jesus* (Los Angeles, 1913), 21.

[16]See the popular handbook for turn-of-the-century premillennialists: W. E. Blackstone, *Jesus Is Coming*, rev. ed. (New York: Fleming H. Revell, 1908).

[17]On the other hand, a more positive view of the relationship between premillennialism and social reform was taken by others. See

Grant Wacker, "The Holy Spirit and the Spirit of the Age in American Protestantism, 1880–1910," *Journal of American History* 72 (June 1985): 45–62.

[18]Ibid., 7.

[19]D. L. Moody, "The Return of Our Lord," in *The American Evangelicals, 1800–1900,* ed. W. G. McLoughlin (New York: Harper and Row, 1968), 185.

[20]For a thorough study of missionary movements in this period, see William R. Hutchison, *Errand Into the World* (Chicago: University of Chicago Press, 1987).

[21]A. B. Simpson, *Larger Outlooks on Missionary Lands* (New York: The Christian Alliance Publishing Co., 1893). Simpson was widely recognized for his innovations in communicating missionary needs. He devised pictorial missionary journals. See Robert Niklaus, John Sawin, and Samuel Stoesz, *All For Jesus: God at Work in the Christian and Missionary Alliance Over One Hundred Years* (Camp Hill, PA: Christian Publications, 1986).

[22]Gordon's fullest expression of his end-times views is in his book, *Ecce Venit.* See Joel Carpenter's preface to *The Premillennial Second Coming: Two Early Champions* (New York: Garland Publishing Inc., forthcoming).

[23]The perception of Christian Science as an archenemy and fundamental threat to the gospel is intriguing. When early Pentecostals listed teachings they opposed, Christian Science usually ranked high; early Pentecostal periodicals contain many articles exposing the errors of Christian Science, suggesting that they felt especially threatened by it. Preoccupation with Christian Science waned during the 1920s when Christian Science came to be perceived simply as one of a long list of unorthodox groups.

[24]A. J. Gordon, *The Ministry of Healing* (New York: The Christian Alliance Publishing Co., 1882), 146ff.

[25]Edith L. Blumhofer, "Jesus Is Victor: A Study in the Life of Johann Christoph Blumhardt," *Paraclete* 19 (Spring 1985): 1–5; see also Gordon, *Healing,* 158ff.

[26]Gordon, *Healing,* 22–38. Gordon stated explicitly: "Christ's ministry was a two-fold ministry, effecting constantly the souls and the bodies of men. 'Thy sins are forgiven thee,' and 'Be whole of thy plague,' are parallel announcements of the Saviour's work which are found constantly running on side by side." Ibid., 19. See also Ernest Gordon, *Adoniram Judson Gordon* (New York: Fleming H. Revell, 1896).

[27]Ibid., 45–57.

[28]Ibid., 64.

[29]Ibid., 72. Pages 72–86 discuss this subject.

[30]Ibid., 75.

[31]See, for example, Benjamin Warfield, *Counterfeit Miracles* (New York: Oxford University Press, 1931), a book which was a compilation of Warfield's earlier lectures on the subject. Warfield maintained that the neglect of "means" like medicine and surgery was "the essence of fanaticism." Others concurred. Writing in the *Methodist Review,* George Hammell stated: "The fanaticism of unauthorized faith consists in the misapplication of divine promises to the affairs of practical life.... It finds manifestation ... in the so-called 'faith-cure' movement." George M. Hammell, "Religion and Fanaticism," *Methodist Review* 70 (July 1888): 534.

[32]It seems evident, however, that Simpson had prayed for restoration to health and had anticipated divine physical quickening before this experience. His diary reveals that before he arrived in New York late in 1879, he had cultivated a spirituality that centered in complete dependence on Christ for spiritual, physical, economic and social well-being. See A. B. Simpson, "Diary," 1879, 1880, Historical Collection, Nyack, NY: Nyack College.

[33]A. P. Thompson, *The Life of A. B. Simpson* (New York: The Christian Alliance Publishing Co., 1920), 75; A. B. Simpson, "Divine Healing," *Word, Work and the World* 7 (September 1886): 158.

[34]A. B. Simpson, *The Gospel of Healing* (Harrisburg, PA: Christian Publications, Inc., 1915), 163; Simpson, "Divine Healing," 158.

[35]Simpson later changed the name of his healing home to Berachah. See "The New Berachah Home," *Word, Work and the World* 7 (September 1886): 186.

[36]*Word, Work and the World* 4 (October 1883): 172; Simpson, *Gospel of Healing,* 1888 edition, 83–84. The last two sentences quoted were replaced with the following: "To a greater or less extent, the gift of tongues has been continuous in the Church of Christ and along with many counterfeits has undoubtedly been realized in the present generation."

[37]Simpson, *Gospel of Healing,* 37–38.

[38]Ibid., 72. Simpson was never fully understood by all in the Alliance on the subject of "divine life." For an example of continuing inability to comprehend his views, see the letters under "Questions About Divine Healing," *The Alliance Witness* 122 (February 4, 1987): 29.

[39]John A. Dowie, "The Everlasting Gospel of the Kingdom of God Declared and Defended," *Leaves of Healing* V (July 1899): 713.

[40]Simpson, *Gospel of Healing,* 183; "Inquiries and Answers," *Word, Work and the World* 7 (November 1886): 339–340.

Pierson, who also affirmed the availability of divine healing, deemed "means" appropriate as long as one's reliance was truly on God. Simpson, Gordon, Pierson, R. A. Torrey, and their associates unanimously affirmed the necessity of exercise and hygiene. They concurred that the advances of medical science were impressive but not "omniscient or omnipotent." See Pierson, *Forward Movements*, 405. Because they did not declare medical science "a work of the Devil," and because they taught that God might use sickness to chasten or discipline, Dowie unequivocally opposed their teaching and efforts. He also publicly criticized Moody's reluctance to identify with healing teaching. During Torrey's tenure at Moody Bible Institute, Torrey became desperate about the condition of his daughter, who was dying of diphtheria. He and his wife had decided to forego medical help and to pray for her healing. When she seemed to get weaker, he asked Dowie to pray for her. Dowie exploited the incident, using it to slander both Moody and Torrey. *Leaves of Healing* 5 (8 April 1899): 457–464.

[41]John Alexander Dowie, "A Letter to the Friends of Zion Tabernacle," *Leaves of Healing* I (1895): 257.

[42]John Alexander Dowie, "The Ministry of an Apostle—Is it for Today?" in *Champion of the Faith,* ed. Gordon Lindsay (Dallas: Christ for the Nations, 1979), 124–125.

[43]Over the years lists of prohibitions were prominently displayed in Zion. See copies in the Assemblies of God Archives, Springfield, MO.

[44]Mrs. M. B. Woodworth-Etter, *Signs and Wonders God Wrought in the Ministry for Forty Years* (Chicago: Hammond Press, 1916), 28. This strand of pietist, holiness-oriented Quakerism in Ohio and Indiana is described more fully in Byron Lindley Osborne, *The Malone Story: The Dream of Two Quaker Young People* (Newton, KS, 1970); and Thomas Hamm, *The Transformation of American Quakerism: Orthodox Friends, 1800–1907* (Bloomington, IN: University Press, 1988).

[45]Any record of her activities during the first decade of this century has not come to light.

[46]For a thorough account of Woodworth-Etter's life, see Wayne E. Warner, *The Woman Evangelist: The Life and Times of Charismatic Evangelist Maria B. Woodworth-Etter* (Metuchen, NJ: The Scarecrow Press, Inc., 1986).

Chapter 2: Origins of Pentecostalism: The Holy Spirit as "Pentecostal Fire"

[1]For Pierson's biography, see Delavan Pierson, *Arthur T. Pierson* (New York: Fleming H. Revell, 1912). See also Dana Roberts, "Forward Movements of Nineteenth-Century Evangelicalism," (Ph.D. diss., Yale University, 1984).

[2]In fact, party lines were not rigidly drawn, and on some matters there was considerable crossing over. D. L. Moody, for example, hailed as a conservative Protestant evangelist, demonstrated none of the rancor of later fundamentalism, sharing his pulpit with men whose identification with "liberal" Protestants in other settings was well-

known. Later generations whose perceptions of "liberal" and "conservative" or "fundamentalist" are colored by the party divisions of the twentieth-century fundamentalist-modernist controversy may well have difficulty admitting the shared concerns and even the similarities among those who later were labeled with an unacceptable party name. The ambiguity of the familiar terms must be recognized if one wishes to understand accurately the aspirations of late nineteenth-century American Protestants.

3Walter Rauschenbusch, "The New Evangelism," in *American Protestant Thought: The Liberal Era,* ed. William R. Hutchison (New York: Harper and Row, 1968), 112–113.

4Ibid., 111.

5Ibid., 115–116. Winthrop Hudson, ed., *Walter Rauschenbusch* (New York: Paulist Press, 1984), contains many passages that illumine the piety of this eminent social gospeler.

6See, for example, Barbara Brown Zikmund, "The Struggle for the Right to Preach," in *Women and Religion in America, Volume 1: The Nineteenth Century,* eds., Rosemary Radford Ruether and Rosemary Skinner Keller (San Francisco: Harper & Row, 1981), 193–241.

7Pierson, *Forward Movements,* 1–2.

8For an account of the holiness movement, see Charles Edwin Jones, *Perfectionist Persuasion* (Metuchen, NJ: Scarecrow Press, Inc., 1974). For the story of one of its primary advocates, see Charles Edward White, *The Beauty of Holiness: Phoebe Palmer as Theologian, Revivalist, Feminist, and Humanitarian* (Grand Rapids: Zondervan Publishing House, 1986).

9G. D. Watson, *A Holiness Manual* (Dallas: Chandler Publications, n.d.), 13.

10Ibid., 14.

11Ibid., 76–77.

12J. W. Horne, "Sermon," in *Penuel; or Face to Face with God,* ed. A. McLean and J. W. Eaton (New York: W. C. Palmer, Jr., 1869), 26.

13Ibid., 27.

14Ibid.

15R. F. Reynolds, "Let the Holy Ghost Come In," in *The Best of All,* hymnal, 87.

16B. M. Adams, "Sermon," in *Penuel,* 65.

17Timothy L. Smith, *Revivalism and Social Reform* (New York: Harper and Row, 1957).

18Horne, "Sermon," 65.

19J. E. French, "This Is Like Heaven to Me," in *The Best of All,* 181.

[20]Lelia Morris, "Baptized with the Holy Ghost," in *The Best of All*, 94.

[21]John Brown, "Feasting with my Lord," in *The Best of All*, 123.

[22]E. E. Hewitt, "Since I Found My Savior," in *The Best of All*, 173.

[23]Lelia Morris, "Nearer, Still Nearer," in *The Best of All*, 63.

[24]J. M. Kirk, "Since the Comforter Has Come," in *Songs of the Evening Light*, 38.

[25]*Hymns of Glorious Praise*, George W. Robinson, "I Am His, and He Is Mine" Springfield, MO: Gospel Publishing House, 1969), 289.

[26]L. L. Pickett, "It Is For Us All Today," in *The Best of All*, 187.

> Have you ever felt the power of the Pentecostal fire
> Burning up all carnal nature, cleansing out all base desire,
> Going through and through your spirit, cleansing all its stain away?
> Oh I'm glad, so glad to tell you,
> It is for us all today.
>
> Jesus offers this blest cleansing unto all His children dear,
> Fully, freely purifying, banishing all doubt and fear,
> It will help you, O my brother, when you sing and when you pray;
> He is waiting now to give it,
> It is for us all today.
>
> Some have thought they could not live it while they dwell on earth below,
> But in this they were mistaken, for the Bible tells us so,
> And the Spirit now is with us,
> He can keep us all the way;
> Then by faith why not receive it?
> It is for us all today.

[27]*Journal*, General Conference, M. E. Church, South 1894, 25–26.

[28]This stress on "faith" living was certainly as common outside the Wesleyan-oriented holiness movement as within its ranks. It was simply the conviction that God would supply temporal needs. For some, it meant giving up visible means of support to pursue religious work without a regular salary. It encouraged people to pray for whatever they needed. There was often a close relationship between advocacy of such "faith" living and the belief that God intervened miraculously to heal sickness in response to faith.

[29]John P. Brooks, *The Divine Church* (El Dorado Springs, MO: Witt Printing Co., 1960), 271. First published in 1891, this book articulated a vision of the basic incompatability of religious organizations and spiritual movements.

[30]Ibid., 283. This attitude toward religious institutions paralleled Darby's impatience with denominations.

[31]Although it is difficult to generalize about the people who accepted "come outist" logic, some students of the movement have tried. For example, Carl Oblinger described the typical *come outer*: "Those who left were most likely to be artisans with obsolete trades, tenant and small farmers, small-town laborers forced into the new cities, and the less educated." Although the holiness movement affected Methodists of all kinds, then, those who ultimately separated from the denomination "usually considered themselves on the fringe of both the church and the mainstream of society." See Carl Oblinger, *Religious Mimesis* (Evanston, IL: Institute for the Study of American Religion, 1973); J. Gordon Melton and Robert L. Moore, *The Cult Experience: Responding to the New Religious Pluralism* (New York: The Pilgrim Press, 1982), 24.

Although some who came from separatist holiness ranks into Pentecostalism fit the above stereotype, further study is needed to reconstruct the composition of local congregations and use census and other public records to draw a social composite of the group.

[32]William G. Schell, "Biblical Trace of the Church," in *Songs of the Evening Light,* 20.

[33]Charles Price Jones, "Autobiographical Sketch," in *History of the Church of Christ (Holiness) U.S.A. 1895–1965,* ed. Ottho B. Cobbins (New York: Vantage Press, 1966), 25.

[34]Ibid., 27, 28.

[35]Ibid., 28.

[36]For a general treatment of this subject, see Barbara Brown Zikmund, "The Struggle for the Right to Preach," 193–241; Letha Dawson Scanzoni and Susan Setta, "Women in Evangelical, Holiness, and Pentecostal Traditions," in *Women and Religion in America: 1900–1968, Volume 3,* eds. Rosemary R. Ruther and Rosemary S. Keller (San Francisco: Harper & Row, 1986), 223–234; Phoebe Palmer, *The Promise of the Father* (Boston: Henry V. Degen, 1859); *Holiness Tracts Defending the Ministry of Women,* ed. Donald Dayton (New York: Garland Publishing, Inc., 1985); A. J. Gordon, "The Ministry of Women," *Missionary Review of the World* 7 (December 1894): 910–921.

[37]Quoted in A. P. Fitt, *Moody Still Lives* (New York: Fleming H. Revell Company, 1936), 28. See also R. A. Torrey's pamphlet, "Why God Used D. L. Moody" (Chicago: The Bible Institute Colportage Association, 1923).

[38]D. L. Moody, "Testimony of D. L. Moody," *Institute Tie* 1 (Septem-

ber 1900): 2; R. A. Torrey, "D. L. Moody, the Unity of His Life," *Institute Tie* 1 (March 1901): 202.

[39] R. A. Torrey, *The Fundamental Doctrines of the Christian Faith* (New York: George H. Doran Company, 1918), 115. Ernest Sandeen, a historian of fundamentalism, notes the extent of this focus on the personhood of the Spirit as well as on the relationship of the Holy Spirit to individuals among contemporary millenarians. Ernest Sandeen, *The Roots of Fundamentalism* (Chicago: University of Chicago Press, 1970), 178.

[40] Ibid.

[41] A. B. Simpson, *A Larger Christian Life* (New York: Christian Alliance Publishing Company, 1890).

[42] R. A. Torrey, *The Person and Work of the Holy Spirit* (Grand Rapids: Baker Book House, 1974), 97.

[43] Ibid., 94.

[44] R. A. Torrey, *What the Bible Teaches* (Chicago: Fleming H. Revell Company, 1898), 251.

[45] Torrey, *Fundamental Doctrines*, 227.

[46] Ibid., 244.

[47] Torrey, "D. L. Moody," 203; Torrey, "Why God Used D. L. Moody."

[48] R. A. Torrey, *The Baptism with the Holy Spirit* (Chicago: Fleming H. Revell Company, 1895).

[49] Gordon's book was entitled *The Ministry of the Spirit* (Chicago: Fleming H. Revell, 1894). For a consideration of the Pentecostal direction Gordon's work took see C. Allyn Russell, "Adoniram Judson Gordon: Nineteenth-Century Fundamentalist," *American Baptist Quarterly* 4 (March 1985): 61–89.

[50] Torrey, *Baptism*, 14–15; Gordon, *Ministry of the Spirit*, 67ff; A. B. Simpson, "Principles of Christian Life and Holiness," *Word, Work, and the World* 7 (October, 1886): 205–207.

[51] D. L. Moody, "Question Drawer," in *College Students at Northfield*, ed. T. J. Shanks (New York, 1888), 205.

[52] Torrey, *Baptism*, 28.

[53] D. L. Moody, "Enduement for Service," in *D. L. Moody at Home*, ed. T. J. Shanks (New York, 1886), 255.

[54] Torrey, *Baptism*, 28. He urged Christian workers to "stop [their] work right where [they were] and not go on with it until [they had been] clothed with power from on high." Ibid., 24–25. A. B. Simpson concurred: "We are not fit to represent God in the world or to do any spiritual work for Him until we receive the Holy Ghost." A. B. Simpson, *The Holy Spirit, or Power from on High*, vol. 1 (Harrisburg, PA: Christian Publications, Inc., 1895), 82.

⁵⁵Moody, "Question Drawer," 204–205.

⁵⁶Ibid.

⁵⁷Torrey, *Baptism*, 66; see also Moody, "Question Drawer," 205.

⁵⁸See, for example, Talbot W. Chambers, review of *The Baptism with the Holy Spirit*, by R. A. Torrey, in *The Presbyterian and Reformed Review* 6 (October 1895): 789–790; Review of *How to Obtain Fulness of Power*, by R. A. Torrey, in *The Presbyterian Quarterly* 12 (January 1898): 125. The *Presbyterian Quarterly* also took issue with Baptist A. J. Gordon's advocacy of similar views. One reviewer noted that contemporary use of premillennial views made the entire system of Christian belief Christocentric and insisted that the Second Coming was its focal point. Gordon and others, the article correctly observed, suggested that premillennialism was "the mountaintop from which the whole landscape of the gospel" was to be understood. See D. N. McLauchlin, review of *How Christ Came to Church*, by A. J. Gordon, in *The Presbyterian Quarterly* 10 (October 1896): 530. Certainly premillennialism provided an incentive for holiness and spiritual power that resulted in this phase of the emphasis on a walk in the Spirit and the baptism with the Holy Spirit.

⁵⁹Moody, "Enduement for Service," 261.

⁶⁰D. L. Moody, "Consecration and Concentration," in *A College of Colleges*, ed. T. J. Shanks (New York, 1887), 217.

⁶¹Roberts, "Forward Movements"; Pierson, *Pierson*.

⁶²Arthur T. Pierson, "An Appeal to Disciples Everywhere," in *Pierson*, 195.

⁶³John Pollock, *The Cambridge Seven* (London: InterVarsity Fellowship, 1956).

⁶⁴John R. Mott, *Addresses and Papers*, vol. 1 (New York: Association Press 1946), 4ff.

⁶⁵Grant Wacker, "The Holy Spirit and the Spirit of the Age in American Protestantism, 1880–1910," *Journal of American History* (1985): 45–62.

⁶⁶See, for example, Charles Finney, "The Essential Elements of Christian Experience," in *Gospel Themes* (New York: Fleming H. Revell, 1876), 398–417.

⁶⁷Hannah Whitall Smith, *The Unselfishness of God and How I Discovered It: A Spiritual Autobiography* (New York: Fleming H. Revell Company, 1903), 190.

⁶⁸Hannah Whitall Smith's book of this title, first published in 1875, remains in print as a classic statement of her higher life views.

⁶⁹John C. Pollock, *The Keswick Story* (London: Hodder and Stoughton 1964), 48; *Signs of Our Times*, a periodical edited by an Anglican clergyman M. Baxter (with a circulation between sixty and seventy

thousand), documented the progress of "higher life" teaching in Britain.

[70]A. T. Pierson, *The Keswick Convention* (New York: Funk and Wagnalls Co., 1900); Pierson, *Forward Movements,* 32–33. Some Keswick participants resented Pierson's effort to define their message; they dismissed it as a typically American attempt to codify something that could never be captured in words.

[71]F. G. Bottome, "Full Salvation," in *Songs of Victory* (London: Pickering and Inglis, n.d.), 253.

[72]Pierson, *Forward Movements,* 33.

[73]For the story of Simpson and the Christian and Missionary Alliance, see Niklaus, *All for Jesus.*

[74]This tract (which, substantially edited, remains in print) appeared in several contemporary periodicals, including the October 1885 issue of Simpson's *Word, Work, and the World.*

[75]For an observation about the relationship between Christocentrism and premillennialism, see D. M. McLauchlin, review of *How Christ Came to Church.* Many non-premillennialists, especially evangelical liberals, nurtured a similar Christocentric emphasis on religious experience.

[76]Simpson, *Larger Life,* 40.

[77]Ibid., 39.

[78]A. B. Simpson, *Wholly Sanctified* (Harrisburg, PA: Christian Publications, 1925), 14.

[79]A. B. Simpson, *The Holy Spirit, or Power from on High,* vol. 2 (Harrisburg, PA: Christian Publications, 1895), 277–286.

[80]Simpson, *Wholly Sanctified,* 17.

[81]Simpson, *Larger Life,* 82.

[82]D. L. Moody, "Christ and the Holy Spirit," in *Northfield,* ed. Shanks, 170ff.

[83]D. L. Moody in Emma Moody Fitt's Scrapbook, Moodyana Collection, Moody Bible Institute, Chicago.

Chapter 3: Charles Parham and the Apostolic Faith

[1]Norma Souders of Souders Historical Farm-Museum, Cheney, KS, to the author, 3 October 1987. Much work remains to be done in sorting out the details in the narrative Parham wrote. Most Pentecostals have accepted it without question, but a search for documentation indicates that Parham's account is unreliable at important points.

[2]Trinity Reformed Church (which in 1957 became Trinity United Church of Christ) was served by a home missions pastor, Isaac Brown, and met in Morton Center schoolhouse just outside Cheney from April

22, 1883, until May 31, 1885, when its permanent facility was completed. It is likely that the meetings were in this school building.

[3]Charles Parham, *A Voice Crying in the Wilderness* (n.p., 1902), 15.

[4]*Cheney Journal,* 19 December 1885.

[5]In the past it has been virtually impossible to document links between Parham and the larger religious subculture of which his early ministry was part. Parham attributed his views directly to the Bible and the Holy Spirit. His accounts convey the sense that no parts of the Apostolic Faith were mediated through others. This link with Bolton and the Church of God of the General Eldership provides the first concrete evidence of the early influence of contemporary charismatic views. Local Cheney newspapers are the best source for such information. Bolton's ministry can be traced in C. H. Forney, *History of the Churches of God in the U.S. of North America* (Findlay, OH: Churches of God, 1914).

[6]"Mrs. Harriet Parham Was a Wife and Mother of Devotion," *The Cheney Sentinel,* clipping in Parham Papers, Assemblies of God Archives.

[7]See, for example, *Cheney Blade,* 11 January 1889.

[8]*The Cheney Sentinel,* 30 May 1901.

[9]*Parham,* 5.

[10]Ralph W. Decker, Jr., Registrar, to Edith L. Blumhofer, 11 December 1986. Parham's account is not substantiated by college records. He reported that he had entered college at 16, which would have been in 1889. See Parham, *Parham,* 5. The school year at Southwestern College ran from September to June. Even this brief schooling was interrupted by Parham's illness. The *Cheney Herald* for May 19, 1892, reported that Parham had been brought home from school, suffering from inflammatory rheumatism.

[11]Parham, *Voice Crying,* 18–19.

[12]*Cheney Herald,* 20 June 1893.

[13]William E. Connally, *History of Kansas State and People,* vol. 3 (Chicago: American Historical Society, 1928), 1324.

[14]Ibid., 19.

[15]See, for example, Charles B. Driscoll, "Major Prophets of Holy Kansas," *American Mercury* 8 (May 1926): 18–26, which is a Mencken-like recital of religious excesses in Kansas.

[16]Parham, *Voice Crying,* 138.

[17]This date is given in Sarah Parham's biography of her husband. See Parham, *Parham,* 29. Sarah Parham's obituary (published by the family in their own paper) gives the date of her marriage as December 29, 1895. The *Cheney Sentinel* reported on December 17, 1896, that Parham would be married on December 31. See *The Apostolic Faith,*

January to February 1938, 3. Sarah Parham's name is also in question: In an issue of *The Apostolic Faith* in January 1900, Parham referred to her as Eleanore Sarah Parham. Later references are to Sarah Eleanore Parham. The *Cheney Sentinel* listed her as S. Eleanor Thistlethwaite. These are but two of the more minor inaccuracies in a story punctuated with inconsistencies.

[18]Charles Parham, "The Sources of Disease," *The Apostolic Faith,* August 1912, 2.

[19]Ibid., 3.

[20]Sarah Parham, *Life of Charles F. Parham* (Baxter Springs, KS: 1930), 31–34. It is impossible to document Parham's knowledge (or lack of knowledge) of other contemporary teachers of healing. Like others with similar religious inclinations, Parham attributed his religious insights to the immediate dealing of the Holy Spirit with his spirit. Within two years, it is clear that he knew several prominent advocates of healing at least by reputation.

[21]*The Apostolic Faith,* 1 January 1900, 8.

[22]Ibid., 7. Parham's paper reprinted the story from the *Topeka Daily Journal.*

[23]*The Apostolic Faith,* 1 January 1900. His advertising of a negative statement about Dowie is interesting since later in the year he visited Dowie's Zion as part of his quest to discover contemporary teachers of New Testament views of the Holy Spirit.

[24]Ibid., 39.

[25]Vinson Synan, *The Holiness-Pentecostal Movement in the United States* (Grand Rapids: William B. Eerdmans Publishing Co., 1971), 61ff.

[26]Parham, *Voice Crying,* 21.

[27]This may simply be another part of his story which he preferred not to tell. It is unlikely that he spent two years leading a Methodist congregation without participating in infant baptism or baptism by sprinkling or pouring.

[28]Charles Parham, "Baptism," *The Apostolic Faith,* October, 1912, 5.

[29]Ibid.

[30]Charles F. Parham, "Baptism," *The Apostolic Faith,* October 1912 supplement, 4–5. This is a reprint of a portion of his *Voice Crying in the Wilderness* (1902).

[31]Parham, *Voice Crying,* 101–118. For a sense of the conservative evangelical response to Herzl, see his obituary, taken from the *New York Sun,* published in *Living Truth,* August, 1904, 466–468.

[32]Report from the *Topeka Daily Journal,* reprinted in *The Apostolic Faith,* 1 January 1900, 7.

[33]Parham, *Parham*, 48.

[34]Ibid., 51.

[35]*Topeka Daily Capital* 7 (December 1901): 3.

[36]*Topeka Daily Capital* 6 (January 1901): 2. Later reports in the same paper were less charitable. A story about the destruction of the mansion by fire in December 1901 noted that Parham's followers had been supported by charity. See *Topeka Daily Capital* 7 (December 1901): 3.

[37]Sandford complained that "none of his counselors went all the way with the Sermon on the Mount," finding fault particularly with "what they didn't say" about "victorious" living. See Frank S. Murray, *The Sublimity of Faith* (Amherst, NH: The Kingdom Press, 1981), 155.

[38]The best account of Sandford's life and work is William Hiss, "Shiloh: Frank W. Sandford and the Kingdom: 1893–1948" (Ph.D. diss., Tufts University, 1978.

[39]See, for example, E. P. Woodward, *Sandfordism: An Exposure of the Claims, Purposes, Methods, Predictions and Threats of Rev. F. W. Sandford, the "Apostle" of Shiloh, Main* (Portland, ME: Safeguard Publishing Co., 1902).

[40]Such claims seem to have been popular. Parham reported in 1912: "I have met eight or ten Elijahs, all the major prophets and some of the minor ones, Adam, God, David, at least fifty claiming to be Jesus, about thirty of the two witnesses (both male and female), all the twelve apostles, the fifth angel, three who were the Devil, eight who were the virgin Mary." *The Apostolic Faith*, September 1912, 12. See Driscoll, "Major Prophets" for reference to some of these.

[41]Quoted in Murray, *Sublimity of Faith*, 162.

[42]Ibid.

[43]Ibid., 157.

[44]Ibid., 288–289.

[45]There are notable similarities between Sandford and John Alexander Dowie, founder of Zion City, IL. For example, Dowie had bands of "seventies" who also engaged in door-to-door visitation work; both men also declared themselves Elijah in 1901.

[46]Ibid., 232.

[47]It is probable that the group stopped at several independent ministries along the way. Parham recorded visiting several places, and the *Topeka Daily Capital* also stated that he had traveled "overland" and "held gospel meetings" along the way. See Parham, *Parham*, 48; *Topeka Daily Capital* 6 (January 1901): 2.

[48]Parham, *Voice Crying*, 32.

[49]Ibid.

[50]Agnes Ozman, "The First One to Speak in Tongues," *Latter Rain Evangel*, January 1909, 2.

[51]See the description of his teachings in the ad for Bethel Divine Healing Home and Mission, *The Apostolic Faith*, 1 January 1900, 8.

[52]Ibid., 86–87, 75.

[53]See her account of her life: Agnes Nevada Ozman LaBerge, *What God Hath Wrought* (Chicago: Herald Publishing Co., n.d.).

[54]Agnes Ozman, "A Witness to First Scenes," *The Apostolic Faith*, Dec.–Jan. 1912–1913, 4.

[55]Ibid.

[56]The date (day) is in dispute, as are many other details of the story. Pentecostals have usually accepted Parham's account uncritically, but on close examination, it contains many questionable details. Parham later claimed that he had laid hands on Ozman during the watchnight service, which had been attended by some 115 people. This figure is arrived at by adding the estimated audience in Ozman's and Parham's accounts. He attached eschatological significance to the timing of the event, claiming that, just as the new century dawned, tongues speech had been restored in a setting remarkably similar to that described in Acts—an upper room in which approximately 120 people waited expectantly; later 12 ministers, with hands uplifted, were reported to have spoken in tongues simultaneously, as "cloven tongues of fire" appeared over their heads.

[57]Ozman, "A Witness," 4; Lawrence, *Apostolic Faith*, 52 also notes this stress on Acts 19.

[58]Acts 19:6.

[59]Ozman, "A Witness," 4. She continued to hold to this position. See Ozman, "First One to Speak in Tongues," 2.

[60]Parham, *Parham*, 67. Ozman's several-page account is quoted in full on pages 65–68.

[61]Parham, *Parham*, 52–53. The *Topeka Daily Capital* 6 (January 1901): 2, published a lengthy specimen of the so-called "writing under the inspiration of the Holy Spirit." It is likely that the writer (whose name was cited as Auswin) was Ozman.

[62]LaBerge, *What God Hath Wrought*, 29.

[63]Ozman in Parham, *Parham*, 67. Following her prayer in English, she claimed that she prayed in tongues in a language understood by a visiting Bohemian. This would be the first of many claims that speaking in tongues was a known language understood as a human language by someone present.

[64]Robert Anderson suggested that Parham had already concluded that Spirit baptism would be attested by speech in foreign languages when he assigned his students the task of searching for the biblical

evidence in Acts. The assignment, Anderson posits, was designed to "make them believe the doctrine was not his own 'man-made' idea, but came by revelation." (See Robert Anderson, *Vision of the Disinherited* [New York: Oxford University Press, 1979], 44). Anderson concludes that Parham's story, which remains virtually unchallenged as the accepted account, is simply "too pat to be true" (p. 54). The inconsistencies in the narrative, when taken with other inconsistencies in the Parham account of his early ministry, support Anderson's doubts about Parham's credibility.

[65]He had visited A. B. Simpson's Christian and Missionary Alliance; John Alexander Dowie's Zion; the Malones' (a Friends' family) efforts in Cleveland. See Parham, *Parham*, 48.

[66]*Topeka Journal* 7 (January 1901): 4. A. B. Simpson anticipated a similar event.

[67]Although he claimed that he had declared his willingness to serve in Africa (or on the streets, in the slums, in life or death), he claimed never to have "felt a call" to Africa. Most of his efforts encouraged others to pursue dimensions of personal religious experience. His Bible school was not primarily intended to equip workers to evangelize but rather to explore "deep" matters pertaining to Christian experience.

[68]Parham later refined his view of evidential tongues to include a clear distinction between the gift of tongues and tongues as evidence, though he always held that both involved actual languages. Writing in 1912 he noted: "The only point wherein we differ now from the first teaching regarding Pentecost is that neither the gift of tongues or any other of the nine gifts of the Spirit are the evidence of the baptism. If you have the gift of a tongue you can use it as you do your English, both in speaking and understanding it.... Those who receive the baptism of the Holy Ghost can only speak as the Spirit gives utterance, while those who have the gift of tongues can use it at will and understand it." "Editorial," *The Apostolic Faith*, August 1912, 6.

[69]*Topeka Daily Capital* 6 (January 1901): 2.

[70]*Topeka Daily Capital* 7 (December 1901): 3; *Topeka Journal* 7 (January 1901): 4.

[71]Parham, *Parham*, 75.

[72]Ibid., 75.

[73]Ibid., 74.

[74]Ozman, "A Witness," 4.

[75]Ibid.

[76]Ibid.

[77]Ibid. Ozman began to share her experience of January 1, 1901, only after she heard reports in Omaha of the Azusa Street awakening in 1906. (See LaBerge, *What God Hath Wrought*, 39.) Between 1901 and 1906, she did not identify herself as a Pentecostal. In 1915, in a letter

to Evangelist Maria Woodworth-Etter, testifying of being healed in one of her meetings, Ozman included some lines about her experience at Parham's school: "I got into the flesh and was under a cloud spiritually, and was willing to lay down the baptism because of criticism and censure." Maria Woodworth-Etter, *A Diary of Signs and Wonders* (Tulsa: Harrison House, reprint, 1916 ed.), 431–432.

[78]Parham, *Parham*, 81.

[79]Parham's followers rented the Grand Leader Building on Main Street, a 50- by 110-foot facility which "never accommodated the crowds." Lawrence, *Apostolic Faith*, 53.

[80]The local papers in Cheney, Kansas, continued to report his activities and to manifest pride in his efforts.

[81]Ibid. For an account of this phase of Parham's work, see Ethel E. Goss, *The Winds of God: The Story of the Early Pentecostal Days (1901–1914) in the Life of Howard A. Goss* (New York: Comet Press Books, 1958). Goss later became an executive of the Assemblies of God. Goss' unpublished diary is in the archives of the United Pentecostal Church, Hazelwood, MO. A copy is in the Assemblies of God Archives.

[82]Charles Parham, "Hell," *The Apostolic Faith*, September 1912, 11.

[83]Goss, *Winds of God*, 14–15.

[84]Ibid., 17; quoted in Parham, *Parham*, 76.

[85]"Houstonians Witness the Performance of Miracles," *Houston Chronicle*, 13 August 1905.

[86]Rilda Cole, Houston, to Apostolic Faith adherents, Baxter Springs, KS, 1 August 1905, in Parham Papers, Assemblies of God Archives.

[87]Goss, *Winds of God*, 35, 38.

[88]For one participant's account, see Goss, *Winds*, 30ff.

[89]Ibid., 34ff.

[90]For Seymour, see Douglas Nelson's dissertation, "For Such a Time as This: The Story of William J. Seymour and the Azusa Street Revival" (Ph.D. diss., University of Birmingham, 1981); James Tinney, "William J. Seymour: Father of Modern-Day Pentecostalism," *Journal of the Interdenominational Theological Center* 4 (Fall 1979): 34–44.

[91]The Evening Light Saints believed they lived "in the evening of the last dispensation of time." They shared fully the persuasion that primitive Christianity was the ideal for the contemporary church: "The pure gospel is shining now as it never has shone since the days of primitive Christianity." See the preface to *Songs of the Evening Light*. The conviction that they lived in the day of restoration was the subject of numerous songs in the hymnal, several of which were written by William G. Schell, later an Assemblies of God minister.

[92]See the testimony of a black woman who was healed. Rilda Cole to Apostolic Faith adherents, Baxter Springs, KS.

[93]Howard Goss, "Reminiscences," in *Apostolic Faith*, Lawrence, 64.

[94]Parham, *Voice Crying*, 106–107.

[95]Lawrence, *Apostolic Faith*, 55.

[96]Alma White, *Demons and Tongues* (Zarephath, NJ: Pillar of Fire Publishers, 1949), 68–69.

[97]The account contained in Goss, *Winds of God*, 35–36, varies at significant points. According to Goss, who was a student at the Houston school, Lucy Farrow obtained money from Parham to spread his views in Los Angeles. Her request for assistance resulted in the Bible school students' providing funds to permit William Seymour to join her.

[98]William J. Seymour to W. F. Carothers, 12 July 1906, in the author's possession. Seymour specifically requested credentials so that he could qualify for clergy discounted fares on the railroad. This indicates that Parham had formally registered his Apostolic Faith Movement.

[99]William J. Seymour, *Doctrine and Discipline of the Azusa Street Apostolic Faith Mission of Los Angeles* (Published by the author, 1915), 2; quoted in Tinney, "William J. Seymour," 39.

[100]Tinney, "William J. Seymour," 39.

[101]Charles F. Parham, "Free Love,"*The Apostolic Faith*, December 1912, 4.

[102]Editorial, *The Apostolic Faith*, October 1912, 6.

[103]Ibid.

[104]In 1907, Parham and another man were arrested in San Antonio and charged with "an unnatural act." The outcome is unclear: Charges may have been dropped. See the *San Antonio Light* (July 1907): 1. In 1916, Voliva printed a purported copy of a confession and affidavit sworn by Parham before I. C. Baker, District Attorney, San Antonio which reads as follows: "I hereby confess my guilt in the commission of the crime of sodomy with one J. J. Jourdan in San Antonio, Texas, on the 18th day of July 1907. Witness my hand in San Antonio, Texas, this 18th day of July 1907." This confession was purportedly witnessed by Charles Stevens, the arresting officer. See poster in the Assemblies of God Archives.

[105]"A Crisis at Hand," *The Household of God* (May 1909): 5.

Chapter 4: The "Nazareth" of Los Angeles: Azusa Street and Beyond

[1]William Seymour, "Bro. Seymour's Call," *The Apostolic Faith*, September 1906, 1.

[2]Seymour notes that three people—Lucy Farrow, J. A. Warren, and he—had been "sent" by the Lord from Houston to Los Angeles "as messengers of the full gospel." Farrow had first "brought the full

Gospel," and had been "greatly used as she laid her hands on many who have received the Pentecost and the gift of tongues." By September, Farrow had left Los Angeles to carry the message to her home city, Norfolk, VA. *The Apostolic Faith,* September 1906, 1.

³Ibid.

⁴Dr. Cecil Robeck of Fuller Seminary is working on an examination of public documents to gather information about known participants in Seymour's meetings.

⁵Frank J. Ewart, *The Phenomenon of Pentecost* (St. Louis: Pentecostal Publishing House, 1947), 36–37; *The Apostolic Faith,* September 1906, 1; Bartleman, *How Pentecost Came to Los Angeles* (Los Angeles: n.p., 1925), 43.

⁶Bartleman, *Pentecost,* 44.

⁷*The Apostolic Faith,* September 1906, 1.

⁸Anderson, *Vision,* 62–63.

⁹Evan Hopkins, "The Teaching of the Revival," in *The Story of the Welsh Revival Told by Eyewitnesses* (New York: Fleming H. Revell, 1905), 73.

¹⁰Edith Blumhofer, "The Welsh Revival," *Paraclete* 20 (Summer, 1986): 1–5.

¹¹The *Times* (London), 13 February 1905, 9d.

¹²Evan Roberts, "A Message to the World," in *The Story of the Welsh Revival,* 6.

¹³G. Campbell Morgan, "The Lesson of the Revival," in *The Story of the Welsh Revival,* 37.

¹⁴Ibid., 39.

¹⁵The *Times* (London), 3 January 1905, 12b.

¹⁶The *Times* (London), 31 January 1905, 7c.

¹⁷Ibid.

¹⁸W. T. Stead, "The Story of the Awakening," in *The Story of the Welsh Revival,* 64.

¹⁹Ibid., 66.

²⁰See, for example, Jessie Penn-Lewis, *The Awakening in Wales* (New York: Fleming H. Revell, 1905). Penn-Lewis considered the central question raised by the revival to be one addressed to believers: "Have you received the Holy Ghost since you believed?"

²¹Morgan, "Lesson," 50, 44.

²²*The Apostolic Faith,* 12 May 1906, 7.

²³A. S. Worrell, "Wonderful Works Going on in Los Angeles," *Gospel Witness* 16 (September 1906): 30.

²⁴Bartleman, *Pentecost,* 54.

[25]Bartleman, *Pentecost*, 62. Though agreeing that tongues speech was a contemporary possibility, Smale objected strongly to the teaching on tongues as *uniform* intial evidence. He also noted the inaccuracy of Bartleman's implication that the New Testament Church had split over Pentecostal teaching. In fact, Smale reported, "only about a dozen have withdrawn from the Church, and mainly such as had not been its elements of strength." Joseph Smale, "The Gift of Tongues," *Living Truth* (January, 1907): 40.

[26]"A Chicago Evangelist's Pentecost," *The Apostolic Faith,* Feb. to March 1907, 4.

[27]Bartleman, *Pentecost,* 58.

[28]Glenn Cook, "The Azusa Street Meeting: Some High Lights of this Outpouring," 2. This pamphlet is in the Assemblies of God Archives. Cook, who served for a time as business manager at Azusa Street, shared Parham's persuasion that the baptism in the Holy Spirit represented a "sealing" with tremendous significance for one's participation in end-times events. (See Cook's pamphlet, p. 4.) It is striking that this adulation comes from three men whose inability to emulate Seymour's humility made them parties to bitter divisions in Pentecostal ranks.

[29]This reference is from Bartleman, *Pentecost,* 19.

[30]"Beginning of World Wide Revival," *The Apostolic Faith,* 1 January 1907, 1.

[31]Ibid.

[32]*The Apostolic Faith,* 1 September 1906, 3.

[33]"The Apostolic Faith Movement," *The Apostolic Faith,* September 1906, 2.

[34]"This Same Jesus," *The Apostolic Faith,* October 1906, 3.

[35]Bartleman, *Pentecost,* 89. At the same time, however, observers noted that events mocked pretensions to unity. Joseph Smale wrote late in 1906: "In the city there are already four hostile camps of those who unduly magnify the tongues, which prove that the tongues have not brought Pentecost to Los Angeles. When Pentecost comes we shall see the union of the Lord's people." Joseph Smale, "The Gift of Tongues," *Living Truth* (January 1907): 40.

[36]*The Apostolic Faith,* October 1906, 1.

[37]*The Apostolic Faith,* September 1906, 1. This is the only reference I have found claiming that signing was accepted as a language evidencing Spirit baptism.

[38]*The Apostolic Faith,* September 1906, 1.

[39]*The Apostolic Faith,* September, 1906, 1.

[40]Bartleman, *Pentecost,* 68, 84.

[41]Ibid., 68.

[42]Ibid.

[43]Ibid, 84.

[44]*The Upper Room* 1 (June 1909): 4.

[45]Ibid. Seymour noted that in the first five months about one hundred fifty had received Spirit baptism at Azusa Street. Many others, of course, testified to the experience elsewhere. See *The Apostolic Faith*, September 1906, 1.

[46]Parham, *Parham*, 163. Smale also noted the similarity of the "manifestations" with those among local spiritualists. He also reported at Azusa Street "the imitation of animal sounds such as the dog, coyote, cat and fowl." See Joseph Smale, "The Gift of Tongues," *Living Truth* (January 1907): 39.

[47]Charles F. Parham, "Baptism of the Holy Ghost," *The Apostolic Faith*, October 1912, 9.

[48]Charles F. Parham, "Leadership," *The Apostolic Faith*, June 1912, 7–8. Parham consistently attributed to Azusa Street anything that he considered "fanatical." Comments like the following surface frequently in his later writings: "All these events are records of work done previous to the awful plunge into fanaticism in Azuza [sic] St. While good may have resulted in part from the work that sprung out of Azuza mission because of the elements of truth the message contained, yet the accompanying fleshly windsucking, body-shaking tomfoolery has done unredeemable damage to the cause." See "Lest We Forget," *The Apostolic Faith*, July 1912, 6.

[49]Bartleman, *Pentecost*, 54. Bartleman also noted that, at the time, whites far outnumbered blacks at Azusa Street.

[50]Charles F. Parham, "Free-Love," *The Apostolic Faith*, December 1912, 4.

[51]Ibid.

[52]Parham, *Parham*, 163–164.

[53]Bartleman, *Pentecost*, 49.

[54]W. F. Carothers in *Apostolic Faith*, Lawrence, 57.

Chapter 5: Some Early Pentecostal Centers

[1]Bernice Lee, "When God Breathed on Zion," *Bread of Life* (October 1981): 10, 11, 13.

[2]*Waukegan Daily Gazette* 15 (October 1906).

[3]*The Cheney Sentinel* 5 (October 1906).

[4]Parham, *Parham*, 156–157. The *Waukegan Daily Sun* 15 (November 1906) reported that as many as three hundred attended a single house meeting.

[5]In 1907, for example, Marie Burgess (who married Robert Brown

in 1909) responded to Parham's request that she take the Pentecostal message to New York City. She remained to establish an influential Assemblies of God church, Glad Tidings Tabernacle. For many years, Glad Tidings led Assemblies of God congregations in foreign missions giving. When she died in 1971, Brown had served her congregation for 64 years.

[6]Gordon P. Gardiner, "The Apostle of Divine Healing," *Bread of Life* 6 (March 1957): 15.

[7]Elnora L. Lee, comp., *C. H. Mason, A Man Greatly Used of God* (Memphis, TN: Women's Department, Churches of God in Christ, 1967), 7–8.

[8]Elsie W. Mason, *The Man: Charles Harrison Mason,* Pioneer Series (Memphis, TN: Church of God in Christ, 1979), 14.

[9]Lee, *Mason,* 8.

[10]Ibid., 19.

[11]In 1916, he conducted a camp meeting for whites at the invitation of city authorities in Nashville, Tennessee. The city auditorium (seating some seven thousand) was placed at his disposal. In 1919, C. M. Grace, a white man from Little Rock, Arkansas, sponsored a meeting for whites in an auditorium seating some seven thousand. Mason reported that "God wonderfully brought his power among both white and black, sanctifying, baptizing and healing." Lee, *Mason,* 13–14.

[12]Both L. P. Adams and August Feick, one of Maria Woodworth-Etter's assistants, were associated with a white branch of the Churches of God in Christ. During the 1920s Mason made a serious effort to formalize such a group. See correspondence, August Feick to J. W. Welch, 6 April 1926, Assemblies of God Archives. Feick surrendered his Assemblies of God credentials to participate.

[13]Parham claimed he had no use for incorporation, and specifically ridiculed those Pentecostals who sought clergy discounts: "I would hate to give such a testimony to the world that my God was a pauper and compelled me to ride on half-fare, or confess my little faith in trusting God for full fare." *The Apostolic Faith,* September 1912, 9. However, six years earlier, Seymour, while still submitting to Parham's leadership, had applied to him for credentials specifically to obtain the rail discount. William J. Seymour to W. F. Carothers, July 1906, copy in the author's possession.

[14]"Came 3,000 Miles for His Pentecost," *The Apostolic Faith,* December 1906, 3.

[15]Ibid.; see also *The Apostolic Faith,* January 1907.

[16]Ibid.; during 1906 and 1907 the paper regularly carried reports from Cashwell.

[17]"Pentecost in North Carolina," *The Apostolic Faith,* January 1907, 1.

¹⁸"Hundreds Baptized in the South," *The Apostolic Faith,* Feb. to March, 1907, 3.

¹⁹Ibid.

²⁰Quoted in James R. Goff, "The Pentecostal Catalyst to the South: G. B. Cashwell, 1906–1908," unpublished paper, Assemblies of God Archives.

²¹John T. Benson, *Pentecostal Mission* (Nashville, TN: Trevecca Press, 1977), 20.

²²The school later became Trevecca College, which is operated by the Church of the Nazarene.

²³Pentecostal Alliance Mission Minutes, 6 January 1908, Assemblies of God Archives.

²⁴The Pentecostal Mission united with the Church of the Nazarene. See Benson, *Pentecostal Mission.* H. G. Rodgers was ordained by the group in 1901; M. M. Pinson served it as an evangelist from 1902. *Living Waters* contains numerous reports of their meetings.

²⁵Tomlinson had a fascinating background. Like Parham, he had been influenced by a visit to Sandford's Shiloh. As a colporteur for the American Bible Society, he had traveled throughout western North Carolina and eastern Tennessee, where he met a group of restorationists who had withdrawn from local churches under the leadership of Richard Spurling and had formed the Christian Union. In 1896, the group had experienced revival, during which speaking in tongues had been a common but uncomprehended occurrence. In 1903, Tomlinson claimed a divine communication, informing him that *the* (exclusive) Church of God had been instituted by the group. See Charles Conn, *Like A Mighty Army* (Cleveland, TN: Pathway Press, 1955); A. J. Tomlinson, *Diary,* ed. Homer Tomlinson (New York: The Church of God, World Headquarters, 1949–1955).

²⁶Robert M. Anderson's account differs.

²⁷*The Christian and Missionary Alliance,* 8 June 1907, 205.

²⁸A. W. Vian, "Further News from Nyack, New York," *The Household of God* (November 1907): 6.

²⁹For Myland's story, see J. Kevin Butcher, "The Holiness and Pentecostal Labors of David Wesley Myland: 1890–1918" (Master's thesis, Dallas Theological Seminary, 1983).

³⁰G. A. Cook, "Pentecostal Power in Indianapolis," *The Apostolic Faith,* Feb. to March 1907, 3; Alice Reynolds Flower, "How Pentecost Came to Indianapolis," unpublished ms., Assemblies of God Archives. An Elder Henry Prentiss also came from Azusa Street to Indianapolis. He became pastor of a predominantly black mission in the city. See Morris Golder, *The Life and Works of Bishop Garfield Thomas Haywood,* (n.p., 1977), 3.

³¹Flower began publishing an eight-page Pentecostal monthly which

he called *Pentecost* in August 1908. His mailing address at the time was at the Apostolic Faith Mission. Note the continued use of the designation "apostolic faith" in areas where Parham's personal influence had not been strong.

[32]The repetition of a pattern in which people claimed to be "led" to accept healing, "faith" living, premillennialism and other such teachings is striking. In totally disparate settings men and women reached similar conclusions about "Bible" Christianity. The Pentecostal movement brought some of them together.

[33]For the story of the origins of Elim, see Susan A. Duncan, *Trials and Triumphs of a Faith Life* (Rochester, NY: Elim Publishing House, 1910).

[34]Elizabeth Baker, *Chronicles of a Faith Life* (Rochester, NY: The Du Bois Press, n.d.), 117ff.

[35]Ibid., 61–62.

[36]For a student perspective on the school, see Marion Meloon, *Ivan Spencer: Willow in the Wind* (Plainfield, NJ: Logos International, 1974).

[37]Ibid., 64.

[38]Ibid., 63. Several of the Duncan sisters visited Wales, and in 1914 and 1915 they still corresponded with Evan Roberts' brother about the Welsh religious scene. See letters in *Trust*. One of them also visited Pandita Ramabai in India before Elim had become Pentecostal. The number of these independent evangelicals who supported Ramabai is striking: From Moody's associates in the 1880s to Torrey's worldwide tour that coincided with the Welsh Revival to early Pentecostal evangelists, Ramabai's work attracted considerable and diffuse American interest. Of special interest is Pandita Ramabai, *The Baptism of the Holy Ghost and Fire* (Kedgaon, India: Mukti Missions Press, 1906).

[39]Ibid., 64.

[40]Ibid., 65.

[41]Ibid., 68.

[42]Baker, *Chronicles,* 127.

[43]Ibid., 130.

[44]Ibid.

[45]Ibid., 63. Susan Duncan noted in 1910 that they turned away nearly as many as they were able to accept. Among the Assemblies of God leaders who participated in some way at Elim were Noel Perkin, Ralph Riggs, Gayle Lewis, Charles W. H. Scott, and Wilfred Brown, two of whom were general superintendents, and all of whom served as resident executive presbyters during the 1950s.

[46]For the congregation's 75th anniversary, it authorized a brief history: Lois Ephraim, *The Stone Church, 1906–1981* (Worth, IL: Charles

E. Brinkman Publishers, 1981). The best source for the early Pentecostal character of the congregation is its monthly publication, *The Latter Rain Evangel.*

[47]Quoted in Gordon P. Gardiner, "Out of Zion . . . Into All the World," *Bread of Life* 31 (April 1982): 7.

[48]William Piper, *The Latter Rain Evangel,* October 1908.

[49]Graves later affiliated with the Assemblies of God. His family contributed in various ways to the Assemblies of God. His son Arthur served as president of Southeastern College, Lakeland; his daughter, Irene, became the wife of Myer Pearlman, noted teacher and author; another son, Carl, served as a missionary to Sri Lanka.

[50]Parham sensed a threat to his own claims as "Projector" of the movement in Piper's popularity and the successful conventions he held. Claiming that Piper was influenced by a "spiritualistic medium" in his congregation, Parham wrote to him, warning that if Piper (who had accepted negative rumors about Parham and had written to Parham, forbidding him to come to the Stone Church) continued to harbor critical attitudes, he would die within two years. "Six months before the two years were up," Parham recorded, "he took sick with a desperate case of erysipelas and died." See "Leadership," *The Apostolic Faith,* 1912, 8.

[51]Immigrants and their children were well represented in the early Pentecostal movement. During the first year, for example, the success of the movement among Swedish Americans in certain areas was noted by Seymour's publication. See *The Apostolic Faith,* April 1907, 2. See also Frederick Link to Robert C. Cunningham, 9 March 1951, Assemblies of God Archives, which refers to Elder Sangreen who led "the Swedish work" of the North Avenue Mission. This later became the Lake View Church. Danish and Norwegians formed a mission-based congregation, as did some Italians led by a husband-wife team named Franciscone.

[52]William Durham, "The Church," *Pentecostal Testimony* vol. 2, no. 1, 14.

[53]William Durham, "What Is the Evidence of the Baptism in the Holy Ghost?" *Pentecostal Testimony* vol. 2, no. 1, 4.

[54]Ibid.

[55]Ibid.

[56]William Durham, "Personal Testimony of Pastor Durham," *Pentecostal Testimony* 2 (August 1912): 3.

[57]His failure to proclaim crisis sanctification did not immediately alienate him from Azusa Street. Jennie Moore, a remarkable woman who later married Seymour, visited Durham's mission at 943 West North Avenue and wrote in the January 1908 *Apostolic Faith* that the mission was "truly a blessed place—many Spirit-filled men and women and children."

[58]William Durham, "The Great Battle of 1911," *Pentecostal Testimony* vol. 2, no. 1, 7.

[59]William Durham, "The Gospel of Christ," *Pentecostal Testimony* vol. 2, no. 1, 9.

[60]As Durham traveled to various camp meetings and conventions, he won key individuals to his viewpoint, among whom were Pinson, Rodgers, and Howard Goss. Parham reported that he had prayed that he or Durham, whichever was wrong on sanctification, would die. When Durham died in 1912 at the age of 39, Parham smugly noted: "How signally God has answered." See *The Apostolic Faith,* supplement, October 1912.

[61]"My Testimony How I Came to Pentecost," Frederick Link file, Assemblies of God Archives. Link reported that he received Spirit baptism on May 30, 1910, and the next Sunday Durham ordained him to the ministry. Like most Pentecostals, the assembled congregation regarded the attendant demonstration of power (Link reported that "the Holy Ghost fell" on him and he was unable to return to his seat; the congregation then broke forth in "waves in song of the Spirit") as evidence that God signally approved the occasion.

[62]Lucy Farrow did not stay in Virginia long, however. Seymour's *Apostolic Faith* reported in December 1906 that after meetings in Virginia, in which about two hundred had been saved—most of whom had also spoken in tongues—Farrow was on her way to Africa with a party of missionaries from the mission. She and four others were going to Monrovia, Liberia.

[63]Howard Goss noted that "everyone for whom she prayed" spoke in tongues. Goss, *Winds of God,* 56.

[64]Ibid., 57.

[65]Goss, *Winds of God,* 79. But Parham associated with some of his southern followers prominently in 1908 when he was the featured speaker at an Alabama camp meeting. See announcements in *Word and Work.* Apparently there was considerable disagreement about his alleged "fall." In 1912, he seemed convinced that he was gaining more acceptance and opposition was finally waning. See editorials and reports in his *Apostolic Faith,* 1912 and 1913.

[66]Bell file, Assemblies of God Archives.

[67]Goss, *Winds of God,* 123.

[68]M. M. Pinson to J. R. Flower, 19 December 1950, Assemblies of God Archives.

[69]J. R. Flower to M. M. Pinson, 4 January 1950, Assemblies of God Archives. Flower quotes minutes of a meeting at Slocumb, Alabama on February 10, 1911.

[70]Goss, *Winds of God,* 163.

[71]Ibid.

[72]Ibid.

[73]J. R. Flower to M. M. Pinson, 4 January 1950. Pinson file, Assemblies of God Archives.

[74]Brumback dates this merger in 1913, but the existence of the paper, edited by Bell, in August 1912 disproves this.

[75]"Glory and Unity at the Eureka Springs Camp!" *Word and Witness,* 20 August 1912, 1.

[76]*Word and Witness,* 20 August 1912, 2.

[77]Ibid.

[78]Ibid. Some whose future contribution to the Assemblies of God has been well documented include Harry Bowley, Hugh Cadwalder, A. B. Cox, W. T. Gaston, B. F. Lawrence, Burt McCafferty, J. W. Welch, and Agnes Ozman LaBerge. "Ordained Elders, Pastors, Ministers, Evangelists and Missionaries of the Churches of God in Christ with Their Stations for 1914," *Word and Witness,* 20 December 1913, 4. The number of women is approximate since many ministers used their initials. It seems evident that women were identified by their full first names or by the prefixes Miss or Mrs., but it is not certain that all were so designated.

[79]Ibid., 2

[80]See, for example, Levi Lupton, "Testimony," *New Acts* 3 (February 1907): 3.

[81]See, for example, *The Apostolic Faith,* December 1906, 4, which contains a letter from a man in Minneapolis who received Spirit baptism as a result of reading reports in the paper and personal correspondence. The same issue, p. 3, contains Cashwell's testimony and that of T. B. Barratt of Norway.

Chapter 6: The Pentecostal Life-style: "Days of Heaven on Earth"

[1]James Hunter makes a similar observation about the larger evangelical community, which Pentecostals consider themselves part of, in his book *Evangelicalism: The Coming Generation* (Chicago: University of Chicago Press, 1987).

[2]Baker, *Chronicles,* 125.

[3]Gordon P. Gardiner, "Out of Zion . . . Into the World," *Bread of Life* 31 (February 1982): 6.

[4]Baker, *Chronicles,* 133.

[5]Ibid., 65.

[6]Donald Gee, *Pentecost* (Springfield, MO: Gospel Publishing House, 1932), 37.

[7]Goss, *Winds of God,* 124.

[8]Both Ethel Goss, *The Winds of God,* and Sarah Parham, *The Life of Charles F. Parham,* recount numerous instances of worship in such varied settings. Garfield Haywood reminisced that those who attended his mission in Indianapolis in 1908 often "would board the street-car praising and blessing God on their journey home." See Golder, *Bishop Garfield Thomas Haywood,* 32.

[9]Lee, *Mason,* 12.

[10]*The Apostolic Faith,* January 1907, 1.

[11]Gee, *Pentecost,* 10.

[12]David Wesley Myland, *The Latter Rain Covenant and Pentecostal Power* (Chicago: The Evangel Publishing House, 1910), 39.

[13]Albert Weaver, "Camp Meeting, Alliance, Ohio," *Word and Work,* August 1907, 215.

[14]*Pentecost* 2 (Nov. to Dec. 1910): 9.

[15]Ibid.

[16]Ibid. See also Myland, *Latter Rain Covenant,* 39–40.

[17]Gee, *Pentecost,* 21.

[18]*Hymns of Glorious Praise,* George W. Robinson, "I Am His, and He Is Mine" (Springfield, MO: Gospel Publishing House, 1969), 289.

[19]S. A. Jamieson, *How a Presbyterian Minister Received the Baptism,* Evangel Tract no. 657, 5.

[20]Goss, *Winds of God,* 132.

[21]Howard Goss cites typical titles from Pentecostal hymnals. Goss, *Winds of God,* 131–133.

[22]Margaret Cragin, "Elim Home, Rochester, N.Y." *Word and Work,* March 1908, 84.

[23]*Word and Work* contains many songs "given" in tongues and interpretation. Mrs. E. W. Vinton (Mary Vinton), who, with her husband, had attended the Azusa Street meetings, played a prominent role in the extension of Pentecostal teaching in the Northeast. She frequently contributed lengthy songs.

[24]Haywood compiled songs that he claimed were "inspired by the Holy Ghost" and published them under the title *The Bridegroom Cometh.* Golder, *Bishop Garfield Thomas Haywood,* 24.

[25]Wayne Warner, "Herbert Buffum," *Heritage* 6 (Fall 1986): 11–16.

[26]Golder, *Bishop Garfield Thomas Haywood,* 32.

[27]Ibid., 28.

[28]"Bible Teaching on Marriage and Divorce," *The Apostolic Faith,* January 1907, 3.

[29]*The Apostolic Faith,* December 1906, 3.

[30]Golder, *Bishop Garfield Thomas Haywood,* 31.

[31]Mrs. A. F. Rawson, "Apostolic Faith Mission," *Word and Work,* February 1908, 49.

[32]*Word and Work* included a brief statement on "Utility of Tongues," assigning the gift "four definite uses:"

1. facility in preaching the gospel in other languages

2. the edification of the church

3. self edification

4. a "sign" to unbelievers

("Better have tongues than magic lanterns to draw the people," the paper urged.) See *Word and Work,* June 1907, 162.

[33]Of the many sources that could be cited, C. H. Mason's account is typical. See Lee, *Mason,* 9, for example. When J. A. Jeter (who accompanied Mason to Azusa Street) criticized the mission, Mason noted that "the enemy had put into the ear of Brother Jeter to find fault."

[34]Myland, *Latter Rain Covenant,* 93.

[35]A Massachusetts publication, *Word and Work,* contains many reports of such experiences. It regularly carried prophecies about the imminent destruction of New York, Chicago, and Boston and testimonies from individuals who had "fallen under the power" for hours at a time. The magazine implies that the significance of such experiences lay in their demonstration of the reality of (seemingly pointless) supernatural intervention in believers' daily lives.

[36]Addie M. Otis, "Upward Attraction," *Word and Work,* March 1908, 67.

[37]"Some Marked Features," *The Upper Room* (June 1909): 4.

[38]For an analysis of this method, see Butcher, "David Wesley Myland."

[39]See Butcher, "Myland." For an example of the application of this hermeneutic, see Myland, *Latter Rain Covenant,* 23.

[40]Myland, *Latter Rain Covenant,* 1.

[41]"What Is Meant by The Latter Rain?" *The Christian and Missionary Alliance,* 19 October 1907, 38.

[42]Ibid.

[43]Ibid.

[44]Ibid.

[45]Julia Morton Plummer, "The Bridegroom Cometh," *Word and Work,* March 1908, 76.

[46]W. C. Stevens, "The Latter Rain," *Word and Work,* July 1908, 17.

[47]See, for example, May Mabette Anderson, "The Latter Rain and Its Counterfeit," *Living Truth* (June, July, August 1907).

[48]Myland's own hymn *The Latter Rain Song* became a well-known

Pentecostal favorite. For the story of its composition and its full text, see *Bread of Life* 30 (November 1981): 16.

William G. Schell, who ministered in the Assemblies of God for many years, wrote a song expressing the typical restorationist attitude toward history. Published by the Evening Light Saints before the Pentecostal movement came about, the song expressed a viewpoint to which some holiness restorationist groups assented as well:

> The church of the morning bright
> Like crystal so clear her light
> Triumphant, she knew no fears
> In finest white linen dressed
> Pure holiness she possessed two hundred and seventy
> years.
>
> The sun went down ere his time,
> The moon also ceased to shine,
> Left Zion in bitter tears;
> No star then appeared in sight,
> Oh long, dreary Papal night! Twelve hundred and sixty
> years.
>
> The sun coming up next day,
> Dispersing the night away,
> Caused popedom to grope in fears
> The mists not all cleared away,
> There followed a cloudy day three hundred and fifty
> years.
>
> We welcome the evening light
> The gospel so clear and bright,
> Breaks forth as in days of yore
> The mists are all cleared away,
> All hail the supernal day! The sun shall go down no
> more.

"Biblical Trace of the Church," in *Songs of the Evening Light*, 20.

[49]W. C. Stevens, "The Latter Rain," 17. Stevens had anticipated the latter rain at least since 1892 and had given a report of the Pentecostal "visitation" at Nyack Missionary Training Institute to the Old Orchard Beach Convention in 1907. See S. G. Otis, "Camp Meeting at Old Orchard, Maine," *Word and Work*, September 1907, 243.

[50]Anderson, *Vision*, 195–222.

[51]Goss, *Winds of God*, 78.

[52]Several of the movement's critics accused them of an appalling

lack of evangelistic zeal and a concomitant tendency to gather in "select," "spiritual" groups to pursue "deeper" experiences. See chapter 8 of this book, "Is the Present Tongues Movement of God?"

[53]Addie M. Otis, "Let Him Come In," *Word and Work,* September 1908.

[54]Abbie C. Morrow, "Church Amusements," tract, 2.

[55]Ibid., 3, 5, 6.

[56]"Pentecostal Backsliders," *The Household of God* (March 1910): 13.

[57]Ibid.

[58]Ibid.

[59]"Gospel Letter," *Word and Work,* April 1908, 111.

[60]*Word and Work,* January 1908, 5.

[61]Ibid.

[62]Golder, *Bishop Garfield Thomas Haywood,* 10.

[63]"Testimonials From Prairie Dell," *Gold Tried in the Fire* 4 (December 1910): 3.

[64]Ibid., 4. In spite of such emphases, some believed the movement tolerated worldliness. See letter from Mary A. Baker in *The Household of God* (May 1909): 10.

[65]"Wearing of God; Adorning the Body," *The Household of God* (May 1909): 7.

[66]Milton Grotz, "Eat and Drink to the Glory of God," tract (Christian Workers' Union, 1914), 2,3.

[67]These were published as part of the Christian Workers Union's Words of Life Series in 1913 and 1914 respectively.

Chapter 7: The Pentecostal Life-style: "Let Us Labor for the Master"

[1]This overwhelming desire to "work for Jesus" was complemented in some settings by teaching on "tarrying" and "waiting on God." In this regard, A. B. Simpson's influence was strong. The spirituality early Pentecostals discovered in Alliance branches around the country had been influenced by Simpson's tract *The Power of Stillness,* which was reprinted in numerous Pentecostal publications. The essence of Simpson's teaching (which was never generally understood by either his movement or the majority of American Pentecostals) was that "God was waiting in the depth of my being to talk with me, if I would only get still enough to hear Him." Simpson gave the following as his testimony of the "power" he discovered:

> After awhile when the other voices ceased, or I ceased to hear them, there was a still small voice in the depth of my being. As I listened it became to me the power of prayer,

> and the voice of wisdom, and the voice of duty, and I did
> not need to think so hard or pray so hard, or trust so hard,
> but that "still small voice" of the Holy Spirit in my heart
> was God's prayer in my secret soul, was God's life and
> strength for soul and body, and became the substance of
> all knowledge, and all blessing, for it was the living God
> Himself as my life and my all.

Testimonies referring to *audible* commands are scattered in early issues of periodicals of the day, like *Word and Work.*

²See, for example, Frank Bartleman, *How Pentecost Came to Los Angeles,* or LaBerge, *What God Hath Wrought.* The number and variety of their activities suggest something of the instability of many people who were attracted to Pentecostalism.

³See, for example, Seeley D. Kinne, "The Pentecostal Movement and the Conversion of Sinners," *The Household of God* (May 1909): 15.

⁴Goss, *Winds of God,* 52.

⁵Ibid. Mabel Smith was widely known as one who had a "special" gift of tongues. It was reported that she gave a message in every meeting she attended, and that these were marked by "great blessing." Smith had been one of two women who had attempted to penetrate Dowie's Zion with Pentecostalism in 1904, but their followers had been forced to leave the town and their work had been halted by city authorities. See Bernice Lee, "When God Breathed on Zion," *Bread of Life* (October 1981): 7–8.

⁶Ibid., 51. See also Carrie Judd Montgomery's autobiography, *Under His Wings: The Story of My Life* (Oakland, CA: Triumphs of Faith, 1936), 170.

⁷"Pentecost Proved," *New Acts* 3 (April 1907): 4.

⁸See, for example, Kinne, "The Pentecostal Movement," 15.

⁹The degree of association among early Pentecostal leaders is striking. Historians of Pentecostalism who have emphasized the geographic isolation of various Pentecostal groups from one another have neglected to examine the rich records preserved in early Pentecostal periodicals that attest frequent shared activities. Camp meetings in particular brought together ministers from diverse backgrounds and far-flung parts of the country. Rail travel must have been relatively easy, since people moved regularly from one place to another. Alliance, Ohio; Rochester, New York; Durant, Florida; Eureka Springs, Arkansas; Beulah Heights Camp Ground, Cleveland, Ohio; Old Orchard Beach, Maine—these and many more places were the sites of regular camp meetings in the years before the Assemblies of God organized. Two of the sites were used by the Christian and Missionary Alliance, whose conventions became opportunities for Pentecostal fellowship.

¹⁰Pentecostal publications announced the camp meetings and con-

ventions. Several papers enjoyed circulation in the thousands of copies per month and helped provide scattered Pentecostals a sense of participation in the broader movement. The same periodicals also carried reports of the conventions and camp meetings, often in considerable detail.

[11]Some attributed persecution primarily to the Catholic Church. See, for example, "The Mark of the Beast: Great Persecutions Breaking Out Against Liberty of God's People in Many Places, Proving the 'Time of the End' Is at Hand," *The Christian Evangel,* 11 July 1914, 1; "Hot Times in Maryland," *The Christian Evangel,* 25 July 1914, 1.

[12]See, for example, Walter J. Higgins, *Pioneering in Pentecost,* (privately published, 1958).

[13]*The Apostolic Faith,* for example, reported over several months the cross-country journey of a party that had left Los Angeles for Africa and had stopped numerous times to preach the "full gospel."

[14]For example, Cyrus Fockler and Fred Bosworth succeeded in pioneering Milwaukee Gospel Tabernacle, the first English Pentecostal assembly in that city, as a result of the healing of Alice Baumbach, who had tuberculosis of the spine. See "Out of Zion . . . Into All the World," *Bread of Life* 30 (November 1981): 13–14.

[15]E. N. Bell, "Some Complaints," *Word and Witness,* 20 March 1914, 1. Bell maintained that the New Testament recognized women only as "helpers" in the gospel and recommended that those who felt "called" should be "permanently attached to some mission and take up some regular and systematic work for the Lord under the proper oversight of some good brother whom God has placed in charge of the work." While he (perhaps grudgingly) tolerated the women "God has blessed," he insisted: "We confess there is no scriptural precept or example for such independent leadership by women."

[16]Rachel A. Sizelove, *A Sparkling Fountain for the Whole Earth,* Assemblies of God Archives.

[17]Smith was apparently received as one who demonstrated the utility of tongues. A sampling of issues of *Word and Work* for 1907 document this.

[18]Parham claimed that he had long anticipated a restoration of tongues for the proclamation of the gospel. However, well before the Pentecostal movement advanced considerable support for the view that evangelism could be accomplished by exercising the gift of tongues, W. W. Simpson, a Missionary Alliance missionary in south China had expressed to A. B. Simpson (no relation) a conviction that he (W. W.) should seek the gift of tongues rather than engage in language study. A. B. Simpson prudently encouraged him to augment his prayers for a linguistic "gift" with traditional language study.

[19]See, for example, *The Latter Rain Evangel; The Good Report; Pentecost.*

[20]Gordon Lindsay, ed., *The John G. Lake Sermons* (Dallas: Voice of Healing Publishing Co., 1949), 12–13.

[21]*The Apostolic Faith,* November 1906, 2.

[22]*The Apostolic Faith,* January 1907, 3.

[23]Daniel W. Kerr, "Spontaneous Theology," *Weekly Evangel,* 17 April 1915, 3.

[24]E. N. Bell, "The Recurrence of Doctrine," *The Christian Evangel,* 26 September 1914, 3.

[25]John Lake to Charles Parham, 24 March 1927, Parham file, Assemblies of God Archives.

[26]G. D. Clementson, *Charles Hamilton Pridgeon* (Pittsburgh: The Evangelization Society of the Pittsburgh Bible Institute, 1963), 130ff.

[27]Charles Mason voiced similar sentiments. See his "Marriage," in *Mason,* Lee, comp., 48–50. Mason insisted that espousal of marital purity opened opportunities for "seducing spirits, working in dreams or in visions."

[28]See, for example, announcement in *New Acts* 3 (July and August 1907): 6. See also C. E. McPherson, *Life of Levi Lupton* (Alliance, OH, 1911).

[29]"Summer Bible School," *Word and Work* 30 (August 1908): 24; see also Lupton's paper, *The New Acts.*

[30]*Latter Rain Evangel,* July 1912, 12.

[31]Butcher, "David Wesley Myland," 108.

[32]See report by Mrs. R. H. (Eleanor) Gardiner, "Notes From Ebenezer Bible Institute," *Weekly Evangel,* 17 April 1915, 3.

[33]D. C. O. Opperman file, Assemblies of God Archives.

[34]This was several months before Parham took Pentecostal teaching to Zion City. Opperman traveled with Parham and attended Parham's Apostolic Faith Camp Meeting in Galena, Kansas.

[35]A gifted evangelist, Hall wrote several songs: *Jesus* and *Deeper in Thy Love, O Jesus* are probably his best-known. He also wrote a popular chorus:

> God is moving by His Spirit,
> Moving in all the earth;
> Signs and wonders when God moveth—
> Move, O Lord, in me.

[36]*Latter Rain Evangel,* December 1908, 19.

[37]Goss, *Winds of God,* 127–128.

[38]Baker, *Chronicles,* 120.

[39]William Durham, "Bible Schools and Training Homes," *The Gospel Witness* (circa 1913): 5.

[40]Ibid.

[41]Rachel Sizelove, for example, wrote: "Because I had had to die out to my own church, the Free Methodist Church, I had been opposed to organizations and churchanity, afraid of getting wrapped up in formality." Sizelove, *A Sparkling Fountain,* 11.

[42]William Durham, "Organization," *The Gospel Witness* 1 (circa 1913): 11.

[43]The pages of Parham's *Apostolic Faith* often contain bitter denunciations of people Parham thought aspired to leadership. Among such were Glenn Cook, Levi Lupton, William Piper, and William Durham.

[44]See, for example, Robert Jaffray, "Speaking in Tongues," *The Christian and Missionary Alliance,* 13 March 1909, 395–397.

Chapter 8: "Is the Present Tongues Movement of God?" Evangelicals Encounter Pentecostalism

[1]Alma White, *The Story of My Life and the Pillar of Fire,* vol. 3, (Zarephath, NJ: Pillar of Fire, 1936), 139.

[2]Ibid., 116.

[3]Quoted in "What They Say of Us," *Gold Tried in the Fire* 6 (April 1913): 6.

[4]Ibid., 7.

[5]Ibid.

[6]Jennie A. Jolley, comp., *As an Angel of Light, or Bible Tongues and Holiness and Their Counterfeits* (New York: Vantage Press, 1964).

[7]See, for example, Jolley, *Angel of Light,* 15, 21.

[8]E. E. Shelhammer, "Best Counterfeit," in Jolley, *Angel of Light,* 16.

[9]Beverly Carradine, *A Box of Treasure* (Chicago: The Christian Witness Co., 1910), 83–85.

[10]A. B. Simpson "Diary," 1906–1919, Historical Collection, Nyack NY: Nyack College.

[11]*The Christian and Missionary Alliance,* 22 September 1906, 177.

[12]Ibid.

[13]*The Christian and Missionary Alliance,* 24 November 1906, 322.

[14]William T. MacArthur, "The Promise of the Father and 'Speaking with Tongues' in Chicago," *The Christian and Missionary Alliance,* 26 January 1907, 40.

[15]*The Christian and Missionary Alliance,* 2 February 1907, 49; see

also "Annual Report of President and General Superintendent of the Christian and Missionary Alliance" (Springfield, MO: Assemblies of God Archives, Alliance Collection, 1907).

[16]Ibid.

[17]*The Christian and Missionary Alliance,* 8 June 1907, 205.

[18]"Annual Report," 1907.

[19]Ibid.

[20]Ibid.

[21]*Word and Work,* 1907–1911 passim, for an indication of the degree to which Pentecostalism influenced local Alliance gatherings that never separated from the Alliance.

[22]"Beulah Park Convention," *The Christian and Missionary Alliance* 14 (September 1907): 128.

[23]Ibid.

[24]"Annual Report," 1907.

[25]Jaffray, "Speaking in Tongues," 395.

[26]"The Fifteenth Annual Report of the Christian and Missionary Alliance" (Springfield, MO: Assemblies of God Archives, Alliance Collection), 10.

[27]Ibid., 11.

[28]Ibid., 13.

[29]"Official Statement of the Board of the Christian and Missionary Alliance Setting Forth Its Position with Reference to 'Tongues' and the Baptism of the Spirit," Assemblies of God Archives.

[30]George N. Eldridge, *Personal Reminiscences* (Los Angeles: East Coast Publishing Co., n.d.). Eldridge had considerable experience in the ministry, and almost immediately after affiliating with the General Council of the Assemblies of God, he became, first, a general presbyter, then, a district superintendent.

[31]Niklaus, *All for Jesus,* 115.

[32]For Pierson's story, see Delavan Pierson, *Arthur T. Pierson* (New York: Fleming H. Revell Co., 1912).

[33]He clearly tied it to the Welsh Revival and Pandita Ramabai's orphanage and home for widows in India. See A. T. Pierson, "Speaking With Tongues," *Missionary Review of the World* 30 (July 1907): 487: "During the last few years, at sundry centers, notably Los Angeles, California, parts of India and China, Sweden and Wales, have recurred unusual and to some extent abnormal, manifestations, similar in character; supposed by some, and claimed by others, to be due to a supernatural gift of speaking with tongues."

[34]Ibid., 490.

[35]Ibid.

[36]Ibid., 492.

[37]A. T. Pierson, "Speaking With Tongues," *Missionary Review of the World* 30 (September 1907): 682.

[38]Ibid., 682–683.

[39]Ibid., 684.

[40]Ibid.

[41]Ibid.

[42]R. A. Torrey, *Is the Present Tongues Movement of God?* (Los Angeles: Biola Book Room, n.d.), 4. Surprisingly Parham (against whom Torrey directed some of his ire) concurred on this score, claiming that "free love" had pervaded Pentecostal ranks—his own excluded, of course. In fact, the moral failures of several prominent early Pentecostals seemed to lend support to such charges, although the frequency of such failures may not have exceeded that in other comparable religious movements.

[43]Ibid., 7. Such accusations are frequent in anti-Pentecostal literature, and they are not directed only against leaders. In a tract entitled *Spirit Manifestations and the Gift of Tongues,* the well-known British prophecy and biblical student Sir Robert Anderson detailed the "fall" of an exemplary Christian who "gave himself up unreservedly to the Spirit's guidance" with the result that "the Bible became less and less his study" until he "no longer needed the written Word." "The details of the disaster," Anderson observed, "would gratify none save the prurient and the profane." Quoted in Louis S. Bauman, *The Tongues Movement* (Winona Lake, IN: BMH Books, 1963 rev. ed.), 32–33.

[44]H. A. Ironside, *The Apostolic Faith Missions and the So-Called Second Pentecost* (New York: Louizeaux Brothers, Inc., n.d.), 15. Internal evidence suggests strongly that the pamphlet was written in 1914 or 1915.

[45]For an interesting later perspective on this, see Wilfred C. Meloon, *We've Been Robbed, Or A Dispensationalist Looks at the Baptism of the Holy Ghost* (Plainfield, NJ: Logos International, 1971).

[46]"Mark of the Beast," 1; "Hot Times in Maryland," *The Christian Evangel,* 25 July 1914, 1; see also *Word and Witness* (June 1914).

[47]This account, written by Haywood in 1924 is published in Golder, *Bishop Garfield Thomas Haywood,* 32. Garfield Haywood was born in 1880, the year that James Garfield was elected president.

[48]See Walter J. Higgins, *Pioneering in Pentecost* (privately published, 1958) passim, and Lou Ella Vaughn, *Brush Arbor Birthright* (Springfield, MO: Gospel Publishing House, 1986), 65.

[49]William Durham, "The Great Crisis," *The Gospel Witness* 1 (1914): 14.

[50]William Durham, "Organization" *The Gospel Witness* 1, 13. (Edited and published by Harry Van Loon, Los Angeles, CA, circa 1914).

Chapter 9: The Formation of the General Council of the Assemblies of God

[1]General Council Minutes, 1914, 3. This figure comes from the information under "conference committee" which explicitly states that the committee included one member from each state and foreign country represented. John Lake seems to have been accepted as representing both Pennsylvania and South Africa.

[2]Woodworth-Etter, *A Diary of Signs and Wonders*, 329, 330–333; 316–319.

[3]William B. McCafferty to J. R. Flower, 19 August 1939, Assemblies of God Archives.

[4]*Word and Witness*, 20 December 1913, 1.

[5]*Word and Witness*, 20 March 1914, 1.

[6]Ibid.

[7]*Word and Witness*, 20 December 1913, 1.

[8]Ibid.

[9]Ibid.

[10]General Council Minutes, 1914, 4.

[11]General Countil Minutes, 1914, 4.

[12]General Council Minutes, 1914, 5.

[13]"General Council Special," *Word and Witness*, 20 May 1914, 1.

[14]"Great November Meeting of Assemblies of God at the Stone Church, Chicago," *The Christian Evangel*, 12 September 1914, 1.

[15]"Hot Springs Assembly; God's Glory Present," *Word and Witness*, 20 April 1914, 1.

[16]"Open for Propositions," *Word and Witness*, 20 December 1913, 2.

[17]See, for example, Opperman's note in the announcement for his own Bible school that began at Hot Springs on January 1, 1914, "The Bible School is Soon to be Held in Hot Springs, Ark.," *Word and Witness*, 20 December 1913, 1.

[18]"The Gospel School," *Word and Witness*, 20 August 1914, 3.

[19]"Some Complaints," *Word and Witness*, 20 January 1914, 2.

[20]E. N. Bell, "Women Elders," *The Christian Evangel*, 15 August 1914, 2.

[21]Ibid.

[22]*Word and Witness*, 20 January 1914, 2.

[23]Although a later General Council (1935) granted women the right to ordination as pastors and although the General Council has always embraced some who have differed on this matter, the sense of the first resolution on women's "rights and offices" persists in the history of

the movement. It is most clearly evident in the absence of women on the various presbyteries as well as in the small and declining percentage of women pastors. It is also evident in the language of the constitution and bylaws.

[24]This was done in response to the request of two missionaries to India, Hattie Hacker and Jennie Kirkland. See Executive Presbytery Minutes, November 1914, 23; Executive Presbytery Minutes, 5 July 1922. The earliest ordination certificates used a format that accommodated both men and women: e.g., having blanks for the pronoun.

[25]For a more detailed consideration of the evolution of attitudes toward women in ministry in the Assemblies of God, see chapter 14.

[26]General Council Minutes, April 1914, 8.

[27]Ibid.

[28]"General Council Special," 1.

[29]*Word and Witness,* 20 March 1914, 2.

[30]E. N. Bell and J. R. Flower, "In Doctrines," *The Christian Evangel* 1 August 1914, 2.

[31]*The Christian Evangel,* 1 August 1914, 1.

[32]"General Council Special," 1.

[33]Ibid., 1. Note the heavy reliance placed on "outward" or subjective confirmations: loud praises or other evidences of spiritual fervor, confirmation by tongues and interpretation, ratification by other respected individuals. A comparison of Bell's description of this event with the way other Pentecostals typically evaluated similar occurrences is striking, for Assemblies of God leaders tended to distrust such charismatic phenomena as evidence when other Pentecostals (like A. J. Tomlinson) introduced it.

[34]There is considerable uncertainty about who actually attended the Hot Springs General Council. The official list was published in the fall of 1914, and contains the names of many who did not attend. In an undated ministers' letter in the Assemblies of God Archives, J. R. Flower solicited the names of any individuals known to have attended. He reported that the original list had been destroyed. He listed 74 known participants, 58 of whom had signed the official application for a charter. Committee appointments as documented in the General Council Minutes, 1914, indicate the presence of at least four others. In response to Flower's request, both W. B. McCafferty and H. G. Rodgers sent in additional names. Rodgers' list, which is the longest of the three, includes 161 names. Further evidence of the approximate size is offered by the well-known group picture containing 141 people. It is known, however, that all participants were not photographed.

[35]One could have assumed, for example, that H. G. Rodgers was organizing a rival Assemblies of God. He announced a "general convention of Pentecostal Saints and Assemblies of God of the southern

states" in November of 1914. See *The Christian Evangel,* 31 October 1914. There was no ill feeling, however, about this or other seemingly conflicting ventures—such as the operation of at least three training schools advertised in the official papers. This simply demonstrates the looseness of the organization.

[36]"For Strangers, Who Are We?" *Word and Witness,* 20 May 1914, 1.

[37]*The Christian Evangel,* 22 August 1914, 1,2; 12 December 1914, 2.

[38]See, for example, E. N. Bell, "Bible Order v. Fanaticism," *Word and Witness,* 20 March 1914, 2; "Hot Springs Assembly: God's Glory Present," *Word and Witness,* 20 April 1914, 1; also an article Bell recommended, Elizabeth Sisson, "Organization of Organism," *Latter Rain Evangel,* March 1914, 20–23. See also J. R. Flower, "Great November Meeting," *The Christian Evangel,* 12 September 1914, 1.

[39]Flower, "November Meeting."

[40]The official announcement in the General Council Minutes, April 1914, (see page 7) lists only Bell. That Flower also taught is clear from his own unpublished narrative, "History of the Assemblies of God," 24, Assemblies of God Archives.

[41]Flower, "History of the Assemblies of God," 24.

[42]*The Christian Evangel,* 24 October 1914, 2. There were eventually several letters in this series. Written by a sympathetic Christian, Charles E. Reynolds (J. R. Flower's father-in-law), they contained timely advice.

Chapter 10: Defining Doctrine, 1914–1918

[1]A. G. Garr, "That 'Yellow Book'," *Word and Witness,* 20 April 1914, 3.

[2]This is evident in notes of a Bible study on sanctification conducted by M. M. Pinson at the Hot Springs General Council. Pinson had spent twenty-one months at a holiness Bible School (sponsored by the Pentecostal Mission in Nashville) before being convinced of the error of holiness teaching. Bible study notes are in the Assemblies of God Archives.

[3]Lawrence, *Apostolic Faith,* 48ff.

[4]Pinson, Bible study notes, 4.

[5]Charles F. Parham, "The Sources of Disease: Sanctification of Spirit, Soul and Body Only Real Antidote for Sickness," *The Apostolic Faith,* August 1912, 4. Parham explicitly charged that the emergence of "free love," "affinity-foolism," and "soul mating" among Durham's adherents stemmed from his negation of crisis sanctification. "All the people . . . who had ever had a tinge of free-love," he fumed, had "swallowed [Durham] and his teaching whole." See Charles F. Parham, "Free Love," *The Apostolic Faith,* December 1912, 5.

[6]Ironside, *Apostolic Faith Missions*, 6.

[7]J. M. Pike, "The Second Blessing," *Word and Witness*, 20 December 1913, 2.

[8]Ibid.

[9]Ibid.

[10]Ibid. On the subject of sanctification, see also H. L. Lawler, "The Flesh: What Is It?" *Word and Work*, 20 February 1913, 4; *The Christian Evangel*, 21 November 1914, 2.

[11]"The Dress Fad," *Word and Witness*, 20 June 1913, 2.

[12]See, for example, "Believers in Sanctification," *Word and Work*, October 1914, 3.

[13]General Council Minutes, 1916, 11.

[14]"World-Wide Apostolic Faith Camp Meeting," *Word and Witness*, 20 March 1913, 1.

[15]Ibid.

[16]M. M. Pinson, "From Los Angeles World-Wide Camp Meeting," *Word and Witness*, 20 May 1913, 1. The numbers varied: while Pinson reported from 75 to 100 ministers, Woodworth-Etter quoted R. J. Scott's claim that there were 200. See Woodworth-Etter, *A Diary of Signs and Wonders*, 250.

[17]Pinson, "World-Wide Camp Meeting," 1.

[18]Woodworth-Etter, *A Diary of Signs and Wonders*, 250.

[19]Pinson, "World-Wide Camp Meeting," 1.

[20]Flower, "History of the Assemblies of God," 24–A. Early proponents often highlighted their distinctive usage with capital letters; thus, THE NAME, THE NEW THING, et al.

[21]Frank J. Ewart, *The Phenomenon of Pentecost* (Houston: Herald Publishing House, 1947; Hazelwood, MO: World Aflame Press, rev. ed., 1975), 94ff. (page references are to revised edition; it should be further noted that quotations do not always correspond between the two editions). McAlister says that George Studd, his wife, and several women were the source of the revelation that God was about to do "a New Thing." That conviction stemmed from their claim that for the meetings they had been given Isaiah 43:19, "Behold, I will do a new thing. . . ." See R. E. McAlister, "Is the 'New Thing' New?" *Truth Advocate* (August 1949): p.16.

[22]Ewart, *Pentecost*, 106.

[23]Ibid.

[24]Ibid., 110.

[25]Ibid., 112.

[26]Ibid., 113.

[27]See, for example, *Word and Witness* (May 1915): 4; A. G. Garr, "Have You Been Baptized in the Name of Jesus Christ?" *Victorious Gospel* (Spring 1915): 3.

[28]Quoted in Paul D. Dugas, comp., *The Life and Writings of Elder G. T. Haywood* (Portland, OR: Apostolic Book Publishers, 1984), 22.

[29]Beverly Carradine, *A Box of Treasure* (Chicago: The Christian Witness Co., 1910), 175.

[30]Ibid.

[31]The Executive Presbytery had taken steps to prepare a Pentecostal hymnal in November of 1914. Kerr, Andrew Fraser, and F. F. Bosworth had been appointed a committee to compile the book. See Executive Presbytery Minutes, 25 November 1914, 5. What resulted is uncertain. However, the 1923 General Council adopted a similar resolution, and the following year a full-page ad in the *Pentecostal Evangel* announced, "We now have our own / PENTECOSTAL SONG BOOK / *Songs of Pentecostal Fellowship*," *Pentecostal Evangel*, August 30, 1924, 16.

[32]John G. Lake to Charles Fox Parham, 24 March 1927, 2–3, Assemblies of God Archives.

[33]Quoted in Carl Brumback, *Suddenly From Heaven* (Springfield, MO: Gospel Publishing House, 1961), 202.

[34]J. R. Flower, "Editorial Comment on Issue," *Weekly Evangel*, 17 July 1915, 1.

[35]Ibid.

[36]Ibid.

[37]E. N. Bell, "Editorial Statement on Preliminary Statement Which Appears Above," *Word and Witness*, June 1915, 1.

[38]Ibid.

[39]Ibid.

[40]See, for example, E. N. Bell, "The Sad New Issue," *Word and Witness*, June 1915, 2,3.

[41]Rodgers left the General Council in 1916, but initiated steps in 1921 that resulted in his return to the Fellowship. See correspondence, Rodgers file, Assemblies of God Secretariat.

[42]E. N. Bell, "There is Safety in Counsel," *Weekly Evangel*, 18 September 1915, 1. The same article also appeared in the October issue of *Word and Witness*.

[43]Bell to J. C. Brickey, 20 August 1920, 1. Assemblies of God Archives.

[44]"Personal Statement," *Weekly Evangel*, 18 September 1915, 4. This article also appeared in the October 1915 issue of *Word and Witness*, 4.

⁴⁵See, for example, J. R. Flower, "The Lord's Supper," *Weekly Evangel,* 24 July 1915, 1; E. N. Bell, "Jesus, the Great Life-Giving Spirit," *Weekly Evangel,* 17 July 1915, 2; E. N. Bell, "To Act in the Name of Another," *Word and Witness,* May 1915, 2 (essentially a study of what the Bible said about acting in Jesus' name, it was the first of this genre of articles that sought to address issues raised by Oneness teaching; an abbreviated version appeared simultaneously in the May 1 issue of the *Weekly Evangel).*

⁴⁶Oneness advocates offered for distribution text by Bell that they claimed was the unamended version. See pamphlet, "Who Is Jesus Christ?" Assemblies of God Archives.

⁴⁷*Word and Witness,* September 1915, 1.

⁴⁸*Weekly Evangel,* 16 October 1915, 2.

⁴⁹General Council Minutes, 1915, 5.

⁵⁰Flower, "History of the Assemblies of God," 26.

⁵¹Brumback, *Suddenly From Heaven,* 203. See also Goss, *Winds of God,* 155. It is not clear whether Goss is referring to meetings of the General Council or the Church of God in Christ, which he was a member of prior to joining the Council in 1914. He does use the term "conference" to describe the meetings rather the (A/G) term "council," and he left the organization in 1916, after the fourth meeting of the Council.

⁵²Flower implies that Haywood had been a member of the General Council. See Flower, "History of the Assemblies of God," 28.

⁵³Ibid., 27.

⁵⁴General Council Minutes, 1916, 3.

⁵⁵Frodsham's appointment to this committee is interesting, since this was the first General Council he attended. A young and talented man, Frodsham had migrated from England, where he had edited a Pentecostal periodical called *Victory.* In 1916 he was living in California. Welch later recounted that at the 1916 General Council, the respected "Mother" Mary Arthur of Galena, Kansas, had confirmed his own impression that Frodsham was "God's man" for the *Evangel.* The paper had carried several articles by him that had given him some visibility in the Assemblies of God. From 1916, Frodsham served as the *Evangel's* assistant editor. From 1921 until 1949 (with a brief break in 1929), Frodsham was editor. From 1916 until 1919, he also served the Fellowship as general secretary. See Faith Campbell, *Prophet With a Pen* (Springfield, MO: Gospel Publishing House, 1974).

⁵⁶General Council Minutes, 1916, 10.

⁵⁷Flower, "History of the Assemblies of God," 28.

⁵⁸Robert Anderson has argued that the Oneness controversy within the Assemblies of God should be understood as a political strategy

dominated by Flower to reorganize the leadership of the Fellowship. See Anderson, *Vision*, 183ff.

[59]Flower, "History of the Assemblies of God," 29.

[60]The name of the *Evangel* was changed several times: On March 13, 1915, the publication was changed from *The Christian Evangel* to *Weekly Evangel*. On June 1, 1918, it was changed back to *The Christian Evangel*. Finally on October 18, 1919, it became the *Pentecostal Evangel*, the name it still bears today.

[61]See, for example, F. F. Bosworth, "Confirming the Word by Signs Following: Jesus Saves, Heals and Baptizes," *Latter Rain Evangel*, December 1908, 7–8. This report of Bosworth's tent campaign in Plymouth, Indiana, included accounts of Bernice Lee and others having spoken in tongues and having been understood by foreigners present.

[62]See Bosworth's account included in Woodworth-Etter, *A Diary of Signs and Wonders*, 172–175.

[63]William Piper, founder of the Stone Church, for example, had not dogmatically accepted evidential tongues; neither did the numerous former Dowieites who banded together to form the Zion Faith Homes; Agnes Ozman had voiced her doubts in Piper's *Latter Rain Evangel*; even J. R. Flower had pointed out the tendencies of overzealous espousal of evidential tongues in his magazine, *Pentecost*.

[64]F. F. Bosworth, "Do All Speak With Tongues?" booklet (New York: The Christian Alliance Publishing Co., n.d.) 3.

[65]Ibid., 4.

[66]F. F. Bosworth to J. W. Welch, 24 July 1918, Assemblies of God Archives.

[67]Ibid.

[68]General Council Minutes, 1918, 8.

[69]Probably the only other prominent individual who left the General Council with Bosworth was his brother, B. B. Bosworth, who established a lifelong affiliation with the Christian and Missionary Alliance. F. F. Bosworth later left the Alliance for independent ministry, achieving prominence as a healing evangelist and later identifying with the emerging healing revival of the late 1940s. See obituary of the Bosworth brothers (who died less than a month apart), *Alliance Weekly*, 23 April 1958, 15.

[70]The full list includes R. L. Erickson, pastor of the Stone Church: dismissed on a morals charge; Howard Goss, Bennett Lawrence, D. C. O. Opperman, and H. G. Rodgers: withdrew over the "new issue" (Rodgers later returned); C. B. Fockler, W. F. Carothers, and John Sinclair: withdrew because of their distaste for organization; Andrew L. Fraser; F. F. Bosworth: resigned because of disagreement over tongues.

Chapter 11: Communicating the Faith: Proceeding into the Second Generation

[1]By 1918, the General Presbytery had voted to request all ministers to surrender any credentials other than those of the General Council. General Presbytery Minutes, 9 September 1918, 1.

[2]Frederick Lewis Allen, *Only Yesterday* (New York: Harper and Row, 1964), 76.

[3]Aimee Semple McPherson, *This Is That* (Los Angeles: Bridal Call Publishing Co., 1921), 149ff.

[4]Several autobiographical accounts give her view of her expanding efforts. The most recent is Aimee Semple McPherson, *The Story of My Life* (Waco, TX: Word Books, 1973). The first, *This is That*, was published in 1923 and contains sermons, testimonies, and pictures of her meetings.

[5]McPherson to Welch and Bell, 28 March 1922, McPherson file, Assemblies of God Secretariat.

[6]For the story of the Open Bible Standard Churches, see Robert Bryant Mitchell, *Heritage and Horizons* (Des Moines: Open Bible Publishers, 1982).

[7]Charles Price, *The Story of My Life* (Pasadena: Privately published, 1935).

[8]Jamieson file, Assemblies of God Secretariat; S. A. Jamieson, "How a Presbyterian Preacher Received the Baptism," pamphlet (Kansas City, MO: Gospel Union Publishing Co., n.d.).

[9]Eloise M. Richey, *What God Hath Wrought in the Life of Raymond T. Richey* (Houston: United Prayer and Workers' League, 1937), 30–31.

[10]Warren Collins file, Assemblies of God Secretariat.

[11]*Hattiesburg American,* 16 October 1920, 8; 18 October 1920, 8; 21 October 1920, 7; 25 October 1920, 8; 26 October 1920, 8; 27 October 1920, 8; 30 October 1920, 8; 1 November 1920, 8; 2 November 1920, 8; 3 November 1920, 8; 5 November 1920, 8; 8 November 1920, 8.

[12]For several years, Richey was out of fellowship with the Assemblies of God. Throughout his life, his efforts had an independent character. In the 1920s questions were raised about the validity of his marriage. His wife, Eloise Mae Richey (whom acquaintances respected as a "spiritual" woman), had had a prior marriage annulled. A. P. Collins had performed the ceremony uniting Eloise and Raymond. Richey's most vocal opponents sought to censure Collins for his role. Collins, a mild-tempered man, responded with unaccustomed vigor. Although the incident was trivial, it helped focus attention on the persistent need for a clear policy regarding irregular marital situations affecting the clergy.

¹³John Lake to Charles Parham, 24 March 1927, Assemblies of God Archives. W. F. Carothers shared these sentiments. His sympathy with Lake can be understood best by a comparison of his 1909 book, *Church Government,* with the situation in the Assemblies of God in the 1920s. See also Carothers' letter of resignation, Carothers file, Assemblies of God Secretariat.

¹⁴General Council Minutes, 1941, 66.

¹⁵Welch moved to California; Flower accepted a pastorate in Scranton, Pennsylvania. For the next ten years he and his wife, Alice, gave invaluable leadership to the Eastern District. Eastern Bible Institute (now Valley Forge Christian College) resulted largely from their efforts. See Welch and Flower files, Assemblies of God Archives.

¹⁶General Council Minutes, 1929, 85.

¹⁷Fred Vogler to J. R. Evans, 5 December 1932, Vogler minister's file, Assemblies of God Archives.

¹⁸Although treatment of the issue is uneven, it is clear from many tracts, sermons, and songs that an informal Pentecostal consensus opposed the use of alcohol. Parham, however, had opposed Prohibition both because he opposed strong government and because he distrusted leaders of the Prohibition movement. He advocated, rather, the removal of all taxes on liquor. He had insisted that as long as the government had a vested interest in the liquor industry, it would thrive. See H. W. Schermer, "Civic Righteousness," *The Apostolic Faith,* October 1913, 15–17. Parham had a dim view of political leadership. "The average politician," he claimed, "does not know whether Christ was crucified on Calvary or shot at Bunker Hill." *The Apostolic Faith,* December 1914, 9.

¹⁹For her story, see "From the Footlights to the Light of the Cross, or From Movieland to Canaanland," *Full Gospel Messenger* (June 1931): 2, 3, 8.

²⁰Pennington's marriage had collapsed before she began evangelizing. In 1950 she resigned from the Assemblies of God, taking with her the church in Louisiana she was pastoring. Her daughter, Edith Lorraine (born in 1927), assisted her mother's later efforts.

²¹See, for example, Carothers file, Assemblies of God Secretariat.

²²See, for example, miscellaneous correspondence in the P. C. Nelson Room of the library at Southwestern College, Waxahachie, TX.

²³Fred Vogler file, Assemblies of God Archives.

²⁴Robert and Marie Brown, for example, had a small home in New Jersey and visited relatives and friends in Great Britain.

²⁵General Council Minutes, 1935, 97.

²⁶Ibid, 96–97.

²⁷These statistics, given in the General Council Minutes of 1939 and

1941, very likely do not tell the whole story. Year after year a substantial number of congregations failed to report; the difficulty of coming up with accurate figures from the past is well known.

Chapter 12: "Into All the World . . . Unto All People": Publishing and Missions

[1]Both of the first editors at Gospel Publishing House had edited papers for several years before the General Council formed. J. Roswell Flower was barely twenty years old in 1908 when he first published *Pentecost*, a monthly that he later turned over to A. S. Copley in Kansas City. (Copley changed the title to *Grace and Glory* and continued to publish the paper, giving its message a self-consciously Reformed theological cast that set it apart from most Pentecostal publications.) With the encouragement of D. Wesley Myland, in 1911 Flower and his wife, Alice, began to issue the *The Christian Evangel*. Eudorus Bell, who served for a time as editor of both *The Christian Evangel* and *Word and Witness,* had begun his publishing efforts with a four-page monthly, *The Apostolic Faith*. (There were several papers using this name. Parham's was published in various places and renumbered at least five times; Florence Crawford's was issued from Portland, Oregon, after she left Seymour, who had published it in Los Angeles. Several of Parham's supporters published papers of the same name which had primarily local circulation.)

[2]People whose articles appeared regularly in respected papers frequently found their ministries considerably extended. In the Assemblies of God alone, for example—at least partly on the strength of several articles—Stanley Frodsham became one of the framers of the Statement of Fundamental Truths and an executive of the Fellowship during the first General Council he attended; Lilian Yeomans, whose articles appeared regularly in the *Pentecostal Evangel* in the 1920s, gained acclaim far beyond that which her classes at Aimee Semple McPherson's L.I.F.E. Bible College would have warranted; Elizabeth Sisson, who was seventy-four years old when she received credentials in 1917, became a highly respected teacher in the Assemblies of God largely through her writings; and Ernest Williams' articles extended his influence throughout the constituency, contributing to his election as general superintendent in 1929.

[3]Seymour's *Apostolic Faith,* for example, carried the following announcement: "If you know of any hungry souls to whom you wish the paper sent, send in their addresses and as the Lord permits, we will send the paper. We are having 5,000 of this issue printed. The money came in answer to prayer. The next issue will come out as He permits." *The Apostolic Faith,* September 1906, 4. Parham offered his *Apostolic Faith* "free of charge to all who desire[d] it" but noted that he would "receive donations of any amount" to defray publishing costs.

(The first song included in an early hymnal used by Pentecostals,

The Best of All, expressed the simple confidence that "the Lord will provide":

> In some way or other the Lord will provide;
> It may not be my way, it may not be thy way,
> And yet in His own way, "The Lord will provide.")

⁴Seymour had claimed, for example, "The Lord showed us before starting this paper that it was to be free. We were not to tax the people.... It was to be a Holy Ghost paper, and it was to be free indeed.... It costs a cent a copy to send it anywhere in the world, and the Lord can afford that." *The Apostolic Faith,* December 1906, 2. In extreme cases, this included a reluctance to sign articles or to acknowledge editors: "The writers and workers in the office live by faith," Seymour noted. "All work for the honor and glory of God. This we believe will be a real protection to the paper to keep it pure, for unless one is filled with the love of God, they do not covet to work without honor or money." *The Apostolic Faith,* December 1906, 2. See also "Pentecostal Testimony," *The Household of God* (May 1909): 10: "If the Lord ordered the paper published, and the faith was perfect in God, not in men, the money would come."

⁵Ibid.

⁶*Word and Work,* April 1907, 112.

⁷J. R. Flower's *Pentecost,* for example, regularly contained unofficial directories of Apostolic Faith missions and missionaries, which Flower endeavored to keep updated.

⁸*Word and Witness* had its origins in the doctrinal dispute over sanctification. M. M. Pinson had been a corresponding editor for Mrs. E. A. Sexton's *Bridegroom's Messenger,* a monthly holiness-Pentecostal publication originally published by G. B. Cashwell and later issued from Atlanta. When Sexton refused to publish articles advocating Pinson's "finished work" views, he broke his relationship with the paper. Pinson decided to publish his own periodical to advocate "correct" teaching on sanctification. He used the Nashville, Tennessee, publishing facilities of the Pentecostal Mission's John Benson until Benson discontinued his service to tongues-speaking Pentecostals. At about the same time, Pinson learned of Bell's *Apostolic Faith.* The two men decided to combine their efforts. Bell assumed editorial responsibility. Taking the size of the *Apostolic Faith* and the name of Pinson's *Word and Witness,* the paper played a dynamic role in facilitating the events that climaxed in the creation of the General Council. M. M. Pinson to J. R. Flower, 23 January 1949, Pinson file, Assemblies of God Archives.

Parham noted that the proliferation of papers, many of which were edited by people who lacked both financial resources and sustained inclination, did not strengthen the movement. "The curse of this movement," he complained in December 1912, "has been the starting of papers and getting people to subscribe for them and perhaps receive a copy or two, and then no more, for the thing has played out." *The Apostolic Faith,* December 1912, 6.

⁹*Weekly Evangel,* 16 October 1915, 2.

¹⁰General Council Minutes, 1915, 7.

¹¹Since 1914, the two papers had become increasingly similar. Material sent in for one was often repeated in the other; copy that did not fit into one usually found its way into the other.

¹²General Council Minutes, 1919, 24.

¹³Flower, "History of the Assemblies of God," 31.

¹⁴Frodsham was appointed—rather than elected—to the position. By action of the General Presbytery in 1920, several positions became appointive: editor of the *Evangel,* manager of the publishing house, missionary secretary-treasurer. General Presbytery Minutes, 27 September 1920. See also the 1920 General Council Minutes, pp. 21-22.

¹⁵His interest in the progress of Pentecostalism elsewhere provoked considerable criticism, however. Welch, for example, felt that Frodsham unduly favored non-Council ministers and especially that he unacceptably promoted his British friends. John Welch to J. R. Evans, 8 January 1926, Welch file, Assemblies of God Archives.

¹⁶General Council Minutes, 1919, 11.

¹⁷Ibid.

¹⁸Ibid.

¹⁹Combined General Council Minutes, 1925, 53.

²⁰Ibid., 25.

²¹General Council Minutes 1919, 10–11.

²²*Weekly Evangel,* 12 February 1916, 8.

²³Ibid.

²⁴Combined General Council Minutes, 1925, 44–45.

²⁵These books reveal the predominantly white and rural assumptions and biases of the reading constituency.

²⁶Charles Parham's paper, *The Apostolic Faith,* is a noteworthy exception. It reflected the virtual absence of missionary motivation among his followers after 1906.

²⁷Such was the case with Levi Lupton. Lupton, an evangelical Quaker who had formed an evangelistic society well before he identified with Pentecostalism, threw the weight of his influence behind Pentecostal missions—until his adulterous relationship with his secretary was exposed in 1910.

²⁸From 1909, when Thomas Barratt went to India, regular reports

of the progress of Pentecostalism in India appeared in *Confidence* as well as in many American periodicals.

[29]Early in 1909, for example, Blanche Hamilton, an Alliance missionary in India, wrote: "Nearly all of the missionaries are baptized here, and have the gift of tongues also." She noted that Indians were speaking English, a circumstance also reported by Minnie Abrams, who worked with the highly esteemed Pandita Ramabai. "What wonderful days!" Hamilton concluded. "A Portion of a Letter from C. and M. A. Missionary," *The Household of God* (May 1909): 6.

[30]An example of the missionaries who embraced Pentecostalism on the field is Alice Eveline Luce. The oldest child of an Anglican rector, Luce went to India at twenty-two in 1896 under the Episcopal Missionary Society. While in India, on February 10, 1910, she received the baptism in the Holy Spirit. Returning to England in 1912 as an invalid, she continued to serve the Episcopal Missionary Society until 1914, when she moved to California. In 1915, she helped inaugurate Assemblies of God efforts among Latin Americans. Luce file, Assemblies of God Secretariat.

[31]Quoted in Noel Perkin, "Our First Five Years," *Pentecostal Evangel,* 25 October 1964, 14.

[32]See, for example, Florence L. Burpee, "What Denomination Are You?" *Weekly Evangel,* 26 February 1916, 7.

[33]General Council Minutes, 23 November 1914, 12.

[34]Some were undoubtedly unaware of the extent of American support for missions; others disdained non-Pentecostal efforts as ineffective; some disparaged the confusion of culture and religion that they observed among missionaries. They particularly distrusted those missionaries who became sensitive in unacceptable ways to the needs of the host culture.

[35]It is unclear precisely how or if this affected the actual status of women. The wording of the resolution, given below, suggests that women may not have been ordained (except as evangelists)—although some were licensed—between about 1925 and 1935:

> Resolved, That we recommend no persons be ordained as missionaries. Persons qualified for the full ministry, whether called to the home work or the foreign field, should be ordained to the ministry. Those not qualified for the ministry should not be ordained even though endorsed for the foreign field as workers.

Many missionaries, male and female, were sent out without ordination, but with Council endorsement. Such endorsement, however, did not include the right to perform any ordinances of the church. Since women did not qualify for ordination to the "full ministry" in the United States, it seems clear that under the above resolution they also no longer qualified for ordination as missionaries.

³⁶Susan Easton, "Application for Credentials," Easton file, Assemblies of God Secretariat.

³⁷General Council Minutes, 1919, 8.

³⁸Ibid., 9.

³⁹Flower, "History of the Assemblies of God," 31.

⁴⁰"Missionary Treasurer's Report," General Council Minutes, 1919, 7–10.

⁴¹General Council Minutes, 1919, 19.

⁴²Quoted in Noel Perkin, "Our First Five Years," 14.

⁴³Quoted in Noel Perkin, "Highlights of the 20s (1920–1924)," *Pentecostal Evangel,* 29 November 1964, 17.

⁴⁴Ibid., 18.

⁴⁵Ibid.

⁴⁶"In Memoriam," *Pentecostal Evangel,* 16 August 1924, 7.

⁴⁷General Council Minutes, 1925, 47.

⁴⁸Pentecostals shared this sense of impending cataclysm with fundamentalists. Rooted largely in their Darbyite dispensational eschatology, it discounted the positive accomplishments of the era (which liberals hailed as progress) and proclaimed imminent judgment. Pentecostalism—and, in fact, fundamentalism—had had another eschatological option. Assemblies of God leaders frequently cited the writings of A. J. Gordon, a historicist (rather than a futurist) premillennialist. Gordon acknoweldged progress, but saw evil advancing with good. He anticipated Christ's premillennial return but rejected the totally negative view of culture that eventually prevailed among most American premillennialists (popularized through the Scofield Bible). Gordon's views, expressed, for example, in his book *Ecce Venit,* promote a radically different worldview than those espoused in the virtual handbook of American premillennialism, William Blackstone's *Jesus Is Coming.* The Assemblies of God accepted some but not all of Gordon's emphases. It is interesting to speculate about the differences embracing the worldview posited by Gordon might have made in premillennialists' attitudes toward culture. For the differences between historicist and futurist premillennialists, see Ernest Sandeen, *The Roots of Fundamentalism.*

⁴⁹For an examination of the relation of missionaries' translating the Scriptures to the arousing of national pride in Third-World cultures, see Lamin Manneh, "Christian Missions and the Western Guilt Complex," *The Christian Century,* 8 April 1987, 330–334.

⁵⁰General Council Minutes, 1929, 58.

⁵¹General Council Minutes, 1925, 57.

⁵²Noel Perkin, "Personal Testimony," unpublished ms., Assemblies of God Archives, 3. Perkin later questioned whether this experience

of tongues speech in fact constituted Spirit baptism marked by evidential tongues. Since he had spoken in tongues during fervent prayer, he concluded in the mid-1920s that the tongues had not been evidential. By that time, he was an Assemblies of God pastor. His suggestion that he resign until he was satisfied that his experience in fact conformed to Assemblies of God expectations was rejected. Perkin file, Assemblies of God Secretariat.

[53]Ibid., 5.

[54]In action related to the adoption of a constitution and bylaws in 1927, the title of the Fellowship's chief executive officer was changed from chairman to general superintendent.

[55]Noel Perkin, "Coordination and Advance," *Pentecostal Evangel*, 27 December 1964, 11.

[56]Ibid.

[57]Perkin, "Coordination and Advance," *Pentecostal Evangel*, 27 December 1964, 11.

[58]*Weekly Evangel*, 19 August 1916, 12.

[59]General Council Minutes, 1929, 72.

[60]General Council Minutes, 1933, 60.

[61]Noel Perkin, "Call to Advance," *Pentecostal Evangel*, 24 January 1965, 9.

[62]General Council Minutes, 1931, 58.

[63]General Council Minutes, 1933, 59.

[64]General Council Minutes, 1937, 92.

[65]The two were released in 1940 but were arrested again when they sought to procure exit visas to return to the United States. Katherine Voronaeff finally reached the U. S. in 1960, after having spent twenty years in Russian prisons. Her husband's fate is unknown.

[66]General Council Minutes, 1933, 109.

[67]General Council Minutes, 1931, 53.

[68]Ibid., 53.

[69]Ibid., 64.

[70]Ibid., 57.

[71]General Council Minutes, 1941, 86.

[72]Ibid., 87.

Chapter 13: Education and Home Missions

[1]Opperman's unpublished diary notes his qualifications for leadership in education. Like many other Pentecostals, he had moved frequently and had known economic hardship. His family moved from Indiana to Missouri to Florida, and returned to Indiana after his

father's death in 1888. Opperman picked, sized, and packed oranges to help support the family; in Indiana, he worked on farms in the summer and attended school in the winter. His educational background was meager for one who won a reputation for leadership in education—although it amounted to more than that of many Pentecostals. Opperman attended a Dunkard college in Mt. Morris, Illionois, for two terms. In 1899, he studied for two months at Moody Bible Institute. After teaching for several years, he enrolled for two summer terms (1900 and 1901) at Illinois State Normal School. In September 1901, he began teaching in John Alexander Dowie's newly founded Zion City, where he eventually became a school administrator until sickness in 1905 forced him to move to Texas. D. C. O. Opperman, "Diary," Assemblies of God Archives.

²Chisolm's school in Mississippi continued under other leadership. See the *Weekly Evangel,* 28 August 1915, 3. Chisolm's name appears on only one General Council roster, published in the fall of 1914.

³See, for example, articles in the issues of *Weekly Evangel* for 24 July 1915 and 28 August 1915.

⁴*Ozark School Herald* (April 1916): 1.

⁵Hugh Barbour, *The Quakers in Puritan England* (New Haven: Yale University Press, 1964), 158.

⁶Opperman was killed in a car-train accident in California.

⁷Luce's file documents both her concerns and activities relating to correspondence education. Assemblies of God Secretariat.

⁸Executive Presbytery Minutes, 25 November 1919.

⁹General Presbytery Minutes, 25 September 1920; 27 September 1920.

¹⁰Executive Presbytery Minutes, 1 August 1922.

¹¹Executive Presbytery Minutes, 2 August 1922.

¹²Executive Presbytery Minutes, 2 August 1922. The men whose decisions transformed Central Bible Institute from an idea to a reality were E. N. Bell, J. W. Welch, D. W. Kerr, Stanley H. Frodsham, and Herman L. Harvey. Three other men sat with these executives and participated in discussions, but did not vote: Williard Peirce, Bert Williams, and Samuel A. Jamieson. The custom of inviting Fellowship leaders or former executives to attend sessions of both the General and the Executive Presbyteries continued throughout the 1920s.

¹³Executive Presbytery Minutes, 5 January 1923. These instructions to "proceed to the east" would seem to indicate that the executives already knew whom they would invite, although the minutes contain no proposed names.

¹⁴Executive Presbytery Minutes, 9 November 1923.

¹⁵"My Journey to the Unknown Sanctuary," *Pentecostal Evangel,* 31 July 1943, quoted in Brumback, *Suddenly from Heaven,* 237.

[16]Pearlman wrote both adult student and adult teacher's quarterlies for Gospel Publishing House and initiated the immensely popular servicemen's publication *Reveille*. For his biography, see Irene Pearlman, *Myer Pearlman and His Friends* (Springfield, MO: privately published, 1953).

[17]This was also true at other Bible institutes, where short-term training, evening classes, and summer programs attracted many who never completed the full programs. For a study of several key Bible institutes, see Virginia Brereton, "The Formation of American Bible Schools, 1880–1940," Ed.D thesis, Columbia University, 1981.

[18]Allen, *Only Yesterday*, 51.

[19]General Council Minutes, 1929, 83.

[20]W. I. Evans, *This River Must Flow* (Springfield, MO: Gospel Publishing House, 1954), 13–14.

[21]Quoted in Kenneth D. Barney, "The Aftermath of Pentecost," *Paraclete* 21 (Summer 1987): 14.

[22]General Council Minutes, 1931, 85.

[23]General Council Minutes, 1935, 100–101.

[24]For Vogler's biography, see Edith L. Blumhofer, "Fred Vogler," unpublished manuscript, Assemblies of God Archives.

[25]The decision to separate missions from publishing had been a result of growth rather than of a recognition of movement in a new direction.

[26]General Council Minutes, 1937, 104.

[27]Ibid., 105.

[28]Ibid., 108.

[29]David Moberg, *The Church as a Social Institution: The Sociology of American Religion* (Grand Rapids: Baker Book House, 1984), 120.

[30]General Council Minutes, 1937, 61.

[31]General Council Minutes, 1939, 61.

[32]Ibid., 61–62.

[33]General Council Minutes, 1941, 58.

[34]Ibid., 62.

[35]General Council Minutes, 1941, 77.

Chapter 14: Pilgrims and Citizens: Some Dilemmas of Dual Allegiance

[1]Robert Anderson discusses thoroughly the subject of Pentecostals and society in *Vision*, Anderson, 195–222.

[2]Six stanzas of this old hymn "Am I a Soldier of the Cross?" were

included in *The Best of All,* a hymnal used widely in early Assemblies of God congregations, 121.

[3]Lelia Morris, "Victory All the Time," in *The Best of All,* 5.

[4]Lelia Morris, "On the Firing Line," in *The Best of All,* 3, 4.

[5]See especially Mrs. Clarence Shreffler's letter, published April 21, 1917, 4, and "The Great War and the Speedy Return of Our Lord: Light on the Present Crisis," *Weekly Evangel,* 10 April 1917, 3. The same issue cited H. Grattan Guinness, *Light for the Last Days* (1886), to the effect that those living in 1917 would "have reached one of the most important, perhaps the most momentous of these terminal years of crisis." For Washington's vision, see the *Weekly Evangel,* 25 March 1916, 5,8,9.

[6]The vision was printed in tract form, entitled "General Washington's Vision," and circulated by the Christian Workers Union in Framingham, MA.

[7]*Weekly Evangel,* 22 April 1916, 6. As the war ended without the anticipated climax of Christ's return, Bell and Frodsham signed an appeal issued through *The Christian Evangel,* 24 August 1918, for readers to join in two days of prayer (November 3 and 4, 1918) "inviting Jesus, our heavenly Bridegroom, to come back." Still convinced that "the time [had] come for Jesus to return," the two expressed what was to be the final official effort to actualize this conviction of many Pentecostals.

[8]Alexander Boddy, "Is the European War Justifiable?" *The Christian Evangel,* 12 December 1914, 1.

[9]William B. McCafferty, "Shall Christians Go to War?" *The Christian Evangel,* 16 January 1915, 1.

[10]Frank Bartleman, "Present Day Conditions," *The Christian Evangel,* 5 June 1915, 1; Frank Bartleman, "The European War," *The Christian Evangel,* 10 July 1915, 1; Frank Bartleman, "What Will the Harvest Be?" *The Christian Evangel,* 7 August 1915, 1–2. For a thorough consideration of Bartleman's views on war and other social issues, see Cecil M. Robeck's introduction to Frank Bartleman, *Witness to Pentecost* (New York: Garland Publishing, Inc., 1985).

[11]Other Pentecostals shared Bartleman's conviction that the war was economically motivated. The April 29, 1916, issue of the *Weekly Evangel,* 7, published a poem by George T. Sisler entitled "War 'Profits' ":

> ". . . Do you to whom people have granted great power
>
> Make boast of the work you have done,
>
> In hurling poor men at other men's throats
>
> With a longing to kill and to burn?
>
> Know ye not that these men you have fired with hate,

With a hunger and thirst for strife,
Will at last stand with you there where all shall bow
down
To a mighty omnipotent Christ?

". . . Then 'what doth it profit?' this question so old,
Yet with meaning and force still new,
Is asked of you now as you stand with the power,
And the wealth you have gained about you.

When you know that those men—filled with anger and
hate—
Whom you spurred on with your greed and lust,
Must with you finally stand at the judgment bar
And be judged by a God who is just?"

[12]Frank Bartleman, "War and the Christian," pamphlet, Assemblies of God Archives, 3.

[13]Ibid.

[14]Ibid.

[15]Stanley Frodsham, "Our Heavenly Citizenship," *Weekly Evangel,* 11 September 1915, 3. See also Howard N. Kenyon, "A Social History of the Assemblies of God: Race Relations, Women and Ministry, and Attitudes toward War" (Ph.D. diss., Baylor University, 1987).

[16]It is significant that the Booth-Clibborns and Bartleman chose during the war to side with Oneness Pentecostals, among whom the radical restorationist vision of the early movement survived longer.

[17]S. H. Booth-Clibborn, *Should a Christian Fight?* (Swengel, PA: Bible Truth Depot, n.d.), 39.

[18]Ibid., 38.

[19]Ibid., 39–40; see also S. H. Booth-Clibborn, "The Christian and War. Is It Too Late?" *Weekly Evangel,* 28 April 1917, 5; 19 May 1917, 4, 5.

[20]Quoted from "Blood Against Blood" by A. S. Booth-Clibborn, "What Is War?" *Weekly Evangel,* 21 April 1917, 2. Booth-Clibborn attributes the sentence quoted to John Wesley.

[21]"Compulsory Military Service: An English Conscientious Objector's Testimony" *Weekly Evangel,* 28 April 1917, 7.

[22]*Weekly Evangel,* 25 March 1916, 5, 8, 9.

[23]Frank Bartleman, "In the Last Days," *Word and Work,* September 1916, 393.

[24]"The Pentecostal Movement and the Conscription Law," *Weekly Evangel,* 4 August 1917, 6,7.

[25]Ibid. Frodsham's pacifistic views are especially significant when one recalls his strong ties to his British background.

[26]Ibid. In its appeal to the Sermon on the Mount, this resolution demonstrates how different Pentecostal dispensationalism was from fundamentalist dispensationalism.

[27]Ibid.

[28]Roger Robins, "Attitudes Toward War and Peace in the Assemblies of God," 31, unpublished ms., Assemblies of God Archives. See also Jay Beamon, "Pentecostal Pacifism: The Origin, Development and Rejection of Pacific Belief Among Pentecostals" (M. Div. Thesis, North American Baptist Seminary, 1982).

[29]W. I. Evans file, Assemblies of God Archives.

[30]General Council Minutes, 1917, 17–18.

[31]Dispensationalists divided along similar lines, with a small faction, dominated by Plymouth Brethren views, opting for pacifism. See Ernest Sandeen, *The Roots of Fundamentalism*. (Assemblies of God publications carried articles by non-Pentecostal prophecy teachers who shared their sense of the eschatological import of the war. See, for example, C. I. Scofield, "The War in the Light of Prophecy," *Weekly Evangel,* 28 October 1916, 6, 7; citation from H. Grattan Guinness in "Signs in the Heavens Above," *Weekly Evangel,* 10 April 1917, 3; Mrs. Reader Harris, "Nearing the End of the Pentecostal Age," *Weekly Evangel,* 15 July 1916, 7, 9.)

[32]E. N. Bell, "Questions and Answers," *Weekly Evangel,* 19 October 1918, 5.

[33]In his retirement, Ernest Williams, reflecting on the contrast in Assemblies of God attitudes toward the two world wars, expressed this sentiment to the author in an interview in Springfield, MO, June 18, 1976.

[34]Anderson, *Vision,* 222.

[35]R. Laurence Moore, *Religious Outsiders and the Making of Americans* (New York: Oxford University Press, 1986), 143.

[36]See, for example, standard articles like those of Letha Dawson Scanzoni and Susan Setta, "Women in Evangelical, Holiness, and Pentecostal Traditions," in *Women and Religion, Volume 3,* 223–265; and Nancy Hardesty, Lucille Sider Dayton, and Donald W. Dayton, "Women in the Holiness Movement: Feminism in the Evangelical Tradition," in *Women of Spirit,* ed. Eleanor McLaughlin (New York: Simon and Schuster, 1979), 226–254.

[37]Charles H. Barfoot and Gerald T. Sheppard, "Prophetic Vs. Priestly Religion: The Changing Role of Women Clergy in Classical Pentecostal Churches," *Review of Religious Research,* 22 September 1980, 2–10.

436 / NOTES TO PAGES 357-362

³⁸Elizabeth Sisson's testimony, "God's Prayer House," *Triumphs of Faith*, 28 (1908) 230ff.

³⁹See, for example, Virginia Lieson Brereton, "Preparing Women for the Lord's Work," in *Women in New Worlds*, eds. Rosemary Skinner Keller, Louise L. Queen, Hilah F. Thomas (Nashville, TN: Abingdon, 1982), 1: 178–199; Virginia Lieson Brereton and Christa Ressmeyer Klein, "American Women in Ministry," in *Women in American Religion* ed. Janet Wilson James (Philadelphia: University of Pennsylvania, 1980), 171–190; Barbara Welter, "She Hath Done What She Could," in *Women in American Religion*, 111–126; Janette Hassey, *No Time for Silence* (Grand Rapids: Zondervan, 1986), 123–143.

⁴⁰See, for example, Martha Tomhave Blauvelt, "Women and Revivalism," in *Women and Religion in America, Volume 1*, eds. Rosemary Ruether and Rosemary Keller, 1–47; for the use of the text "Your sons and your daughters shall prophesy" to legitimate women's ministry, see Barbara Brown Zikmund, "The Struggle for the Right to Preach," 193–241.

⁴¹See, for example, W. F. Carothers, "The Gift of Interpretation," *The Latter Rain Evangel*, October 1910, 7–10.

⁴²W. F. Carothers, *Church Government* (Houston: J. V. Dealy Co., 1909), 43.

⁴³Ibid., 44–45.

⁴⁴Ibid., 44.

⁴⁵Ibid.

⁴⁶Ibid., 46.

⁴⁷Ibid., 45.

⁴⁸Ibid., 47.

⁴⁹Carothers, "Gift of Interpretation," 9.

⁵⁰Baker, *Chronicles*, 117.

⁵¹See, for example, A. J. Gordon, "The Ministry of Women," *Missionary Review of the World* (December 1894): 910–921; A. T. Pierson, "Woman as a Factor in the World's Evangelization," *Missionary Review of the World* (July 1895): 520; Mrs. A. J. Gordon, "Women as Evangelists," appendix 3 in Hassey, *No Time for Silence*, 157–161.

⁵²Janette Hassey overstates women's involvement in the Alliance in *No Time for Silence*, 15–19. The largest number of women to serve on the Alliance Board of Managers at one time was six. They served in 1893 with twenty-four men. A historical statement of the Alliance attitude toward women in ministry is contained in "Report of the Board of Managers Regarding the Role of Women in Ministry in The Christian and Missionary Alliance," Christian and Missionary Alliance Minutes 1981, 307–328.

⁵³For a description of these restrictions, see Leslie A. Andrews, "Re-

stricted Freedom: A. B. Simpson's View of Women," in *The Birth of a Vision* eds. David F. Hartzfeld and Charles Nienkirchen (Alberta, Canada: Horizon House Publishers 1986), 219–240.

[54]Albert B. Simpson, *The Holy Spirit, or Power from on High* (New York: Christian Alliance Publishing Co., 1895), 112.

[55]A. B. Simpson, *Christ in the Bible: 1 Corinthians*, 124–127. This book was part of a series published from 1888 by Simpson's Word, Work and the World Publishing Co., New York.

[56]A. B. Simpson, *Christ in the Bible: Romans*, 286. This was part of a series published from 1888 by Simpson's Word, Work and the World Publishing Co. in New York.

[57]F. L. Chapell, *Eleventh-Hour Laborers* (New York: Christian Alliance Publishing Co., 1898), 59–65.

[58]Ibid.

[59]General Council Minutes, 1914, 1. Early General Council Minutes do not state, however, that delegates had to be men.

[60]Ibid., 7.

[61]Ibid.

[62]General Council Minutes, 1915, 3.

[63]General Council Minutes, 1919, 7.

[64]See ad in the *Weekly Evangel*, 1 January 1916, 9.

[65]General Council Minutes, 1920, 9, 48. One should not overlook two facts: In 1920, women first exercised their new privilege of voting in a national election and Aimee Semple McPherson preached to the General Council.

[66]E. N. Bell, "Questions and Answers," *Weekly Evangel*, 29 January and 5 February, 1916, 8.

[67]Ibid.

[68]E. N. Bell, "Questions and Answers," *Weekly Evangel*, 2 September 1916, 8.

[69]Ibid.

[70]E. N. Bell, "Questions and Answers," *Weekly Evangel*, 10 March 1917, 9.

[71]E. N. Bell, "Questions and Answers," *Weekly Evangel*, 22 July 1916, 8.

[72]Frank Bartleman, "Flapper Evangelists, Fashion's Fools," tract, privately published, circa 1920. Assemblies of God Archives.

[73]Elaine Lawless, "Women's Speech in the Pentecostal Religious Service" (Ph.D. diss., Indiana University, 1982).

[74]Executive Presbytery Minutes, 23 November 1914, 1.

[75]Ibid.

[76]General Council Minutes, 1931, 58.

[77]Ibid.

[78]For the circumstances surrounding the ordination of Esther McDowell, see Esther McDowell file, Assemblies of God Secretariat.

[79]Figures from the 1936 religious census demonstrate that her denomination had some 65.5 males for each 100 females; for the Assemblies of God, the figure was 58.7. See Barfoot and Sheppard, "Prophetic vs. Priestly Religion," 3.

[80]General Council Minutes, 1935, 111.

[81]Ernest Williams' file, Assemblies of God Archives. "May Women Preach?" Typed.

[82]Brereton, "Preparing Women," 184.

[83]Barbara Brown Zikmund, "Winning Ordination for Women in Mainstream Protestant Churches," in *Women and Religion, Volume 3,* 339–340.

[84]John Roach Straton's pamphlet, "Does the Bible Forbid Women To Preach and Pray in Public?" in Hassey, *No Time for Silence,* 189–210.

Bibliography

Addie M. Otis. "Upward Attraction." *Word and Work*, March 1908, 67.

Allen, Frederick Lewis. *Only Yesterday.* New York:Harper and Row, 1964.

Anderson, May Mabette. "The Latter Rain and Its Counterfeit." *Living Truth* (June, July, August 1907).

Anderson, Robert. *Vision of the Disinherited.* New York: Oxford University Press, 1979.

Andrews, Leslie A. "Restricted Freedom: A. B. Simpson's View of Women." In *The Birth of a Vision*, eds. David F. Hartzfeld and Charles Nienkirchen. Alberta, Canada:Horizon House Publishers 1986.

Baker, Elizabeth. *Chronicles of a Faith Life.* Rochester, NY: The Du Bois Press, n.d.

Baker, Mary A. Letter. *The Household of God* (May 1909): 10.

Barbour, Hugh. *The Quakers in Puritan England.* New Haven: Yale University Press, 1964.

Barfoot, Charles H., and Gerald T. Sheppard. "Prophetic Vs. Priestly Religion: The Changing Role of Women Clergy in Classical Pentecostal Churches." *Review of Religious Research*, 22 September 1980, 2–10.

Barney, E. Warren, and Andrew L. Byers, eds. *Songs of the Evening Light.* Moundsville, WV: Gospel Trumpet Publishing Company, 1897.

Barney, Kenneth D. "The Aftermath of Pentecost." *Paraclete* 21 (Summer 1987): 14.

Bartleman, Frank. *How Pentecost Came to Los Angeles.* Los Angeles: n.p., 1925.

_____. "The European War." *The Christian Evangel,* 10 July 1915, 1.

_____. "Flapper Evangelists, Fashion's Fools." Tract. Privately published, circa 1920. Assemblies of God Archives.

_____. "In the Last Days." *Word and Work,* September 1916, 393.

_____. "Present Day Conditions." *The Christian Evangel,* 5 June 1915, 1.

_____. "War and the Christian." Pamphlet. Assemblies of God Archives.

_____. "What Will the Harvest Be?" *The Christian Evangel,* 7 August 1915, 1–2.

Bauman, Louis S. *The Tongues Movement.* Winona Lake, IN: BMH Books, 1963.

Beamon, Jay. "Pentecostal Pacifism: The Origin, Development and Rejection of Pacific Belief Among Pentecostals." M.Div. thesis, North American Baptist Seminary, 1982.

Bell, E. N. "Bible Order v. Fanaticism." *Word and Witness,* 20 March 1914, 2.

_____. "Editorial Statement on Preliminary Statement Which Appears Above." *Word and Witness,* June 1915, 1.

_____. "Jesus, the Great Life-Giving Spirit." *Weekly Evangel,* 17 July 1915, 2.

_____. "Questions and Answers." *Weekly Evangel,* 29 January and 5 February 1916, 8; 22 July 1916, 8; 2 September 1916, 8; 10 March 1917, 9; 19 October 1918, 5.

_____. "The Recurrence of Doctrine." *The Christian Evangel,* 26 September 1914, 3.

_____. "The Sad New Issue." *Word and Witness,* June 1915, 2,3.

_____. "Some Complaints." *Word and Witness,* 20 March 1914, 1.

_____. "There is Safety in Counsel." *Weekly Evangel,* 18 September 1915, 1.

_____. "To Act in the Name of Another." *Word and Witness,* May 1915, 2.

_____. "Who Is Jesus Christ?" Pamphlet. Assemblies of God Archives.

_____. "Women Elders." *The Christian Evangel,* 15 August 1914, 2.

Bell, E. N., and J. R. Flower. "In Doctrines." *The Christian Evangel,* 1 August 1914, 2.

Benson, John T. *Pentecostal Mission.* Nashville, TN: Trevecca Press, 1977.

Blackstone, W. E. *Jesus Is Coming.* rev. ed. New York: Fleming H. Revell, 1908.

Blauvelt, Martha Tomhave. "Women and Revivalism." In *Women and Religion in America, Volume 1,* eds. Rosemary Ruether and Rosemary Keller, 1–47.

Blumhofer, Edith L. "Fred Vogler," unpublished manuscript, Assemblies of God Archives.

_____. "Jesus Is Victor: A Study in the Life of Johann Christoph Blumhardt." *Paraclete* 19 (Spring 1985): 1–5.

_____. "The Welsh Revival." *Paraclete* 20 (Summer 1986): 1–5.

Boddy, Alexander. "Is the European War Justifiable?" *The Christian Evangel,* 12 December 1914, 1.

Booth-Clibborn, A. S. "What Is War?" *Weekly Evangel,* 21 April 1917, 2. Booth-Clibborn, S. H. *Should a Christian Fight?* Swengel, PA: Bible Truth Depot, n.d.

_____. "The Christian and War. Is It Too Late?" *Weekly Evangel,* 28 April 1917, 5; 19 May 1917, 4, 5.

Bosworth, F. F. "Confirming the Word by Signs Following: Jesus Saves, Heals and Baptizes." *Latter Rain Evangel,* December 1908, 7–8.

_____. "Do All Speak With Tongues?" Booklet New York: The Christian Alliance Publishing Co., n.d. 3.

Bottome, F. G. "Full Salvation." In *Songs of Victory.* London: Pickering and Inglis, n.d.

Brereton, Virginia Lieson. "The Formation of American Bible Schools, 1880–1940." Ed.D. thesis, Columbia University, 1981.

_____. "Preparing Women for the Lord's Work." In *Women in New Worlds,* eds. Rosemary Skinner Keller, Louise L. Queen, Hilah F. Thomas Nashville, TN: Abingdon, 1982.

Brereton, Virginia Lieson, and Christa Ressmeyer Klein. "American Women in Ministry." In *Women in American Religion,* ed. Janet Wilson James, 171–190. Philadelphia:University of Pennsylvania, 1980.

Broadbent, E. H. *The Pilgrim Church.* London: Pickering & Inglis, 1931.

Brooks, John P. *The Divine Church a Treatise on the Origin, Constitution, Order, and Ordinances of the Church; Being a Vindication of the New Testament Ecclesia and an Exposure of the Anti-Scriptural Character of the Modern Church of Sect.* Columbia, MO: Herald Publishing House, 1891; reprint, El Dorado Springs, MO: Witt Printing Co., 1960.

_____. *The Divine Church.* El Dorado Springs, MO: Witt Printing Co., 1960.

Brown, John. "Feasting with my Lord." In *The Best of All,* 123.

Brumback, Carl. *Suddenly From Heaven.* Springfield, MO: Gospel Publishing House, 1961.

Burpee, Florence L. "What Denomination Are You?" *Weekly Evangel,* 26 February 1916, 7.

Butcher, J. Kevin. "The Holiness and Pentecostal Labors of David Wesley Myland: 1890–1918." M.A. thesis, Dallas Theological Seminary, 1983.

Campbell, Faith. *Prophet With a Pen.* Springfield, MO:Gospel Publishing House, 1974.

Carothers, W. F. *Church Government.* Houston: J. V. Dealy Co., 1909.

————. "The Gift of Interpretation." *The Latter Rain Evangel,* October 1910, 7–10.

Carradine, Beverly. *A Box of Treasure.* Chicago: The Christian Witness Co., 1910.

Chambers, Talbot W. Review of *The Baptism with the Holy Spirit,* by R. A. Torrey. In *The Presbyterian and Reformed Review* 6 (October 1895): 789–790.

Chapell, F. L. *Eleventh-Hour Laborers.* New York: Christian Alliance Publishing Co., 1898.

Clementson, G. D. *Charles Hamilton Pridgeon.* Pittsburgh: The Evangelization Society of the Pittsburgh Bible Institute, 1963.

Conn, Charles. *Like A Mighty Army.* Cleveland, TN: Pathway Press, 1955.

Connally, William E. *History of Kansas State and People.* Vol. 3. Chicago: American Historical Society, 1928.

Cook, G. A. "Pentecostal Power in Indianapolis." *The Apostolic Faith,* Feb. to March 1907, 3. Cragin, Margaret. "Elim Home, Rochester, N.Y." *Word and Work,* March 1908, 84.

Dayton, Donald. *The Theological Roots of Pentecostalism.* Grand Rapids: Zondervan, 1987.

————, ed. *Holiness Tracts Defending the Ministry of Women.* New York: Garland Publishing, Inc., 1985.

Dowie, John A. "The Everlasting Gospel of the Kingdom of God Declared and Defended." *Leaves of Healing* V (July 1899): 713.

————. "A Letter to the Friends of Zion Tabernacle." *Leaves of Healing* I (1895): 257.

————. "The Ministry of an Apostle—Is it for Today?" In *Champion of the Faith,* ed. Gordon Lindsay. Dallas: Christ for the Nations, 1979.

Driscoll, Charles B. "Major Prophets of Holy Kansas." *American Mercury* 8 (May 1926): 18–26.

Dugas, Paul D. comp. *The Life and Writings of Elder G. T. Haywood.* Portland, OR:Apostolic Book Publishers, 1984.

Duncan, Susan A. *Trials and Triumphs of a Faith Life.* Rochester, NY: Elim Publishing House, 1910.

Durham, William. "Bible Schools and Training Homes." *The Gospel Witness*, circa 1913: 5.

_____. "The Church." *Pentecostal Testimony* vol. 2, no. 1, 14.

_____. "The Gospel of Christ." *Pentecostal Testimony* vol. 2, no. 1, 9.

_____. "The Great Battle of 1911." *Pentecostal Testimony,* vol. 2, no. 1, 7.

_____. "The Great Crisis." *The Gospel Witness* 1 (1914): 14.

_____. "Organization." *The Gospel Witness* 1 (circa 1913): 11.

_____. "Personal Testimony of Pastor Durham." *Pentecostal Testimony* 2 (August 1912): 3.

_____. "What Is the Evidence of the Baptism in the Holy Ghost?" *Pentecostal Testimony,* vol. 2, no. 1, 4.

Eldridge, George N. *Personal Reminiscences.* Los Angeles: East Coast Publishing Co., n.d.

Ephraim, Lois. *The Stone Church, 1906–1981.* Worth, IL: Charles E. Brinkman Publishers, 1981.

Evans, W. I. *This River Must Flow.* Springfield, MO: Gospel Publishing House, 1954.

Ewart, Frank J. *The Phenomenon of Pentecost.* St. Louis: Pentecostal Publishing House, 1947. Rev. ed., Hazelwood, MO: World Aflame Press, 1975.

Finney, Charles. "The Essential Elements of Christian Experience." In *Gospel Themes.* New York: Fleming H. Revell, 1876.

Fitt, A. P. *Moody Still Lives.* New York: Fleming H. Revell Company, 1936.

Flower, Alice Reynolds. "How Pentecost Came to Indianapolis," unpublished manuscript.

Flower, J. R. "Editorial Comment on Issue." *Weekly Evangel,* 17 July 1915, 1.

_____. "Great November Meeting." *The Christian Evangel,* 12 September 1914, 1.

_____. "The Lord's Supper." *Weekly Evangel,* 24 July 1915, 1.

Forney, C. H. *History of the Churches of God in the U.S. of North America.* Findlay, OH: Churches of God, 1914.

French, J. E. "This Is Like Heaven to Me." In *The Best of All,* 181.

Frodsham, Stanley. "Our Heavenly Citizenship." *Weekly Evangel,* 11 September 1915, 3.

Gardiner, Gordon P. "The Apostle of Divine Healing." *Bread of Life* 6 (March 1957): 15.

————. "Out of Zion . . . Into the World." *Bread of Life* 31 (February 1982): 6.

Gardiner, Mrs. R. H. (Eleanor). "Notes From Ebenezer Bible Institute." *Weekly Evangel,* 17 April 1915, 3.

Garr, A. G. "Have You Been Baptized in the Name of Jesus Christ?" *Victorious Gospel* (Spring 1915): 3.

————. "That 'Yellow Book'." *Word and Witness,* 20 April 1914, 3.

Gee, Donald. *Pentecost.* Springfield, MO: Gospel Publishing House, 1932.

Goff, James R. "The Pentecostal Catalyst to the South: G. B. Cashwell, 1906–1908," unpublished manuscript.

Golder, Morris. *The Life and Works of Bishop Garfield Thomas Haywood.* n.p., 1977.

Gordon, A. J. *Ecce Venit.* New York: Fleming H. Revell, 1889.

————. *The Ministry of the Spirit.* Chicago: Fleming H. Revell, 1894.

————. *The Ministry of Healing.* New York: The Christian Alliance Publishing Co., 1882.

————. "The Ministry of Women." *Missionary Review of the World* 7 (December 1894): 910–921.

Gordon, Ernest. *Adoniram Judson Gordon.* New York: Fleming H. Revell, 1896.

Gordon, Mrs. A. J. "Women as Evangelists." Appendix 3 in Hassey, *No Time for Silence,* 157–161.

Goss, Ethel E. *The Winds of God: The Story of the Early Pentecostal Days (1901–1914) in the Life of Howard A. Goss.* New York: Comet Press Books, 1958.

Grotz, Milton. "Eat and Drink to the Glory of God." Tract. Christian Workers Union, 1914.

Guinness, H. Grattan. "Signs in the Heavens Above." *Weekly Evangel,* 10 April 1917, 3. Hamm, Thomas. *The Transformation of American Quakerism: Orthodox Friends, 1800–1907.* Bloomington, IN: University Press, 1988.

Hammell, George M. "Religion and Fanaticism." *Methodist Review* 70 (July 1888): 534.

Hardesty, Nancy, Lucille Sider Dayton, and Donald W. Dayton. "Women in the Holiness Movement: Feminism in the Evangelical Tradition." In *Women of Spirit,* ed. Eleanor McLaughlin, 226–254. New York: Simon and Schuster, 1979.

Harris, Mrs. Reader. "Nearing the End of the Pentecostal Age." *Weekly Evangel,* 15 July 1916, 7, 9.

Hewitt, E. E. "Since I Found My Savior." In *The Best of All,* 173.

Higgins, Walter J. *Pioneering in Pentecost.* Privately published, 1958.

Hiss, William. "Shiloh: Frank W. Sandford and the Kingdom: 1893–1948." Ph.D. diss., Tufts University, 1978.

Hopkins, Evan. "The Teaching of the Revival." In *The Story of the Welsh Revival Told by Eyewitnesses*. New York: Fleming H. Revell, 1905.

Hudson, Winthrop, ed. *Walter Rauschenbusch*. New York: Paulist Press, 1984.

Hunter, James. *Evangelicalism: The Coming Generation*. Chicago: University of Chicago Press, 1987.

Hutchison, William R. *Errand Into the World*. Chicago: University of Chicago Press, 1987.

Ironside, H. A. *The Apostolic Faith Missions and the So-Called Second Pentecost*. New York: Louizeaux Brothers, Inc., n.d.

Jaffray, Robert. "Speaking in Tongues." *The Christian and Missionary Alliance*, 13 March 1909, 395–397.

Jamieson, S. A. "How a Presbyterian Preacher Received the Baptism." Pamphlet. Kansas City, MO: Gospel Union Publishing Co., n.d.

Janette Hassey. *No Time for Silence*. Grand Rapids: Zondervan, 1986.

Jolley, Jennie A., comp. *As an Angel of Light, or Bible Tongues and Holiness and Their Counterfeits*. New York: Vantage Press, 1964.

Jones, Charles Edwin. *Perfectionist Persuasion*. Metuchen, NJ: Scarecrow Press, Inc., 1974.

Jones, Charles Price. "Autobiographical Sketch." In *History of the Church of Christ (Holiness) U.S.A. 1895–1965*, ed. Ottho B. Cobbins. New York: Vantage Press, 1966.

Kenyon, Howard N. "A Social History of the Assemblies of God: Race Relations, Women and Ministry, and Attitudes toward War." Ph.D. diss., Baylor University, 1987.

Kerr, Daniel W. "Spontaneous Theology." *Weekly Evangel*, 17 April 1915, 3.

Kinne, Seeley D. "The Pentecostal Movement and the Conversion of Sinners." *The Household of God* (May 1909): 15.

Kirk, J. M. "Since the Comforter Has Come." In *Songs of the Evening Light*, 38.

LaBerge, Agnes Nevada Ozman. *What God Hath Wrought*. Chicago: Herald Publishing Co., n.d.

Lawler, H. L. "The Flesh: What Is It?" *Word and Work*, 20 February 1913, 4.

Lawless, Elaine. "Women's Speech in the Pentecostal Religious Service." Ph.D. diss., Indiana University, 1982.

Lawrence, Bennett F. *The Apostolic Faith Restored*. With an Introduction by John W. Welch. St. Louis: Gospel Publishing House, 1916.

Lee, Bernice. "When God Breathed on Zion." *Bread of Life* (October 1981): 7–8, 10, 11, 13.

Lee, Elnora L., comp. *C. H. Mason, A Man Greatly Used of God.* Memphis, TN: Women's Department, Churches of God in Christ, 1967.

Lindsay, Gordon, ed. *The John G. Lake Sermons.* Dallas: Voice of Healing Publishing Co., 1949.

Lupton, Levi. "Testimony." *New Acts* 3 (February 1907): 3.

MacArthur, William T. "The Promise of the Father and 'Speaking with Tongues' in Chicago." *The Christian and Missionary Alliance,* 26 January 1907, 40.

Manneh, Lamin. "Christian Missions and the Western Guilt Complex." *The Christian Century,* 8 April 1987, 330–334.

Mason, Elsie W. *The Man: Charles Harrison Mason.* Memphis, TN: Church of God in Christ, 1979.

McAlister, R. E. "Is the 'New Thing' New?" *Truth Advocate* (August 1949): 16.

McCafferty, William B. "Shall Christians Go to War?" *The Christian Evangel,* 16 January 1915, 1.

McLauchlin, D. N. Review of *How Christ Came to Church,* by A. J. Gordon. In *The Presbyterian Quarterly* 10 (October 1896): 530.

McLean, A., and J. W. Eaton, eds. *Penuel; or Face to Face with God.* New York: W. C. Palmer, Jr., 1869.

McPherson, Aimee Semple. *The Story of My Life.* Waco, TX: Word Books, 1973.

————. *This Is That.* Los Angeles: Bridal Call Publishing Co., 1921.

McPherson, C. E. *Life of Levi Lupton.* Alliance, OH, 1911.

Meloon, Marion. *Ivan Spencer: Willow in the Wind.* Plainfield, NJ: Logos International, 1974.

Meloon, Wilfred C. *We've Been Robbed, Or A Dispensationalist Looks at the Baptism of the Holy Ghost.* Plainfield, NJ: Logos International, 1971.

Melton, J. Gordon, and Robert L. Moore. *The Cult Experience: Responding to the New Religious Pluralism.* New York: The Pilgrim Press, 1982.

Mitchell, Robert Bryant. *Heritage and Horizons.* Des Moines: Open Bible Publishers, 1982.

Moberg, David. *The Church as a Social Institution: The Sociology of American Religion.* Grand Rapids: Baker Book House, 1984.

Montgomery, Carrie Judd. *Under His Wings: The Story of My Life.* Oakland, CA: Triumphs of Faith, 1936.

Moody, D. L. "Consecration and Concentration." In *A College of Colleges,* ed. T. J. Shanks. New York, 1887.

_____. "Enduement for Service." In *D. L. Moody at Home,* ed. T. J. Shanks. New York, 1886.

_____. "Question Drawer." In *College Students at Northfield,* ed. T. J. Shanks. New York, n.p., 1888.

_____. "The Return of Our Lord." In *The American Evangelicals, 1800–1900,* ed. W. G. McLoughlin. New York: Harper and Row, 1968.

_____. "Testimony of D. L. Moody." *Institute Tie* 1 (September 1900): 2.

Moore, R. Laurence. *Religious Outsiders and the Making of Americans.* New York: Oxford University Press, 1986.

Morris, Lelia. "Baptized with the Holy Ghost." In *The Best of All,* 94.

_____. "Nearer, Still Nearer." In *The Best of All,* 63.

_____. "On the Firing Line." In *The Best of All,* 3, 4.

Mott, John R. *Addresses and Papers.* Vol. 1. New York: Association Press, 1946.

Murray, Frank S. *The Sublimity of Faith.* Amherst, NH: The Kingdom Press, 1981.

Myland, David Wesley. *The Latter Rain Covenant and Pentecostal Power.* Chicago: The Evangel Publishing House, 1910.

Nelson, Douglas. "For Such a Time as This: The Story of William J. Seymour and the Azusa Street Revival." Ph.D. diss., University of Birmingham, 1981.

Niklaus, Robert L., John S. Sawin, and Samuel J. Stoesz. *All for Jesus: God at Work in the Christian and Missionary Alliance Over One Hundred Years.* Camp Hill, PA: Christian Publications, 1986.

Oblinger, Carl. *Religious Mimesis.* Evanston, IL: Institute for the Study of American Religion, 1973.

Osborne, Byron Lindley. *The Malone Story: The Dream of Two Quaker Young People.* Newton, KS, 1970.

Otis, Addie M. "Let Him Come In." *Word and Work,* September 1908.

Otis, S. G. "Camp Meeting at Old Orchard, Maine." *Word and Work,* September 1907, 243.

Ozman, Agnes. "A Witness to First Scenes." *The Apostolic Faith,* Dec.–Jan. 1912–1913, 4.

_____. "The First One to Speak in Tongues." *Latter Rain Evangel,* January 1909, 2.

Palmer, Phoebe. *The Promise of the Father.* Boston: Henry V. Degen, 1859.

Parham, Charles F. "Baptism of the Holy Ghost." *The Apostolic Faith*, October 1912, 9.

———. "Free Love." *The Apostolic Faith*, December 1912, 4–5.

———. "Hell." *The Apostolic Faith*, September 1912, 11.

———. "Leadership." *The Apostolic Faith*, June 1912, 7–8.

———. "The Sources of Disease: Sanctification of Spirit, Soul and Body Only Real Antidote for Sickness." *The Apostolic Faith*, August 1912, 4.

———. *Voice Crying in the Wilderness*. n.p., 1902.

Parham, Sarah. *Life of Charles F. Parham*. Baxter Springs, KS: 1930.

Pearlman, Irene. *Myer Pearlman and His Friends*. Springfield, MO: privately published, 1953.

Pennington, Edith Mae. "From the Footlights to the Light of the Cross, or From Movieland to Canaanland." *Full Gospel Messenger* (June 1931): 2, 3, 8.

Penn-Lewis, Jessie. *The Awakening in Wales*. New York: Fleming H. Revell, 1905.

Perkin, Noel. "Call to Advance." *Pentecostal Evangel*, 24 January 1965, 9.

———. "Coordination and Advance." *Pentecostal Evangel*, 27 December 1964, 11.

———. *Forward Movements of the Last Half Century*. New York: Funk & Wagnalls, 1900.

———. "Highlights of the 20s (1920–1924)." *Pentecostal Evangel*, 29 November 1964, 17.

———. "Our First Five Years." *Pentecostal Evangel*, 25 October 1964, 14.

Pickett, L. L. "It Is For Us All Today." In *The Best of All*, 187.

Pierson, A. T. *The Keswick Convention*. New York: Funk and Wagnalls Co., 1900.

———. "Speaking With Tongues." *Missionary Review of the World* 30 (July 1907): 487.

———. "Speaking With Tongues—II." *Missionary Review of the World* 30 (September 1907): 682.

———. "Woman as a Factor in the World's Evangelization." *Missionary Review of the World* (July 1895): 520.

Pierson, Delavan. *Arthur T. Pierson*. New York:Fleming H. Revell Co., 1912.

Pike, J. M. "The Second Blessing." *Word and Witness*, 20 December 1913, 2.

Pinson, M. M. "From Los Angeles World-Wide Camp Meeting." *Word and Witness*, 20 May 1913, 1.

Plummer, Julia Morton. "The Bridegroom Cometh." *Word and Work*, March 1908, 76.

Pollock, John C. *The Cambridge Seven.* London: InterVarsity Fellowship, 1956.

_____. *The Keswick Story.* London: Hodder and Stoughton, 1964.

Price, Charles. *The Story of My Life.* Pasadena: Privately published, 1935.

Ramabai, Pandita. *The Baptism of the Holy Ghost and Fire.* Kedgaon, India: Mukti Missions Press, 1906.

Rauschenbusch, Walter. "The New Evangelism." In *American Protestant Thought: The Liberal Era*, ed. William R. Hutchison. New York: Harper and Row, 1968.

Rawson, Mrs. A. F. "Apostolic Faith Mission." *Word and Work*, February 1908, 49.

Reynolds, R. F. "Let the Holy Ghost Come In." In *The Best of All*, 87.

Richey, Eloise M. *What God Hath Wrought in the Life of Raymond T. Richey.* Houston: United Prayer and Workers' League, 1937.

Robeck, Cecil M. Introduction to *Witness to Pentecost*, by Frank Bartleman. New York: Garland Publishing, Inc., 1985.

Roberts, Dana. "Forward Movements of Nineteenth-Century Evangelicalism." Ph.D. diss., Yale University, 1984.

Robins, Roger. "Attitudes Toward War and Peace in the Assemblies of God," unpublished ms., Assemblies of God Archives.

Robinson, George W. "I Am His, and He Is Mine." In *Hymns of Glorious Praise*, 289. Springfield, MO: Gospel Publishing House, 1969.

Russell, C. Allyn. "Adoniram Judson Gordon: Nineteenth-Century Fundamentalist." *American Baptist Quarterly* 4 (March 1985): 61–89.

Sandeen, Ernest. *The Roots of Fundamentalism.* Chicago: University of Chicago Press, 1970.

Scanzoni, Letha Dawson, and Susan Setta. "Women in Evangelical, Holiness, and Pentecostal Traditions." In *Women and Religion in America: 1900–1968, Volume 3*, eds. Rosemary R. Ruther and Rosemary S. Keller, 223–234. San Francisco: Harper & Row, 1986.

Schermer, H. W. "Civic Righteousness." *The Apostolic Faith*, October 1913, 15–17.

Scofield, C. I. "The War in the Light of Prophecy." *Weekly Evangel*, 28 October 1916, 6, 7.

Seymour, William J. *Doctrine and Discipline of the Azusa Street Apostolic Faith Mission of Los Angeles.* Published by the author, 1915.

"Bro. Seymour's Call." *The Apostolic Faith,* September 1906, 1.

Simpson, A. B. *Christ in the Bible: 1 Corinthians.* New York: Word, Work and the World Publishing Co., 1888.

————. *Christ in the Bible: Romans.* New York: Word, Work and the World Publishing Co., 1888.

————. "Diary," 1879, 1880, Historical Collection, Nyack, NY: Nyack College.

————. "Divine Healing." *Word, Work, and the World* 7 (September 1886): 158.

————. *The Gospel of Healing.* Harrisburg, PA: Christian Publications, Inc., 1915.

————. *The Holy Spirit, or Power from on High.* New York: Christian Alliance Publishing Co., 1895.

————. *The Holy Spirit, or Power from on High.* Vols. 1, 2. Harrisburg, PA: Christian Publications, Inc., 1895.

————. *A Larger Christian Life.* New York: Christian Alliance Publishing Company, 1890.

————. *Larger Outlooks on Missionary Lands.* New York: The Christian Alliance Publishing Co., 1893.

————. "Principles of Christian Life and Holiness." *Word, Work, and the World* 7 (October 1886): 205–207.

————. *Wholly Sanctified.* Harrisburg, PA: Christian Publications, 1925.

Sisson, Elizabeth. "God's Prayer House." *Triumphs of Faith* 28 (1908): 230ff.

————. "Organization of Organism." *Latter Rain Evangel,* March 1914, 20–23.

Sizelove, Rachel A. *A Sparkling Fountain for the Whole Earth.* Tract. Assemblies of God Archives.

Smale, Joseph. "The Gift of Tongues." *Living Truth* (January 1907): 39, 40.

Smith, Hannah Whitall. *The Unselfishness of God and How I Discovered It: A Spiritual Autobiography.* New York: Fleming H. Revell Company, 1903.

Smith, Timothy L. *Revivalism and Social Reform.* New York: Harper and Row, 1957.

Stevens, W. C. "The Latter Rain." *Word and Work,* July 1908, 17.

Straton, John Roach. "Does the Bible Forbid Women To Preach and Pray in Public?" In Hassey, *No Time for Silence,* 189–210.

Synan, Vinson. *The Holiness-Pentecostal Movement in the United States.* Grand Rapids: William B. Eerdmans Publishing Co., 1971.

Thompson, A. P. *The Life of A. B. Simpson.* New York: The Christian Alliance Publishing Co., 1920.

Tinney, James. "William J. Seymour: Father of Modern-Day Pentecostalism." *Journal of the Interdenominational Theological Center* 4 (Fall 1979): 34–44.

Tomlinson, A. J. *Diary,* ed. Homer Tomlinson. New York: The Church of God, World Headquarters, 1949–1955.

Torrey, R. A. *The Baptism with the Holy Spirit.* Chicago: Fleming H. Revell Company, 1895.

_____. "D. L. Moody, the Unity of His Life." *Institute Tie* 1 (March 1901): 202.

_____. *The Fundamental Doctrines of the Christian Faith.* New York: George H. Doran Company, 1918.

_____. *Is the Present Tongues Movement of God?* Los Angeles: Biola Book Room, n.d., 4.

_____. *The Person and Work of the Holy Spirit.* Grand Rapids: Baker Book House, 1974.

_____. *The Return of the Lord Jesus.* Los Angeles, n.p., 1913.

_____. Review of *How to Obtain Fulness of Power.* In *The Presbyterian Quarterly* 12 (January 1898): 125.

_____. *What the Bible Teaches.* Chicago: Fleming H. Revell Company, 1898.

_____. "Why God Used D. L. Moody." Chicago: The Bible Institute Colportage Association, 1923.

Vaughn, Lou Ella. *Brush Arbor Birthright.* Springfield, MO: Gospel Publishing House, 1986.

Vian, A. W. "Further News from Nyack, New York." *The Household of God* (November 1907): 6.

Wacker, Grant. "The Holy Spirit and the Spirit of the Age in American Protestantism, 1880–1910." *Journal of American History* (1985): 45–62.

_____. "The Holy Spirit and the Spirit of the Age in American Protestantism, 1880–1910." *Journal of American History* 72 (June 1985): 45–62.

_____. "Marching to Zion." *Church History* 54 (December 1985): 496–511.

Warfield, Benjamin. *Counterfeit Miracles.* New York: Oxford University Press, 1931.

Warner, Wayne E. *The Woman Evangelist: The Life and Times of Charismatic Evangelist Maria B. Woodworth-Etter.* Metuchen, NJ: The Scarecrow Press, Inc., 1986.

_____. "Herbert Buffum." *Heritage* 6 (Fall 1986): 11–16.

Watson, G. D. *A Holiness Manual.* Dallas: Chandler Publications, n.d.

Weaver, Albert. "Camp Meeting, Alliance, Ohio." *Word and Work,* August 1907, 215.

Weber, Timothy. *Living in the Shadow of the Second Coming.* New York: Oxford University Press, 1979.

Welter, Barbara. "She Hath Done What She Could." In *Women in American Religion,* 111–126.

White, Alma. *Demons and Tongues.* Zarephath, NJ: Pillar of Fire Publishers, 1949.

—————. *The Story of My Life and the Pillar of Fire.* Vol. 3. Zarephath, NJ: Pillar of Fire, 1936.

White, Charles Edward. *The Beauty of Holiness: Phoebe Palmer as Theologian, Revivalist, Feminist, and Humanitarian.* Grand Rapids: Zondervan Publishing House, 1986.

Williams, Ernest. "May Women Preach?" Typed. Assemblies of God Archives.

Woodward, E. P. *Sandfordism: An Exposure of the Claims, Purposes, Methods, Predictions and Threats of Rev. F. W. Sandford, the "Apostle" of Shiloh, Maine.* Portland, ME: Safeguard Publishing Co., 1902.

Woodworth-Etter, Maria. *A Diary of Signs and Wonders.* Tulsa: Harrison House, reprint, 1916 ed.

—————. *Signs and Wonders God Wrought in the Ministry for Forty Years.* Chicago: Hammond Press, 1916.

Worrell, A. S. "Wonderful Works Going on in Los Angeles." *Gospel Witness* 16 (September 1906): 30.

Zikmund, Barbara Brown. "The Struggle for the Right to Preach." In *Women and Religion in America, Volume 1: The Nineteenth Century,* eds. Rosemary Radford Ruether and Rosemary Skinner Keller, 193–241. San Francisco: Harper & Row, 1981.

Index

Adams, B. M., 43
Allen, Frederick Lewis, 249
Alliance *(see* Christian and Missionary Alliance)
Altamont Bible and Missionary Institute, 172
Amillennialism *(see* Millennialism)
Anderson, Robert, 153, 415n.43, 421-422n.58
Angelus Temple (Los Angeles), 251
Anglo-Israelism, 75
Apostolic Faith (Bell), 425n.1, 426n.8
Apostolic Faith (Parham) *(see also Everlasting Gospel),* 73, 425n.3, 427n.26
Apostolic Faith (Seymour), 103, 425n.3, 426n.4
Apostolic Faith Movement, 103–105, 108, 115, 118, 126, 152, 163, 218, 359, 363
formation of, 67–84, 396n.98
spread of, 85–92
in Texas and Arkansas, 130–134
Argue, Andrew Harvey, 129, 199, 248, 254, 297
Argue, Beulah, 254
Argue, Watson, 254, 273pl., 368
Argue, Zelma, 254, 264, 269
Arthur, Mary (Mother Arthur), 86, 165, 421n.55
Assemblies of God Bible schools, 316–321

Canyonville Bible Academy, 320
Central Bible Institute, 317–318
endorsement of, 332
Glad Tidings Bible Institute, 332
Midwest Bible School, 317
North Central Bible Institute, 324, 333
Northwest Bible Institute, 324, 333
Southwestern Bible School, 320
Assemblies of God foreign missions program, 285–307, 312pl.
department organized, 263, 291–297
missions giving, 212, 289, 296
outreaches: Brazil, 306–307; China, 286–287; 300, 306; Eastern Europe, 305; Egypt, 307; India, 286–287; Nigeria, 307
women in missions, 289–290
Assemblies of God, General Council of the
constitution and bylaws of, 202–203, 258
credentials issued by, 210
cultural issues, 344
dissensions, internal, 213
doctrine: defining of, 217–243; sanctification, 217–221; Trinity, 221–239

as end-times people, 347
Executive Presbytery, 203–204, 215pl.
field representatives, 248
formation of, 197–213, 417n.34
General Presbytery, 237
growth chart, 263
headquarters, 245pl.
marriage and divorce, statement on, 208
ministerial training, 204–206
ministers, dismissal and rehabilitation of, 259
purpose of, 200–202
relocation of, 206, 212, 238–239
resolution on military service, 352
Statement of Fundamental Truths, 236
war, early views of, 344–355
women, attitudes toward, 355–372
women ordained, 290
women's rights, statement on, 206–208
Assemblies of God General Councils
appointed committees, 199, 283, 290, 319, 324, 331
sessions: (April 1914), 197–198, 214pl.; (November 1914), 211–213; (October 1915), 232–235; (October 1916), 235–238; (September 1917), 238–239; (September 1918), 239–243, 247; (1920), 364–365; (1914–1921, annually), 247; (September 1923), 319; (1925), 319; (1935), 304, 368; (1937), 329; (1939), 332; (1941), 306
Assemblies of God Home Missions and Education Department (see also Education), 327–336
Assemblies of God movement, 343–372
Azusa Street mission (see also Pacific Coast Apostolic Faith Movement), 98–100, 104–107, 113, 118, 124, 112pl., 168, 399n.46
reports on, 103, 106, 108, 131, 133, 148

Baker, David, 72
Baker, Mrs. E. V. (see also Duncan sisters), 123, 140pl., 361
Ball, Henry C., 254, 291, 301
Ball, Sunshine, 301
Balliet, Emil, 316
Bamford, Annie (Mother Bamford), 320
Baptism in the Holy Spirit (see also Tongues speaking)
non-Wesleyan teaching on, 50–57
Wesleyan teaching on, 41–45
Baptism, water (see also New Issue), 223, 233
rebaptism, 224, 230, 232
Barratt, Thomas B., 190, 286, 427-428n.28
Bartleman, Frank, 98, 99, 107
Azusa Street, statement on, 105–106, 107
diary, 99
evangelism world tour, 147
pacifistic views of, 349–350, 351
women in ministry, views on, 366
Barton, Victor, 79
Bell, Eudorus N., 136pl., 218, 229–233, 238–239
committee on resolutions, 235
education, 131, 173
editor, 133, 199, 200, 210, 211, 219, 281, 289
death, 248, 258
executive presbyter, 204
foreign missions committee, 290
General Council chairman, 202, 225, 247
general superintendent, 317
holiness views, 220
manager of GPH, 283–284

military service, views on, 352
New Issue, 230–234
nonpacifistic views, 354
Spirit baptism, 129, 131
women, views on, 206, 365–366, 370, 411n.15
Bender, Gottfried, 323
Bennett, Belle, 370
Berachah, 382n.35
Berean Bible Institute, 292
Bethel Bible School, 76, 80–81
Bethel Bible Training School, 315, 323, 339pl.
Bethel Healing Home, 73
Beulah Heights Bible Institute, 315
Beulah Park Convention, 186
Bible baptism (see Tongues speaking; Baptism in the Holy Spirit)
Blanchard, Ora (Mrs. Noel Perkin), 298
Bliss, Philip P., 39
Blumhardt, Johann Christoph, 27
Boardman, William Edwin, 27, 58
Boddy, Alexander, 348–349, 353
Boddy, John Thomas, 282, 315
Bolton, C. S., 69
Booth, Catherine, 50, 350
Booth-Clibborn, Arthur, 351
Booth-Clibborn, Eric, 295
Booth-Clibborn, Samuel H., 350
Booth, William, 350
Bosworth, B. B., 422n.69
Bosworth, Fred Francis, 111pl., 115, 239–242, 245pl., 422n.69, 422n.70
Bowley, Harry, 254
Boyd, Frank, 318, 323
Boyer, Margaret (Mrs. Fred Vogler), 327
Britton, Blanche, 336
Brooks, J. H., 47–48
Brooks, John P., 19
Brown, Marie (see Burgess), 253, 270pl., 356

Brown, Robert, 199, 242–243, 253, 259, 270pl.
Buffum, Herbert, 146, 157, 181
Burgess, Marie (later Marie Burgess Brown), 115, 127, 165, 362, 399-400n.5
Burroughs, F. G., 46
Cadwalder, Hugh, 254
Calhoun, Etta, 299
Cambridge Seven, 57
Campbell, Alexander, 19, 238
Campbell, Jean (later Mrs. L. C. Hall), 127
Canada, A. G., 131
Canada, Pentecostal Assemblies of, 254
Carlson, G. Raymond, 336
Carmichael, Adele, 269
Carothers, Warren Fay, 89, 130, 175, 359–361, 422n.70
Carradine, Beverly, 119, 182, 227
Cashwell, Gaston Barnabas, 118–121, 164, 426n.8
Central Bible Institute, 317–318, 338pl., 431n.12
Chapell, F. L., 363
Chicago Avenue Church (Moody), 192
Chisolm, Robert Benjamin, 205, 314, 337pl.
Christian and Missionary Alliance, 25, 61, 237
  baptism in the Holy Spirit, 121–123, 183, 189
  tongues, views on, 241
Christian and Missionary Alliance School (see Missionary Training Institute)
Christian Catholic Church, 20, 33, 114
Christian day schools, 321
Christian Evangel (see also *Weekly Evangel* and *Pentecostal Evangel*), 171, 204, 205 230, 280, 281, 425n.1
Christian Science, 381n.23
Christian Workers' Union, The, 155, 280

Christ's Ambassadors, 255
Church of God, 21
Church of God of the General
    Eldership, 69
Churches of God in Christ, 49,
    116, 133-134, 405n.78
Collier, Harry L., 253, 265
Collins, Archibald P., 243, 255,
    353-354, 423n.12
  Clergy Reference Committee,
    199-200
  executive presbyter, 204
  General Council chairman,
    211, 212, 233, 248
  tongues, view of, 241
Collins, Warren, 256
Confidence, 348
Cook, Glenn, 244pl., 398n.28
  Azusa Street participant, 109,
    117, 123,
  New Issue, 235
  Pentecostal teaching of, 224
Copley, Albert, 327, 425n.1
Cox, A. B., 194, 322
Craig, Mary (Mrs. Robert J.),
    254, 315
Craig, Robert J., 250, 254, 315,
    322
Crawford, Florence, 99, 261, 356,
    425n.1
Cullis, Charles, 27, 29

Darby, John Nelson, 22-24
Dispensationalism, 23, 153, 193,
    380n.12, 429n.48
Disciples of Christ, 19
Divine healing, 26-36, 164, 250,
    382n.31, 382-383n.40
  at Azusa Street, 104
  as doctrine of "foursquare"
    gospel, 18
  message of, 86, 104
  opposition to, 382n.31
  testimonies of, 72-73, 81-82,
    86, 255-256, 373-376, 411n.14
Doney, W. I., 293
Dowie, John Alexander, 20-21,
    28, 31-34, 37pl., 78, 113, 115

Leaves of Healing, 38pl.
Draper, Mark, 254
Draper, Minnie, 165, 315
Duncan, James, 123
Duncan sisters, 123, 164, 170, 361,
    402n.38
Duncan, Susan, 124
Durham, William H., 126, 128,
    136pl., 138pl.
  baptism in the Holy Spirit, 129
  Bible school training, 173
  death, 130, 195, 404n.60
  North Avenue Mission, 126,
    128, 130
  sanctification, views on, 129,
    221
Easton, Susan, 290
Ebenezer Chapel and Bible
    Training Institute, 170-171
Ecclesia Mission, 79
Ecumenical efforts, 379n.9
Education
  Bible schools utilized by As-
    semblies of God, 313-316, 329
  education department, 328
  General Council Bible schools,
    316-321, 324-327
  promoters of, 313
  secular, Council's response to,
    321-324, 329
Eldridge, George N., 122, 189,
    254, 290, 316, 414n.30
Elim (see also Rochester Bible
    and Missionary Training
    School), 123-126, 298, 361
  becomes Pentecostal, 125, 145
  ministerial training, 173
  provides leaders for Assem-
    blies of God, 363, 402n.45
  Trust, 124
  worship services, 168
End times, 169
Erickson, R. L., 204, 288, 422n.70
Etter, Maria Woodworth (see
    Woodworth-Etter, Maria)
Evangelical Alliance, 379n.9
Evans, James R., 254, 258, 262,
    298

Evans, W. I., 189, 322, 353
Evening Light Saints, The, 48, 395n.91
Everlasting Gospel, 92
Ewart, Frank pastor, 223–225, 226–227, 235

Faith living, 123, 124, 147–148, 149, 201, 385n.28
at Bible schools, 169, 172, 173, 206
in Christian service, 76, 105, 106, 166, 280
for healing, 28, 32
Farrow, Lucy, 89, 90, 130, 396-397n.2, 404n.62
Faux, William, 283, 297, 318
Federal Council of Churches, 379n.9
Finney, Charles G., 58
Fisher, Elmer, 107
Fisher, Warren, 224
Flower, Alice Reynolds, 123, 170, 424n.15
Flower, J. Roswell, 123, 270pl., 401-402n.31, 424n.15
baptism in Holy Spirit, 163
editor, 425n.1
Oneness, views on, 228–230
positions held, 202, 204, 211, 232, 263, 281, 292, 327
student, 170
tongues, views on, 144, 422n.63
Fockler, Cyrus, 198, 204, 422n.70
Follette, John Wright, 173
Forrester, Hazel Fairchild, 323
Fraser, A. L., 422n.70
Friends, Society of (Quakers), 34, 314, 383n.44
Frodsham, Stanley, 421n.55
editor, 282, 427n.14, 427n.15
Foreign Missions Committee member, 290
views, 350, 352
writer, 425n.2
Full Gospel School, 340pl.

Gannon, Theodore, 268, 335

Garr, A. G., 241
Gaston, William T., 210, 248, 258–259
General Councils (*see* Assemblies of God General Councils
General superintendents of the Assemblies of God, 298–299
Gibeah (Bible school), 170, 327
Gifts of the Spirit (*see* spiritual gifts)
Glad Tidings Bible Institute, 315, 340pl., 341pl., 400n.5
Goben, John, 252
Gordon, Adoniram Judson, 53, 55, 429n.48
healing, views on, 28–29, 32
premillenialism, views on, 25–26, 388n.58
women in ministry, views on, 50, 362
Gortner, J. Narver, 254, 283, 316, 328, 332
Gospel Publishing House (*see also Pentecostal Evangel*), 215pl., 309pl.
evangelistic arm, 279, 281
formation of, 206, 212
growth of, 283–285
Sunday school/children's materials, production of, 284–285
Gospel School, 170, 177pl., 205, 206
Gospel Tabernacle, 184
Goss, Ethel, 131–132, 165, 356
Goss, Howard A., 143, 145, 172, 175, 229, 422n.70
and Apostolic Faith Movement, 131, 132
positions held, 130, 199, 212, 404n.60
water baptism, views on, 225, 232
Goss, Millicent, 165
Graves, F. A., 115, 127, 135pl., 318, 403n.49
Gray, Frank, 254

Greisen, Victor G., 267

Hall, Lemuel C., 127, 130, 131, 171, 225, 288, 412n.35
Hammond, Elmer, 300
Hammond, Hattie, 264, 269
Hardin, Ben, 254, 336
Harriman, Nathan, 79
Harris, Thoro, 146
Harvey, Esther, 293
Harvey, James, 291, 293
Hatch, Carl, 255
Haywood, Garfield Thomas, 146, 157, 194, 224, 225, 227, 233, 235
Healing (see Divine healing)
Herzl, Theodor, 75
Higgins, Walter, 194
Holiness, 35–36, 40, 119, 180
  vs. carnality, 153, 156
  General Council issue, 213, 332
Holmes, Nickels John, 172
Holy Ghost and Us Bible School, 77
Holy Spirit (see Baptism in the Holy Spirit)
Home for Faith and Physical Healing, 29
Hopkins, Evan, 100
Horne, J. W., 42, 44

Ironside, Harry, 192–193, 219
Irwin, Benjamin F., 74

Jaffray, Robert, 186–187, 191
Jamieson, Samuel, 144–145, 236, 243, 253–254, 317
Jeffrey, Ralph, 253
Jehovah's Witnesses, 22
Jeter, J. A., 116
Jolley, Jennie, 182
Jones, Charles Price, 49, 116, 222
Juergensen, Carl, 293

Kammerer, J. Z., 285
Kerr, Daniel W., 167, 209, 235, 241
  Bible school work, 316, 317, 318

positions held, 204, 283, 293
  Statement of Fundamental Truths, work on, 236
Keswick, 59–60, 348, 380n.13, 389n.70
Keys, Leland, 316
King, Joseph Hillary, 163
Kinney, Helen (Mrs. Frank Sandford), 77
Knapp, Phoebe Palmer, 42

Lake, John, 111pl., 115, 166, 257
La Luz Apostolica, 291
Latin American District Council of the Assemblies of God, 301
Latter-Day Saints, The Church of Jesus Christ of, 19, 20
Latter rain, 125, 134, 346
  dispensationalists reject views of, 193
  early Pentecostals, view of, 150–153
  as end-times event, 100
  produced missions emphasis, 286
  Simpson's, (A. B.), influence on, 183
Lawrence, Bennett F., 13, 15, 211, 327, 422n.70
Legalism, 153–154
Leonard, Thomas K., 202, 204, 252
  Gospel School founder, 170, 205, 206
Lewis, Gayle, 254, 268, 324
L.I.F.E. Bible College, 252
Lindberg, Hilda (Mrs. W. I. Evans), 323
Lindquist, Frank, 254
Link, Frederick, 129, 404n.61
London Missionary Conference, 57
Louizeaux Brothers' Bible Truth Depot, 193
Lucas, Christian, 315
Luce, Alice Eveline, 291, 301, 316, 428n.30

Lupton, Levi, 134, 163, 170, 182, 427n.27

MacArthur, William T., 184–185
Manley, William, 280
Marriage, 169, 208, 412n.27, 423n.12
Mason, Charles H., 49, 116, 143, 210
McAlister, R. E., 223–224, 225, 254
McCafferty, William B., 254, 349, 354
McClendon, Millicent *(see* Goss, Millicent)
McClurkan, J. O., 117, 119
McDowell, David, 243, 258, 260, 367
McKinney, C. A., 298
McPhair, William, 316
McPherson, Aimee Semple, 272pl., 437n.65
  Angelus Temple, 251
  Bridal Call, 50
  family, 249–250
  impact on the Assemblies of God, 252
  leaves Assemblies of God, 368
  L.I.F.E. Bible College, 252, 253
  radio broadcast, 260
McPherson, Harold, 250, 368
Menzie, James, 254
Merian, Lillian (Mrs. Ralph Riggs), 267
Merritt, Stephen, 82
Methodism, American, 41–42, 47
Meyer, Frederick Brotherton, 59
Millenialism, 18–26, 117, 148, 154, 286, 380n.11, 380n.14, 388n.58
Miller, Harriet, 69–70
Miller, Jacob, 233
Millsaps, Ruth, 254
Millsaps, Willie T., 254, 267
Milwaukee Gospel Tabernacle, 411n.14
Missionary Alliance *(see also* Christian and Missionary

Alliance), 61
Missionary Institute, 184, 185
Missionary Review of the World, 25, 28, 190
Missionary Training Institute, 82, 122, 123, 151, 315, 318, 322
Montgomery, Carrie Judd, 147, 162, 254, 371
Montgomery, Helen Barrett, 370
Moody Bible Institute, 57, 77, 171, 173, 184, 192
Moody, Dwight L., 24, 25, 60, 383n.2
  Holy Spirit, views on, 51, 54, 55, 56, 63
  Northfield conferences, 27, 55–56, 57
Moral failures, 415n.42, 422n.70
Morgan, G. Campbell, 59, 101
Morris, Lelia, 43, 45, 345
Morrow, Abbie C., 155, 356
Mueller, George, 39, 124
Murray, Andrew, 59
Myland, David Wesley, 145
  baptism in the Holy Spirit, 122
  Bible school work, 170, 171, 327
Nash, Oscar E., 335
Needham, Harold, 254, 316, 324
Nelson, Peter, C., 268, 320, 322, 324
Neshoba Holiness School, 205, 431n.2
Ness, Henry, 268, 333
New Acts, The, 134, 162
New Issue *(see also* Baptism, water), 230–231
Nikoloff, Nicholas, 305
North Avenue Mission, 128–130
Northwest Bible Institute, 333, 339pl.
Norton, Will, 291
Oneness, 235, 237, 238, 421n.45, 421n.58
Open Bible Standard, 252
Opperman, D. C. O., 130, 132, 215pl., 422n.70, 430n.1, 431n.6

baptism in the Holy Spirit, 163
Bible school work, 170–172,
200, 313, 314
Clergy Reference Committee,
199
death, 315
evangelism, 131, 198, 200
General Council participant,
204, 205, 211, 225, 236
Oneness embraced, 238
rebaptism, statement on, 232
Osterberg, Arthur, 254, 255
Otis, S. G., 280
Ozark Bible and Literary School,
314–315, 337pl.
Ozman, Agnes, 81–83, 84, 86

Pacific Coast Apostolic Faith
Movement, 109
Pacifistic views, 347, 349–350,
352–254
Page, Albert, 309pl.
Parham, Charles Fox, 74–77,
93pl., 94pl., 95pl., 171, 390n.5,
390n.10, 393n.56, 396n.104,
400n.13, 403n.50, 404n.65,
412n.34
    Apostolic Faith Movement,
    founder, 67
    Azusa, views of, 108, 399n.48
    early life, 68–70
    family, 72
    healing, 72, 73
    ministry of, 70–74, 95pl., 108–
    109, 114, 130
    and Prohibition, 424n.18
    role in Pentecostal move-
    ment, 68
    sanctification, views on, 219
    tongues, view of, 83–85, 393-
    394n.64, 394n.68, 411n.18
Parham, William, 69–70
Pearlman, Myer, 316, 318–319,
323, 432n.16
Peirce, Willard, 316, 317, 318
Peniel Bible Institute, 339pl.
Pennington, Edith Lorraine,
424n.20

Pennington, Edith Mae (nee
Patterson), 264–265, 269,
424n.20
Pennington, J. B., 264–265
Pentecostal Association of the
Mississippi Valley, 120
Pentecostal Evangel (see also
Weekly Evangel; Christian
Evangel), 259, 261, 266, 283,
309pl., 354, 421n.55
    controversial issues ad-
    dressed, 349–354
    editors of, 263, 281, 315
    title changes, 239, 282–283,
    422n.60
Pentecostalism, 26, 61, 153, 154,
192, 257, 301, 402n.32
    classical, 237
    during wartime, 355
    development of, 26, 27–28, 35,
    51, 63–64, 110, 179
    foreign missions and, 286
    institutions' response to, 193
    Oneness, 15, 237–238,
    opposition to, 180, 187, 193, 198
    organization of, attitudes to-
    ward, 174, 199–200
    restorationist influence, 15, 18,
    19, 20
    Welsh Revival influence, 100
Pentecostals, early day, 141
    association among, 410n.9
    Christianity vs. culture, 153–
    159
    faith life of, 147–150
    immigrants, 403n.51
    latter rain, view of, 150–151
    organization, view of, 174, 199–
    200
    spiritual gifts, 149
    worship of, 142–146
Pentecostal Union (see Pillar of
Fire)
Perkin, Noel, 263, 297–299, 301–
303, 304, 367, 429-430n.52
Perkins, Jessie, 293–294
Petersen, Bartlett, 336
Peterson, Paul, 305

Phillips, Dorothy, 307
Phillips, Everett, 307
Pickett, L. L., 46
Pierson, Arthur T., 25, 41, 382n.40
background, 39, 40
baptism in Holy Spirit, 180, 191–192
Keswick conventions, 59–60, 389n.70
Missionary Review of the World, 190
Northfield conferences, 56
premillenialist views, 22, 25
Pike, J. M., 117
Pillar of Fire, 181
Pinson, Mack M., 119–120, 200, 222, 241
General Council participant, 204, 243
holiness views, 218, 404n.60, 418n.2
missions, 301
Pentecostal Mission, 137pl.
sanctification, views, 426n.8
tongues as initial evidence, 242
Piper, Irene, 162
Piper, Lydia Markley, 127, 199
Piper, William Hamner, 126–127, 150, 403n.50, 422n.63
Pittsburgh Bible Institute, 169
Plymouth Brethren, 19, 23, 380n.13
Pocock, W., 298
Pope, W. H., 241
Postmillenialism *(see* Millenialism)
Premillennialism *(see* Millenialism)
Price, Charles, 253, 256, 264, 270pl., 271pl.
Pridgeon, Charles Hamilton, 169
Prophecy, 22–23, 166, 207, 345
Prophecies, 148, 407n.35

Rader, Paul, 368
Ramabai, Pandita, 402n.38, · 414n.33

Rauschenbush, Walter, 40–41
Rawson, A. F. (Mrs.), 148
Reckley, Etta, 254, 336
Reiff, Anna, 127, 356
Restorationism, 15, 18–22, 359, 379n.9
Reveille, 432n.16
Reynolds, Alice (later Alice Reynolds Flower), 123
Richey, Eli N., 115, 254, 255
Richey, Eloise Mae, 423n.12
Richey, Raymond T., 255–256, 320–321, 351, 423n.12
Riggs, Ralph M., 172, 266–267, 268, 323, 324
Riggins, S. J., 84–85
Roberts, L. V., 194, 231, 244pl.
Robinson, Charles Elmo, 115, 285
Robinson, Daisy, 115
Rochester Bible and Missionary Training School, 123, 124, 125–126, 140pl., 173
Rodgers, Henry G., 119, 120, 132, 225, 231, 404n.60, 417n.35, 420n.41, 422n.70
Roselli, Joseph, 254
Russian and Eastern European Mission, 305
Russellites *(see* Jehovah's Witnesses)

Salmon, John, 122
Salvation Army, The, 48, 50, 193, 250, 255, 295, 350
Sanctification *(see also* Holiness), 63, 97, 213, 217–221
crisis, 44, 48, 90, 129, 220, 403n.57
instantaneous, 57
progressive, 52, 57
Sandford, Frank, 20, 77–81, 86
Savell, James O., 243, 253, 324
Schaeppe, John, 223
Schell, William G., 233, 281, 408n.48
Schmidt, Gustav, 305
Schoonmaker, Christian, 293, 297, 298

Schoonmaker, Violet, 293
Scott, Charles, 336
Scott, R. J., 222, 223
Second Blessing (see Sanctification)
Second Coming, 24, 104, 106, 286, 346, 358, 371, 380n.14, 388n.58
Semple, Aimee (see McPherson, Aimee Semple)
Semple, Robert James, 249
Sexton, Mother E. A., 138pl., 426n.8
Seymour, William J., 89–91, 97–99, 104–105, 111pl., 163, 180
Shelhammer, E. E., 182
Shields, Guy, 320
Shiloh ministry (Sandford), 78–79, 80, 86
Shiloh Tabernacle (Dowie), 37pl., 114
Sikes, Edwin, 270pl.
Simpson, Albert B., 61, 65pl., 409-410n.1, 411n.18
  baptism in the Holy Spirit, 52, 180, 387n.54
  Christian and Missionary Alliance founder, 25, 61–63, 183
  gospel song composer, 61–62, 122
  healing ministry, 29–31
  Missionary Training Institute, 122, 123, 151, 318, 322
  sanctification, views on, 63
  tongues, views on, 30
  women, views on, 362
Simpson, William W., 287, 290, 293, 300, 323, 411n.18
Sinclair, John, 204, 422n.70
Sisson, Elizabeth, 165, 357, 361, 425n.2
Sizelove, Rachel, 165, 413n.41
Slager, George, 293, 298
Slager, Harriet, 293
Smale, Joseph, 99–100, 102, 398n.25, 398n.35
Smith, Mabel, 114, 162, 165
Smith, R. D. E., 253, 411n.17

Southern Bible School, 256, 320
Southern California Bible College, 316
Southwestern Assemblies of God College (see also Southern Bible School), 321
Spanish, ministry to the (see also Latin American District Council of the Assemblies of God), 291, 301, 316
Spiritual gifts, 168
Spurgeon, Charles, 190
Stead, W. T., 102
Steelberg, Wesley, 254–255, 268
Stevens, William C., 122, 151, 153, 408n.49
Stone, Barton, 238
Stone Church, 126–127, 204, 211, 422n.63
Studd, George B., 199, 222
Student Volunteer Movement (SVM), 25, 57, 301
Sunday, Billy, 249
Sunday schools, Assemblies of God, 266–269, 330
Swift, Allan, 315, 323

Terry, Neeley, 90
Tomlinson, Ambrose J., 79, 120, 132, 163, 401n.25
Tongues speaking, 92, 143, 145, 228, 393n.63, 422n.61, 422n.63
  Alliance position at beginning of century, 82, 183–189
  baptism in the Holy Spirit, 51–55, 191–192
  gift of tongues, 30, 407n.32, 410n.5, 411n.18, 414n.33, 428n.29
  as initial physical evidence, 119, 179, 429-430n.52
  by Japanese, 291
  McPherson, Aimee Semple, 129, 161, 226, 315
  as missionary speech, 162, 285
  opposition to, 128, 168, 180, 181–183, 190, 192, 194, 205–

206, 240–242
Parham's view of, 83–85, 108
Piper, William, accepts tongues, 126
premillenialism, views on, 24
proclaiming the message of, 97, 116–123, 163
sanctification, views on, 52–53
Seymour, William J., experience of, 98
Torrey, Reuben Archer, 180
Towner, D. E., 252
Tozer, Aiden Wilson, 189
Trasher, Lillian, 163, 293, 356
Trudel, Dorothea, 27
Trust, 124
Tunmore, Joseph, 242, 243, 283
Turnbull, Louis, 254

United Prayer and Worker's League, 255
Upper Room, The, 107, 149
Upper Room Mission, 107
Urshan, Andrew, 297

VanLoon, Harry, 235
Van Meter, Flem, 170, 254, 327
Victoria Hall mission, 107
Victorious Gospel, The, 107–108
Vogler, Fred, 340pl.
  Assemblies of God leader, 243, 254, 268
  early life, 327
  Kansas district superintendent, 265, 325
  national education secretary, 328, 331–333
  student at Gibeah, 170
Vogler, Margaret, 170
Voliva, Wilbur Glenn, 114
Voronaeff, John, 300, 304, 430n.65
Voronaeff, Katherine, 300, 304, 430n.65

Waggoner, Harold, 293
Waggoner, John, 254
Walthall, W. Jethro, 218, 241, 254

Wannenmacher, Helen Innes, 3pl., 115, 367
Wannenmacher, Joseph P., 3pl., 336, 373–377
Ward, A. G., 254
Ward, C. M., 325
Warren, J. A., 89
Watchword, 28
Water baptism (see Baptism, water)
Watson, George D., 42
Webb, Bert, 268, 336
Weekly Evangel (see also Christian Evangel; Pentecostal Evangel), 230, 239, 281–282,
Welch, John W., 243, 318
  Central Bible Institute, 325
  editor, 281
  executive presbyter, 204
  Foreign Missions Committee, 290
  General Council chairman, 233, 235, 247–248
  General Council Committee, 283
Welsh Revival, 100–103, 414n.33
Wengler, Jessie, 294–295
Wesley, Charles, 41
Wesley, John, 41, 220
Wesleyan teaching on holiness, 53, 58, 61, 63
  on Holy Spirit, 41–50
Whipple, Edith, 300
White, Alma, 90, 181
Whittle, Daniel W., 39
Willard, Frances, 50
Williams, Ernest S., 248, 253, 263, 268, 302, 323, 369, 425n.2
Williams, Laura, 261
Wilson, Aaron A., 254
Women, 15, 34, 212, 299, 364, 366, 369, 416-417n.23
  in Alliance outreaches, 362
  early Pentecostals' views on, 158, 411n.15
  General Council issue, 206–208
  holiness movements, views on, 50

as missionaries, 289, 303, 366
ordination of, 367, 368, 370, 416-
417n.23, 417n.24, 428n.35
Plymouth Brethren, views on,
23
in public ministry, 34, 50, 164–
166, 194, 363
restorationist views on, 359–
361
vote at General Councils, 365,
437n.65
Women's Missionary Council
(WMC), 299
Wood, Alice, 294
Woodworth-Etter, Maria B., 28,
34–36, 38pl., 69
Pentecostal meetings, 198–199,
222–223, 227, 240
Word and Witness, 133–134, 200–
202, 203, 204, 280, 239, 425n.1,
426n.8
Word and Work, 280
World Evangelization Com-
pany, 134
World-Wide Apostolic Faith
Camp Meeting, 222, 226
Worrell, A. S., 103
Wright, Ethel *(see* Goss, Ethel)

Yellow Books, 217
Yeomans, Lilian, 116, 165, 252,
425n.2
Young, D. J., 116

Ziese, Anna, 294
Zion City, 32–33, 113–116, 127,
255, 324, 327
Zion Faith Homes, 422n.63